Visual
Scalability Handbook

Damon Allison
Ben Hyrman

wrox

Wrox Press Ltd. ®

Visual Basic .NET Scalability Handbook

© 2002 Wrox Press

All rights reserved. No part of this book may be reproduced, stored in a retrieval system or transmitted in any form or by any means, without the prior written permission of the publisher, except in the case of brief quotations embodied in critical articles or reviews.

The authors and publisher have made every effort in the preparation of this book to ensure the accuracy of the information. However, the information contained in this book is sold without warranty, either express or implied. Neither the authors, Wrox Press, nor its dealers or distributors, will be held liable for any damages caused or alleged to be caused either directly or indirectly by this book.

First published October 2002

Published by Wrox Press Ltd,
Arden House, 1102 Warwick Road, Acocks Green,
Birmingham, B27 6BH
United Kingdom
Printed in the United States
ISBN 1-86100-788-4

Trademark Acknowledgments

Wrox has endeavored to provide trademark information about all the companies and products mentioned in this book by the appropriate use of capitals. However, Wrox cannot guarantee the accuracy of this information.

Credits

Authors
Damon Allison
Ben Hyrman

Editor
Nick Manning

Technical Reviewers
Neil Davidson
Damien Foggon
Mark Horner
Andrew Krowczyk
Phil Powers-DeGeorge
Ciaran Roarty

Project Manager
Beckie Stones

Index
Michael Brinkman
Andrew Criddle

Production & Layout
Neil Lote

Proof Reader
Chris Smith

Cover
Natalie O'Donnell

Managing Editor
Jan Kolasinski

About the Authors

Damon Allison
Damon is an IT consultant in Minneapolis, MN focusing on implementing Microsoft technologies. Arguably, Damon has a life outside programming. He enjoys playing golf and has high hopes that someday he'll be good at it.

Dad, I miss you, pal.

Ben Hyrman
Ben lives in Minneapolis, Minnesota with his wife, Dawn, and a rambunctious dog, Bandit. Ben keeps himself busy during the day as a Program Architect for Best Buy. On weekends, when they're not out kayaking, Ben and his wife enjoy touring the country, having put 30,000 miles on their car this year alone.

I would like to thank my loving wife, Dawn, for her patience and support during the writing of this book. I would like to thank Damon for being the driver behind completing this book. Lastly, I would like to thank our editor, Nick, for his ongoing support and feedback throughout the writing process.

VB.NET

Scalability

Handbook

Table of Contents

Table of Contents

Introduction 1

Who is this Book For 1
What Does this Book Cover 2

Chapter 1: Introduction to Scalability 5

Scalability Primer 5
Microsoft and Scalability 6
   Microsoft: Pre-.NET 7
   The .NET Effect 7
Where do We Go from Here? 8

Scalability Myths 9
Scalability is Not Performance 10
Scalability is Not Reliability 11

Why Scalability? 11
Planned Growth Happens 12
   Current Baseline Indicators 12
   Trends 12
Unplanned Growth (Really) Happens 13
   Charles Schwab 14

Scalability Issues 15
Scalability Issues with Visual Basic and DNA 15
   Threading 15
   Session 17
   DCOM 19
   Caching 22
   Windows DNA Scalability Limitations Recap 24
Common VB Scalability Design Pitfalls 24
   Using Inline SQL Instead of Stored Procedures 25
   External Resource Misuse 26
   Inefficient Recordset Creation and Use 26
   Improper usage of Visual Basic Objects 27
   Maintaining a Stateful Middle Tier 27
   Creating Resource-Intensive Tier Interfaces 27
   Improper OO Design 29

Table of Contents

Welcome .NET   29
.NET Threading   30
Session   32
- Easy to Use   33
- Cookieless Browser Support   33
- Session Hosting Capabilities   33

Middle-Tier Application Hosting   34
- Remoting   34
- Web Services   35

Caching   36
- @OutputCache   36
- Programmatic Cache Access   37

Visual Basic Does .NET   37
Setting the Stage   38

MyInvestmentWatch.com   38
Environment Diagram   39
The Database Tier   40
The Application Tier   41
User Interface Tier   41
User Object   42
- User Object Examination   42

Scalability Options   46
- Hardware Scaling   46
- All or Nothing Design   47
- Resource Lifetimes   49
- Ad hoc SQL Usage   50
- Session State   50
- Web Farm Possibilities   51

Summary   52

Chapter 2: Planning for Scalability   55

Plan or Fail   55
Microsoft Wants to Help, Really   57
- Planning Without a Safety .NET   57
- It's a .NEW World   59
- .NET Today   60

Where do we go from here?   61

Types of Scaling   62
Scaling Up   63
- Make it Faster   63
- Make it Bigger   64
- Best Practice for Scaling Up   64

Scaling Out   66
- Scaling Out Across Tiers   66
- Scaling Out a Single Tier   67
- Best Practices for Scaling Out   70

Tying it all Together   72
- Start Small   72
- Start Right   73
- Grow Big   74

The .NET Landscape   76
    Retraining   76
    The Common Language Runtime   77
        The Impact of the CLR on Planning   77
    Language Selection   77
    Code Migration   78
    Assembly Deployment   79
    Conclusion   80

Ready, Set, Plan   80
    Clearly Define Requirements   81
    Understand the Environment   81
    Align with Business Vision   82
    Take a Holistic View   83
    Determine Expected Load on the System   83
        Concurrent Users   84
        Transactions   84
        Integration   85
        Maintenance   85
        Trends   85
    Benchmark   86
        Benchmarking an Existing System   86
        Prototype During Design   87
        Benchmarking Before Rollout   87
    Determine Growth of the System   88
    Plan for the Unexpected   88
    Measure, Measure, Measure   89
    Create an Environment Growth Plan   89
    Plan for Design   90

Design Guidelines   90
    No Shortcuts   90
    Don't Reinvent the Wheel   91
    Don't Reuse a Flat Wheel   92
    Embrace the Tier   92
        Beware the Monolithic Application   92
        Beware the Intertwined Design   93
        .NET Makes Tiers Happy   94
    Reduce Round-trips   94
        Code   94
        Stored Procedures   95
        The Secret ASP.NET Scalability Weapon   95
    Determine Critical Path   95
    Design Interchangeable Objects   96
    Sequence Around Expected Load   96
        Application Integration   96
        Sequence out Non-User Processing   99
        Create a Reporting Environment   99
    Design for the Future   101

Summary   101

Table of Contents

Chapter 3: The Data Tier — 105

Database Design — 106
- Design Decisions — 107
  - Choosing a Platform — 107
- Normalization — 108
  - First Normal Form — 109
  - Second Normal Form — 110
  - Third Normal Form — 111
  - Normalization and Scalability — 112
- Stored Procedures — 114
  - Stored Procedure Lifecycle — 114
  - Stored Procedures and Scalability — 115
  - Stored Procedures and ADO.NET — 115
- Indexes — 116
  - Clustered Indexes — 116
  - Nonclustered Indexes — 117
  - Index Performance Tuning Tips — 117
  - Using the SQL Profiler — 118
  - Index Tuning Wizard — 119

ADO.NET — 121
- ADO.NET at a Glance — 122
  - Familiar Programming Model — 122
  - Support for N-Tier Programming Model — 122
  - Native XML Support — 123
- ADO.NET Object Model — 123
  - .NET Data Providers — 124
  - ADO.NET DataSet — 129
  - ADO.NET DataView — 136
- ADO.NET and Scalability — 141

MyInvestmentWatch.com Data Tier — 142
- Data-Access Layer: Goals — 143
  - Reuse — 144
  - Provide Abstraction — 144
  - Stateless Design — 144
  - Improved Performance Testing — 145
- Database Design — 145
  - First Normal Form — 146
  - Second Normal Form — 146
  - Third Normal Form — 147
- Stored Procedures — 147
- Data-Access Layer: Application Logic — 148
  - DAL Object Model — 148
  - Creating the Interfaces — 149
  - Implementing the Interfaces — 152
  - Data Access Layer: Highlights — 162
  - Data Access Layer: Possible Improvements — 163
- Summary — 163

iv

Chapter 4: The Middle Tier — 167

Middle-Tier Definition — 169
- Middle-Tier Benefits — 169
  - Scalability — 169
  - Reusability — 170
  - Integration — 170
  - Deployment — 171
  - Benefits Summary — 171
- Middle-Tier Drawbacks — 171
  - Performance — 172
  - Configuration — 172

Middle-Tier Design — 172
- Logical Middle Tier — 172
  - Managing Interfaces — 173
- Physical Middle Tier — 178
  - Performance in a Physical Middle Tier — 179

.NET Middle Tier — 180
- .NET Remoting — 181
  - Terminology — 183
  - Creating a Remoting-Accessible Object — 186
  - Remoting and the Middle Tier — 193
- Web Services — 193
  - Web Services Defined — 194
  - Web Service Example — 197
  - Web Services and the Middle Tier — 202
  - Additional Web Services Concerns — 203

MyInvestmentWatch.com Middle Tier — 203
- Determining the Middle-Tier Environment — 203
- Creating the Object Model — 205
  - User — 206
  - Stocks — 209
  - Stock — 213
  - StockQuotes — 217
  - StockQuote — 218
  - NewsArticles — 219
  - NewsArticle — 220
  - Hits — 221
  - Hit — 223
  - Using the Logical Middle Tier — 224
- Possible Improvements — 226
  - Error Handling — 227
  - Searching/Sorting Techniques — 227
  - Additional Functionality — 228

Summary — 228

Table of Contents

Chapter 5: The Presentation Tier — 231

Rationale for a Web-Based UI — 231
Advantages of a Web-Based UI — 231
- Fewer Deployment Targets — 232
- Consistent Deployment Platform — 232
- Easier Collaboration with External Partners — 232
- Easier Support for Multiple Clients — 232

Disadvantages of a Web-Based UI — 232
- Less Functionality — 233
- Slower Response Times (Perceived and Actual) — 233
- Client Processing Power Not Leveraged — 233

ASP.NET Scalability — 233
Compiled Code — 234
Caching — 234
Session Management in a Web Farm — 234
Where do We Go from Here? — 235

Our User Interface — 235
Page Flow — 235
- User Login — 235
- View Individual Stock — 236

Code Highlights — 237
Design Goals — 242

Caching — 243
Where the Cache Fits — 244
Output Caching — 246
- The @OutputCache Directive — 247
- Output Caching Sequence — 250
- Using Output Caching — 251

Partial Page Caching — 262
Programmatic Caching — 265
- Cache Item Dependencies — 266
- Cache Item Priorities — 269
- Cache Events — 270

Caching Best Practices — 272
- Start with No Caching at All — 272
- Don't Cache Data that Must be Up-To-Date on Each View — 272
- Don't Try to Cache Everything — 272
- Don't Cache Items that will Expire Quickly — 272
- Don't Cache Rarely Used Data — 272
- Cache Items that are Expensive to Create — 273
- Cache Items that Can be Used by Multiple Clients — 273
- Don't Use VaryByParam="*" — 273

State Management — 273
Session Management — 274
- No State — 276
- In-process — 276
- State Server — 278
- SQL Server — 281
- Best Practices for Session Management — 283

vi

View State	284
ViewState and Scalability	285
Best Practices	286
Our Revised User Interface	**287**
Code Highlights	287
Summary	**291**

Chapter 6: Measuring Scalability   295

Application Testing	**296**
Unit Testing	297
Unit Test Example	298
Strengths of Unit Testing	300
Unit Testing, Performance, and Scalability	301
Stress Testing	302
Common Performance Limitations	302
Importance of Tools in Testing	305
Application Monitoring Tools	**306**
Our First Test	306
Code Profiler	311
Profiling Test Cases	312
Profiler Strengths	316
Profiler Limitations	317
Performance Monitor	317
Performance Monitor and Distributed Applications	318
Microsoft Application Center Test	320
Configuring Application Center Test	321
Tools Summary	326
Code Instrumentation	**327**
Tracing	328
Tracing 101 – Establishing Tracing	328
Tracing 102	332
Tracing and Performance Monitor	335
Instrumentation and Scalability Measuring	339
Summary	**340**

Appendix A: MyInvestmentWatch.com Database Layout   343

Database Design	**343**
Users	344
Companies	345
StockQuotes	345
UserStocks	346
UserHits	347
News	347
NewsTraffic	348
UserLogins	348

Appendix B: Support, Errata, and Code Download 351

How to Download the Sample Code for the Book 351
Errata 352
E-Mail Support 352
p2p.wrox.com 353

Index 355

VB.NET

Scalability

Handbook

Introduction

Introduction

Developers have always been expected to build robust applications that meet a business need. In today's economy, however, there is also an increasing need to build applications that can rapidly scale to meet both planned and unexpected growth in user numbers and demands. This could mean more users, or the same level of users demanding more and more from your application.

With the introduction of .NET, Microsoft has enhanced the Visual Basic developer's capability to produce scalable n-tier applications built using solid object-oriented techniques. To be able to take advantage of more and better hardware, your application must be designed with scalability in mind from the outset.

This book presents a tier-by-tier break down of the issues involved in producing scalable applications. At the data tier you will learn how effective database design, stored procedures, and indexes impact on scalability. At the data-access layer you will see how to leverage the advances of ADO.NET. At the middle tier, which typically contains the bulk of the application's business logic, you will see how to design and build a scalable tier capable of supporting multiple presentation options. At the presentation tier you will learn how to benefit from the new features of ASP.NET, such as effective caching and state management.

Who is this Book For

All books in the Visual Basic .NET Handbook series are aimed at practicing Visual Basic .NET programmers who need to learn how to complete a specific task. This book is no different and will be the ideal companion for any developer who needs to build scalable, enterprise-level applications capable of rapidly meeting both planned and unexpected growth in today's business environment.

To gain the most from this book you will need a copy of Visual Basic .NET or Visual Studio .NET and SQL Server 2000.

What Does this Book Cover

This book covers all the ground that a developer needs to know in order to build scalable applications. Below is an outline of what each chapter contains.

Chapter 1 – Introduction to Scalability

In this chapter we introduce the issues involved in scaling applications to meet the needs of today's enterprises. We discuss the limitations of the Windows DNA model and the tremendous benefits that come with .NET. We also introduce MyInvestmentWatch.com, which is the demonstration application that we'll be using throughout this book.

Chapter 2 – Planning for Scalability

Scalability must be planned for, and designed into, applications right from the outset. The decisions that you make at the design and early development phases will have the largest affects on your application's ability to scale. This chapter covers both scaling up and scaling out from a best practices viewpoint.

Chapter 3 – The Data Tier

The data tier is extremely important for scalability as it is one of the, if not the, most resource-intensive parts of an application. We cover the design of both the database and the data access layer in this chapter. For the database, we discuss normalization, stored procedures, and indexes. For the data-access layer, we examine the huge advances in scalability made by ADO.NET, including the new disconnected `DataSet` object. We then build the database and data-access layer for our demonstration application.

Chapter 4 – The Middle Tier

The middle tier is generally where the majority of an application's business logic is contained. In this chapter we discuss the benefits of a separate middle tier and how to design an effective one from both the logical and physical perspective. We cover two of the most important topics for anyone developing a middle tier in .NET, namely .NET Remoting and Web Services. We then show you how we implement the middle tier in our demonstration application.

Chapter 5 – The Presentation Tier

The presentation tier is expected to manage and respond to user requests and must be capable of scaling to support the expected average and peak numbers of concurrent users. The main focus of this chapter is on the advances made by ASP.NET with regards to scalability, such as caching and state management. We conclude the chapter with the implementation of the presentation tier in our demonstration application.

Chapter 6 – Measuring Scalability

Measuring your application's performance and ability to scale is vital throughout its entire life time. In this chapter we cover techniques such as unit testing, stress testing, and code instrumentation. We also cover the tools we can use to help us monitor our applications such as code profilers, the Windows performance Monitor, and Application Center Test.

Appendix A – MyInvestmentWatch.com Database layout

This appendix is a handy reference for the structure of the database used in our MyInvestmentWatch.com demonstration web site.

Appendix B – Support, Errata, and Code Download

This appendix tells you about the support available from Wrox for this book, how to view or submit any errata, and how to download the code available at the Wrox web site.

Nick Manning
Editor – VB.NET Handbook Series, Wrox Press

VB.NET

Scalability

Handbook

1

Introduction to Scalability

Developers have always been expected to build robust systems that meet a business need. In today's economy, however, there is also an increasing need to build applications that can rapidly scale to meet new user demand. This has been most apparent in the many web sites where outages due to the system failing under its own weight have made the headlines.

Scalability Primer

It is no secret that users expect more out of today's applications. Users expect a rich, customized user interface with dynamic, personalized content delivered to their home PC, office laptop, or portable phone. Developers must balance this need, and their own desire, to add functionality and "cool" features to applications with the fact that they must support not only more clients, but also more types of clients.

Clients come in many flavors, from traditional Windows Win32-based applications, to HTML-based web applications, to handheld devices. As trends point towards growing bandwidth, faster processors, and higher competition between information providers, the underlying application architecture and code design must be built with scalability in mind to meet the growing demands of serving not only a proliferation in clients, but also a proliferation in client devices.

Businesses demand and expect scalability of their applications. Businesses need applications that can both rapidly scale up to meet growing business needs and scale down when a system is underutilized. In addition, businesses expect applications that can rapidly respond to new needs. An application that has no, or few, reports may suddenly be called upon to deliver ad hoc reports to a large base of users.

Quite simply, businesses demand and expect software that responds rapidly to new challenges. In other words, the need is for nimble software that requires minimal effort to meet new demands, and scalability is one of the cornerstones of nimble software.

A scalable system is one that can be expanded to meet greater user loads, and changing user behaviors, without modifying its existing architecture and design, or at least ensuring these modifications have as little impact as possible. If the expected system usage doubles suddenly, or the system undergoes rather heavy peak loads, a scalable system will have the ability to meet these challenges without incurring huge expense, or worse, recoding. If the underlying code is designed properly, scaling a system is surprisingly painless. On the contrary, if the underlying application code design did not consider growth, or the changing nature of system usage, meeting the increased demand or peak usage scenarios may not be possible.

To be more precise, one goal of application design, namely scalability, should be to deliver a system that meets current and future capacity needs within the problem domain. Obviously, not every application needs to handle the traffic of today's largest sites or be expected to handle 400% more users tomorrow than it did today, but it must be able to handle expected growth. Regardless of the exact application growth expectations, the architect, infrastructure support personnel, and most importantly developers, must answer the question: "How well positioned is my system to handle a potentially large increase in users?"

Another aspect of scalability that is especially apparent in today's economy is the need to build systems that can also scale down to meet reduced usage needs. A system that requires a large amount of hardware to even function will not serve a company well when expenses must be trimmed.

No matter what your role in software development, the last position you want to be in is explaining how you need to recode or redesign a system to meet growth predictions. Once a system is designed, it becomes costly and time consuming to enhance. Understanding scalability concerns at the design phase enables you to understand, predict, and avoid common practices that lead into non-scalable systems. Of course, you can't be expected to design a system that will meet unforeseen needs or unstated requirements. However, you will also want to ensure that you do not pigeon-hole your system into a brittle and non-scalable design from the start.

Microsoft and Scalability

Microsoft has, over time, gained the reputation of creating non-scalable server software, or, at least, of creating architectures that could only achieve scalability with a large effort. With the introduction of .NET, Microsoft has taken great strides towards silencing its critics. Let's take a look at Microsoft's product offerings with an eye on scalability.

Microsoft: Pre-.NET

Over time Microsoft has been improving scalability in its products. With the advent of Windows NT4 Symmetric Multi-Processor (SMP) technology and cluster-capable applications like Microsoft SQL Server, great strides were taken to improve system scalability. Windows 2000 and COM+ followed NT's lead and continued to lay the foundations for the developer to create scalable applications.

For many applications, Visual Basic 6 was the ideal programming language choice in Microsoft environments. Creating fully functional user interfaces in Visual Basic, for example, was extremely easy. You tied visual controls to a user interface form, handled events, and perhaps talked to COM components or a database.

When it came to creating scalable web applications, however, Visual Basic's limitations started to become noticeable. In fact, for certain aspects of a highly scalable system, the limitations started to make Visual Basic unusable. Perhaps the most common complaint that plagued the use of Visual Basic was the all too common line: "Visual Basic can't scale".

Threading in particular was limited in Visual Basic. If you created COM components in Visual Basic 6, your threading options were limited. You simply couldn't take advantage of the same threading options you could in C++. Because of the limitations the language imposed on its developers, developers shied away from Visual Basic 6 for many enterprise systems. Developers and architects who wanted to squeeze every last ounce of performance out of their hardware sacrificed the simplicity of VB for the power of C++.

Besides performance limitations, Visual Basic was limited in its support for Object Oriented (OO) programming. OO concepts were not supported in Visual Basic version 3. Bits started to appear in version 4, but were still only minimally supported in later versions of VB (VB6). For instance, implementation inheritance, parameterized constructors, and method overloading were not available in VB6. To an OO developer coming from another programming language to VB, these shortcomings were enough to turn them off to the language. Despite VB's ease of use and Rapid Application Design characteristics, the language proved to be limiting. True OO programmers just couldn't live with these limitations and opted to program in a more OO-centric language like C++ or Java.

The .NET Effect

Building further on Windows 2000 and COM+, the .NET platform enables developers to design more robust systems by abstracting even more of the plumbing into the Framework. .NET introduces a unified type system, versioning, side-by-side deployment, Remoting, and integrated web service support, to name a few features. From a more holistic aspect, .NET gives the developer freedom in design and productivity savings allowing them to concentrate on building more scalable systems. Technically, these advances are crucial to making scalable systems.

Chapter 1: Introduction to Scalability

With the introduction of .NET, Visual Basic has matured to become a first class player in the programming language arena. Virtually all of the OO concepts that once limited Visual Basic's usage have been incorporated into the language. Implementation inheritance and popular concepts like polymorphism, multiple interface inheritance, overloading, and constructors are available to the developer.

Visual Basic .NET is only missing a few features that its cousin language C# incorporates. VB.NET cannot call into 'unsafe' code (code that directly accesses memory or hardware) and cannot perform operator overloading where languages like C# can. However, these features are of questionable importance to the average development project.

With the industry focus turning from client-based Windows Form applications to web-based ASP.NET applications, more pressure is being put on the server and the language used at the server level. As mentioned previously, Visual Basic's space in enterprise applications has traditionally suffered because of the limitations imposed by Visual Basic itself. With .NET, those limitations are lifted and Visual Basic is more than capable of performing enterprise-level duties.

Where do We Go from Here?

The goal of this book is to introduce you to developing scalable applications with VB.NET. As developers, Microsoft .NET and the .NET Framework provide us with many critical code and system-level improvements that traditional unmanaged COM and Windows DNA failed to provide.

In this chapter, we will cover:

- **Scalability Myths** – There are common myths that need to be examined and explained to give a more concrete understanding of scalability. In particular, scalability is commonly confused with two other 'abilities': performance and reliability. While there are correlations between the different 'abilities', designing systems for scalability differs from the others.

- **Why Scalability?** – We will also examine common technological trends to determine how important scalability is in today's computing environment. We will present case studies illustrating the importance of creating a scalable application and what happens when systems are designed without fully understanding the impact growth has on a system.

- **Scalability Issues** – We just briefly scratched the surface on the limitations VB6 forced on the developer. In this section, we will examine these limitations in more detail while keeping an eye on what .NET does to solve the issues.

- **Welcome .NET** – With the advent of .NET, many things that previously posed problems to Visual Basic developers are no longer an issue. We will examine the huge strides made by this revolutionary new Microsoft platform.

- **Sample Application (MyInvestmentWatch.com)** – Throughout the book, we will be looking at code and discussing limitations and performance improvements, many of which plagued pre-.NET systems. We will show how these previous limitations are overcome with the .NET Framework. In particular, we will dissect an existing ASP/VB application and show, chapter by chapter, the work needed to address the existing scalability problems during a migration to VB.NET. This is not a book about converting VB6 to VB.NET or converting ASP to ASP.NET, but since many of the performance improvements that .NET offers address previous ASP or Windows DNA shortcomings, a comparison between pre-NET and .NET code will allow you to more fully understand and take advantage of what the .NET platform has to offer. We think you will agree that .NET has made some very exciting advances in terms of scalability.

Scalability Myths

Scalability is often confused with other 'abilities' and system characteristics that are discussed during systems design. It becomes important to distinguish scalability apart from these other 'abilities' because of their subtle differences. In order to set the record straight, what we need to do is compare scalability to its close relatives: performance and reliability. Examine the concept of scalability closely in order to be able to effectively compare it to other system metrics. Keep these definitions and concepts in your mind as you read on. Scalability has the following characteristics:

- Scalability is the ability of a computer application or product (hardware or software) to continue to function well as it (or its context) is changed in size or volume in order to meet a user need. Typically, the scaling is to a larger size or volume. The move can be of the product itself (for example, a line of computer systems of different sizes in terms of storage, RAM, and so forth) or to a new context (for example, a new operating system).

- Scalability is roughly defined as the ability of an application to support a much larger number of users than it was initially designed for. For example, a web application written for a maximum of 100 simultaneous users may not be scalable (that is, it may not operate as required in terms of functionality or performance when the number of users increases to 300, 500, 10,000, or one million). Scalability depends not only on the software but also on the capabilities of the servers and the hardware.

Scalability is Not Performance

> **Myth: Making a system highly scalable will also make it extremely fast.**

While planning for scalability and planning for performance often include the same tasks, the goals are different. The goal of scalability is to support as many users at a time as possible while the goal of performance is to accomplish a task as quickly as possible. Obviously, the two concepts are closely connected. The ability to process users faster will ultimately help with scalability, but as you will see, there are some decisions made for scalability's sake that could hinder performance.

To illustrate, let's break out the trusty bank analogy. One teller can assist a customer in 5 minutes. Adding a second teller does not decrease the time needed to process a single customer. However, it allows more customers to be helped simultaneously. We've just scaled our system, the bank, linearly to double the number of concurrent users we can support, but we haven't decreased the time spent to process any single request.

A key concept of scalability is to design an application so that it can be partitioned and spread across multiple servers. Adding a physical middle tier will increase scalability, assuming the application has been properly designed, but it will decrease performance as multiple process and network boundaries must be crossed. Conversely, you may combine functions and objects together for speed, which, in turn, will decrease scalability as it will hinder the ability to partition the application.

However, things are not as dire as they may sound. Scalability and performance are not mutually exclusive concepts. As you will see, the concepts we follow to create a scalable system will also assist in creating a rather fast application. For example, caching data on the front end to minimize roundtrips to the database will help with both scalability and performance. Other considerations that will assist with performance include minimizing database calls, minimizing state management, and minimizing communication between layers.

Because scalability and performance are rather intertwined, it becomes important to write and test code for performance considerations. However, it is also important to not over-optimize needlessly. That is, do not spend inordinate amounts of time optimizing a report that will only run once a month when there are likely many other places that optimizations would be felt immediately. It becomes interesting to note that while applications tend to grow in size, the core of the application that consumes the majority of the resources tends to be relatively small. Writing solid test scripts, using code analysis tools like profilers, and monitoring system performance with Windows system tools are concepts you will want to understand when coding.

Scalability is Not Reliability

> **Myth:** Making a system highly scalable will also make it highly reliable.

The infrastructure of a system built for reliability, especially a Windows-based system, will share characteristics with the infrastructure of a system built for scalability. For example, both will often have clustered web servers and database servers. However, the goal of each is different.

The goal of building a highly reliable application is to create a system that is both able to resist failure and to recover from failure with a minimal loss of data. It should quickly become evident that certain things, such as a load-balanced web server, will help with both scalability and reliability. By adding a second web server, we've increased scalability, and we've provided a server that can take over handling user requests if the first server fails.

However, some considerations for reliability do not assist with scalability at all. You might deploy an active-passive SQL Server cluster so that, if the active server goes down, the passive node takes over immediately. This greatly improves system reliability, but does not assist with scalability at all. The passive cluster has done nothing for the goal of scalability since it has not increased our ability to handle more concurrent users.

We should also mention that the applications mentioned in this book are not focused on building reliability into our application. Redundancy, fault tolerance, and reliability are very broad topics that would take another book (or three) of this size to properly document. Where appropriate, we will point out possible reliability improvements at each tier of the application and it should be rather apparent where features will be applicable. For example, session management, a concept that was difficult to make reliable and to avoid losing in a server crash, is much easier with ASP.NET and SQL Server Session Manager, and happens to be achieved by the same method as we will follow to achieve scalability.

Why Scalability?

You are likely reading this book because you already know at least some of the answer to this question. Of course, there are many reasons for scalability, and we will discuss a few of them in this section.

Planned Growth Happens

By looking at the current baseline indicators and trends in the application's environment, we can predict the rate of system change. Easily overlooked, determining your current baseline performance and spotting trends allow the application to be designed for scalability.

Current Baseline Indicators

Change is inevitable. As businesses evolve, so do system demands. By following general planning practices, we can typically predict future system needs. We can examine the current usage patterns and feel fairly confident in our predictions for the foreseeable future.

Systems growth tends to mirror the trend of the business. If the size of the business is increasing, systems can be predicted to increase at a proportional rate. The average application will have a fairly linear growth path and a known time span. Of course, these growth characteristics are only for typical systems, and will not reflect well the growth of a web site for the next big game system.

When examining systems, it becomes important to determine the current system's usage and baselines. Questions you need to ask yourself concerning scalability when designing or planning architecture requirements include:

- What is the current usage pattern and how do the current systems perform given these conditions?
- What has been your historical growth rate and will your systems be able to match the growth rate in years to come?
- What is the planned growth rate, both for the business and for the system?
- Which parts of the application can be scaled significantly by a small investment?
- Which parts of the application will take a significant investment to meet demand?
- Which systems are critical to the heart of the business and how can they handle the expected growth rate?

By asking ourselves these questions, we begin to determine a scalability baseline. These assumptions and parameters will set the constraints for our system. By determining a baseline performance, we position ourselves well for inevitable business change.

Trends

When discussing planned growth, special considerations are required for system usage trends. For example, retail vendors need to pay specific attention to the Christmas season. In a normal corporate work environment, where the major processing is done during the business day, usage trends can be spotted by examining the peak and non-peak system performance during the day.

Examining your system for trends is important from a system administration and development standpoint. System administration must examine network-related traffic, CPU utilization, and hardware resource performance during the information gathering period. Developers need to examine their application usage patterns on an application-by-application basis. If an application is performing poorly under heavy load, then profilers, tracers, and diagnostic information can be coded into the application to give the developer a better understanding of which parts of the code are bottlenecks.

Performance monitoring from both a system architecture and developer standpoint is an extremely important concept for growth planning. We will cover low-level system and code performance tools in Chapter 6, *Measuring Scalability*.

Unplanned Growth (Really) Happens

Planned growth is relatively easy to deal with from a scalability standpoint because, like the name suggests, it is planned for and can be predicted (for the most part). Obviously, not all business indicators can be predicted. From a system's standpoint, unplanned growth tests limitations and system scalability.

Unplanned growth includes environmental changes, mergers, and acquisitions outside the realm of typical business activity. Merging systems, interfacing with new systems, or transferring data between systems can fundamentally change the system and code architecture.

As system designers, we cannot plan for every scenario that could potentially occur, nor would we want to. Designing a system to the scalability principles we define in this book can assist your system to be more nimble and better able to meet the challenge.

While we cannot completely plan for the unexpected, asking the right questions will help. Examples include:

- What pieces of your system can be separated or replaced? For example, what would have to be rewritten if your database changed from SQL Server to Oracle, or visa versa?

- At the code level, are components designed as independent black boxes, which enable the system pieces to be somewhat interchangeable? For example, if you take credit card payments and your credit card processing vendor files for bankruptcy, how difficult would it be to replace the vendor? Would your database need to be altered drastically?

- Is your code compliant with standard protocols and languages? If you inherited systems, how easily could you adapt to language integration? Defining common formats, like standard XML document conventions, gives the system the ability to absorb change and scale well to meet new demands.

Environmental considerations of the industry must also be taken into account. Say, for example, that you sell concert tickets to a local market. If a popular band is selling tickets through your web site, the site will undergo a huge amount of stress in a short period of time. While these events are not completely unpredictable, they are serious and need to be taken into consideration. If the site is not scalable, your business may lose future opportunities to host ticket sales for large selling concerts. Similarly, a news site will experience a large increase in traffic in response to important world events.

In the unplanned growth scenario, not only must an application be scalable, there must be enough planning done up front to be able to rapidly scale a system on short notice. In practice, it's not practical to order and install fifteen new servers immediately to meet new demand. Generally, it is standard practice to keep spare hardware sitting idle just to meet spikes in system load. Of course this approach isn't necessarily the most appealing either. Planning will greatly assist with determining and sizing the environment properly in order to keep enough hardware on standby without overly wasting hardware.

A very well documented example of unplanned growth is found by examining the systems and environmental trends surrounding Charles Schwab in the late 1990's. During the late 1990's, online investment became wildly popular as investors saw the potential to drive their own portfolios online. Charles Schwab, a leader in traditional portfolio investment, struggled with designing scalable systems. The case study illustrates real-world lessons learned that can be applied to systems of all sizes.

Charles Schwab

In October of 1997, Charles Schwab had a problem. Its web site was too popular. On October 27th the stock market dropped 7.5%, representing one of the largest stock market drops in history. The following day, October 28th, the stock market rebounded with one of the largest gains in history. Due to the heavy trading involved with this market volatility, schwab.com experienced a melt down. Thanks to a Herculean effort, and plenty of extra hardware, capacity was doubled within days. Of course, this would have been for naught if Charles Schwab's systems weren't scalable.

Charles Schwab learned from this experience and reacted. Capacity planning efforts were formalized and an additional buffer room to account for trading spikes was added. By 1998, schwab.com was processing 10,000 simultaneous trades during peak trading. Within a year, it was processing upwards of 100,000 simultaneous trades.

Within this same time frame, Charles Schwab upgraded its existing RS/6000-based web farm to 88 IBM RS/6000 servers and increased its back-end application servers to four IBM OS/390 mainframes. To further meet growing demands in 1999, it installed 66 more RS/6000s, for a total of 154 web servers, and two more OS/390s. This increase in capacity allowed it to process over 200,000 simultaneous trades.

Obviously, an amazing amount of hardware was involved in delivering such impressive capacity abilities. However, equally important, Charles Schwab designed applications that could scale with hardware growth. While you may never need a system that must support even 10,000 concurrent users, you may need a system that can not only quickly scale but also has enough spare capacity to meet spikes in demands.

Scalability Issues

In this section we are going to take a more technical look at the landscape for Microsoft developers. In particular, we are concerned with pinpointing the scalability limitations in Windows DNA, which was Microsoft's pre-.NET strategy for developing enterprise applications. It promoted the creation of an n-tier logical design for applications and code reuse; the user interface tier consisted of a Windows or ASP user interface, the middle tier consisted of COM and DCOM objects for hosting business logic, and the data tier consisted of the SQL Server data storage engine.

However, effectively building Windows DNA application was not a trivial undertaking. Even worse, the problems were made more difficult when using Visual Basic. All of this has changed with the introduction of the .NET platform.

Microsoft has held nothing back in its fight to win respect in the enterprise development arena with the introduction of .NET. As the company turned its focus from client-based applications to distributed applications, the issues presented with DNA needed to be addressed. We will discuss these changes later in the chapter.

Scalability Issues with Visual Basic and DNA

While DNA was a major step forward for Microsoft in its quest to embrace enterprise development, it still presented some hurdles that often kept businesses away. The constraints of Visual Basic further compounded, and even introduced, problems in this architecture. The focus of this section is on these problems with using Visual Basic.

It is these constraints that further kept enterprises from embracing Windows DNA. The fact that another language, such as C++, was required to truly harness the power of DNA often led companies to evaluate Java instead. As we will discuss further on, Microsoft has addressed these concerns both in the form of Visual Basic .NET and the underlying Framework.

Threading

It was difficult to program scalable web applications with Visual Basic 6 because of the limitations imposed by its threading model. It didn't offer the free-threading model that Visual C++ developers enjoyed.

15

Chapter 1: Introduction to Scalability

In COM-speak, objects could have multiple threading models, most notably Multi-Threaded Apartments (MTA) and Single-Threaded Apartments (STA). Visual Basic objects could not take advantage of the different threading models, as they were limited to STA threading. Using these objects across multiple requests (and accessed via different threads) severely impacted on scalability, especially with regards to ASP.

An object in an STA threading model is limited to executing on the current thread. Objects created with Visual Basic are limited by what is called thread affinity, which means they can only be accessed by the thread that originally created them.

For an ASP application, if the object was created and destroyed within a single page request, the performance was not hindered by the threading model because the same thread was used to access the object for its entire lifetime. However, if you stored the VB object and stored it into the session (remember the session can be accessed by any thread that Internet Information Server is running), only the thread that it resided on could use it. Internet Information Server (IIS) then had to route every request to that object through the single thread. Further, these requests had to be blocked until they were completed. Because of this, ASP would not even allow a VB COM object to be created within the `Application` object. Rather, these objects had to be instantiated within each session. This often led to VB developers storing objects in each user session even if they legitimately belonged in the application space.

The IIS Threading Model

Thread affinity was one of the most noticeable and limiting scalability concerns found in ASP. If IIS could access the object from any of its worker threads, we would be able to alleviate the threading bottleneck.

IIS, being a scalable application, uses a server process (`InetInfo.exe`) that was designed to accommodate huge numbers of simultaneous users. To process massive amounts of traffic, IIS maintains its own thread management system that helps increase its performance. The worker threads are commonly referred to as the thread pool. As IIS handles requests, `InetInfo.exe` retrieves a thread from the pool. The default pool is ten worker threads, but can be configured if further control is needed.

This model allows IIS to perform faster and respond to more clients at a time, at the cost of some efficiency. Creating objects is a time-consuming process. Allowing IIS to spin up these objects before they are needed will subsequently save time while handling client requests. Limiting IIS's threading model by using thread-specific VB objects at the session and application scope negated the benefits of the multithreaded web server.

The threading architecture of IIS is most efficient when it has the flexibility to dispatch any thread in the pool to service an incoming request. However, as you can see, when you assign a Visual Basic object to an ASP Session variable, IIS must locate (and possibly block on) the one thread that created the object. While IIS is capable of serializing all future requests over the same thread, this situation doesn't allow IIS to make the most of its thread-pooling scheme. An incoming request can be blocked while waiting for one thread to free up, while several other worker threads are idle.

VB and the ASP Application Object

The `Application` object posed several problems in terms of how threading impacted on the ability to use VB-based COM objects. When assigning an STA object in the `Application` collection, all clients using the object would be limited to the thread the object resided on. This meant that each client request to this VB object would have to wait for the request in front to complete. Thankfully the ASP runtime does not allow us to assign STA objects. The error "Cannot add object with apartment model behavior to the application intrinsic object" would trigger.

This often led to developers placing these VB objects in the ASP `Session` object. Of course, sometimes this was a necessity to get around the restrictions of the VB threading model. Even if these objects were rather global in nature and could be used across an entire ASP application, they had to be placed within each user session. This approach was certainly not ideal for many reasons. For one, it wasted valuable system resources, such as RAM, since a separate copy had to be loaded in each session. Even worse, due to the nature of the ASP session, this approach was not without its problems either.

Session

`Session` is an interesting object because it allows you to maintain a history of the current user. It is powerful in that it is unique to a user and extremely easy to program. No longer were the HTTP connections completely stateless, since the user-specific information was saved to the session. Of course, one problem with sessions in ASP was that they required the user to allow cookies in order to work properly. While not necessarily a scalability problem, this could potentially severely hamper the usefulness of the `Session`.

The ASP `Session` suffered from other serious scalability concerns. First, `Session` was tied to the ASP process. If the process was terminated, the session state was lost. Also, the `Session` could not adapt to multi-server scenarios such as web farms. You'll want to keep these session limitations fresh in your memory for when we discuss the ASP.NET session state manager. Many improvements that have gone into the ASP.NET session were the result of lessons learned from these ASP session shortcomings.

Session Required Cookies

Since sessions are cookie-based, the user could disable cookies and effectively eliminate using sessions entirely. What is needed is a method that allows the web developer to use a cookie-less session.

One possible scenario was to determine programmatically if cookies were being refused. By storing a method into the session that redirected the user to a second page and checked for the cookie, we could find out if the cookie was being rejected or accepted. If the session variable was retained in session on the second page, we would know cookies were enabled and could program for cookie acceptance.

Session was Tied to ASP Process

The ASP session database was maintained in the web server's memory space. If the web server process was terminated, either on purpose or unexpectedly, all session state was lost. Because users could be in the middle of the application when the process was restarted, they were subject to having an invalid state. If the pages weren't designed with the ability to do a friendly redirect if the session was lost, the user often was rudely interrupted.

What was needed, something that IIS 5 did not provide, was a method to save sessions in a manner that isn't tied to a specific machine.

Session was Not Scalable in Web Farm Scenarios

The limitations of the `Session` handicapped ASP when scaling in a web farm. Ideally, any server in the farm should be able to respond to any client request at any point. This allows the client load to be fully, and equally, distributed across the entire farm.

However, as you recall, the ASP `Session` is bound on a specific server. This means that the user request must be routed back to the same server each time. At any point, a given server could be overburdened responding to clients while another server could be underutilized.

From another point of view, this drawback was also detrimental because, if the server crashed, all session state on the server would be lost. Of course, the user would be routed to a functioning server on the next request, but they still lost any state to that point.

Session State Alternatives

The `Session` object, which was once promising, had serious limitations. In order to work around these limitations, many companies decided to implement their own session manager. In particular, the goal was to build a session with the following characteristics:

- Not tied to cookies
- Accessible by every server in a web farm
- Not tied to the stability of a single machine or process

As we will discuss further in Chapter 5, ASP.NET has answered this need in a big way. ASP.NET still allows session state to be maintained on the server responding to the request. However, it also provides two alternatives that work wonderfully in a web farm. One option is to store state in a special session state server. Another is to utilize SQL Server to persist session information.

Storing State Outside of Session

The ASP session could be avoided by holding state outside of the session. Turning off session in the ASP layer had performance improvements of its own. Because the ASP process did not need to maintain a session cache, the code performance actually improved because the server could optimize the incoming requests. Session could either be disabled in the IIS MMC console or via this directive:

```
<%@ENABLESESSIONSTATE=False %>
```

In order to maintain state in this environment, the information must be sent to the client between each page request. The main benefit to this approach is the resources required for session management were very low.

The problem with storing information at the client is that variables need to be maintained between page requests. If the user had cookies disabled, you were left with using either the hidden fields in a form or querystring variables. The querystring was limited in the amount of data you could store and forms required each page to be posted back on each request (every page was required to be in an ASP `<form>` tag, regardless if there were form elements like a textbox).

Maintaining a shopping cart (or anything dynamic) between pages in this environment is costly and puts unnecessary pressure on the front-end logic to handle state management. This places an unneeded strain on development and maintenance as well. However, it was often the best method for creating highly scalable ASP applications that could work across browsers.

After we have reviewed all the alternative session state management scenarios with ASP, we realize how little option we actually had when planning for a scalable system. The limitations imposed by the ASP session manager were too restricting for truly scalable systems.

DCOM

When DCOM was released, Microsoft took a step forward in scalable architecture. DCOM extends COM by allowing different machines to communicate, so COM developers could now use their current skills for creating distributed applications. DCOM handled all the plumbing associated with the details of delivering the call and marshaling the parameters for you. That is, developers could write the same code as they always had been, while Microsoft handled the workings of getting these objects to exist on separate servers.

With COM, the client and component resided on the same physical machine. The client would create an instance of the object and use it directly, as illustrated in Figure 1:

Chapter 1: Introduction to Scalability

Figure 1

```
Client ●────────▶○ Component
```

With DCOM, the same object could be created on a different physical machine. The Remote Procedure Call (RPC) call was transparent to the developer, as illustrated by Figure 2:

Figure 2

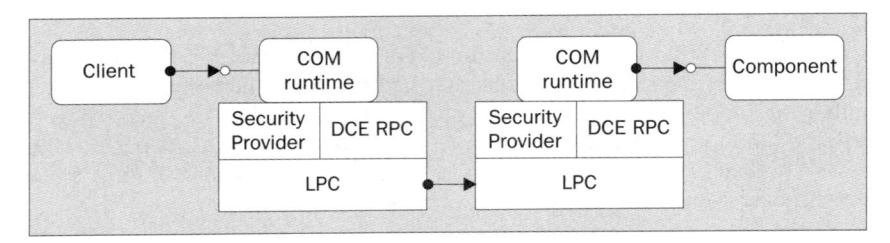

```
            ┌─────────┐                    ┌─────────┐
Client ●──▶○│  COM    │                    │  COM    │○◀──● Component
            │ runtime │                    │ runtime │
            ├────┬────┤                    ├────┬────┤
            │Sec.│DCE │                    │Sec.│DCE │
            │Prov│RPC │                    │Prov│RPC │
            ├────┴────┤                    ├────┴────┤
            │   LPC   │●──────────────────▶│   LPC   │
            └─────────┘                    └─────────┘
```

Advantages of DCOM

DCOM promoted reuse. The same set of logic written as a COM component was now capable of being exposed to a wider range of applications without much, if any, modification. For example, a COM component meant for handling logic for a Windows client could now be used from a web application.

DCOM did wonders for application scalability. Components could now execute under a physical context on a remote location. Expensive processes could be sent off to work on another box, reducing the application's processor load.

Deployment with DCOM was relatively painless when compared to COM. The object could be deployed to a single location (server) and client applications could be configured to use the DCOM instance. If upgrades were made to the COM object, the deployment consisted of replacing the COM object on the server machine only. Of course, DLL Hell was still a problem in this scenario, but at least the upgrade was centralized.

Limitations with DCOM

Multiprocessing was limited to an object that used a free-threaded model. DCOM provided Symmetric Multi-Processing (SMP) support by maintaining a thread pool optimized for the number of processors on the machine. The threading manager was a welcome sign for developers since a thread pool is rather difficult to write. Creating too many threads resulted in a large amount of thread context switches, thereby slowing down performance instead of increasing it. Too few threads wouldn't fully utilize the other processor(s).

Most Internet-based applications use one port. For example, web traffic has traditionally used port 80, FTP traffic resides on port 21, and SMTP uses port 25. When designing firewalls, network administrators would limit traffic to these specific ports and deny access to all other ports for increased security.

Dynamic Port Assignment

DCOM dynamically assigns ports between 1,024 and 65,535 to each process that is servicing a remote object. To make matters more difficult, DCOM assigns both a TCP and UDP port to each process. The client could discover the port associated with a particular object by using the DCOM Service Control Manager (SCM). The SCM, however, required that port 135 be opened for both TCP and UDP.

For many networks, dynamic port allocation was detrimental to network firewall configuration. Many administrators created separate logical segments of their networks to handle web traffic and kept their databases and middle-tier DCOM objects running on a different segment of the network. If the web tier and middle tier are on different network segments, as is common, then the firewall must be configured to leave open the range of ports DCOM requires between the network segments. This presents a serious security breakdown.

Microsoft's developers picked up on the shortcoming of DCOM and implemented a feature to restrict the port range DCOM uses for communications. They also enabled the machine to be configured to use TCP only.

In order to configure the range of ports, the following registry settings must be edited to the appropriate values mentioned in the table. The key to edit is:

```
HKEY_LOCAL_MACHINE\Software\Microsoft\Rpc\Internet
```

Name	Type	Description
`Ports`	`REG_MULTI_SZ`	One or more port ranges. The options below determine the meaning of this named value.
`PortsInternetAvailable`	`REG_SZ`	Always set this to `Y`.
`UseInternetPorts`	`REG_SZ`	If this value is set to `Y`, then the `Ports` named value indicates which ports should be used for DCOM applications. If this value is set to `N`, then the `Ports` named value indicates which ports should NOT be used for DCOM applications.

Chapter 1: Introduction to Scalability

The actual keys and values aren't terribly difficult to implement; however, networks were still weary of DCOM between a firewall. It took far too much configuration and planning to make it run right. In addition, the documentation was not straightforward. Network administrators and developers alike spent many a late hour preparing their networks for the successful launch of DCOM applications.

COM+ Functionality to DCOM

The introduction of Windows 2000 brought with it many useful developer features. COM+ provided object pooling, queued components, loosely coupled events, and a host of other useful application-tier functionality. These COM+ enhancements to DCOM were a welcome addition to the developer toolbox.

While the advances were attractive, the limitations DCOM imposed on the network continued to wreak havoc and prevented DCOM implementations. Alternatives to DCOM, most notably Enterprise Java Beans (EJB), began to find their way into enterprise applications.

Caching

Caching provides an important aspect to scalability. Basically, caching allows processing work to be saved for later use. This requires that the data is somewhat static in nature. However, caching is especially useful when multiple clients use the same data. For example, it may be desirable to store the fifty states in the US in a database. However, it is not necessary to dynamically read this data for every client request to enter an address. Rather, the data can be read once, cached, and then the cached data can be used for subsequent requests.

ASP had no inherent support for caching. This required that a third-party solution be found and implemented or that a custom solution built. While the custom solution is not necessarily a difficult undertaking, it does require some forethought. As we will explore in Chapter 5, ASP.NET provides wonderful caching support. Of course, this is exposed in a straightforward and easy to use manner as well.

Shared Property Manager

COM provided a caching mechanism called the Shared Property Manager (SPM) that allowed components within the same server process to share information. Data or values that were static or time consuming to retrieve were stored in the SPM and could be retrieved by any object created in the same process.

The SPM gave the developer an easy-access caching mechanism to use at the COM layer. However attractive, the SPM suffered scalability limitations in much the same fashion that the ASP session was limited by being hosted in a single machine.

Scalability Issues

Since the middle-tier application layer where COM resides is traditionally resource intensive, it becomes an attractive layer to scale to multiple physical machines. Like session, if multiple machines are used to host DCOM processes, each machine (and process) maintains its own collection of SPM variables in memory. If the data is not truly static (perhaps it is retrieved from a database), the Shared Property Manager variables can grow out of sync.

Similar to scaling ASP applications to a web farm, when the COM layer is scaled to multiple machines in a web environment, each request can potentially be handled by a different machine. If the Shared Property Manager is out of sync between the machines, unpredictable results can occur.

Client (Page) Caching

Caching web pages in a client browser was another method commonly found in ASP applications. By adding HTTP headers to an outgoing web request, web developers could tell a browser not to re-hit the web site for a new copy of the page.

Because browser navigation is unpredictable in nature, page-level caching represented a quality performance improvement. Users in a web application have the ability to return to previous pages or forward to already existing pages without regenerating the page from the ASP application. If the user clicks the 'Back' button on the browser for example, or navigates to a page already seen, a new request is issued to the web application to return the same information.

Page-level caching was an excellent mechanism for caching static data. Requiring a user to re-hit a site for static content is a performance drain on the application and the user's resources. If the page, while static in nature, is an ASP page, then the page must be reprocessed. Even if the page simply had an ASP extension, it still had to be reprocessed. For either ASP or strict HTML pages, the HTML must be re-downloaded. Static content benefited from caching since it did not change between requests.

However, page-level caching failed for caching dynamic data. Caching dynamic data is not only a bad practice, but it is also annoying for users. Page caching was not typically enabled for dynamic sites. Common practices for disabling page caching included any of the following ASP lines of code:

```
Response.Expires = -1

Response.ExpiresAbsolute=#Jan 1, 1950 00:00:00#

Response.AddHeader "Pragma", "no-cache"

Response.AddHeader "cache-control", "no-store"
```

23

Unfortunately, these options disabled caching for the entire page. It is often preferable to have a mix of cached and dynamic data on a page. For instance, on a page with a menu that is standard for every user, and a user-specific greeting, it would be desirable to cache the menu while leaving the user greeting as dynamic.

For truly enterprise systems, implementing page-level caching and middle tier caching meant purchasing a third-party caching application server or implementing your own caching mechanism. Neither alternative was particularly attractive and left the developer with much to be desired at the caching level.

Windows DNA Scalability Limitations Recap

Windows DNA provided necessary and important technological advancements over its predecessor technologies. Any technology that introduces as many features as Windows DNA did is bound to face some limitations. In Windows DNA, one of the primary concerns was platform scalability.

It is very important to understand the limitations that VB and ASP imposed on developers to appreciate the advances found in .NET. .NET gained much of its strength from the lessons learned with the COM and ASP layers. Understanding the limitations imposed by COM and ASP gives us a better appreciation of the changes introduced in the .NET Framework.

Common VB Scalability Design Pitfalls

Scalability limitations were not only imposed by the Windows DNA platform, the Visual Basic language and common developer design pitfalls also introduced scalability concerns to applications. As mentioned at the start of this chapter, the Visual Basic language was limited in functionality. The OO deficiencies themselves were serious enough to persuade developers to use alternative languages.

However feature limiting, Visual Basic's rise in popularity proved the language's benefits far outweighed its shortcomings. Using Visual Basic for writing client applications (and web applications) for Microsoft platforms proved to be a more approachable alternative to the more difficult-to-master C++.

Visual Basic's straightforward and simple programming environment and documentation focused primarily on creating user interfaces. When Visual Basic was developed, its focus was initially on rapid Windows applications and user interfaces. Initial material from Microsoft and from the popular press raved about the simplicity of creating user interfaces.

Visual Basic's popularity thrived in the business community. Tech-savvy business people were writing with Office VBA (and VB itself) and creating rather powerful business applications very quickly.

With the rise of a new programming community built from non-traditional programmers, the Visual Basic code structure was often unwieldy. Many of the fundamentals learned by schooled application developers were not being utilized.

It has been documented that even though class design has been a feature of Visual Basic since 1995, only a small percentage of Visual Basic developers use such capabilities to their full extent. As .NET is introduced, OO fundamentals are crucial to understand for Visual Basic developers making the transition to .NET.

An important requirement when building scalable systems is recognizing how code, and design, affects application performance. The application developer has the most important role to play in designing scalable systems. By understanding the design practices used in traditional Visual Basic applications that were proven difficult to scale, we can prepare ourselves for developing scalable applications with .NET.

Common design pitfalls found in Windows DNA include:

- Using inline SQL statements instead of stored procedures
- External resource misuse
- Inefficient `Recordset` creation and use
- Improper usage of Visual Basic objects
- Maintaining a stateful middle tier
- Creating resource-intensive tier interfaces
- Improper OO design

Using Inline SQL Instead of Stored Procedures

Inline SQL is subject to performance limitations that stored procedures can avoid. When discussing scalable systems, the performance between tiers is critical to monitor. Inline SQL requires more data to be transferred between the application layer and database, so is not as efficient as stored procedures.

Stored procedure usage is detailed in depth during Chapter 3. At the high level, stored procedures provide the following performance benefits over inline SQL:

- Stored procedures provide a layer of security not found in inline SQL
- Stored procedures allow faster execution times since an in-memory version of the procedure can be used for all subsequent calls after the initial call
- Stored procedures reduce network traffic since only parameters, not SQL code, is transmitted over the network
- Stored procedures insulate your application by providing a layer of abstraction between the code and the database

Perhaps one of the biggest advantages of stored procedures is in how databases treat any action that must be performed. A database will determine the best method for executing a statement. For inline SQL, these plans must be recreated each time. However, a stored procedure will save these execution plans for reuse every subsequent time.

External Resource Misuse

Applications use the services of external resources. Understanding the proper usage of the external resource is critical to avoid locking and contentions. It is important for resource-intensive objects, like database connections and file-system resources, to obtain locks late and release locks early to avoid resource locking.

Some external resources, such as database connections, are in limited supply. While it is easy to keep connections available in Visual Basic code, doing so consumes resources that would better serve other clients. Eventually, ADO introduced the ability to disconnect recordsets. This is carried further in ADO.NET

Inefficient Recordset Creation and Use

The `Recordset` object is the de facto standard for retrieving data from a database and is trivial to create and use. It is not, however, trivial to create and use *properly*. Traditionally, `Recordset` objects limited scalability. Some common bad practices were developed around recordsets, including:

- Stored procedures and database functionality was under-utilized because of the ease of use of the `Recordset`. Functionality that was meant for the data tier was being handled, often inefficiently, by recordsets, not stored procedures.

- Recordsets were created with non-optimal settings. The cursor location defaulted to the server side, which was not efficient for many cases, such as updating data. A client cursor would have proven to be more efficient in many scenarios. However, since it was not the `Recordset` default parameter, many failed to understand the differences between the cursors.

- Record locking types were not used properly to efficiently deal with concurrency. Data that was read-only in nature was not being locked as such.

- Recordsets were not disconnected. This meant that the recordset would maintain a connection to the database for its lifetime, causing valuable connections to remain open.

- Extra data was retrieved. Doing a `Select * From` query often resulted in too much data being returned where a limited set of fields could have been specified.

Improper usage of Visual Basic Objects

As mentioned earlier, ASP `Session` and VB objects lead to serious scalability limitations found in ASP code. Still, Visual Basic objects were being held in the `Application` and `Session` objects in ASP. Many reasons contributed to developers using VB applications in session:

- Complicated threading models. Visual Basic developers have, in general, never needed to understand STA and MTA threading models.
- Lack of quality documentation.
- No immediate performance drawbacks. When developers tested applications with VB components in the middle tier, scalability limitations were not readily apparent.

Maintaining a Stateful Middle Tier

Maintaining middle-tier state sounds attractive. Once a resource is obtained, it can be used throughout the life of the user's session. However, this can severely affect an applicantion's scalability.

The alternative to maintaining a stateful middle tier is creating and destroying the resource for every page request. While such a process has traditionally involved a great deal of overhead, COM+ helps alleviate the overhead by allowing for connection and object pooling.

Creating Resource-Intensive Tier Interfaces

Interfaces between tiers (COM and ASP, for example) that are resource intensive will kill application performance and scalability. Resource-intensive tiers are often called "chatty" tiers since they require a great deal of communication in their interaction with one another. When objects are communicating between tiers, the goal is to accomplish as much as possible with as few calls as possible.

Let's take a look at an example of a simple VB6 object called `Customer`:

```
Private mFirstName As String
Private mMiddleName As String
Private mLastName As String
Private mEMailAddress As String

Public Property Get FirstName() As String
   FirstName = mFirstName
End Property

Public Property Let FirstName(ByVal Value As String)
   mFirstName = Value
End Property
```

```
    Public Property Get MiddleName() As String
        MiddleName = mMiddleName
    End Property

    Public Property Let MiddleName(ByVal Value As String)
        mMiddleName = Value
    End Property

    Public Property Get LastName() As String
        LastName = mLastName
    End Property

    Public Property Let LastName(ByVal Value As String)
        mLastName = Value
    End Property

    Public Property Get EMailAddress() As String
        EMailAddress = mEMailAddress
    End Property

    Public Property Let EMailAddress(ByVal Value As String)
        mEMailAddress = Value
    End Property

    Public Sub Load(ByVal sFirstName, ByVal sMiddleName, _
                    ByVal sLastName, ByVal sEMailAddress)
        FirstName = sFirstName
        MiddleName = sMiddleName
        LastName = sLastName
        EMailAddress = sEMailAddress
    End Sub
```

This `Customer` object's simplicity is by design. We have properties that can be retrieved and set. Whenever a `Property Let` is called by the calling code, the parameter needs to be marshaled over to the object, the property set, and execution returned to the calling code. If the calling code is residing in ASP on one box and the `Customer` object is installed in COM+ on another box, each call between layers is expensive.

A much more efficient way to set the properties of this object is demonstrated by the `Load()` method, which accepts the values for all parameters, so the overhead of setting up four property set calls can be reduced to one. Setting properties individually is an example of a "chatty" interface because it requires a lot of communication to function. Setting properties via the `Load()` method is considered a "chunky" interface because it saves on wire-time overhead.

Here is an example of a small client application that demonstrates the use of a "chunky" and "chatty" coding practice. Chunky interfaces are heavily favored in a scalable system:

```
Sub main()

    ' "Chatty" user - each property set requires a round trip to object.
    Dim ChattyUser As New Customer
    With ChattyUser
       .FirstName = "Robert"
       .MiddleName = "Alexander"
       .LastName = "Smith"
       .EMailAddress = "chaz@myInvestmentWatch.com"
    End With

    ' "Chunky" User - all properties set in single call
    Dim ChunkyUser As New Customer
    ChunkyUser.Load "Bandit", "Dog", "Hyrman", _
                    "Ruff@myInvestmentWatch.com"
End Sub
```

Improper OO Design

OO design in VB was underutilized. Because OO was not a native concept to the Visual Basic language or its developers, unorthodox object designs had the potential to find their way into systems.

The most common use of improper OO design revolves around creating a "one-size-fits-all" object capable of handling multiple unrelated functions. For example, a class had a `ConvertString()` method and a `DoesRecordExistInDB()` method defined in the same class module. Or perhaps functions were grouped according to purpose (for example string objects grouped into the same class); however, the objects were more function bases than true OO objects.

> **Keep in mind that OO design is the heart of developing for .NET. Traditionally, Visual Basic developers have not been as exposed to OO concepts as have developers specializing in other languages. When making the transition from VB6 to VB.NET, one of the learning curves facing the developer is to become versed with OO skills. A good OO design enables applications to perform much more efficiently and is a major benefit for scalable applications.**

Welcome .NET

By now you're probably painfully reminded of the limitations and frustrations of previous Microsoft technologies and coding practices. Thankfully the wait for a platform that provides the infrastructure for scalability is over with the release of .NET, which has improved upon Windows DNA in many respects, most notably in terms of overall performance and scalability.

Throughout the rest of this book, the discussion will be concerned with .NET scalability tips and tricks. Knowing the limitations that were imposed by COM gives us a more appreciative eye when viewing the features of .NET. Since this is not an introduction to either .NET or VB.NET, we will be skipping over the .NET platform and VB.NET language introductory material to focus in depth on scalability features.

Let's revisit the Windows DNA scalability limitations and find out how .NET has improved in the areas of:

- Threading
- Session
- Middle-tier application hosting
- Caching
- VB Language enhancements

.NET Threading

Remember STA, MTA, free threading, neutral threading, or the free-threaded marshaller from COM? Forget them! .NET has only one type of thread and it doesn't have any of the limitations of the previous threading models. Visual Basic .NET itself, in previous versions limited to creating objects running under the STA threading model, now creates threads in the same fashion as any other language.

Creating and using a thread in Visual Basic .NET is straight forward and trivial. To prove this statement, the following code is all that is required to execute a thread from within VB.NET:

```
Imports System
Imports System.Threading

Public Class Server

  'This method is called when the thread is started.
  Public Sub DoSomething()
    Console.WriteLine("Server.DoSomething is starting")

    'Pause a moment to provide a delay to make threads more apparent.
    Thread.Sleep(3000)
    Console.WriteLine("Server.DoSomething is ending")
  End Sub
End Class

Public Class Simple

  Public Shared Sub Main()
    Console.WriteLine("Main() Application Starting")
```

```vbnet
        Dim serverObject As New Server()

        ' Create the thread object, telling the thread where to start
        ' executing when the thread is started.
        Dim InstanceCaller As New _
            Thread(New ThreadStart(AddressOf serverObject.DoSomething))

        ' Start the thread.
        InstanceCaller.Start()

        Console.WriteLine("Main() Application Ending")
        Console.ReadLine()
    End Sub
End Class
```

To execute the application, save the file as `thread.vb` and compile the code with the following command line:

> **vbc thread.vb**

When the code is compiled and executed, it produces the following output:

```
C:\Scalability\Chapter 1>Thread
Main() Application Starting
Main() Application Ending
Server.DoSomething is starting
Server.DoSomething is ending
```

That is all we needed to create a multi-threaded application! If we look at the code, all we needed was to create a thread and start it:

```vbnet
        ' Create the thread object, telling the thread where to start
        ' executing when the thread is started.
        Dim InstanceCaller As New _
            Thread(New ThreadStart(AddressOf serverObject.DoSomething))

        ' Start the thread.
        InstanceCaller.Start()
```

Creating a new instance of a `Thread` object actually creates a 'managed' thread. We call the thread managed since it executes under the watchful eye of the Common Language Runtime (CLR). The `ThreadStart` parameter of the `Thread` object's constructor is a delegate object that tells the thread where to start when the `Start()` method is called. One thing to note is that the execution order is not guaranteed.

If you look at the code carefully, you may be wondering why calling the `Start()` method did not print the line Server.DoSomething() is starting before the Main() Application Ending line. The reason the `Main()` method was ended before the thread's code was executed has to do with the asynchronous nature of the `Start()` call. The `Start()` call submits an asynchronous request into the CLR and returns immediately. The code running in the `Main()` method executed before the asynchronous request could start. The timing of the additional thread started is not guaranteed. If you are interested in examining the thread status, call the `IsAlive` property to determine if the thread has been started.

.NET has made the concept of threading much simpler to understand when compared to COM. There is a unified threading model and the `System.Threading` namespace where threading classes are found is both logical and functional for the developer to understand.

.NET threading is also more functional than threading found in COM. The limitations imposed by COM's (and particularly VB objects') threading models in the ASP.NET `Session` and `Application` objects have been lifted. Objects written in any .NET managed language, including VB.NET, can be held within session or application without concern for limiting scalability by contending threads.

In order to remain scalable, threading in .NET still requires a bit of knowledge of how the system scheduler handles threads. It is possible to overuse threads and actually make a system run slower than if threading was avoided. While threading is simple to implement, its simplicity hides a much more sinister complexity. Threading introduces problems with guaranteeing execution order, concurrency, and resource contention. Because of this, the effective use of threading is by no means a trivial developer concept and all uses of threading should be tested and well thought through before being implemented in a production environment. For more information on threading in .NET, refer to *Visual Basic .NET Threading Handbook*, ISBN 1-86100-713-2.

Session

Session improvements in .NET are numerous and were eagerly anticipated by developers. Here is an overview of a few of the major session enhancements:

- ❑ Easy to use for traditional ASP developers
- ❑ Support for browsers that do not use cookies
- ❑ Ability to host session in a dedicated process or database
- ❑ Completely independent of the ASP.NET process and can be maintained if the ASP.NET application is terminated

Easy to Use

Using sessions in ASP.NET is similar to using sessions in ASP from a coding standpoint, except the ASP.NET `Session` object is vastly more functional. The ASP.NET `Session` object has the familiar properties of `Session.Contents`, and `Session.Item` that were available to the ASP developer. The theory behind session as a user-specific data storage location has not changed, it's the improvements built into the `Session` object that make it vastly more functional than in ASP.

Cookieless Browser Support

One of the most noticeable improvements found in ASP.NET sessions is the ability to support browsers that don't support cookies. Instead of storing the session ID as a cookie, the ASP.NET runtime can insert the session ID directly into the URL when returning a page to the user. The beauty of the process is the fact that the developer can configure this option directly in an ASP.NET configuration file without adding an extra line of code.

Session Hosting Capabilities

The ASP.NET sessions can be hosted either in-process, in a dedicated process, or in SQL mode that will store session into a SQL Server database. Depending on your needs, the three different modes allow for vast flexibility in how the session is stored.

Like many other system aspects with the ASP.NET environment, the session state storage host can be configured via an ASP.NET configuration file. The different options allow for a session that is not dependent on the ASP process. Let's look at some of the pros and cons for each session state storage host mode:

In-Process

The in-process ASP.NET session model is fast. There is no need to cross process borders between the ASP.NET process and the state server to retrieve objects or values from the session.

A limitation of the in-process model is the fact that the ASP.NET session remains tied to ASP.NET worker process. If the ASP.NET worker process is terminated, either expectedly or unexpectedly, the session state is lost. This is similar behavior to the ASP session and should be used when losing a session would not be detrimental to the application.

Out-of-Process

Hosting the session state out-of-process allows the session state to be independent of the ASP.NET worker process. The session is stored in a special server called a state server, which resides in the memory space of another server. The out-of-process model removes the session's dependency on the ASP.NET worker process. If the ASP.NET process terminates, the new ASP.NET process will have access to the same `Session` objects that the previous process had. Hosting the ASP.NET session out-of-process also allows us to use the session from multiple computers (web-farm) or multiple ASP.NET working processes on the same computer. Scalability of the application is greatly improved since we have the ability to add ASP.NET machines to handle the processing without needing to concern ourselves with session management.

Objects stored in session are serialized. When an object is requested from a state server, the object is serialized and sent between processes to the ASP.NET application process. The ASP.NET process retrieves the object in binary format and re-creates the live object instance. The retrieval is still very fast since the objects remain in memory on the state server; however, the serialization must take place between processes.

The out-of-process model removes the session's dependency on the ASP.NET process; however, the session's lifetime remains dependent on the state server process. If the state server process terminates, the session is lost.

SQL Mode
Out-of-process session hosting provides a great deal of flexibility and convenience for developers; however, the dependency of the session on the state server process remains. In many web farms and application environments, such a dependency is tolerable. If your application demands the absolute best reliability, the SQL Session mode is available. Of course, along with this, you'll need access to a SQL Server database where ASP.NET can install the necessary tables.

The SQL Mode for session storage uses a SQL Server instance for storing state. The session is serialized in the same fashion as the state server but instead of retaining the session in a process memory space, it is stored into a database. A SQL Server instance is more reliable than a process and thus the session state itself is more reliable.

We will expand on these alternatives, as well as the advantages and disadvantages of each, in Chapter 5.

Middle-Tier Application Hosting

Middle-tier functionality previously hosted by COM and COM+ is greatly improved with the .NET Framework. .NET provides two middle-tier application hosting technologies called Remoting and Web Services that are poised to not only replace, but revolutionize, what COM and DCOM began.

Remoting

.NET Remoting allows much the same functionality as DCOM, but has removed many of the problems and hurdles often faced with DCOM.

Like DCOM, Remoting allows code running on one server to invoke code on another server, effectively separating the application into multiple logical (and perhaps physical) tiers. Offloading the processing to other machines or processes is a technique that allows systems to be designed for scalability. If a specific tier is not performing well, resources can be added to alleviate the bottleneck.

The limiting factor DCOM had was its dependence on a dynamic port range to operate. An object exposed via Remoting is configured by the administrator to use a specific port (and only that port!). Since the port is known in advance, the network administration can make one non-obtrusive firewall change for the application to function. Remoting is advantageous to the developer because they gain scalability at a surprisingly low cost by making objects available between tiers via Remoting. Remoting is advantageous to the network administrator because, unlike DCOM, Remoting is network friendly.

The Remoting infrastructure, in addition to being network friendly, offers tremendous flexibility to the developer to control the process used during Remoting. When objects are created, the data is marshaled between the two Remoting endpoints. The developer can choose how the data is packaged up for delivery and the channel it is delivered on. For example, the Remoting client and server can be configured to use SOAP encoding, to send messages in the verbose but readable format. They can also be configured to use a binary format that is compact and efficient. The client and server can also be configured to use an HTTP channel or TCP channel. The HTTP channel relies on the HTTP protocol, understandable to many varieties of application servers, and the TCP channel is optimized for fast data transfer. If these channels and formatters are still not what the developer desires then custom channels and formatters can be developed and used by the Remoting runtime without difficult configuration. We will cover Remoting in more detail in Chapter 4.

Web Services

Web Services are similar to Remoting in the sense that they both allow scalable, multi-tiered applications to be developed and consumed by clients. Web Services pose an even more exciting prospect in the .NET Framework. While they were, in a sense, bolted onto Visual Basic 6, they are an integral part of the language in Visual Basic .NET.

The draw to web services is their accessibility to a wide variety of applications that are enabled to communicate using ubiquitous internet standards like HTTP, XML, SOAP, and others. Web services, like Remoting, expose a set of callable functionality. Web services, being callable from all types of platforms, use the HTTP protocol for their channel and typically SOAP for the formatter. While SOAP and HTTP are slower than the TCP channel and the binary formatter, they are more flexible since they rely on the industry standards.

Web Services provide an excellent method of providing interfaces into an application in an industry-standard format. Thus, it is possible to provide a layer in front of your application to expose certain services and then consume these services from any client, regardless of technology. In a sense, this is also much of the draw of web-based applications. One fundamental difference is that people are meant to interact with HTML and web pages while applications are meant to interact with Web Services. We will cover Web Services in more detail in Chapter 4.

Caching

Caching is one of the best performance improving aspects of scalable web applications. ASP.NET allows the developer to store pages, parts of pages, controls, or custom objects in memory. ASP.NET provides two primary methods for caching; output caching and programmatic caching. Of course, these two options also have a variety of methods to control specific aspects of caching. We will further explore these options in Chapter 5.

The caching functionality found in .NET gives the ASP.NET developer tremendous scalability improvements that previously required additional products or dedicated caching applications. Understanding how to use the ASP.NET caching facility provides tremendous scalability advancements since it frees us from expensive repetitive lookups.

@OutputCache

ASP.NET output caching, which allows pages or even partial pages to be cached, can be set using the `@OutputCache` directive in an ASP.NET page. The `@OutputCache` directive allows you to specify the duration, in seconds, for which you wish to cache an item before it is refreshed. You can also specify where the cached output will be stored, including on the web server, the client, or even a proxy server in between. Lastly, the `OutputCache` directive will allow the output to be varied by multiple means. For instance, it is possible to cache a separate copy of the output for each different client. In other words, it is possible to have a different cached page for IE 5, IE 6, and Netscape 4.7.

It's even possible to cache by the parameter values sent in as part of the querystring or a form. For example:

```
<%@ OutputCache Duration="60" VaryByParam="productID" %>
```

When a request is made to this ASP.NET page with a form or querystring parameter of `productID=7`, the ASP.NET cache will hold a copy of that page for 60 seconds. Any request coming in for `productID=7` in the next 60 seconds will use the cached item.

When a client makes a new request for `productID=6`, then the resulting output for this page will also be cached for 60 seconds. Keep in mind that both items are cached independently of each other. Since product 7 was requested first, it will expire first. Of course, next time product 7 is request, it will be cached again. We will examine ASP.NET caching in detail in Chapter 5.

Programmatic Cache Access

The `Cache` object can be accessed via code, providing further caching benefits. Items are added to the cache with either an absolute or a sliding expiration time, whichever fits the object best. For example, you could direct an object to expire every ten minutes (absolute expiration) or give the object a sliding expiration. A sliding expiration time starts when the object was last accessed. If the object is given a sliding expiration of twenty minutes, if the object isn't requested for twenty minutes, the object is removed from the cache. If the object is accessed within the twenty minute period, the sliding expiration time is renewed so that the object will remain in the cache for a further twenty minute period.

With parameter-based caching in particular, objects stored in cache can accumulate very quickly. When the cache is reaching capacity, the ASP.NET process will begin to purge cached objects. Objects, when added to the cache, can be assigned a priority. If the object has a high priority value, it will withstand cache purges longer than those with a lower priority.

If an object is expensive to create and is global to users, it is a good candidate for caching. The amount of resources required to retrieve the value help to determine its priority level. Expensive resources should be cached with a high priority level, while those with lower resource retrieval requirements should be cached with a lower priority. ASP.NET caching offers a nice range of useful features; priority is definitely nice to have.

With the ASP.NET runtime periodically checking the cache, a state could occur where one cached object depends on another cached object that has been swept from the cache. In order to prevent invalid states, ASP.NET caching allows you to create dependencies on other cached objects. If one object is removed from the cached, any others with dependencies on the removed object will also be removed.

Assume we have two objects in cache, a `DataSet` and an HTML table that draws its data from the `DataSet`. Both are cached. Since the HTML table derives its data from the `DataSet`, when the `DataSet` is removed from cache, the HTML table object will also need to be removed. If the table object remained in cache and the `DataSet` was recreated with different data, the HTML table would contain invalid information. When adding the HTML table to the cache, we would specify it to be dependent on the `DataSet`. Removing the `DataSet` from cache will also destroy the HTML table to eliminate the possibility of an invalid state.

Visual Basic Does .NET

The .NET Framework has been developed with OO concepts in mind, including support for parameterized constructors, method overloading, inheritance, and vastly improved exception handling to name a few of the improvements. Visual Basic .NET exposes these new features in a robust and accessible manner. Arguably the most anticipated improvement, OO concepts are new to many VB developers. A detailed description of the Visual Basic OO features is detailed in the *Visual Basic .NET Class Design Handbook*, ISBN 1-86100-708-6.

37

Chapter 1: Introduction to Scalability

Not to be overlooked is the fact that ASP.NET code, unlike ASP code, which was uncompiled VBScript or JScript code, is now fully supported by any CLR-compliant language. Of course, this includes VB.NET. ASP.NET is now also compiled to Intermediate Language on the first page request and then simply executed for each additional request, greatly speeding performance. Compiled code is faster than interpreted script and provides a much more efficient user interface. The Visual Basic .NET language itself will not limit the developer in terms of scalability for writing applications for the Microsoft platform as it did in versions past.

Setting the Stage

The .NET platform is far reaching in the changes imposed on the developer. The rest of this book is dedicated to explaining the .NET platform's scalability improvements in greater detail. You will be introduced to the .NET platform at each layer; Database, Middle Tier, and User Interface with a slant on scalability improvements in each tier.

It is not our intention to discuss specific technologies. It is assumed you have a fundamental knowledge of web application development and developing n-tier application architectures.

Each chapter will be independent of all others in nature. Throughout the course of the book we will maintain a sample application titled MyInvestmentWatch.com, a fictitious web application developed to keep track of stock quotes and manage your personal portfolio. The goal is to create a highly scalable application, designed with scalability improvements found in the .NET Framework.

MyInvestmentWatch.com

MyInvestmentWatch.com is a fictitious web site created for this book that is dedicated to helping its customers survive the stock exchange, and even make some money in the process. Over the course of time, the small web application has grown quite popular and is exhibiting scalability problems with its current architecture. Developed for functionality first, performance second, MyInvestmentWatch.com is a typical candidate for improvements.

The typical performance problems are being recognized: slow response time, user complaints, heavy system resource consumption, and expected growth.

The design practices found in the current VB6/ASP (with VBScript)/COM MyInvestmentWatch.com site are similar to those found in many of today's web applications. At the ASP layer, the `Session` object is being used, the COM layer is designed using VB and the limited OO features it provides, and the database is normalized.

Our intention when originally designing the application was not to purposely create a non-scalable system. Granted we understand the limitations proposed in pre-.NET applications, however, our intention was not to create the most bulletproof and high performing system we could, but rather to use the common design practices found in today's development code. Research was done, sample code was read, and newsgroups were queried for design practices around current Windows DNA applications developed in Visual Basic 6.

As the application progresses, we will pick apart the design guidelines and examine each layer in detail as we transition the code base to .NET.

Let's begin by setting the stage of the application by describing our environment.

> The code for the application (including database setup scripts) can be downloaded from the Wrox web site at www.wrox.com.

Environment Diagram

Our environment is very straightforward and typical of the n-tier web applications in production environments today. Perhaps the MyInvestmentWatch.com infrastructure is a bit scaled down, especially for today's enterprise applications, but the tiers are in place and reflective of the common DNA architecture.

We're assuming a complete Microsoft solution for the operating system, Visual Basic 6 for the implementation language, and ASP with VBScript for the front end. Logically, the application is separated into three tiers: Presentation, Business, and Data. The Presentation and Business tiers reside on the same physical machine that we term the Application Tier. Figure 3 illustrates our logical environment.

Figure 3

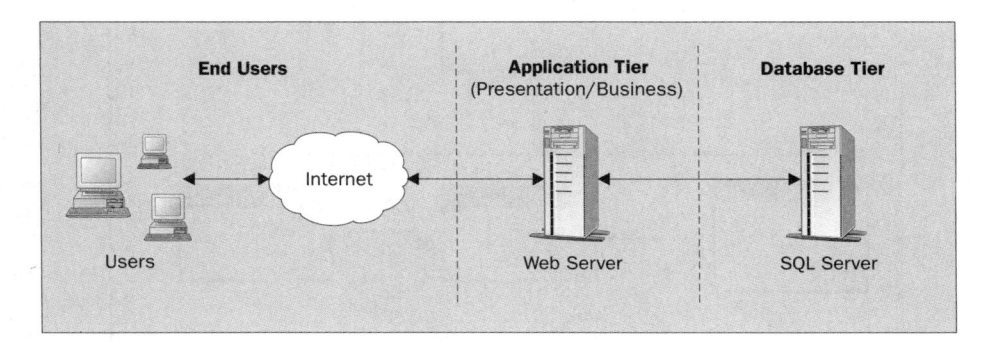

The Database Tier

One thing to note, although it's not directly related to the database tier, is that each class accesses the database directly. This poses a few problems related to scalability. Firstly, it makes it nearly impossible to ensure that all access to the database is uniform and following best practices. Secondly, it introduces a tight cohesion between the application and the data provider. If, for scalability reasons, we need to change out data providers, we must go back to each class and modify the persistence code. As you will see in Chapter 3, we introduce a much more elegant method for dealing with both of these problems.

The database has been designed in SQL Server 2000 with a relational model and assumes the logical primary and foreign key constraints. The actual data stored in the application is fairly simple to understand. Here is a high-level table explanation:

- `Companies` – Represents publicly traded entities. The table's design assumes that a company can have only one stock symbol for simplicity.
- `StockQuotes` – Represents quote prices for the companies on a specific date/time.
- `Users` – Valid login accounts for our system.
- `UserHits` – Requested company ticker stock quotes. Maintains a list of current 'hot' stocks the user has requested.
- `UserStocks` – A list of stocks the user has entered into their online portfolio.

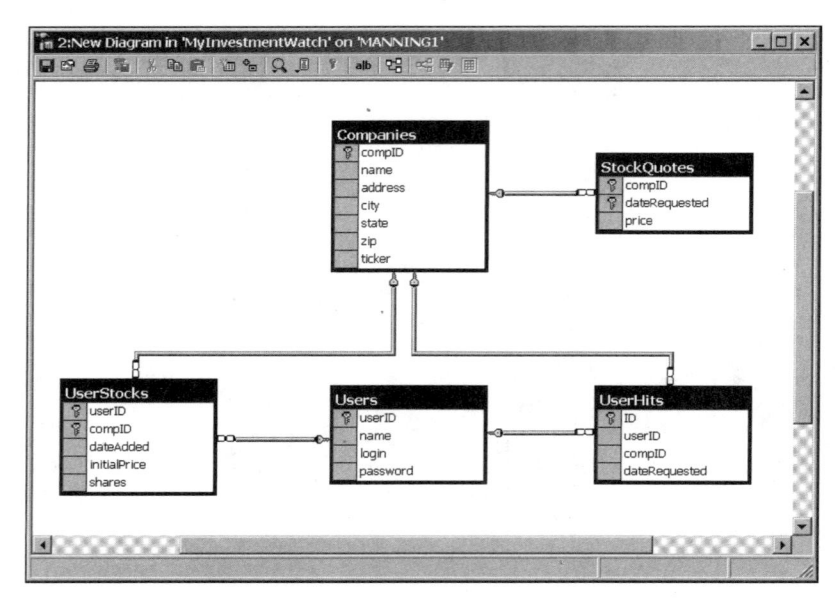

The Application Tier

The application tier consists of a single COM .dll written in Visual Basic 6. It is designed with commonly used OO principles of data encapsulation and uses, in a somewhat limited fashion, the concepts of properties and methods. Events are not used in this middle tier.

Figure 4 shows a UML diagram that illustrates the object model and interface definition for each object.

Figure 4

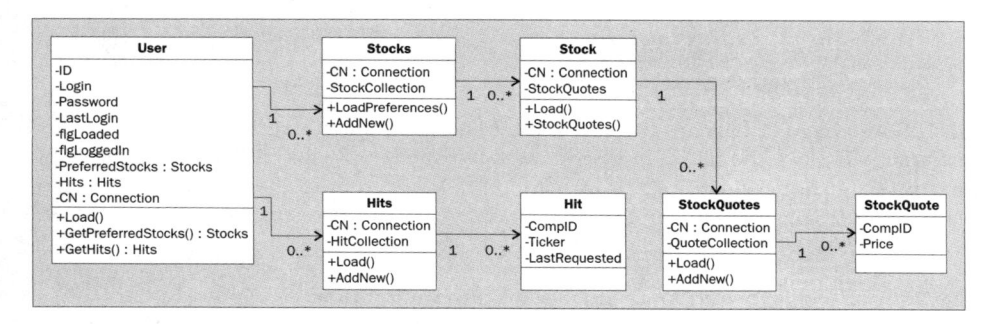

User
-ID
-Login
-Password
-LastLogin
-flgLoaded
-flgLoggedIn
-PreferredStocks : Stocks
-Hits : Hits
-CN : Connection
+Load()
+GetPreferredStocks() : Stocks
+GetHits() : Hits

Stocks
-CN : Connection
-StockCollection
+LoadPreferences()
+AddNew()

Stock
-CN : Connection
-StockQuotes
+Load()
+StockQuotes()

Hits
-CN : Connection
-HitCollection
+Load()
+AddNew()

Hit
-CompID
-Ticker
-LastRequested

StockQuotes
-CN : Connection
-QuoteCollection
+Load()
+AddNew()

StockQuote
-CompID
-Price

This object model is not overly complex, but, as you can see, there is quite a bit happening in this single object. The actual number of objects in the object model is not of concern or limiting our scalability in any way. Nor is it necessarily how these objects are structured that is limiting our scalability. One of the largest problems with these objects, which we will discuss in detail in Chapter 4, is in how they are created, loaded, and utilized. The point to emphasize at this point is this: The object design and architecture layout is structured correctly; it's the implementation of the code that hinders our scalability potential.

User Interface Tier

This piece of the user interface consists of a default ASP page that pulls different include files depending on the state of the user's account. Figure 5 illustrates this graphically.

Chapter 1: Introduction to Scalability

Figure 5

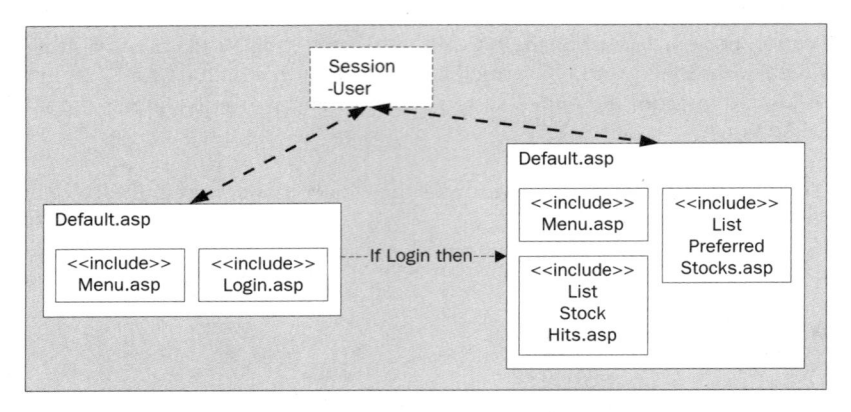

```
                            Session
                             -User
                    ╱         ▲         ╲
                  ╱           │           ╲
                ╱             │             ╲
              ╱               │               ╲
    ┌─────────────────────┐   │   ┌───────────────────────────────────┐
    │ Default.asp         │   │   │ Default.asp                       │
    │ ┌──────────┐ ┌──────────┐ │ │ ┌──────────┐   ┌──────────┐       │
    │ │<<include>>│ │<<include>>│─┼─│<<include>>│   │<<include>>│      │
    │ │ Menu.asp │ │ Login.asp │ │ │ Menu.asp │   │   List    │       │
    │ └──────────┘ └──────────┘ │ │ └──────────┘   │ Preferred │       │
    │      ----If Login then--->│ │ ┌──────────┐   │Stocks.asp│       │
    │                           │ │ │<<include>>│   └──────────┘       │
    │                           │ │ │   List    │                     │
    │                           │ │ │  Stock    │                     │
    │                           │ │ │ Hits.asp  │                     │
    │                           │ │ └──────────┘                     │
    └─────────────────────┘       └───────────────────────────────────┘
```

First off, the include files are used to add fairly encapsulated page snippets. For example, we place the menu in a separate page and simply add it back to each page through the include directive. In this manner, if we need to change the menu, we can make the modifications in a single spot. In ASP.NET, this concept has been refined and expanded greatly through user controls.

The `User` object is stored in session, not an uncommon practice. Knowing the limitations VB threading imposes on our application, we have a candidate for improving scalability by removing this from the `Session` object. However, this would require us to store the information elsewhere and perhaps change the middle tier.

User Object

Let's examine the `User` class in more detail to point out some of the scalability limitations provided by the object's implementation. The `User` object is the center of the application hierarchy and the parent to the other objects. When the `User` object is loaded, the user's recent stock quotes (`Hits`) and portfolio stocks (`PreferredStocks`) are loaded. In terms of OO design, the `User` object has child `Stocks` and `Hits` objects. The `Stocks` and `Hits` objects are custom collection objects that contain `Stock` and `Hit` objects respectively. The `User` object is of high interest since it is ultimately responsible for creating the object model instances.

User Object Examination

The `User` object and its child objects provide the following functionality:

- Log the user into the MyInvestmentWatch.com application
- Store the user's preferred stocks
- Store the stock quote history for each preferred stock
- Store a list of the stocks the user has last requested

The code is as follows (keep in mind that this is VB 6):

```vb
'    User.cls (note: This is VB6)

Option Explicit

Private mID As Integer
Private mLogin As String
Private mName As String
Private mPassword As String
Private mLastLogin As Date
Private mPreferredStocks As Stocks
Private mHits As Hits
Private mCn As ADODB.Connection
Private mflgLoaded As Boolean
Private mflgIsLoggedIn As Boolean

'<instance read/write properties omitted for brevity>

'Note: Passwords are case sensitive.
Public Sub Load(ByVal userName As String, ByVal Password As String)
  Dim rs As New Recordset
  Dim SQL As String

  SQL = "Select * from users where login = '" & userName & "'"

  With rs
    .Source = SQL
    .CursorType = adOpenForwardOnly
    .LockType = adLockReadOnly
    .ActiveConnection = mCn
    .Open
  End With

  If rs.EOF Then
    Err.Raise vbObjectError + 10001, _
       "UserName '" & userName & "' is not valid"
  End If

  If Password <> rs("Password") Then
    Err.Raise vbObjectError + 10001, "Password is incorrect"
  End If

  'You have a valid user.
  mID = rs("userID")
  mName = rs("Name")
  mLogin = rs("Login")
  mPassword = rs("Password")
  'retrieve user preference stocks
  mPreferredStocks.LoadPreferences userID
  'retrieve recently loaded stocks
  mHits.Load userID
```

Chapter 1: Introduction to Scalability

```
        mflgLoaded = True
        mflgIsLoggedIn = True
        rs.Close
        Set rs = Nothing
    End Sub

    Private Sub Class_Initialize()
        Set mPreferredStocks = New Stocks
        Set mHits = New Hits
        Set mCn = New ADODB.Connection
        mCn.Open CONN
        mflgIsLoggedIn = False
    End Sub

    Private Sub Class_Terminate()
        If mCn.State = adStateOpen Then mCn.Close
    End Sub
```

The `Load()` method is responsible for retrieving the object's initial state. The initial state includes initializing the object's hierarchy by calling the children's `Load()` method as well. Because of Visual Basic's constructor limitations (or lack thereof), calling `Load()` to populate state was one alternative used to circumvent the limitations.

Problem: Inefficient Resource Consumption

There are serious performance inefficiencies in how this code handles resources. If you look at the code again, you'll notice that loading the user opens a connection to the database and retrieves some user data. However, after this database call is made, several more `Load()` methods are called. These calls will load subsequent user items, such as the user's preferred stocks. These called routines, in turn, create their own connections to the database. Examine what happens with the following lines of code:

```
'From User
Public Sub Load(ByVal userName As String, ByVal Password As String)
    ...
    'retrieve preferred stocks
    mPreferredStocks.LoadPreferences userID
    'retrieve recently loaded stocks
    mHits.Load userID
    ...
End Sub
```

The inefficiency is a misuse of `Connection` objects. The `User` object maintains a connection to the database at class level. When the `Load()` method of the `Stocks` object is called, `Stocks` also maintains its own connection to the database at class level. The `Hits` class maintains its own connection in similar fashion. This is illustrated in Figure 6.

Figure 6

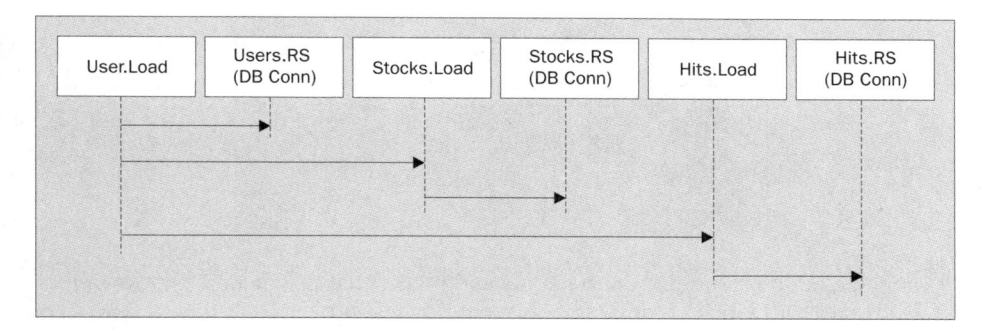

![Figure 6 sequence diagram showing User.Load, Users.RS (DB Conn), Stocks.Load, Stocks.RS (DB Conn), Hits.Load, Hits.RS (DB Conn)]

As we drop further down the class hierarchy, the problem begins to compound. Each `Stock` object within `Stocks` maintains a `Connection` object, as does its child, the `StockQuotes` object. We can now imagine how many connections each `User` object's `Load()` method requires. Figure 7 shows the object hierarchy of the `Stocks` object:

Figure 7

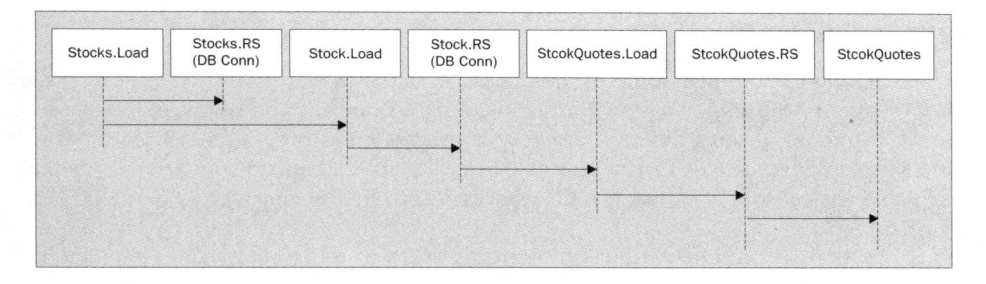

![Figure 7 sequence diagram showing Stocks.Load, Stocks.RS (DB Conn), Stock.Load, Stock.RS (DB Conn), StcokQuotes.Load, StcokQuotes.RS, StcokQuotes]

For example, if a user has five preferred stocks, we have a `Connection` object opened at the `User` object, another opened at the `Stocks` object, five opened at the `Stock` level (one for each object), and five at the `StockQuotes` level (one for each stock). We have a total of twelve connections opened, a horribly inefficient situation. From a holistic view, this can be worse still. Many vendors will also charge by the number of concurrent connections to the database. This may actually hurt the scalability of our project budget as well.

The `Hits` object suffers from similar connection issues, although not as severe as seen with the `Stocks` hierarchy because it has a more shallow depth – see Figure 8.

Figure 8

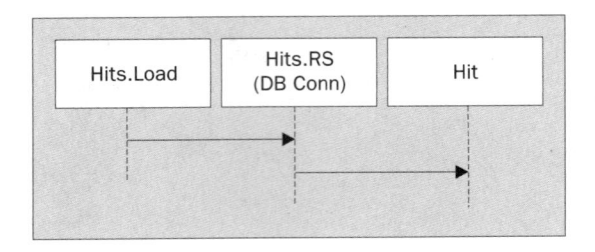

```
┌─────────────────────────────────────────────┐
│   ┌──────────┐   ┌──────────┐   ┌──────┐   │
│   │ Hits.Load│   │ Hits.RS  │   │ Hit  │   │
│   │          │   │ (DB Conn)│   │      │   │
│   └────┬─────┘   └────┬─────┘   └──┬───┘   │
│        │──────────────▶            │        │
│        │              │────────────▶        │
│        │              │            │        │
└─────────────────────────────────────────────┘
```

We can imagine the strain put on the application when a user enters 50 stocks in their preferred stocks list. Such a configuration would maintain over 100 open `Connection` objects while the object is available in memory.

Keep in mind, this is all done whenever a user logs into the site. The mere fact that this entire object model is populated at login can't be helping with the long load times users are experiencing. Also, a new connection to the database is created for each `Load()` method, which puts a large strain on our database.

Scalability Options

It is interesting to note that some of the biggest scalability concerns, such as storing the `User` object in ASP session scope and maintaining a `Connection` object at the class level (for updates, inserts, deletes), are very convenient and programmer friendly. It is these simple conveniences that have caused our scalability concerns and illustrates that the first or easiest solution does not necessarily return the best results.

The application, as presented, functions correctly and was relatively trivial to implement. Now that we have a larger user base for our application, we need to examine the options we have for enhancement with our current architecture and code design.

Hardware Scaling

Let's examine our application architecture again. As you can see, we only have two servers. Our option for scalability, with our existing hardware, is limited. At the application tier, we are limited to scaling up since the ASP session requires execution on one physical box. The database tier can be scaled up or scaled out, so there is room for scalability improvement here. Briefly, scaling up is increasing the capacity of the computer hosting the tier, and scaling out is hosting the tier on multiple computers. (The terms scaling up and scaling out will be explained fully in Chapter 2).

Figure 9

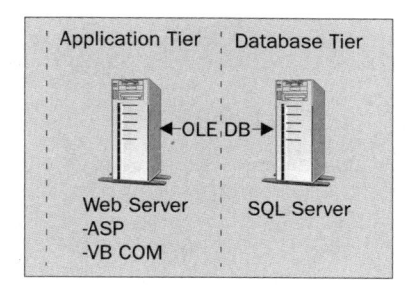

```
        Application Tier │ Database Tier
            ┌──────┐     │   ┌──────┐
            │      │ ◄─OLE.DB─► │      │
            │      │     │   │      │
            └──────┘     │   └──────┘
           Web Server    │   SQL Server
            -ASP         │
            -VB COM      │
```

How are we limited?

Our best option right now is to add more, or faster, processors to each box. This presents a very real limit to how scalable our application is. We can only scale as long as we have room for more processors. While a high-end server, running Windows 2000 Datacenter Server, can support 32 processors, and will likely provide more than enough processing power, this isn't necessarily a favorable option for many IT budgets. We will cover this further in the beginning of Chapter 2.

.NET to the Rescue

As you will see in the rest of the book, .NET is capable of handling our session-related scalability limitations by opening up the session to an out-of-process hosting mechanism. Making the upgrade to .NET will also give us the chance to fix our resource consumption problem. No platform, .NET included, can solve scalability concerns when the code is poorly structured. It becomes important to examine the code structure and apply sound code structure techniques.

All or Nothing Design

When the `User.Load()` event fires, it cascades down the object hierarchy until everything related to a user is loaded. Before the process completes, four objects and two collections must also be loaded. Along the way, a lot of data is returned to our objects.

Let's examine our code. Remember, `Stock.Load()` is repeatedly called by `Stocks.Load()`, which is called in the `User.Load()` sub:

```
'From User
Public Sub Load(ByVal userName As String, ByVal Password As String)
    ...
    'retrieve preferred stocks
    mPreferredStocks.LoadPreferences userID
    'retrieve recently loaded stocks
    mHits.Load userID
    ...
End Sub
```

Chapter 1: Introduction to Scalability

`Stock.Load()` then calls `StockQuotes.Load()`:

```
'From Stock
Public Sub Load(ByVal userID As Long, ByVal CompanyID As Long)
    Dim rs As Recordset
    Dim SQL As String

    SQL = "Select * From UserStocks where userID = " & userID & _
          " and CompID = " & CompanyID & " order by dateAdded desc"

    Set rs = mCn.Execute(SQL)
    ...
    mQuotes.Load CompID
    rs.Close
    Set rs = Nothing
End Sub
```

Here we discover our largest potential producer of large amounts of data. Because this is called for each stock, this function will load historical data for every stock that the user has in their portfolio. As bad, we haven't filtered the SQL statement at all; we're just blindly requesting everything in the table. Likely, that will be a lot data, and a lot of data we're asking the database server to pump back to the client:

```
'From StockQuotes.Load()
Public Function Load(ByVal CompanyID As Long)
    Dim rs As Recordset
    Dim SQL As String

    SQL = "Select * from stockQuotes where compID = " & CompanyID & _
          " order by dateRequested DESC"
    ...
End Function
```

Just to load a user, we will load the stock quote history for every single one of the stocks they own. If an investor only has stock in two companies, and those companies have only been around for a few weeks, then the amount of data being pulled across won't be an issue.

Unnecessary Loading

All of this processing has to happen before the application can return to the user, regardless of whether the user wants to see their preferred stock quotes or not. Meanwhile, the user, who has just clicked the login button, is stuck wondering if they'll ever see their stocks.

If a large amount of data is returned on any given call then a bit of latency will be incurred while the `Recordset` is returned, a collection is created, and objects are instantiated and added to the collection. Each of these seemingly minor tasks will have a detrimental affect on the user's wait time. This is compounded even further when considering that multiple clients will be placing this same load on the database at the same time.

Memory Consumption

When the object is loaded, it remains in the ASP session for the life of the session. With the amount of unnecessary resources and data being loaded and kept open, the ASP process becomes loaded down with unnecessary objects.

Resource Lifetimes

Not only are there too many `Connection` objects open, they are open for too long a time. Scarce resources, like `Connection` objects, should have the shortest lifetime possible to efficiently do their work. The concept of "obtain late, release early" is a fairly common approach to resource lifetime. In our code, the connection is kept open throughout the life of the object, from initialization to termination:

```
Private Sub Class_Initialize()
    ...
    Set mCn = New ADODB.Connection
    mCn.Open CONN
End Sub

Private Sub Class_Terminate()
    If mCn.State = adStateOpen Then mCn.Close
End Sub
```

Objects such as the `StockQuote` object use the connection only for their initial load. One improvement that would cause the least amount of code work would be to have both the `Connection` object's `Open()` and `Close()` methods inside the `Load()` method. However, as we will see with our .NET improvements, it is entirely possible to avoid many of these `Connection` objects altogether.

The OLEDB provider has a nice scalability feature called connection pooling that our code cannot take advantage of. The OLEDB database access libraries will maintain a pool of objects that have identical connection strings. When the connections are released, the OLEDB provider has the ability to keep the released connections ready for use in a pool. When a request is sent from ADO to create another connection, the OLEDB layer has the ability to return the "hot" connection from the pool without physically having to create the connection with the database.

Our code cannot take advantage of OLEDB connection pooling since we do not release our `Connection` references. Even though the `Connection` objects may not be used again by the objects that created them, they cannot be released back to the connection pool since the connection is still being referenced in our code. The OLEDB provider can only pool the connection after it has been released by our application. Holding connections open negates the benefits offered by OLEDB's connection pool.

Ad hoc SQL Usage

One of the more common mistakes involved with data-access code in VB6 is the use of ad hoc or 'dynamic SQL' in place of stored procedures. Dynamic SQL suffers from many limitations that stored procedures tend to eliminate, many of which will be discussed in Chapter 3. An example of dynamic SQL is shown in the following code. Notice how the SQL string is created at run time depending on the current state of the parameters:

```
Public Sub Load(ByVal userName As String, ByVal Password As String)
    Dim rs As New Recordset
    Dim SQL As String

    SQL = "Select * from users where login = '" & userName & "'"
    With rs
        .Source = SQL
        ...
        .Open
    End With
    ...
End Sub
```

Dynamic SQL's Scalability Concerns

The problem is that this is a prepared, or dynamic, SQL statement. This means that the database has to determine the best way to execute the statement every time the user is loaded. Modern databases, such as SQL Server 2000, do their best to cache execution plans and reuse these plans for similar calls. However, not every database supports plan caching. Also, even with a database that does support caching, the cache will have to be accessed to search for the plan, and there is no control over whether the database was able to properly cache the plan or not.

Stored Procedures

Utilizing dynamic SQL makes it much more difficult to tune database access. A better option, as you will see in Chapter 3, is to use stored procedures.

There are many discussions over the virtues and pitfalls of stored procedures; however, stored procedures are an excellent tool for achieving scalability. In essence, you are ensuring that the execution plan is optimized when creating a stored procedure.

Session State

User is a large object and every person on the web site will have a User object. As you can see, we first assign a User object when the session starts. Of course, this object is still very small as the Load() method will not be called until the person actually logs in:

```
Sub Session_OnStart
    set Session("User")=server.CreateObject("StocksComponent.User")
End Sub
```

Scalability Concerns

Storing `User` objects in session is memory intensive and causes threading bottlenecks. As the current design stands, the `User` object can have an unlimited set of preferred stocks and each preferred stock could have an unlimited set of stock quote data. If the preferred stock has 10 quotes, chances are we will not notice the performance hit as the objects are loaded. If the preferred stock has 100 quotes, we will begin to see serious performance (not to mention scalability!) problems.

It is in the `Session` object that the threading limitation with VB's STA threaded objects begins to become truly relevant. An object in an STA thread is limited to executing on the thread that created the object. However, IIS creates a thread pool to handle user requests. This means that IIS must then route every request to that object, the `User` object in our case, through a single thread.

Limiting the threading model of IIS by using thread-specific VB objects in the session negates the benefits of having a multithreaded web server. An incoming request can be blocked while waiting for one thread to free up, while several other worker threads are idle. This severely hurts IIS scalability because it is forced to leave worker threads idle and not serving content to users.

Web Farm Possibilities

Session management is largely a problem in ASP, at least when it comes to managing state in a web farm. In a web farm, multiple servers are configured with the same web pages, data, and components. User requests are routed to whichever server has the spare capacity for a new user.

Scalability Concerns

Web farms are not supported by default in ASP. Sessions are tied to the machine they are created on. If a user is routed to web server 'A' in the first request, they will lose all session information if they are then routed to web server 'B' on the next request.

In our scenario, we need `Session` to store the `User` object. `User` can be a very large object when it is fully instantiated. One option for using a web farm includes sending back the `User` object as hidden form variables to the user's browser. When subsequent requests are made, the data can be read from the browser and the `User` object recreated.

Unfortunately, the `User` object contains just too much data to persist to the client. Imagine the headache of coding the persistence code to retrieve and save the `User` object for every request. Also imagine the overhead of reading the persisted `User` object from the browser into a `User` object and back into persisted data for every request. The size of the object model makes client persistence impracticable.

Chapter 1: Introduction to Scalability

Pinning Users to Web Servers

One option is to modify the ASP pages so that, after the first request, all subsequent requests are routed back to the original server. In other words, the user may be dynamically routed to web server 'C' on the first request. The page should then render all of the links so that each subsequent request is routed back to web server 'C' automatically.

This will prevent the user from losing their session information. However, this will require a fair amount of work to the front end. In addition, the net result is that customer traffic may not truly be distributed to the servers in the farm that have spare capacity. Rather, traffic may clog one server while others sit idle. We will cover various options to tackle these problems both in Chapter 2 and 5.

Summary

Scalability is the ability for a system to handle additional users or volume without undergoing a loss of performance or requiring a great deal of code or administrative redesign. A scalable system will be able to scale up or scale down depending on the change in user load. Scalability is important as systems continually change, both from planned change and unplanned change.

Microsoft DNA, VB6, and COM in particular, had important scalability limitations. Of important interest are:

- VB's STA threading model in respect to the ASP `Session` and `Application` objects.
- Limited session capabilities, which required the ASP session to be tied to the ASP process.
- DCOM introduced a firewall-unfriendly architecture requiring a range of ports to be opened for DCOM traffic. Even though DCOM ports can be limited by registry hacks, DCOM proved to be an administrative nightmare.
- Caching was limited in Windows DNA. The Shared Property Manager required a separate (and perhaps different) state to be held on each web server.

In addition to Windows DNA platform limitations, common coding practices found in VB6 further limited scalability. The following design practices hindered scalability:

- Inline SQL used in place of Stored Procedures
- External resource usage
- Inefficient recordset creation
- Improper use of VB objects
- Maintaining a stateful middle tier
- Improper OO design

Summary

Microsoft, with the introduction of .NET, has taken great strides to provide a platform for scalability, improving on what Windows DNA offered. The .NET threading model is simple and eliminates the issues raised with Windows DNA. The session is vastly improved, allowing for cookieless browser support, and multiple hosting capabilities while continuing to be easy to use. The middle-tier application hosting with Remoting and web services gives much greater flexibility and ease of use when compared to DCOM. The caching features at the ASP.NET layer are completely new to the ASP paradigm and allow the programmer total control over how objects are cached.

The application we will be following throughout the book, MyInvestmentWatch.com, suffers from a few of the commonly found Windows DNA pitfalls and scalability limitations. The object model design highlights resource consumption issues and the use of ASP's `Session` object limits our physical tier separation by requiring the use of a single web server.

We now have a background of where scalability concerns arise and have the knowledge to plan for and design systems that avoid scalability limitations. Armed with the .NET Framework and the Visual Basic .NET language, we address these limitations in the upcoming chapters.

The first step in scalable applications occurs in the planning and design phase. Planning the code design and physical system architecture will lay the foundations on which the application will reside. It's now time to turn our attention to discuss this important topic in scalability.

VB.NET
Scalability
Handbook
2

2

Planning for Scalability

"By failing to prepare you are preparing to fail." – Benjamin Franklin

Plan or Fail

The goal of many systems is to support some business need. These systems must often be developed within the constraints of the guiding principles and technical standards of the company. These systems must also meet the business requirements that are defined as part of the business problem. Assuming the system is intended to be more than a short-term solution, the final product should also closely support the strategic business plan and direction.

Addressing these needs and constraints will, directly or indirectly, define the various traits of a system. For example, if a business requirement is that the system must support a call center that is open all of the time then minimizing downtime will be seen as essential. This will translate to designing your system with reliability as a key trait.

These intended traits of a system must be planned for, and designed for, early in the application development lifecycle. Often, design shortcuts that are taken to quickly develop a system are later seen as "flaws" once the system is hitting its stride in production. Attempting to address these flaws would mean either changing the fundamental structure of the application or coming up with band-aid solutions.

Unfortunately, systems architecture is often viewed as unneeded. After all, everything exists only in code and code is easy to change. This view is flawed. Changing large systems after they have been designed, developed, and deployed is both costly and prone to introducing even more problems. If the underlying structure of an application cannot support scalability, then the underlying structure must be changed.

Chapter 2: Planning for Scalability

Scalability is an often overlooked trait of an enterprise system. There is often a belief that a system can be scaled simply by adding more hardware, or that simply developing a system that will perform fast will ensure that it is scalable. However, as with any other trait, scalability must be planned for, and designed into, a system from the start. It is not a feature you can add later. The decisions you make in the design phase, and early in the development phase, will have the largest effect on the scalability of your application.

Application scalability is a function of hardware and software and the impact of both must be taken into consideration during the planning and design process. It is important to understand the relationship between scaling hardware and software. While either can be done separately, it is the combination of these two that yields the largest gains.

Attempting to scale the hardware of a system, if the software cannot scale, will result in only small gains, and will likely introduce more problems into the system than are being solved. Likewise, it would be rather short-sighted to design and develop highly scalable software, only to deploy to anemic machines that do not support scaling in any manner.

For example, one method we could use to scale MyInvestmentWatch.com is to create a web farm, a function of hardware, to handle user load. However, if you will recall, the software is not designed to take advantage of this. Scaling just the hardware would introduce more problems than it would solve.

Designing for scalability at the start will lead to the highest benefits with, relatively, the least amount of effort. However, care should be taken to not over-scale a system in design or in deployment. For example, if a system must only ever support a few thousand users, then there is little reason to tweak the application to support a few hundred thousand users. If an application must only start by supporting a department, and will be slowly rolled out over a year, then there is no reason to deploy sixty servers from the start.

Another aspect in scalability planning should be to tailor the plan and implementation to the constraints your company must live under. If it is difficult to assemble a team of superb developers for your application, then your scalability design may need to emphasize gains through hardware first. If your organization has a large shared capacity environment that you will be deploying into, then greater emphasis must be placed on achieving scalability through software, while living within the constraints, and gains, of a shared environment.

Throughout this chapter, we will focus on the steps that must go into planning for a scalable system. Of course, scalability is often not the only facet that needs to be considered when building a system. Other traits, such as performance and reliability, deserve consideration as well. These needs can be considered concurrently when planning for scalability. In fact, you will likely find that the goals of scalability will complement other needs within your system.

Microsoft Wants to Help, Really

One of the reasons that scalability with .NET deserves such a strong focus is that Microsoft has made a solid stride towards delivering systems that are now capable of supporting highly scalable applications. After all, it is difficult to deliver a highly scalable system, in a cost effective manner, if the underlying components cannot keep up. Scalability is no longer synonymous with Java and UNIX. Rather, the new offerings from Microsoft, in which .NET plays a large role, are now capable of competing in this arena.

Planning Without a Safety .NET

Microsoft technologies have always faced a problem. Their tools have often been labeled as "toys" and relegated to supporting desktop and department-level applications. For example, NT 4 Enterprise Edition only supported up to 8 processors. To many companies, this was seen as a debilitating weakness that often kept Windows-based solutions relegated to the department level. Microsoft needed a way to better capture the heart of the enterprise.

This pain was also felt across other Microsoft products. The fact that NT 4 only allowed for access to 4 GB of memory hurt SQL Server as well. Databases need memory, and this 4 GB limit kept SQL Server out of the running for really large systems.

With the advent of Windows 2000, Microsoft started to show how serious it was about addressing enterprise needs, especially scalability. Now, the first planning decision that had to be made, Windows or UNIX, wasn't so "cut and dried" any more. One of the large scalability advantages of UNIX was that many vendors were making 16-, and 32- processor servers. With Windows 2000 Datacenter Server and some impressive hardware from the likes of Unisys, businesses had the choice of Windows on a 32-processor server with up to 64 GB of memory.

At the hardware level, things were looking bright. As you will see when we discuss scalability options, scaling up and scaling out, access to larger servers can be critical. Without hardware that can scale up, an application can only scale so far before it must scale out, which brings many infrastructure and support problems with it. Microsoft more than addressed these needs for bigger hardware. However, scaling software across multiple tiers, especially with COM components using DCOM, was still a difficult undertaking.

Application Center, a New Hope

With Application Center 2000, Microsoft bundled together a great tool for scalability. Application Center provided many features, such as a single console to deploy applications across servers. This feature is important because it allows for rapid deployment of an application to a new server, which is vital in fulfilling the need to bring up hardware quickly to meet spikes in user demand. Plus, it helps greatly with on-going support and upgrades to the application. More importantly, Application Center introduced Component Load Balancing (CLB).

Chapter 2: Planning for Scalability

With the advent of COM, Microsoft introduced the Service Control Manager (SCM) to act as the middleman when instantiating objects. Basically, it's this middleman that makes using other objects so painless. You pass the SCM a ProgID and it handles all of the work of locating and loading the corresponding DLL or out-of-process EXE.

With NT 4 and the introduction of DCOM, the SCM was updated to allow for the instantiation of objects on remote servers. This was a huge boon for scalability and scalability planning in that it allowed an application to be spread across multiple tiers.

Before DCOM, a typical application solution was simply a Windows client connecting to a remote database server. Multiple clients running the presentation layer, a set of Windows forms, and business objects would connect directly to the database. The largest problem with this approach is that it creates a deployment and upgrade nightmare. If business rules change then every client must be upgraded, and this is rarely a trivial task. Even worse, some clients could potentially utilize incorrect business logic until they were upgraded.

From a scalability standpoint, one of the failings of this method was that each client had a connection to the database. When properly managed, this was generally not an issue. However, rogue code could inadvertently hold a connection to the database open indefinitely, which had a severely adverse impact on the load on the database server.

To alleviate problems around performing upgrades, a frequently used remedy was to embed business logic in stored procedures on the database. This hindered scalability as the database was now forced to process business rules in addition to managing data.

By allowing components to be run remotely, we could now add an application server as well. This provided several benefits. First, from a supportability standpoint, it centralized object deployment. Second, it removed processing burden from the database. Life was good, but it still wasn't great.

DCOM still had some nasty problems that limited scalability. Not least, the application was bound to only having a single server in the application tier, as DCOM would pin requests to a single server. This meant that, without some interesting workarounds, scalability was still severely limited.

Around the same time, web servers as presentation hosts became popular. This led to the rise of HTML-based applications, thin clients, and a need to distribute and scale applications in a new manner. When faced with the limitations of DCOM, the typical solution was to not take advantage of scaling across multiple tiers. All application logic was pushed back to the web tier. While this solution allowed for scaling through adding more web servers, it also forced an inordinate number of web servers to be deployed to meet demands.

Microsoft then released the Windows Distributed iNternet Architecture (DNA). DNA consolidated and extended COM, DCOM, and Microsoft Transaction Server (MTS) into a single, easy-to-manage bundle. This eased much of the burden of distributed computing on a single server or between two servers. However, it still carried with it the problem of scaling across a server farm.

Application Center and CLB brought with it salvation for many developers. Plus, it made the future exciting. It showed that Microsoft was still marching forward. CLB allowed for scaling at the component level.

CLB extended the SCM yet again. Where DCOM allowed remote COM invocation, CLB allowed dynamic remote COM invocation. Instead of relying on one machine to process all requests, CLB distributes the load across an entire server farm. Application Center constantly monitors the servers in the cluster and distributes work accordingly. This greatly helps with scalability. It further helps with scalability planning because the options for increasing capacity are straightforward and do not make the infrastructure more complex.

Application Center greatly improved the ability of Windows to scale. It also assisted greatly with improving the availability and manageability of applications. However, especially with regards to planning, things were not so good at the language level. Visual Basic and C++, while able to leverage each other through COM, were not on the same playing field.

It's a .NEW World

One of first decisions during planning and design had to be a decision on which language would be used to develop the application. VB allowed for quick development, but thanks to various features such as multi-threading, C++ was better suited for high-throughput sections of code that had to handle multiple simultaneous clients.

This led to design tradeoffs that had to be made along the way. Either VB would be used for the entire application, or VB and C++ COM would be mixed throughout the application. This made design, development, and on-going support difficult.

Language differences also made planning difficult after deployment as well. If it turned out that a VB component was performing poorly, a decision had to be made on whether to focus effort on tuning the existing component or to rewrite that component in C++. The tradeoff when writing in C++ was that the application would increase in complexity, and require a new skill set to support, making this option generally more costly. However, there was also no assurance that tuning the existing VB code would yield the desired results.

Since both options took time, a planning practice often employed was to concurrently do both options. That is, have one team rewrite the component in C++ while another team focused on tuning the VB code. Obviously, this is not a desirable solution as it wastes a significant amount of time and effort.

This pain was often felt on the front end as well. There was no inherent support in IIS and ASP for session management in a web farm. One alternative was to select and implement a third-party session management solution that typically needed to be specifically coded to, which made replacement, if needed, difficult. Another option was to tailor build a custom solution. If a decision on an approach wasn't made, or if the decision was not to implement any solution, then extensive code changes would have to be made after rollout when scaling the front end was required. Neither option was very appealing.

Enter .NET. Whereas COM allowed for interoperability between languages, the Common Language Runtime in .NET actually compiles multiple languages to the same Intermediate Language. Visual Basic .NET retained its rapid development heritage, and it gained the ability to solidly compete, especially with regards to scalability.

This makes it possible for the development team to be chosen based on language preference, rather than the traits of the language and its compiler. In addition, and even more remarkably from a planning and design standpoint, a team can comprise Visual Basic *and* C# developers, all working from the same design and all producing completely compatible code.

The gains of .NET on the front end are just as impressive. Many solutions that had to be custom-built, or purchased and worked into the existing code base, are now part of the framework. For example, page-level and control-level caching is now built into ASP.NET, and session management in a web farm is now seamless to utilize and transparent to your application code.

Session management is easily the single greatest improvement, with regards to scaling out in a web farm, in ASP.NET. Expensive solutions do not need to be created at the start and extensive code rewrites do not need to take place after deployment. Rather, deployment can start small and then infrastructure can easily and quickly scale to meet demands as needed.

.NET has brought along many scalability improvements. Many of these improvements are implemented so that they are transparent to the developer and can be utilized with minimal effort. Just as important, from a planning perspective, all .NET languages are on the same level. No decision has to be made with regards to which language to develop on.

.NET Today

With the advent of .NET, there's been a bit of confusion on what .NET does and doesn't do. It is important to understand these nuances, especially from a planning and design standpoint. .NET replaces COM; .NET does not replace COM+. Well, at least not yet! This means that Application Center may continue to play an important role in your infrastructure.

Plan or Fail

In fact, COM+ is very accessible from .NET; it's conveniently wrapped by the `System.EnterpriseServices` namespace. However, whether you must rely on COM+ or not is largely up to your application needs. COM+ provides several key features, including:

- **Two-Phase Transactional Support** – If you need to ensure a transaction across two or more databases, then you need two-phase commital support. COM+ also allows for a bit of code simplification by automatically handling transactions. However, if you are only updating a single data source, you can easily manually manage transactions and not incur the overhead of calling through to COM+.

- **Loosely Couple Events** – Loosely Coupled Events (LCE) allow a publisher-subscriber model where the subscriber(s) need not be constantly running. LCE also fully abstracts the subscribers from the publisher. If you are simply looking for a publisher-subscriber model, but have full control over both ends of the relationship, then .NET delegates are a more attractive alternative.

- **Component Role-Based Security** – COM+ role-based security allows for component access to be restricted administratively at run time. While this is currently not offered natively to .NET, it is important to note that the .NET Framework has many security models built in which may offer an acceptable alternative.

- **Object Pooling** – A COM+ managed pool is homogenous. All objects are of the same type. The benefit of an object pool is that you can ensure a minimum number of objects are spun up and ready to be utilized by clients. This is highly beneficial with objects that are expensive to create, such as opening database connections.

It is important to understand, if you need these services, you are still bound to COM+, at least for the foreseeable future. However, based on Microsoft's stellar advancements, we can speculate that we will see many of these features wrapped into a .NET-managed, and .NET-centric, library at some point.

Where do we go from here?

"Facts do not cease to exist because they are ignored." – **Aldous Huxley**

In this chapter, we will discuss how to plan and design for scalability. Planning is the single most important step in building a scalable system. Planning is essential to understanding the many factors that will affect your application. Planning will also deliver a clear roadmap to future growth of your system.

61

Chapter 2: Planning for Scalability

In this chapter, we will cover:

- **Types of Scaling** – There are a few ways to scale. We will cover the differences, and the advantages, and the drawbacks of the various options. All are critical to scaling, and will be needed, but will typically come into play at different times. We will cover the best practices for when and how to scale.

- **The .NET Landscape** – This section of the chapter provides general planning and design best practices that are applicable to most environments, but it is equally important to understand the specific challenges and opportunities that are presented with the advent of .NET. The focus of this section will not be on an introduction to the Framework. Rather, we will highlight the planning and environmental changes that come about when moving from Visual Basic 6 to .NET.

- **System Analysis** – Quite a bit of effort must go into planning. Things like determining the expected number of concurrent users may be obvious, but many points are often overlooked early on in planning. Factors such as when batch jobs should be run, and what additional loads they will place on the system, must also be determined.

- **System Design** – The design is the implementation of the planning and analysis phase. The design phase is crucial because it lays the foundation for development. Poor design choices will lead to a poor, or at least complex and time-consuming, code implementation. We will cover the features built into the .NET Framework that greatly assist with scalability. These libraries should be utilized, rather than creating your own solution.

Planning for scalability is not specific to VB.NET. The principles presented in this chapter will assist with most scaling efforts. However, it should also be noted that VB.NET opens many possibilities that make scaling possible, and easy. The .NET Framework contains many advances for designing for scalability. Since these features are readily available, design becomes more about knowing what is available than anything else.

Types of Scaling

Types of scalability could include handling more users, more user requests, more data, or even just new functions and features for the existing users. For example, a system may need to move from supporting 100 concurrent users to 1,000. Or, a system may have the same user base, but suddenly have more active users. If an application supports a call center, the number of concurrent users may stay constant at 100, but the requests per second may increase if the workers are asked to answer more calls per shift. Similarly, a system may need to support a larger load if it is modified to generate ad hoc reports that were not accounted for originally.

There are two basic ways to accomplish scalability. You can either increase the system's underlying speed or give it more processing resources. However, the assumption cannot be that these are mutually exclusive options. Rather, both options will need to be judiciously mixed and matched to provide maximum benefit.

Scaling Up

Scaling up is often referred to as the traditional method of scaling. Scaling up is simple, straightforward, and can typically be the easiest method to scale. It is also generally the least disruptive to existing environments. The solutions are typically referred to as "Big Iron" solutions, because we're implementing bigger servers.

The core idea to scaling up is that existing servers will be expanded to provide better throughput, thereby allowing for more concurrent work. There are two ways to accomplish this, either make the servers faster, or make them bigger.

Make it Faster

The idea here is pretty straightforward. Simply take what you have and make it faster. In other words, upgrade to newer and faster hardware. Often, the main focus will be on putting in the latest and greatest processors. However, don't overlook other important areas such as disk I/O and RAM as upgrade candidates. In fact, in certain scenarios, such as speeding up a database server, adding more RAM and faster disk access will provide the greatest improvement.

Figure 1

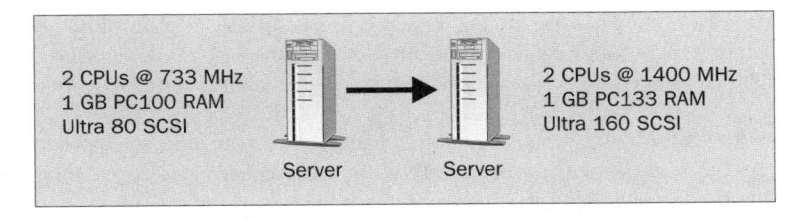

```
2 CPUs @ 733 MHz          2 CPUs @ 1400 MHz
1 GB PC100 RAM            1 GB PC133 RAM
Ultra 80 SCSI             Ultra 160 SCSI

       Server      →          Server
```

The problem with simply making a server faster is that there is a foreseeable and definite limit. If you have a 733 MHz processor in a server with a motherboard that only supports up to a 1 GHz processor, then you are bound to that scalability limit. Unless, of course, you replace the motherboard so that it can support the newest processor.

Even beyond the limits of what is in the server, there is still a hard limit with scaling by speeding up the server. That limit is whatever the current fastest processor is on the market. Plus, you're tied to chip vendors for upgrade paths. If Intel or AMD only releases a new chip every year, then you're stuck with a yearly upgrade schedule. This is great if you only need to upgrade once a year to handle a slight increase in traffic, but otherwise it isn't a practical alternative.

Make it Bigger

The second option for scaling up is to increase the resources available to the existing hardware. In other words, super size. The underlying assumption here is that the hardware has spare room in the first place.

If the server is capable of handling four processors and it only has two installed, then you can easily add two more processors. However, if the server is only capable of two processors, and already has two installed, then no amount of force will let you raise the processing power to four CPUs. Trust us, we've tried.

Figure 2

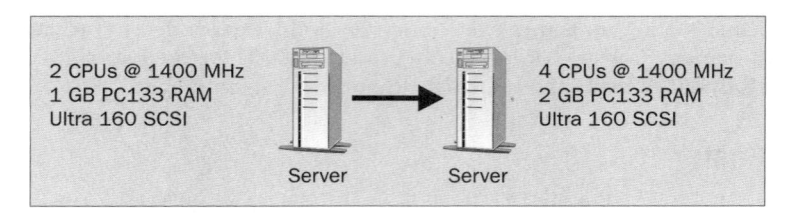

```
2 CPUs @ 1400 MHz          4 CPUs @ 1400 MHz
1 GB PC133 RAM      →      2 GB PC133 RAM
Ultra 160 SCSI             Ultra 160 SCSI

    Server                     Server
```

Scaling up by adding more processors would not be practicable on any level if the underlying operating system did not support it. Windows 2000 Advanced Server can support up to eight processors and Windows 2000 Data Center can scale all the way to 32 processors. Equally as important, the .NET Framework makes taking advantage of these extra processors rather straightforward.

Planning becomes important in this phase. It is probably not practicable to install only servers capable of eight processors. The cost for these servers is prohibitive, even without all eight processors installed. Not only are the server chassis expensive, but Windows 2000 Advanced Server is a good bit more costly than Windows 2000 Server.

However, in the same vein, it is also not practical, from a planning standpoint, to install only dual-capable servers, with both slots filled, if a rapid increase in scalability is required. This is especially true in environments where load-balancing and clustering is a bit more involved than simply plugging in another server, such as on the database tier.

Best Practice for Scaling Up

A best practice for scaling up is to deploy servers that have spare capacity. For instance, to minimize up-front costs, you may want to deploy a web server that can support four processors, but only install two processors. Then, when needed, it becomes a trivial task to install two more processors to bring the server to its full capacity. This will also save on up-front costs for software that is licensed per processor. Of course, as you add more processors, you may need to pay licensing for the software on the system. This additional cost should be accounted for in scalability planning.

The fundamental reason for this approach is that it is much cheaper, both in terms of cost and support, to start off with a single server that can support four processors and only plug in two, than it is to start off with a two processor-capable server and then add a second server to the mix to achieve scalability.

However, deploying servers that can scale up to a very high degree is not the best approach for most servers, either. It is not practical to purchase a server that is capable of 32 processors and then plug in only two processors.

A web server's focus is in delivering content to users quickly. The nature of HTTP makes these clients stateless, which reduces load on the server since the client isn't constantly connected. Due to high I/O needs, generally low processing needs, and little overhead from software, two-, or four-processor servers should be used for web servers.

> **The opposite can be said for web servers that must process SSL requests. These servers typically require more processing power and will be less I/O intensive. However, all of the associated costs and corresponding gains may still not be worthwhile. If your server truly requires a lot of SSL processing then there are specialized solutions, such as hardware-based SSL accelerators that will provide better performance and scalability than any number of processors ever can.**

Installing processors has a diminishing return as the number of processors increases. Generally, the operating system utilizes processors less efficiently as more processors are added. Greater gains can be achieved on this tier by providing high-speed storage and plenty of memory. Also, as Windows 2000 Server only supports up to four processors, you would need to upgrade to Windows 2000 Advanced Server or Datacenter to take advantage of more processors.

Databases must typically support many concurrent requests. The transaction processing requirements are much higher on a database. Databases also carry a greater overhead due to software. Fortunately, database software, such as SQL Server, is written to take maximum advantage of as many resources on the server as possible. Databases scale very well as faster disks, more memory, and more processors are added. In fact, it is this tier that will benefit the most from a larger server.

Therefore, it may be advantageous to install, say, a server that is capable of eight processors and then only install two or four processors to start with. For a very large, process-intensive database, one of those 32 processor servers may actually come in handy. Of course, one thing to keep in mind is that Windows 2000 Advanced Server is needed for scalability up to eight processors, and Datacenter Server will be needed for those big 32 processor servers.

Scaling Out

The idea behind scaling out is to add more servers. Scaling up is the process of adding faster processors, more resources, such as more memory to existing servers, and, in general, just larger servers. Scaling out is the process of spreading processing across multiple and potentially smaller servers.

The principle of scaling out has been around for years. However, thanks in part to the needs of robust Internet sites, scaling out has taken on a new buzzword; n-tier architecture. Scaling out is the heart of the n-tier architecture.

N-tier is an often misused and maligned term. Simply put, an n-tier application is a system that can be spread across any number of tiers. Processing can be spread across multiple servers. For example, you may want to add an application tier to host business objects and a utility tier to handle service components, such as a user authentication component. In theory, there are no limits to n-tier architecture. Practically, however, there are limits due to the infrastructure complexity and associated support costs.

While the concept is simple, the implementation isn't quite so straightforward. However, Microsoft has made achieving scalability in n-tier architecture easier than ever before. With the advent of Network Load Balancing Services, Windows has strong support for scaling out built-in. Microsoft further extended the ability to scale out at the software layer through Application Center 2000. The advancements in .NET take scaling out even further; especially at the web tier with the ability to utilize SQL Server for session management in a web farm (see Chapter 5).

There are two basic means of scaling out. These are scaling out across multiple tiers and scaling out across a single tier. Both will come into play in any planning effort, as both are needed to achieve a high level of scalability. However, the plan for when to implement each, and where to focus efforts, will be different.

Scaling Out Across Tiers

Scaling out across tiers is often the first thing that comes to mind when discussing n-tier architectures. The idea with scaling out across tiers is to add more servers to meet specific needs. Instead of a web server that houses both ASP pages and VB COM business objects, you can scale out by adding an application server to host the VB COM objects. This allows independent scaling of the web and application tiers. Instead of running batch processes on the application tier, a tier that must be tuned to handle a high number of user transactions, a utility (or batch) server may be added to offload long-running jobs.

Figure 3

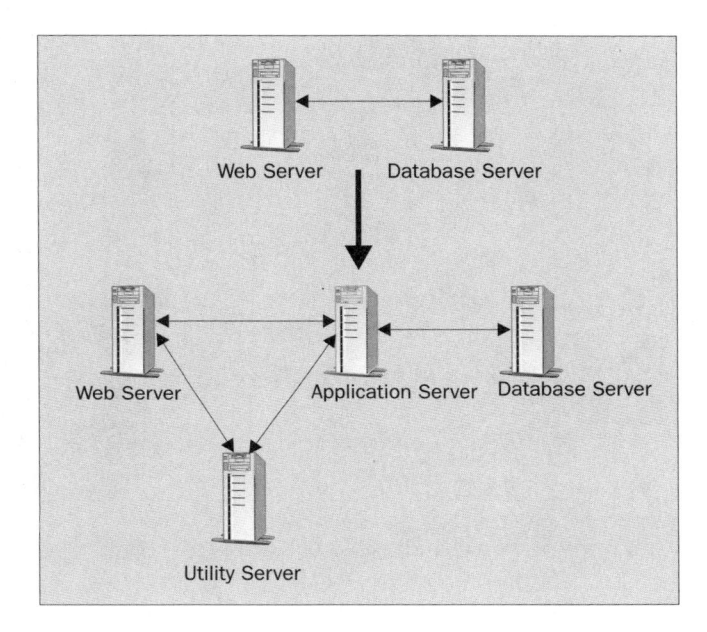

[Diagram showing a Web Server and Database Server at the top, and below them a Web Server, Application Server, and Database Server connected to each other, with a Utility Server connected below.]

There are tradeoffs to scaling out across multiple tiers. Rather than the front-end logic making a local call to a business object, the call must now go across the network to the application server. This imposes a network hop and its associated latency. In addition to a network hop, these tiers are also often separated by firewalls, which can impose restrictions on integration options. In fact, in using ASP and DCOM, this option was unappealing due to the problems with getting DCOM to communicate through a firewall.

One thing to keep in mind is that scaling out across multiple tiers will place more reliance on the network. As such, a slow network will adversely impact on the performance of the application. However, for scalability, adding more tiers can provide an excellent method of segmenting off workload.

Scaling out over multiple tiers allows more granular control for planning capacity growth as well. If the application tier needs more resources, then efforts can be focused solely on the application tier. If reporting needs are such that they can no longer run on the database tier, then a reporting tier can be added.

Scaling Out a Single Tier

Scaling out across tiers is a great first step in gaining scalability. However, you will soon find that specific tiers will become burdened as the user base grows. The web tier may start to experience strains while the application and data tiers still have spare capacity. Or, maybe your application is widely popular and all physical tiers are resource-constrained. The next step is then to scale out a single tier.

Figure 4

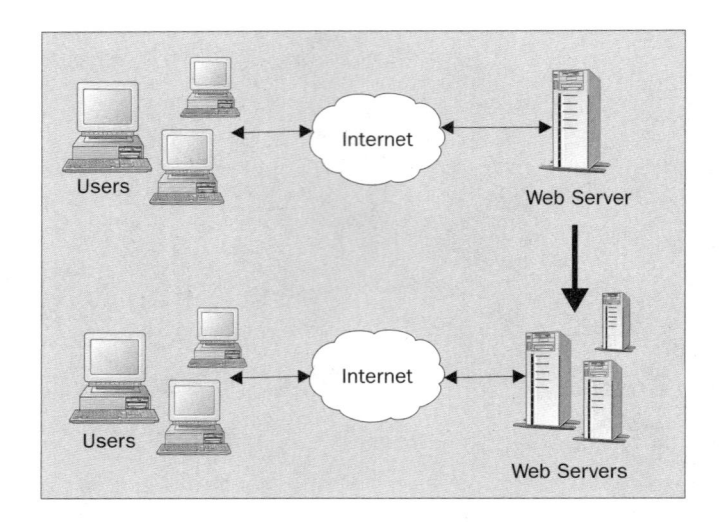

Physically, there are many ways to handle load balancing:

- Round-robin DNS
- Hardware-based load balancing
- Software-based load balancing

Round-Robin DNS

Round-robin DNS (Domain Name Service) is a popular small-scale solution, but will not always achieve effectiveness in a production environment. Round-robin relies on DNS to map to a set of servers. It then passes requests on to each server in order. If a given server fails, round-robin will still attempt to route the request to that failed server.

A consideration with this method of scalability is that it will add a slight amount of complexity into the application design. If a server crashes, the client will receive a timeout error. The client must then reattempt the connection, which will cause the client to be redirected to another server. The failing of this is that, eventually, another client request will be sent to the non-responsive server, causing this new request to timeout. This process will repeat until the server is either removed from the DNS list or restarted. The problems with round-robin DNS can be lessened through actively monitoring the server environment. However, some complexity must still exist within components that must call out to other tiers.

Types of Scaling

Hardware Load Balancers

Hardware-based load balancing requires that a physical piece of hardware sits in front of the servers that will have their loads balanced. A Virtual IP address, or VIP, is assigned to the load balancer, which makes the physical servers transparent to the client. The client has only one entry point, the VIP. The load balancer typically translates each request from the client to the physical IP address of one of the servers and then sends it on to that server. This is called Network Address Translation, or NAT.

Figure 5

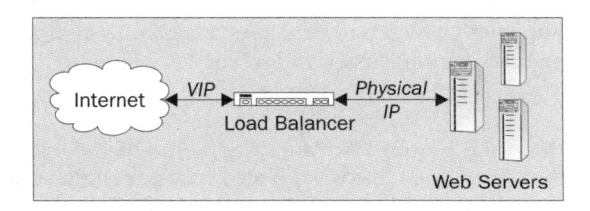

The advantage of hardware load balancers is that they are hardened solutions that scale very well to meet demand. These solutions also tend to be feature-rich and integrate well with many other solutions. A primary disadvantage to this solution is that it is expensive. Also, as is apparent in our diagram above, a single load balancer becomes the single point of failure in the system. Of course, these solutions typically don't crash, but it's probably not a chance you want to take. This means that two load balancers must be purchased to achieve a guaranteed high availability.

Software Load Balancers

Software-based load balancers are implemented with varying degrees of sophistication. However, the challenge they face is the same as a dedicated hardware solution. The goal is to make load balancing transparent to the client. For this discussion, we will only cover Windows 2000 Network Load Balancer (NLB).

NLB is the successor to Windows NT Load Balancing Services (WLBS). Of course, NLB has many enhancements over WLBS and is much easier to set up. NLB ships with Windows 2000 Advanced Server and Windows 2000 Datacenter and can support up to 32 nodes, or servers, within a cluster.

Figure 6

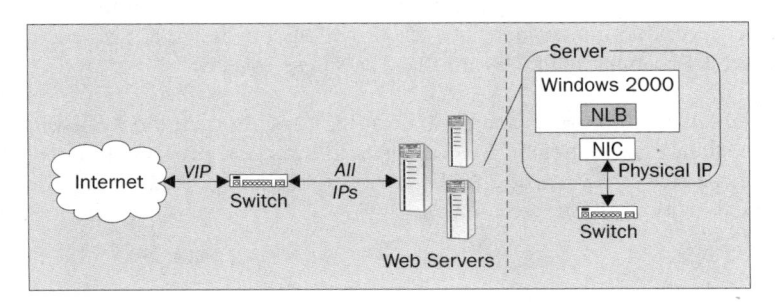

NLB is a fully distributed software solution that can run on your existing hardware. NLB relies on the ability of switches to deliver traffic in parallel to all servers in the cluster. This means that every host is receiving every packet. NLB determines, on a packet-by-packet basis, which host should process the request. That host will then handle the request and all other hosts simply discard their copy of the packet.

The advantage of NLB is that it is typically much more cost effective than an equivalent hardware-based solution. A redundant hardware-based solution will typically cost around $50,000 just for the hardware whereas NLB only requires Windows 2000 Advanced Server, which is $3,000 more than Windows 2000 Server, per server. NLB also provides for redundancy, which will translate to higher system availability. All but one server can be removed from a cluster and it will still continue to respond, although, obviously, not as fast.

One disadvantage is that NLB requires Advanced Server, which could be costly if you are deploying many servers to the cluster. NLB also incurs a slight processing overhead that is not present with a hardware solution. Possibly the biggest drawback is that the burden for all traffic delivery, which must be sent to multiple servers simultaneously, is pushed to the switch, which will run the risk of flooding the switch.

Hardware solutions are hardened and may supply a better solution for your environment. Compared to the software solution, the hardware option will not burden any switches, it will not incur processing overhead on the server, and it does not require a costlier version of Windows. However, both options deserve consideration and evaluation when deciding on an approach to scaling out a single tier.

Generally, if a tier will comprise few enough servers and budget considerations are a concern, then Network Load Balancing may present the best option. If a hardened solution with a wide range of features is preferred, and if enough servers will be deployed to a tier to make the Windows-based option less attractive from a costing standpoint, then consider a hardware-based solution.

Best Practices for Scaling Out

If you are deploying a public-facing web site, then you will likely benefit by deploying three tiers consisting of a web server, an application server, and a database server. This allows greater isolation of business objects behind a public Demilitarized Zone, or DMZ, which is a separate segment on the network designed to separate publicly accessible servers from servers on the private network. It will also better minimize security risks to internal systems that must interact with these business objects.

If your availability requirements are high, or at least higher than the availability of a single server, then scale out each tier. That is, add a second presentation server and a second database server. By starting in this manner, you are poised for rapidly increasing scalability in these two areas.

Types of Scaling

To scale out the web tier, utilize the hardware-based load balancing approach discussed above. While the hardware approach is recommended for the web tier, we would encourage an evaluation of both solutions to determine which will better fit your environment.

To scale out the middle tier, consider using NLB. The rationale for this is that there will, generally, not be as many application servers as web servers. Thus, the cost of a second hardware load balancing option is not necessarily justified.

Conspicuously missing from this discussion is an overview of scaling the database tier. The method for scaling will vary by vendor. This topic will vary by vendor and even by database version.

SQL Server 2000 supports scaling through the use of federated clusters. In this scenario, the database will be installed across all federation member servers, the tables that must be scaled out will be horizontally partitioned, and then distributed partitioned views must be created for these partitioned tables. This method will allow SQL Server 2000 to scale out virtually infinitely.

After adding availability, the next step should be to scale out by adding more tiers. This step could, and likely will, happen in parallel with scaling out each tier. This effort should be tailored to the needs of the particular application. For example, a high-traffic transactional system will benefit from a focus on removing load from the operational database. This can be accomplished by adding a reporting server.

The benefit to scaling out is that the possibilities are virtually boundless. Scaling out is the principle behind Beowulf, a massively scalable system built on relatively cheap hardware. This type of scaling is even finding its way into the ranks of supercomputing. Hewlett Packard built the third-fastest computer in the world by interconnecting 750 servers that each house four Compaq Alpha processors.

This is probably the single biggest asset of scaling out. The entry costs can be relatively low as the solution can start by running on one or two small servers. As increased scalability is required, more servers can easily be added. While it is not likely that you'll be called upon to build the next supercomputer, it is nice to know that you can start with a small solution and quickly scale as your business grows using the same design principles.

Scaling out does not come without cost though. The heart of scaling out is in adding more servers. These additional servers will require additional infrastructure and, more importantly, will require support personnel.

Scaling out, by itself, is only part of the solution. As you will see, both scaling up and scaling out are required in planning for highly scalable solutions. An important part of the planning effort is to determine the right approach for scaling your application. That is, it makes little sense to invest a large sum of money into hardware up-front if growth of the system will be linear and over months, such as a new system rollout in an enterprise. Likewise, it does not make sense to deploy as little hardware as possible if system growth will be exponential and spread over only weeks, or even days, such as with a web site launch. We will now tie it all together and provide some guidance for scalability planning.

Tying it all Together

Applications that need to scale will likely need to incorporate both scaling up and scaling out. However, the extent, and focus, will vary not only by application, but also by tier. An Internet-based application will benefit from a scaled out web tier, whereas a Windows forms-based application will benefit from a scaled out application tier, and an analytical system will benefit from a focus on adding reporting servers and larger database servers.

Start Small

The underlying benefit of scalability is a fundamental benefit that no business should overlook. Scalability allows a company to start an application small and then scale it as needs progress. This means that, if you have a 50-person user base, you don't need to deploy an infrastructure capable of handling 5,000 concurrent users. However, proper planning will easily allow for this type of expansion if, and when, it's needed. In other words, plan big but start small.

With that in mind, start with short-term needs, but with an eye towards expansion. For a database tier, where additional processors will easily allow for database scalability, you should deploy servers with spare capacity to scale up. Instead of deploying a dual processor server, deploy a chassis that is capable of four processors and only install two to start with. While the upfront cost will be slightly higher, the cost for processors and software licenses is the same.

The web tier will benefit from the same approach. However, if you will recall, the needs of web servers are slightly different. While you may not want to install quad processor servers, you should consider a dual processor server. Don't limit yourself by installing a single processor server. More importantly, don't limit your server with regards to subsystem components, such as memory and disk storage. With that in mind, your initial environment, with room for expansion, may look like Figure 7:

Figure 7

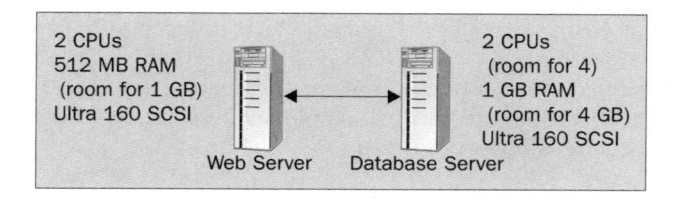

```
2 CPUs                          2 CPUs
512 MB RAM                      (room for 4)
(room for 1 GB)                 1 GB RAM
Ultra 160 SCSI                  (room for 4 GB)
                                Ultra 160 SCSI
Web Server      Database Server
```

Starting small is an ideal approach, at least if you know that requirements will be light to start with. This allows for a right-sized growth of your environment, as it must increasingly handle a larger user base. However, starting small is only part of the equation for a scalable system. You must also start right.

Start Right

Starting with the short-term goals in mind will most likely be the most soothing method of introducing a new system into any business. Starting with the short-term can even be carried to an existing application that is being upgraded to VB.NET. Just don't add more hardware than already exists for the current application.

However, starting small is only part of the planning that must go into a system. You should also make sure you are starting right; otherwise you may be crippling the scalability of your application from the start. If you took starting small literally, then you might be tempted to run ASP.NET, VB.NET business objects, and SQL Server all on the same box. In other words, we must start appropriately.

Scalability, done right, will help with achieving other desired application aspects as well. For example, scalability can help achieve system availability as well. Suppose that a given server is available 95% of the time. That means it is down 5% of the time, or roughly 438 hours per year.

Now, add a second, identical server to the same tier. It too has 95% availability. It too can be down for roughly 438 hours per year. However, the odds of both servers being down at the same time is 5% * 5%. The chance of both servers being down at the same time is now only 0.25%, or 22 hours per year. Just by scaling out a system intelligently from the start, we've increased our availability as well, which is certainly a pleasant side effect. Expanding on our previous diagram for starting small, our environment may start to look like Figure 8:

Figure 8

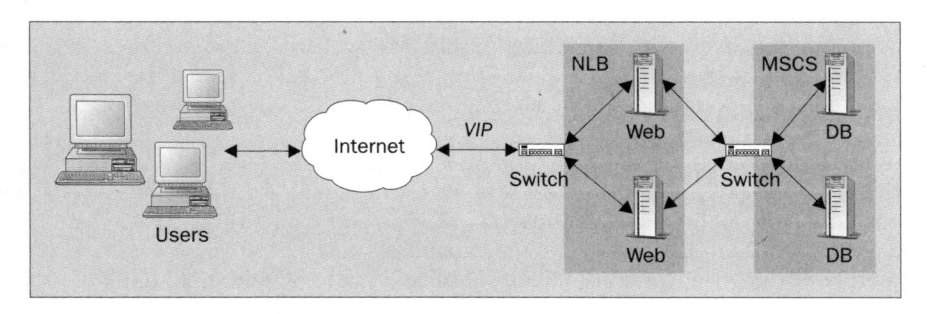

Of course, there are many other factors that may affect your infrastructure needs. For example, in order to provide for stronger security and restricted access to internal network resources, you may need to deploy both a web tier and an application tier. The web tier will reside within the DMZ and the application tier will reside behind the DMZ.

Figure 9

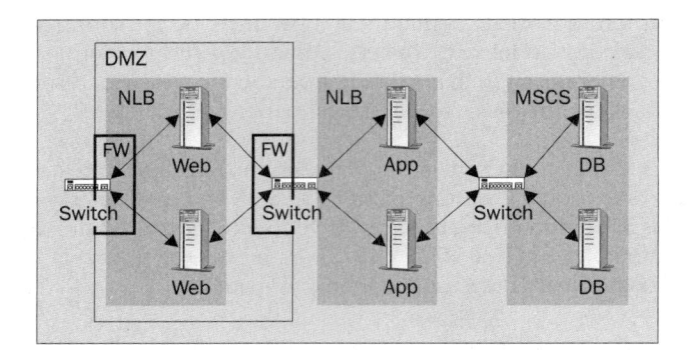

```
┌─────────────────────┐
│ DMZ                 │
│    NLB      NLB           MSCS
│  ┌──┐                          
│  │FW│ Web    FW   App         DB
│  Switch     Switch    Switch
│              
│         Web         App        DB
└─────────────────────┘
```

By trusting only the application servers to the web servers, you can better ensure that, if a web server is compromised, the internal network will not be breached. Of course, network security is much more complicated than that, and is well outside the discussion of this book. However, it is important to understand that some aspects of application deployment will be affected by the network policies at your company.

Grow Big

Starting appropriately provides a solid base for growing the system as the need presents itself. The point is to have in place a system that is nimble enough to support an exponential increase in demand if needed. However, the point of proper scaling is also to properly and effectively manage demand so that we do not add scads of hardware long before it is needed.

By this point, you have an idea of where to start. We've covered the potential application tiers that you will need; a web tier, application tier, and database tier. We've talked about planning big but starting small. Now, let's discuss what's next.

One of the fundamental reasons for planning is to know where and when to focus growth efforts. One of the fundamental reasons for designing for scalability is to further support growth through planning. Through planning and monitoring, capacity can be added as needed. Through proper design, capabilities can be further segmented onto dedicated hardware. This, of course, feeds back into planning and monitoring efforts.

To illustrate a scaled system, so that we can relate this to planning and design, let's speed up the growth of our existing system. The following two diagrams show logical models of our new environment. Keep in mind that there may be multiple physical servers for each logical representation here. Let's go from this:

Types of Scaling

Figure 10

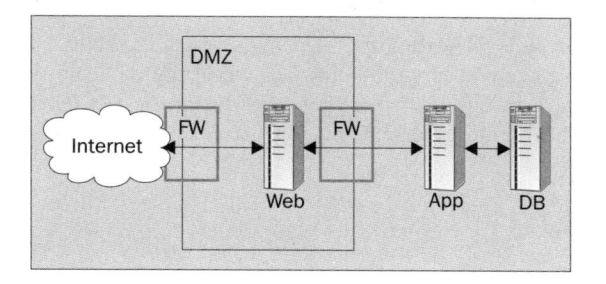

[Figure 10: Diagram showing Internet connected through FW to DMZ containing Web server behind FW, then to App server and DB server]

to this:

Figure 11

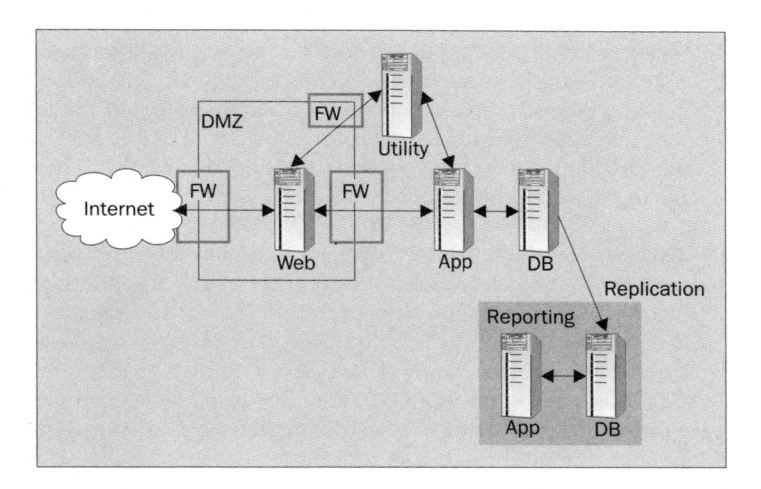

[Figure 11: Diagram showing Internet connected through FW to DMZ containing Web server behind FW, with Utility server connected, then to App server and DB server, with Replication to a Reporting area containing App and DB servers]

This change looks substantial. However, as you will see, with a proper design, nothing in your application will need to be changed. With proper planning, you will have a plan for where to scale first and you will know which area will need focus first.

As you will see in the rest of this chapter, planning and design are the most crucial steps in creating a scalable system. It is at this early stage that the effort expended will yield the greatest results. We've covered the different ways to physically scale a system; now let's cover how to take advantage of those techniques.

75

The .NET Landscape

So far, we've covered general planning and design practices. Many of these practices can apply to any development language and all will apply to Visual Basic .NET. However, in addition to the general planning and design best practices, Visual Basic .NET and the .NET Framework also bring many environmental changes that must also be accounted for.

Retraining

There is a reason why Visual Basic .NET is not called VB7. While the syntax differences between VB6 and VB.NET are small, that is where the similarities end. One of the greatest challenges in adopting VB.NET will be in retraining developers that are accustomed to traditional Visual Basic.

A move to .NET brings many concepts that, while not necessarily foreign to many VB developers, are now exposed in a much more powerful manner. Visual Basic supported interface implementations and allowed for extensibility, and inheritance, through component delegation, or object composition. A 'base' class, such as `Person`, would be instantiated within a new class, such as `Customer`, and this new class would repurpose the calls that it wanted to expose.

Visual Basic .NET allows for much more control and a richer, more powerful approach to building applications. Interfaces are now robust and objects can inherit and extend base classes. In fact, in .NET every class derives from `System.Object`.

Aside from slight syntax differences, many developers will need to learn and embrace Object-Oriented Analysis and Design (OOA&D) and Object-Oriented Programming (OOP) practices. Visual Basic developers who already have a familiarity with these concepts, and have used them to the extent they were supported in Visual Basic, will need to unlearn existing implementation practices and relearn how to apply their knowledge to Visual Basic .NET. For a complete coverage of this subject, see the Wrox Press book *Visual Basic .NET Class Design Handbook*, ISBN 1-86100-708-6.

As if adapting to syntax differences and brushing up OOP skills wasn't enough, there is one more component to preparing for .NET. The .NET Framework brings with it a large set of libraries that expose functionality to tackle many programming needs. An acquaintance with these libraries, and an understanding of how and when to use them, will greatly speed up development.

These revolutionary advances carry over to the web tier as well. ASP is no longer. ASP.NET provides a new paradigm for web-based development. To start with, ASP.NET is compiled. Whereas the script code in ASP was interpreted and run on each page request, pages are now compiled on the first request and then simply run each time after that. We will explore the new ASP.NET features related to scalability in Chapter 5.

Now, before we scare you into not converting from Visual Basic to Visual Basic .NET, the benefits are innumerable. The power of OOP and the robustness of the Framework libraries are worth the move to .NET. As you will see, .NET makes planning and design easier as well.

The Common Language Runtime

Many white papers, presentations, and articles have been written about the Common Language Runtime, or CLR. We will simply examine the CLR from a planning standpoint. From that standpoint, it's important to understand how revolutionary the CLR is for Microsoft development.

The Impact of the CLR on Planning

The CLR provides a common runtime and common services to all managed languages. The CLR manages memory allocation, threads, and resources, and performs garbage collection, all on behalf of the developer. These services span multiple languages with VB.NET and C# being the most well known examples.

The power of the CLR is carried forward to ASP.NET as well. ASP.NET pages are no longer interpreted, as was the case with ASP. Rather, the code is compiled to the Intermediate Language (IL).

As importantly, *all* .NET code is now compiled to Intermediate Language (IL). However, the power of this comes into play when this IL code complies with the Common Language Specification (CLS), which VB.NET does.

It is when multiple languages compile to the same IL and comply with the CLR that things can get truly interesting. An assembly can be consumed by multiple clients. In this manner, a group of objects that are developed in, perhaps, C# can be easily leveraged by VB.NET developers, and vice versa. Managing a multi-language environment is now much easier than it has been.

Language Selection

In the past, a decision had to be made as to which language to use to develop new applications. Visual Basic accelerated development but didn't always provide a complete solution. C++ allowed for more powerful development support, such as multi-threading, but had a much higher barrier to entry. To deliver highly scalable solutions, VB and C++ would often both be utilized to deliver a system.

Language differences were further carried to the UI tier for web-based applications. ASP utilized VBScript, or JScript, not VB. While the differences were slight, this still introduced subtleties, such as the fact that all variables are variants in VBScript.

With the advent of .NET, language selection suddenly seems to matter a whole lot less. All managed languages, such as Visual Basic .NET and C#, compile to IL, and it is this IL that is executed by the CLR. Because all code compiles to the same basic language, all languages are on a much more equal footing. While certain styles or features may be more appealing, depending on development background, language selection no longer needs to be a balance between ease of development and ease of scaling.

This language independence carries over to web-based development as well. ASP.NET is not limited as ASP was to a choice between VBScript and JScript. Rather, any language that is supported by the CLR can be utilized to create dynamic web pages.

The bottom line is that language selection can now be performed solely on the best fit for a given team of developers. This simplifies planning and staffing greatly. Project managers no longer need to search for experienced Visual C++ programmers to tighten critical sections of code, or to add functionality, such as multithreading, that Visual Basic doesn't provide.

Code Migration

You likely have a large amount of legacy development written in Visual Basic 6. Obviously, you don't want to upgrade everything at once. After all, why change a perfectly functional application? However, there are compelling reasons to upgrade at least portions of existing applications to .NET.

Perhaps the strongest candidates for immediate upgrade to the .NET Framework are any current ASP applications. Similarly to ASP, ASP.NET requires no components to be installed on the client machines. As you will see in Chapter 5, the power and benefit of ASP.NET are immediately available and immediately beneficial.

So, there is a seemingly impossible choice to make. Migrate to .NET and take advantage of innumerable new functionalities and features, and experience the pains of retraining and converting code; or, resist migrating any applications and only develop new systems on .NET.

Fortunately, the choice isn't nearly as dire as that. Microsoft has made it extremely simple to integrate existing COM components into .NET. How easy? Examine the following:

```
> tlbimp myObject.dll /out:myNetObject.dll
```

`tlbimp`, a utility provided as part of the Framework SDK, converts the type library information into equivalent definitions in a CLR assembly. Your .NET application then simply needs to reference this new assembly and the interoperability is taken care of for you. For a full discussion of interoperability, see the Wrox Press book *Professional Visual Basic Interoperability: COM and VB6 to .NET*, ISBN 1-186100-565-2.

This presents a likely strategy for converting existing applications to .NET. Start simply. It's likely that your goal will be to gradually migrate to .NET over the course of the application lifecycle. Along the way, keep an eye on which components can be leveraged in developing new systems as well.

For web-based applications, convert the front end to ASP.NET. Then, examine your existing application and determine which components will most easily converted to .NET and which will benefit most from a migration to .NET. Then, migrate the components that most heavily rely on external resources. For example, due to the potential complexity of testing, an interface to a legacy application may be the last component to convert.

Small components with few dependencies on external resources will most easily convert to .NET. Most often, it is service, or utility, components that best fit this profile. The benefit of migrating these components is that they are quick hits for testing the waters, so to speak, with a full-scale migration to .NET, or even a good trial of adopting .NET for new development. Also, these components are now in a managed environment and ready for reuse in new .NET development projects as well.

Assembly Deployment

You all know the drill. Copy the COM DLL to the target server, register it, and then start making calls against the DLL. Things run beautifully, the first time. Then, you're faced with an upgrade.

Enter the phenomenon affectionately known as DLL Hell. In COM, versioning is implicit. There is no way to indicate that your component relies on a specific version of another component. If you add a new version of the component, and your application relied on the previous version, the dependency will break.

The situation is further complicated when deploying a COM component to a web server. In order to replace an existing DLL, all references must be removed and the DLL must be unloaded. Unfortunately, IIS has a habit of not releasing controls in a timely manner. Typically, this leaves only the option of rebooting the server in order to replace a DLL. Obviously, being forced to reboot a production environment is not an ideal solution.

Similar to the notion of COM components is the .NET assembly. However, an assembly is also much more powerful than a COM component. Assemblies, and their interaction with the .NET Runtime, address many of the problems that plagued their COM predecessors.

To resolve versioning problems, .NET enables you to specify the version of the assembly that your application is reliant on. Multiple versions of an assembly are now able to coexist. To further reduce deployment problems, .NET no longer uses the registry. In the past, type information about each component was stored in the registry. Now, this information is simply stored within the assembly as metadata, making the assemblies self-describing.

In fact, it is this self-describing code that brings about one of the greatest deployment features of .NET. Components can now simply be copied, by using the XCOPY command, to the target server. In true infomercial style, "wait, there's more!" Remember that, in the past, all references to a component had to be released before the file could be replaced. The CLR now supports a concept called shadow copy deployment.

Shadow deployment, a function of app domains explicitly and ASP.NET implicitly, allows a new version of a component to be copied over the existing component. All new requests will be handled by the new component. The CLR will keep both objects in memory until all references to the old version are released.

Deployment and versioning, two of the toughest challenges after deployment is complete, are now much easier in .NET. New assemblies can be copied to a production environment without a need to reboot the server, or even stop IIS. Applications that rely on the older version of the assembly will not need to be modified, as both the existing and the new assembly will continue functioning side-by-side. These abilities greatly enhance the availability of an application.

Conclusion

For Visual Basic developers, .NET is not evolutionary, it is revolutionary. Visual Basic .NET fundamentally changes the way VB programmers must think about design and development. In the remaining chapters, we will illustrate this newfound power, and the responsibilities of this power. We will demonstrate the relative ease of use of .NET as we create our highly scalable solution for MyInvestmentWatch.com.

Equally important to understanding the power of .NET is to understand the fundamental need for planning and designing a scalable system. Proper planning at the start will provide a solid base for scalable systems. Poor planning at the start will likely lead to systems that are brittle and fail easily. The focus of the rest of this chapter is to provide an understanding of how to prepare this solid foundation for development in general and developing highly scalable applications specifically.

Ready, Set, Plan

Before you start, don't. With deadlines looming, customers demanding functionality and changes, and a project manager asking about milestones, we want you to do something different. Don't start. Well, don't start development at least.

Poor planning at the start will likely lead to a system that is unwieldy and unable to scale. Proper planning up front will deliver a system that meets current needs, is cost effective, and will scale to meet future demand. We're going to cover what must be considered during this phase.

Clearly Define Requirements

Reactionary statements, such as "it needs to be faster", are very easy requirements to provide but are impossible to design from. "It needs to support a lot of users" is a good place to start from, but these need to be requirements that are both actionable and measurable. Otherwise, you will never know when you're done.

Actionable and measurable is a theme that you'll hear throughout this chapter. Basically, system goals must be stated such that they can be acted upon, and there must be a way to know when you have met each goal. Vague goals are not easily met. Consider these two statements "pages must load fast" and "all pages must render within 5 seconds, with a target of 3 seconds." The first is open for interpretation and will lead to confusion. The second statement is concise, actionable, and measurable.

While these goals must be actionable and measurable, they must also be explicit. A goal of "form must render within 3 seconds" is not enough. Goals must not be open to interpretation. For example, the above goal does not necessarily state that the page must render within three seconds if 1,000 requests are concurrently hitting the same form. If requirements of the system are not explicitly chained, then it could be construed that an application meets the requirements if it sufficiently renders a page for one client request every ten seconds, as opposed to the intent of a thousand client requests per second.

A system that needs to support 50 concurrent users at initial deployment and then scale to support 500 concurrent users will have very different needs from a system that needs to support 10,000 concurrent users at initial deployment and scale to support 50,000 concurrent users. If you don't need to support as much traffic as Yahoo or Amazon, then you don't need to design a system capable of supporting as much traffic as Yahoo or Amazon. Conversely, if you need to support more traffic than WatchMyPaintDry.com, you might want to know that up front as well. The bottom line is that clear requirements will set boundaries around the scope of effort needed in the planning, design, and development efforts.

Understand the Environment

It is important to understand the environment that you are dealing with and the constraints that it will place on your design. This step is not quite as critical for a new system being deployed onto new infrastructure. However, this scenario will be rare; after all, after the first system is deployed, every other deployment will be to an existing environment. Even in this case, it's likely that there will still be constraints that will affect planning and design. Generally, there are three scenarios to consider before starting:

- **Deploying a New Application to a New Environment** – Even if you are creating a new system from the ground up, and deploying to a new infrastructure, you still need to understand how your system will work within the environment. There will always be existing constraints on the environment that will affect planning and design. For example, if your company has a policy against allowing a direct connection from the DMZ to the database, then this is a constraint that will affect your design.

- **Deploying a New Application to an Existing, Shared Environment** – In this scenario, your application is expected to co-exist alongside other applications. This may mean sharing hardware at various tiers, such as existing database servers. It is important to understand how other systems will impact on your application. For instance, if a batch job for another application runs every hour, and will affect throughput to the database that your application depends upon, it would be nice to know about this batch job before searching for the cause of an intermittent slowdown in your application.

- **Upgrading an Existing System** – This can be one of the easiest scenarios in which to understand the existing environment. After all, you already know how your current application fits into the existing environment. You probably also have an idea of where your current application is failing and where it is performing well.

The underlying theme is that you understand the ecosystem your application must live in. This will assist with better planning and design. Of course, this is only a small, but vital, part of system planning.

Align with Business Vision

A system that is developed without accounting for the vision and strategic plan of the company is a system that is doomed. Certain requirements may never be captured for an application that will invariably impact on scalability. If the strategic plan calls for company growth of 15% a year, and the system is not designed to support this annual growth in the user base, then the application will quickly become a chokepoint.

Similarly, it makes little sense to build a system with burgeoning capacity to support a section of the business that will only grow by a small fraction each year. The company business plan will provide an excellent yardstick, along with business requirements, to ensure completeness of predicted system growth. As a side benefit, any shortage in capacity, or too much spare capacity, can be blamed on the delusions of management. While we don't recommend blaming one's boss, it is nice to know that you'll be able to quietly think this fact with smug satisfaction.

Take a Holistic View

This point is of special importance when deploying to a shared environment, where an application will be running alongside one or more other applications, and when you are re-evaluating an existing application. Before any extensive work, or at least before extensive hair-pulling and head-banging, it's time to take a step back and look at what else is going on in the environment. Unless, of course, you enjoy banging your head repeatedly, in which case, we would like to point out the multiple uses of this book, including it being a wonderful surface for smacking one's forehead (unfortunately there are currently no plans for a hardcover edition).

In this step, it should be determined what else in the environment could affect your application. Examples include batch jobs, data backup routines, system extracts, application interfaces, and reporting. After all, what's the point of attempting to troubleshoot a scalability issue in your application if the problem is not your application at all! Surely you've heard the story of the IT team that tried for days and went through countless tuning efforts on an application that was randomly slowing down, only to discover that the problems were caused by a scheduled batch extract that was initiated against the database by another application.

Determine Expected Load on the System

Simply put, understand what you are planning and designing for. The needs of a transactional system that must support a high number of concurrent users are often quite different from the needs of a reporting system that must perform a large number of calculations. Likewise, the impact of a web-based application can be quite different from that of a client-based application.

Understanding the expected load on your application, both short-term and throughout the growth predictions in the business plan, will help you to determine various design needs. Of course, applications do not exist in a void. Many scalability problems that you will face will not necessarily be caused by your design at all. Rather, these issues may arise from how other applications are attempting to interact with your system.

A few key questions to ask during this portion of the planning process are:

- How many concurrent users must the application support?
- How will these users interact with the application?
- How many concurrent transactions, or requests, must the application support?
- What are the integration points with the application?
- What is the maintenance pattern for the application?
- What are the usage trends for the application?

Of course, there are many subsequent questions and issues with each of these topics. Each will affect system scalability, and each can be addressed through design.

Concurrent Users

For many applications, it is the number of concurrent users that must be supported that will impact on system scalability. With regards to concurrent users, there are several important aspects to consider. These are the average number of users that an application must support, the peak number of users expected, and, lastly, how these users are interacting with the system.

Consider our web site, MyInvestmentWatch.com. Arbitrarily, let's say that we have an average of 5,000 concurrent users on the web site. However, the peaks spike to 15,000 concurrent users in the morning when the stock market opens. Unfortunately, from a planning perspective, our infrastructure must support, at a minimum, our peak number of users. This may mean that we will have idle resources the majority of the time, but it also means that we can scale to meet user demand without degradation in performance.

Another important aspect of handling concurrent load has to do with user state management. There are only two basic places to store state, on the server or on the client. In a WinForm environment, the choice may be rather obvious to store state on the client machine. Similarly, due to a desire to support multiple client devices, even for internal-facing applications, the choice for a web-based application is often to store state on the web tier. We will further discuss state management options in Chapter 5.

User Profiling

Concurrency can actually be a bit of a misnomer. That is, after making a request, the user must wait for the page to render and then react to the information. This is referred to as "think-time". For example, on MyInvestmentWatch.com, a user will likely spend some time looking over any charts and news after they click on a stock symbol.

To truly understand the concurrent user load that will be placed on the system, it is important to understand how the users will interact with the system. Creating user scenarios will help greatly with this. For example, a scenario that calls for a user to enter information over several forms translates to a much different load on the system from a scenario that calls for a user to search for multiple stocks in rapid-fire succession.

Transactions

We are not referring to a sales transaction. Rather, a transaction is a series of events, such as a user logging in and performing a search, or background tasks such as the web server recording click stream information, or, even, yes, a user placing an order and conducting a sales transaction.

The purpose of determining transaction throughput is that it can often provide a more meaningful picture of system usage than just a count of concurrent users. For example, knowing that your site will have 500,000 page views in a day, that 100,000 of those page views are of the product detail page, and that the product detail page requires more intensive logic will help with knowing the true load on a system.

Integration

Especially in larger companies, no application stands alone. Eventually, some other application will need to integrate with your application. Of course, this has a direct bearing on scalability. After all, another application calling into your system to retrieve a large amount of data can have a much more detrimental effect than multiple users could ever have.

It is important to understand the integration points, the integration methods, and the general frequencies of these actions. It is one thing for an application to subscribe to asynchronous alerts from your system. It is quite another for a batch job to run every morning and populate summary tables in your database for reporting purposes.

It is important to understand the interaction of these integrations, or at least planned integrations, with your application. This also presents the opportunity for improvements that will immediately benefit scalability. For example, a popular method of integration is to start some scheduled program to retrieve data for the target system.

In other words, this may be a batch job that updates the calling application with data from your system. If this job is scheduled to run at 8 am, and your application experiences its heaviest user load at 8 am, then your scalability is severely hampered as it needs to handle both an influx of users as well as processing demands from the batch job. In this scenario, it may be possible to reschedule the job to a time that does not conflict with peak usage of your system.

Maintenance

If the goal of your system is to support a large number of users or transactions, then one obvious goal of planning should be to sequence actions not directly related to this goal. It's rather obvious that running a backup during peak usage will degrade performance. However, analysis should be done to determine what must be run to support the system that doesn't directly relate to processing transactions.

These support processes should be moved to complement, rather than conflict with, peak user load. Obvious candidates include backups, batch jobs, and logic-intensive reports. Any processing not directly related to supporting transactions will be a candidate for sequencing. During planning, these processes simply need to be identified so that they may be addressed after peak loads are determined.

Trends

Typically, an application will not experience the same load constantly. Rather, there will be spikes in average usage. Of course, these patterns will affect planning as well. After all, it is these spikes that will stress a system.

For example, a retailer will experience much higher volumes during the Christmas shopping season than at any other time in the year. Or, a university's enrollment system will be idle for the majority of the year but must be able to handle the registration load during class sign-up. A system must be able to scale to meet these demands. Identifying these trends during planning will assist both in benchmarking, as you will see, and in determining how the environment must grow to meet these demands.

Benchmark

The goal of a benchmark is simple; its purpose is to determine the load a system can handle as well as weak points in the system design. The reason for a benchmark is simple as well. Basically, benchmarking is a risk-mitigation strategy. It will quickly point out problems and successes along the development cycle.

You should plan to benchmark at several key points throughout development. For an existing application, you should benchmark the system before you start. You should always perform successive benchmarks, or prototypes, during design and development. Finally, you should always benchmark at the end of development. These are not trivial tasks and must be planned for at the start.

Benchmarking an Existing System

If you are planning to upgrade, redesign, or further develop an existing application, then you have a wonderful opportunity to determine the current weak points and strong points of the application before even starting the design. This will allow for a more concerted approach on where to focus design and development efforts.

This benchmark should take a holistic and methodical approach to testing the system. The testing environment should mimic the existing environment as closely as possible. This should include hardware, infrastructure, and any other applications that may be placing a load on the server. The goal is to get a complete snapshot of the current system. If you cannot implement a full testing environment, then try at least to stress the application as thoroughly as possible, and extrapolate your results.

Once you have the environment set up, stress test the application. If the application doesn't break, then stress it further. Measure along the way, see what breaks, and determine where the application will benefit most from redesign.

Now, I'm going to recommend something unconventional, at least unconventional for a VB.NET book. If you are upgrading to VB.NET purely for scalability reasons, and you find that your application meets growth needs for the foreseeable future, then don't upgrade. If the application performs well in the test environment but not in the production environment, then evaluate the production environment and determine the optimizations that can be made there.

However, conversely, if the application does not work well today, a direct upgrade will likely not go well either. Simply upgrading an existing application will likely bring along the design decisions that are adversely impacting scalability today. In this case, reading on will assist greatly with designing for scalability up-front.

Prototype During Design

During design, you will likely encounter portions of your design that you think may not scale well enough. There are two ways to handle these sections of the design. The first option is ignore the potential problem and hope it doesn't materialize. The second option is to prototype the implementation and hammer away at it to see if it meets the requirements.

Frankly, we prefer the second option, as it tends to be the most reliable. The goal here is to build out enough of the design to enable stress testing. In this scenario, you don't necessarily need to emulate the production environment; you simply need to measure how well the potential bottleneck will perform.

When prototyping, consider the following approach. First, plan and design the entire system. Then, identify the potential risk areas. Then, build out these areas fully enough to test. After testing and refining these sections, build out subsequent skeletal portions of the application. After a few iterations, you will have the skeleton of your final application and will have prototyped the design well enough, and frequently enough, to know that the application will scale and perform well. You will likely even start to understand the upper limits of your application's scalability.

Benchmarking Before Rollout

After design, development, and testing, you're done and ready to deploy, right? Well, not exactly. We suggest planning and budgeting time for final stress testing. This final test should again mimic the production environment that the application will be deployed to. If this application is being deployed to a new environment, the task is even easier as you should have the hardware available already.

The goal of this step is to provide a final snapshot of system performance. This will become a baseline for measuring as the system grows. A baseline is crucial, as you will see, in determining trends and growth of your system.

Optionally, this test could stress the application to determine its ceiling for growth. Of course, if you've designed for it, the ceiling could be virtually limitless. Practically, benchmarking before deployment should at least determine requirements are met on the planned hardware.

Ideally, testing at this phase will perfectly simulate production. This should include simulated user load and user interaction, batch jobs that may be running, and other processes that may affect your application. Of course, to know these constraints and specifications, we need to determine the expected load on the system.

Chapter 2: Planning for Scalability

Determine Growth of the System

At this point, you should determine the expected growth of the system. A business system that is in use by the entire company will likely have a growth pattern that matches the expansion of the company. If the business grows 10% a year, then it is a safe bet that the application will need to support a 10% increase in users per year. This type of growth is relatively flat, and easy to predict.. Of course, for a rapidly growing company that is expanding by 25% a year, the growth will be easy to predict but difficult to manage.

Another type of system growth may come in to play with a phased rollout. An application may start small, perhaps being used by a single department or even a single group within a department. This system is then gradually rolled out to the entire business. This type of growth is still linear and predictable, but the growth path is much steeper. In this scenario, monitoring and measuring along the way will help greatly with planning expansion into the system.

Of course, there is another type of growth that is much more difficult to predict. It's not easy to plan for what will happen when a web site is first launched. It's not easy to know how your system would handle an unexpected increase in user volume because your company just merged with its competitor. Unplanned growth happens, and it is the source of nightmares for IT managers everywhere. Fortunately, there are ways to plan for the unexpected as well.

Plan for the Unexpected

Unplanned growth is not a rarity. Nor is it easy to predict or plan for. News sites are deluged when a significant world event occurs. E-commerce web sites are overburdened when a new game system is released. Stock investment sites are saturated with trading in response to market reaction.

If you are launching a new web site, it may be difficult to predict if it will experience an unforeseeable spike in users due to exposure on other sites. Similarly, if your company launches a new product, your sales system may need to handle a large influx of orders. Your business may rapidly expand and expect your system to meet this new demand.

Of course, with proper design, your application will easily be able to meet these new challenges. However, design is only part of the solution. Planning for these unexpected spikes is just as crucial. After all, what's the point of designing a scalable system if there is no spare capacity for it to scale on?

As part of planning for unexpected growth, you must decide how your environment will grow and react. For an application with random spikes in usage, it may be necessary to keep idle hardware ready and active just to handle the inrush. In this situation, it may be prudent to have two, or even three, times the capacity that you would normally need.

Regardless of how unpredictable your system's growth may be, it is possible to plan to handle it. However, again, you must plan up front or you will find yourself scrambling for a solution when the need finally arises. It must be up to you to determine an acceptable buffer.

Conversely, there is another aspect, although not quite as appealing to address, to a highly scalable system. A system that can easily scale up should also be able to scale down as demand lessens. After the first "big push", all of the hardware used to meet demand may no longer be needed. A highly scalable system is able to meet business demands in either direction.

Measure, Measure, Measure

Measuring is so important that we've devoted an entire chapter to the concept. During the entire planning, design, and development phase, your mantra should be measure early, measure often. Performance and load monitoring is one of the best ways to proactively scale a system.

A solid plan will help with knowing when to increase capacity. For example, you might want to add hardware when your hardware is 70% utilized during peak usage. Measuring is also vital for determining where additional hardware will benefit the most. For example, your web tier may be underutilized, even during peak usage, but your database may be struggling to meet demand. Only proper, and consistent, monitoring will point out this capacity need before it becomes a problem.

Trending is important in measurement as well. After all, you must determine if that 70% utilization is an oddity, an unexpected spike, or if represents solid growth. Measurement cannot be sporadic. It must be planned for, it must be timely, and it must be frequent.

Measuring picks up where benchmarking leaves off. Where benchmarking assists early with design and testing, measuring assists with environmental growth and proactively identifying problem areas once the application is in production. Measuring will tie closely into creating an environmental growth plan. The growth plan will lay the roadmap, measuring will pinpoint when to enact portions of the plan.

Create an Environment Growth Plan

A growth plan is, basically, a roadmap for your infrastructure. This plan should outline planned expansion, by tier. It should indicate what will be involved with scaling each tier. In short, the growth plan will remove the surprises with how to scale your application.

Growing an environment is much more involved and complicated than just adding more servers. Moving from a web server to two will involve additional configuration to enable Network Load Balancing. Moving from 32 web servers to 33 will involve configuring a second NLB cluster, as the limit of NLB is 32 nodes. Adding an application tier will affect firewall rules, component deployment, and configuration.

Plan for Design

The focus of the next section is on designing for scalability. A poor design will lead to a poorly implemented system. So, it stands to reason that the proper time for design should be planned for up front.

So far, we've covered the ins and outs of planning. However, planning is only a portion of the entire process. Planning simply lays the groundwork for starting the development of an application. In a sense, planning will enforce allotting enough time for aspects of development that cannot be overlooked.

Designing is where the blueprint is created. This blueprint is what will ultimately be followed to build the application. Proper design is as important in the digital world as it is in the physical world.

Design Guidelines

In this last section of the chapter, we will outline some best practices to follow when designing for scalability.

No Shortcuts

This may be a bit confusing at first. Basically, when faced with meeting user needs, shortcuts are often taken to deliver a solution quickly. These shortcuts lead to detrimental effects on the system, namely forcing the system to process more than originally intended, or to work in ways not originally intended. While these decisions may provide adequate short-term solutions, care should be taken to plan for, and move towards, refactoring these demands onto the proper system and environment.

To give an example, a transactional system, such as a billing system, may originally generate a few basic reports. As reporting needs and complexities grow, such as with trending reports, the load on the system will increase dramatically. This will severely limit the billing system's ability to easily scale. At this point, a decision should be made to create an operational reporting environment to handle all reporting needs.

Conversely, a data warehouse system that is tuned for large batch reads and writes shouldn't be used as the backend for a transactional system. The bottom line is that care should be taken to partition out the portions of the application that would be better suited on another type of system. This should be an on-going task that accompanies every release of an application. Doing so will greatly ease the burden placed on the system and will address the bottlenecks that affect scalability.

Another shortcut that isn't quite as obvious is when a system is first prototyped. Often, portions of a system are prototyped to prove out various concepts. However, under deadline pressure, there is often a push to make these prototypes into production applications. It should be understood up-front that the prototype will be either be thrown away or properly grown into a production system.

Again, shortcuts may need to be taken at the start of design. These shortcuts must be documented and addressed through planning to bring these shortcuts back in line with the original design. Failure to do so will compound scalability issues later.

Don't Reinvent the Wheel

Make sure you understand the capabilities of the .NET Framework before you start. In the remaining chapters of the book, we will highlight the portions of the framework that help with scalability. However, this is not a complete introduction to the framework. Before you expend effort, make sure your need hasn't already been met.

This is one of the most common scalability issues, and perhaps also one of the least obvious. Developers are very creative people and love to solve challenges. Unfortunately, sometimes developers are compelled to solve problems that already have commercial-strength solutions. This is often referred to as the "Not Invented Here" syndrome or the belief that if your company didn't create it, it's not worth using.

From a pure affect on scalability, robust solutions that scale nicely are often overlooked simply because there is a belief that an in-house solution will be better tailored to the problem, often without evaluating if the assumption is correct or not. From a more holistic view, this syndrome can indirectly lead to scalability issues as developers spend time creating solutions not related to the business problem, which takes away time that could be spent redesigning risky portions of the application.

With the advent of the .NET Framework, this syndrome deserves special attention. Many features that previously required custom solutions, whether commercially obtained or built in-house, are now directly part of the Framework. If the Framework does not meet your needs, then extend the Framework. Don't start from scratch if you don't have to. This will provide significant timesaving. The bottom line is, if you don't have to build your own solution then don't.

A business developer should be focused on solving problems for a given domain. In the past, they were often forced to come up with their own solutions for many standard problems, such as caching on the front end, state management in a clustered environment, and even measuring performance and throughput. Much of this is now handled in a robust and elegant manner by the .NET Framework.

Don't Reuse a Flat Wheel

If you're upgrading an existing system, you likely have some interesting solutions for many problems for which ASP and VB didn't provide solutions, or at least not elegant solutions. For example, if you have an ASP application deployed to a web farm, you likely have either a custom or purchased solution for handling session management; or, you've set up your servers to hold client affinity. None of these solutions, to varying degrees, are ideal.

When migrating an application to .NET, evaluate what should be carried over and what should be discarded. Keep in mind, .NET provides an interoperability layer to existing COM components, so the decision may not be as cut and dried as discarding everything that is now solved by the Framework. However, odds are, you'll be much happier with the .NET approach than with any custom solutions you've had to use in the past.

Embrace the Tier

Beware the Monolithic Application

Typically, to scale a system, you must add more hardware. However, generally not every portion of an application will need additional hardware, or at least not the same increase in hardware. This translates to a need to partition an application across multiple infrastructure boundaries. This need must be reflected in the application design.

If a system is incapable of being spread across multiple servers, say more than a single web server and database server, then the scalability limits of the application are very real. At that point, the only scalability option is to add more, or faster, processors to the machine, which is a very finite endpoint.

In the past, a very common design has been to create ASP pages that directly access a database. Presentation logic, business logic, and database connections are all intermingled within each page. This is a good example of a monolithic system. ASP.NET makes this pitfall much easier to avoid, but care should still be taken to segment responsibilities discreetly.

The above example is monolithic because the web tier must run business logic and manage database connections, all in addition to its normal user interface presentation responsibilities. This design is monolithic because it is impossible to separate presentation logic from business logic from database connection logic. By adding a logical layer to handle business logic, we introduce the ability to better handle threading, pooling, and object caching. We also have the possibility to reduce the load on the web server by redeploying the business object layer to a separate physical server.

When designing an application, or even converting an existing application, care should be given to prevent the design from becoming monolithic. Simply put, a monolithic system is one that is clumped together into one unwieldy whole where there are very few, or no, interconnection points that may be spread across systems.

Beware the Intertwined Design

This is a twist on the concept of a monolithic system, and will also lead to non-scalable systems. In this problem, layers share responsibilities in a manner that makes it difficult to segment the application across physical tiers. In this scenario, we may be faced with a middle tier that manages client state, or a database tier that has business logic embedded within stored procedures.

The problem here is several-fold. In cases such as managing client state in the middle tier, the load is further removed from the client, causing unneeded traffic between the web tier and the middle tier. Even worse, it forces the middle tier to be scaled almost linearly with the web tier, whereas, if state were moved from the middle tier, that type of growth is typically not needed. This design will also shackle the built-in capabilities of the .NET Framework.

Rather, application components should be highly granular and loosely coupled. We discuss this further in Chapter 3 with our method of database access. The database access components are highly granular as they only handle data retrieval and editing tasks. In addition, the database access layer provides an interface to develop against and keeps the application from the specific implementation. In this manner, the database can be changed with little impact on the rest of the application.

Some boundary intertwining is not quite so dangerous, nor is it so obvious; for example, embedding business logic within the database. The problem here, from a scalability standpoint, is that undue load is placed on the database server that could be pulled out into a tier that is designed for program logic, such as the middle tier. A slightly less obvious problem is that, by embedding some logic in the database and some logic in the business objects, design improvement opportunities are much harder to spot.

Please note that sometimes scalability enhancements can be achieved by placing business logic within the database tier. An example of this may be where a selection is made, the results are then evaluated, and then another action, such as a second selection, is performed based on the evaluation. In this case, pushing the logic to the database tier will reduce the number of round-trips, which will assist with scalability.

A good rule of thumb is to utilize the database for what it is good at, working with data. Do not move data manipulation to the middle tier that could easily be accomplished during reading from or writing to the database. However, a decision to embed logic should be consciously made with an awareness of the advantages and drawbacks.

.NET Makes Tiers Happy

.NET makes building n-tier applications easier than ever. Components can be separated across tiers and then called via remoting or web services. As you will see in Chapter 4, this power is easy to tap into, and even extend.

.NET also provides excellent support for how an object will be passed, both within the same logical tier and across physical tiers. .NET allows for object serialization and marshaling.

Serialization allows you to specify not only that your object can be passed by value, but also what will be serialized. This allows for greater control over how much data about an object will be passed. Marshalling by reference allows just an object pointer to be passed. All calls to the marshaled object are then proxied back to the host container.

Reduce Round-trips

Crossing process boundaries and, even worse, network boundaries, is costly. These round trips adversely affect scalability in the sense that you will not be able to process as many requests through at a time. These resources can also become constrained quickly if too much data is being needlessly transmitted or if too little data is being frequently transmitted.

Code

The purpose of this design goal is to reduce the amount of communication that must happen between layers. With each network call, you should send enough information to complete the entire action. Consider the following two sections of code. The first illustrates a "chatty" object:

```
Dim ChattyCustomer As customer()
ChattyCustomer = New customer()
ChattyCustomer.FirstName = "Damon"
ChattyCustomer.LastName = "Allison"
```

If this were an object that had to cross a process boundary then a call would need to be made to set each property. Now, consider the following "chunky" code:

```
Dim ChunkyCustomer As customer
ChunkyCustomer = New customer("Ben", "Hyrman")
```

This code leads to the same result, but, again assuming this is a remote object call, it reduces the number of round trips needed.

Stored Procedures

There are many places to look for savings. For example, if the application must perform a query against the database, analyze the results, and then access the database again, then overhead can easily be removed simply by placing the entire sequence within a stored procedure.

In our initial application, once the customer logged in successfully, we would write to a `UserLogin` table. Without a stored procedure, this involved two network round trips. By combining these two functions into a single call, we reduce the network bandwidth used and, to a certain extent, our processing requirements.

Now for word of caution about using stored procedures: As we mentioned before, care should be taken to not intertwine application logic across tiers. Logic that is not core to returning the appropriate data to the business objects for processing should not go within stored procedures. Also, stored procedures cannot take advantage of XCOPY deployment nor are they easily versioned.

The Secret ASP.NET Scalability Weapon

The output cache is your secret weapon in the war on scalability. All static, or semi-static, information should be cached. By caching data, you greatly improve scalability. You can reduce round-trips to the business objects, which is crucial if these objects are on a separate server. If this data is loaded from a database, which is normally the case, then you are reducing load on the database server as well. The caveat here is that you will increase resource use, such as memory, on the web server. This area will be fully covered in Chapter 5.

Determine Critical Path

Not everything needs to happen "right now" – some things simply need to happen. In other words, what events can be made asynchronous and what interactions must be synchronous? The greatest benefit in asynchronous processing with regards to scalability is in the fact that events need not happen immediately. Messages can be queued as they happen and spun off as the receiver has time, which will allow for much better scalability.

Suppose you are logging when a visitor to your web site clicks on an advertisement. The user wants to follow the advertisement right away and you want to log that the ad was clicked. A very common option for this is to synchronously log the click to a database and then navigate the user on to the ad. However, there is likely no reason that the click must be logged before the ad is displayed. In this scenario, the click logging process should be changed to asynchronously write to the database. In this manner, the user can see the ad without having to wait for the logging event, which both decreases customer wait time and increases the throughput of the system as the chokepoint is lessened.

If you are running an e-commerce site, then you likely want to allow people to order items. If you are selling physical items on your web site, then there really is no need to collect payment before you accept an order. In other words, there is no reason to attempt to settle a credit card during the checkout process. Rather, you can accept the order immediately and then perform the necessary authorization and settlement at a later time.

Design Interchangeable Objects

No, the idea isn't to create a design where a `User` object can easily be substituted for a `NewsItem` object. Rather, objects of the same type should be identical with regards to state. In this manner, a client can request any object. ADO.NET connection pooling provides a good example of this design goal.

To utilize connection pooling, each connection must use the same connection string. If the connection string is modified per user, perhaps to add a User ID to the connection string credentials, then the connection cannot be pooled and shared among other system users. In the previous scenario, each connection object is identical; ADO.NET simply returns an available connection from the pool.

To better support interchangeability, you should move state out of your components. Requiring an object to maintain state between function calls hurts interchangeability and scalability. These objects cannot be pooled and must be pinned to a specific client for their lifetime.

Instead, state should be stored externally to the object. The information needed to perform a given action should be passed in only when it is needed to complete the request, and then saved externally again. This design concept fits very well with the design concept of reducing round trips.

Sequence Around Expected Load

There are other factors that will impact on your application's scalability besides the number of concurrent users that you must support. Other applications may need to interface with your system, you may need to perform offline processing, or users may want to run reports and analyze data. All of these tasks can adversely affect performance and scalability. The key is to minimize their impact through proper design. For a discussion of Design Patterns, see the Wrox Press book *Professional Design Patterns in VB.NET: Building Adaptable Applications*, ISBN 1-86100-698-5.

Application Integration

Traditionally, integration between applications has not always been ideal. The source system may run batch jobs to create a file for the target system, or the target system may reach into the source system's API, or the target system may even directly access the source database. All of these methods pose varying problems.

Design Guidelines

Schedule-Based Integration

Each of the above solutions requires the source and target to be tightly coupled together. In the case of the batch job method of integration, the target may not get the information in a timely manner. This is especially true if there are multiple targets, all with different timing needs. The advantage with this approach is that the batch job can be run when user load on the system is lightest.

Real-Time Integration

The advantage of the API integration is that all information is retrieved in real time. More importantly, any business logic is explicitly applied through the API. A key disadvantage is that the target and source are closely tied. If the source changes then the API may change, which will mean the target, or targets, will need to be rewritten as well. However, a large advantage of this is that, if the API is treated as a physical integration point, such as separate object or series of objects to handle integration, then the internals of the application can change without breaking the API.

Another potential disadvantage is that the source application must handle the added load of each interfacing application. If the data needed is large or if the frequency is high then the added load will be great.

Database Integration

The options are slightly different with integrating directly to the database, but they are still not ideal. One method of integration may be to have the target system directly access the source database. You lose the benefit of hiding business logic behind the source API, likely without reducing the load on the source system. This option may be preferred to an API if the database has greater spare capacity or if the API is performing unnecessary calculations and actions.

Another option is in using an Extract, Transfer, and Load, or ETL, tool. An ETL tool is best positioned for database-to-database integration. While it doesn't necessarily fit the bill of this discussion on application-to-application integration, it provides a viable alternative that is worth discussion.

The purpose of an ETL tool is to read large amounts from a source, transform the data into the format expected by the target, and write the transformed data to the target system. The transformation step can include any logic, such as calculations or validation. An ETL tool can be as simple, and cheap, as DTS, which is a free tool that comes with SQL Server, or as complex and costly as an enterprise ETL tool from vendors such as Informatica, Mercator, Ascential, and many others. If you prefer this approach to integration, then make sure to clearly define your criteria and only then start looking for a solution. Also, don't forget to look at DTS, as it packs a lot of power and may suffice for your needs.

Event-Based Integration

The idea behind event-based integration is that the source, or publisher, will notify the target, or subscriber, applications when significant events transpire. For example, traditionally a target system might perform a call against the source system's API to return all newly registered users. With an event-based approach, the source system would notify all subscribers every time a new user registers.

The .NET Framework makes event-based programming easy. In fact, if you've created any Windows Forms in .NET, you've likely used the power of events already. However, events do not need to be relegated to programming the user interface. They bring quite a bit of functionality to the business object tier as well.

However, from an integration standpoint, there are still several problems with just using events. First and foremost, the subscriber is tightly bound to the publisher event model. While the publisher need not know every subscriber, the subscriber must have rather intimate knowledge of which events it is interested in. If the event model changes for the publisher, then every subscriber will need to change. Second, and equally important, the event model must be well thought out during design. To add new events after development, the event model must be expanded, and code may become overly complex. Lastly, the event model of the publisher may be too fine-grained. A subscriber may need to respond to several events in order to retrieve enough information.

For integration between applications, we suggest a more versatile solution. In early 1997, Microsoft released Microsoft Message Queue, or MSMQ. With the advent of .NET, programming to MSMQ is easier than ever before.

The idea behind MSMQ, or any queuing technology, is that a publisher places messages on a queue and any interested subscribers then read from that queue. The messages are read off the queue in the order they are written to it. Just like a queue at a bank, messages are processed in the order they are received. In other words, queues are first in and first out. Unlike our bank example though, we have the advantage of building in the digital world. Our queues can be on different machines, even in different countries! This is illustrated in Figure 12:

Figure 12

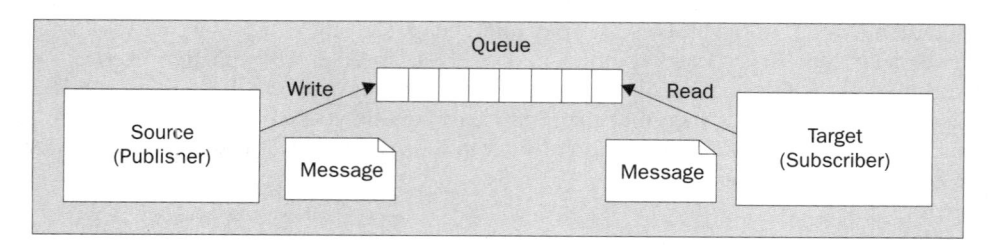

As events happen, the source will publish logical groupings of information. It probably doesn't make sense to publish inventory count along with a new customer registering. However, it makes sense to publish an order header and all related line items as a single message when a customer makes a purchase.

If interoperability with multiple platforms and languages is a concern, then a best practice is to publish to the queue in a format that is easily readable by various subscribers, regardless of technology. Raw XML, or even SOAP, fits this need well. When dealing with only .NET, then simply queuing a serialized object, such as a `CustomerPageVisit` event for our traffic tracking example, is preferable.

We will further examine queue-based programming in Chapter 4. At this point, it is important to understand that event-based programming, when combined with queues, provides a robust and scalable method of integration. Planning and designing for integration up front will greatly speed up efforts to interface applications later. In addition, code changes to the source application during later integration efforts will be minimal or non-existent, which reduces the possibility of introducing bugs into code.

Sequence out Non-User Processing

Any batch jobs, or otherwise long-running processes, should be moved to complement, not contend with, user load whenever possible. For example, MyInvestmentWatch.com experiences its highest user loads at 8 a.m. and right after lunch. Rather than forcing processes to fight for resources at the same time, we can simply move any jobs to when traffic ebbs, such as overnight.

Of course, these types of processes can't always be moved. Or, perhaps there is no low in the number of concurrent users. In this situation, it is beneficial to provide another environment for processing. For example, a group of utility servers to handle non-user load will remove load from the tier that must support users. It is important to realize that many components may be shared, just deployed to several servers. The requirements for each are different though. The goal of the application tier is to support a large number of requests and the goal of the utility server is to support long-running processes.

However, one thing to keep in mind is that both the long-running processes and the transactional requests will, more than likely, impact on the production database. It is important to keep this in mind as every effort should be taken to remove load from the production database, where possible. There is a slightly more specialized approach to removing load from the user environment. That is setting up an environment for reporting.

Create a Reporting Environment

Reporting can place a large strain on any system. Complex reports can involve large amounts of data, extensive calculations, and joins across multiple tables. Generally speaking, operational reporting should never happen against a transactional system.

With regards to building highly scalable systems, planning and designing for an operational reporting environment at the start is important. It is not necessary to purchase hardware for, and implement, this environment immediately. Rather, it is necessary to have the pieces in place to easily move reporting to a separate server when the time comes.

The advice here is to purchase a reporting environment rather than build your own. Reporting is a type of commodity product that will be used by every company in some capacity. As such, building your own reporting environment likely will provide very little competitive advantage. This is the crux of the "buy before build" strategy; it allows a solid, feature-rich tool to be implemented rather than relying on developing in-house solutions.

Database Replication

One option for providing a separate reporting database has already been mentioned, the ETL tool. The main benefit of the ETL tool is that it can easily summarize data during the ETL process, and that it can transfer data between different types of databases. Another option is in database replication.

SQL Server has strong support for replication. Fundamentally, the publisher, or source, database will update one or more subscriber databases in one of two ways. Subscribers can be updated either through transactional or snapshot replication.

Snapshot replication, as the name implies, sends a snapshot, or picture in time, of the publishing database. Snapshot replication requires lesser processing power than transactional replication, as it does not need to constantly monitor for changes. Rather, a snapshot of all data is simply selected from the publisher and sent to the subscriber at a scheduled interval.

The downside of snapshot replication is that the entire data set, not just the deltas, are sent to the subscribers. For large datasets, this method of replication could place too great of a burden on the network. Also, it is important to remember that changes are not immediately available on the subscriber. This may be acceptable for morning or month-end summary reports, but the time lag will not likely be acceptable for any reports that must access the most current information possible.

Transactional replication involves monitoring the transaction log on the publisher and sending changes, such as inserts, updates, and deletes, to all subscribers. These replications generally happen near real-time, but can be scheduled as well. Because only committed changes are sent to subscribers, the network load is much lighter. However, because of the constant monitoring for changes, the processing load on the server will be greater.

Either snapshot or transactional replication provides an excellent solution for moving data to a reporting database. If the need is for timely data then the transactional approach is obviously preferred.

Design for the Future

The bottom line is that it is often not until long after an application has been initially developed and deployed that the pains of a lack of scalability are felt. The idea of a proper design is that an application can start small and quickly scale to meet new demands. A certain amount of this design must involve attempting to future-proof the application. While it is certainly not possible to accurately predict the future, the design principles set forth in this chapter will better allow an application to adapt to change.

Summary

In this chapter, we discussed how to plan and design for scalability. Planning is the single most important step in building a scalable system. One important part of planning is allocating time for design. Proper design will deliver a system that can scale when needed, and where needed.

Planning and proper design deliver the following:

- A proper understanding of the system's requirements
- A solid environmental growth plan
- A correct baseline on the current capacity of the system
- A design that can start small and scale to meet user demand
- An application that is measurable over time

One of the greatest benefits is that the end goal is to remove the potential for surprises that could arise during development and deployment. If it is suddenly apparent that an application is failing in production, a well-designed application will pinpoint where the system is failing. A proper plan will indicate the impact of fixing the weak point.

In this chapter, we covered:

- **Types of Scaling** – There are two basic aspects to scaling. An application can scale up and scale out. An application will need to employ both methods, and likely at different times. Knowing the right balance will assist with implementing a lower cost, "right-sized" solution at the start and still allow for growth as the need arises.
- **The .NET Landscape** – The .NET Framework brings with it many advances. However, it also demands a change in mindset for many developers. These soft-skill changes are as important to planning as the technical aspects of the new features of the Framework.

101

- **System Analysis** – Countless sources can be found on system analysis and design. Within the scope of this chapter, we discussed the points and steps that should be covered when developing a scalable system. It is often difficult to lobby for the time needed for planning, especially when deadlines are tight. However, this step will save overall development time and cost at the start as well as through the lifecycle of the system.

- **System Design** – Poor design choices will lead to a poor, or at least complex and time-consuming, code implementation. Proper design will reduce development costs up-front. Design will also help with reducing maintenance costs and future-proofing an application through techniques such as loosely coupled application integration.

Planning for scalability is not specific to Visual Basic .NET. The principles presented in this chapter will assist with most scaling efforts. However, the .NET Framework and, subsequently, Visual Basic .NET bring many advances for creating highly scalable systems.

Summary

VB.NET

Scalability

Handbook

3

The Data Tier

Similarly to how data is critical to a business, the data tier is critical to an application. The data tier is extremely important for scalability since the database is one of the, if not the, most resource intensive portions of an application. Designing an efficient data tier allows us to alleviate the stress placed on a database and provides the foundation on which scalable applications are built.

The foundation for the data tier begins with the database design. To design a well structured database, we must consider the concepts of normalization, as designing a normalized database helps to eliminate redundancy and provides integrity via table relationships.

A proper level of database normalization will improve scalability by improving performance. Looking at normalization with an eye on the scalability, we must not only determine when to normalize, but when to denormalize. Online Transaction Processing (OLTP) systems, which are write-intensive, will benefit from a highly normalized data store. Online Analytical Processing (OLAP), which are read-intensive, are prime candidates for denormalization. Understanding the fundamentals behind denormalization helps us to determine under which conditions denormalization is appropriate.

Most modern relational databases, including SQL Server, provide additional functionality to enhance the scalability and performance of the database. The proper use of stored procedures and indexes in particular allows us to squeeze even more performance from our application, which leads to faster data retrieval times and improved scalability.

Once the database and stored procedures are implemented, ADO.NET is used to provide the connection, data transfer, and data storage mechanism for communicating with the database. ADO.NET offers vast scalability improvements over traditional ADO. ADO.NET is completely XML-enabled and has much stronger capabilities for reading and writing XML than previously found in ADO. The ability to send and receive XML natively with the `DataSet` simplifies communication with any XML-enabled platform.

The SQL Server .NET managed provider, speaking in the native SQL Server language, is capable of outperforming traditional OLEDB and ODBC data access mechanisms, since it does not need to pass through the layers of interpretation before it hits the data source.

While the SQL Server .NET managed provider provides data source connectivity, the `DataSet` offers a relational, disconnected, multi-table relational data structure where the developer has ultimate control over storing, manipulating, and validating data. The `DataSet` object hierarchy allows us to create relationships between tables and enforce constraints to provide data integrity when updating data. The connectionless nature of the `DataSet` allows us to easily pass the `DataSet` between application tiers. Together, the SQL Server .NET managed provider and the `DataSet` object hierarchy give us the tools necessary to implement data access within our data tier.

An effective data tier relieves the middle tier from performing database access. A separate data tier performs all of the database persistence and provides a more scalable solution than applications having data persistence code intermingled at the middle or user interface tiers.

In this chapter, we implement a data tier for the MyInvestmentWatch.com site using ADO.NET and SQL Server. Using the factory design pattern, we implement a factory object capable of returning instances of our persistence classes. Using an interface-driven approach, we have the capability to add additional classes capable of persisting data to and from a single or multiple data stores within the same data tier.

Database Design

In order to have a highly scalable data tier, we need to have a high quality data storage design and a solid understanding of the database tools available to change, monitor, and evaluate for scalability. Having a highly scalable data tier does not happen by accident. If the design is structured appropriately, it becomes easier and more efficient for the database system to create, read, update, and delete data and allows the database to handle more concurrent users.

A good design also helps the application development and maintenance effort run smoothly. As database needs change over time, a solid database design simplifies the change process. Having a bad database design is costly and time consuming in terms of performance and upgradeability. Whether you are concerned with updating an existing database or creating a new database from scratch, the techniques used in this section are of equal importance.

Design Decisions

Stating the importance of a good database design feels a bit too intuitive to us as system developers. We understand and work first hand with systems and understand how a poorly written query or a poorly structured design leads to complexity, performance issues, and the inability to change the database.

However intuitive the importance of database design might seem, it is interesting to note how many poorly designed systems are in existence today. For some reason, many systems are designed without much consideration for database design or scalability.

Choosing a Platform

The first critical design decision is choosing a platform that will meet the application's scalability needs. Database systems vary widely regarding which hardware and operating systems they support, and their price, scalability options, and tools they provide. Understanding these differences will provide you a solid foundation to make your platform choice.

Understanding Design Principles and Your Platform

Understanding and developing databases is an art. For the database developer, it is important to understand proper database normalization techniques to be able to create a solid relational design. Normalization techniques include both normalizing databases and denormalizing databases. For many systems, normalizing promotes a well structured database design. We will see that in some cases, particularly where high performance is required, denormalized database designs are appropriate as well.

Relational databases, like Oracle and SQL Server, provide developer tools to simplify database creation, performance monitoring, performance tuning, and data manipulation. Understanding the tools provided by the platform eases development and administration.

.NET provides a vastly improved data access layer, ADO.NET. In order to create a high performing data tier, we must understand the tools offered by the database platform. Since we are dealing with Microsoft technologies in the context of this book, we will soon turn our attention to discuss the tools related to Microsoft SQL Server. The tools and techniques discussed here are consistent with the tools provided by other database vendors.

In particular, we will examine the following fundamentals related to database design in conjunction with Microsoft SQL Server. Many of the design topics are general in nature but influence our ability to scale our data tier. The tools and language features we will use are specific to SQL Server and are subject to change between database vendors. The following topics will be discussed:

Chapter 3: The Data Tier

- **Normalization** is the process of developing a structured, organized, and efficient database design
- **Stored Procedures** provide the ability to encapsulate logic at the database layer into a callable procedure that can be optimized by SQL Server
- **Indexes** facilitate fast access to data when the index is used in part of the search criteria
- **Design Tips** provide guidelines for building a highly performing and scalable data tier

Normalization

Before data is presented to the user, before ADO.NET is used to retrieve data, and before stored procedures are written, the database must be designed for scalability. Since the data tier is the foundation for the business logic and user interface, it is extremely important to create an effective database design.

Database administrators and experienced professionals are probably familiar with the concept of normalization. In theory, developing a normalized database design is quite easy to do. In practice, normalization is sometimes glossed over as academic or not 'real-world' enough for true systems. Designing a database system for normalization really isn't complicated and can seriously improve the performance of the database.

Normalization is the process of designing an organized and well structured database. A normalized database eliminates redundant data and creates dependencies between tables of data to ensure the data is consistent. Primary and foreign keys are designed to relate tables together and ensure that database rows cannot be entered unless they meet the criteria established by foreign keys. By eliminating redundant data, we can reduce the amount of space the database consumes. By creating dependencies between tables, we increase the consistency of the data.

In 1970, E. F. Codd began publishing a series of research papers, the first of which was entitled *A Relational Model of Data for Large Shared Data Banks*, which lead to the beginnings of normalization. The levels of normalization are referred to as 'normal forms' and are numbered from 1 to 5. First Normal Form (1NF) is considered the lowest form of normalization and the Fifth (5NF) is the highest. In practice, achieving the third degree of normality (3NF) is considered normalized. Let's briefly discuss each of the first three normal forms to illustrate proper design techniques.

The discussion of normal forms is going to be kept brief. The goal of discussing normalization here is simply to convey an understanding of how to build scalable database designs. A detailed discussion of the intricate points of normalization is beyond the scope of this book. A more detailed description of database design and normalization can be found in the Wrox book *Professional SQL Server 2000 Database Design*, ISBN 1-86100-476-1.

Database Design

First Normal Form

First Normal Form (1NF) is the simplest form of normalization and is quite intuitive. A database is considered in 1NF if the following conditions are met:

- Duplicated columns are eliminated from the same table
- Separate tables are created that group related data and identify each row with a unique identifier

Let's look at the design of a table that is not in 1NF, Orders:

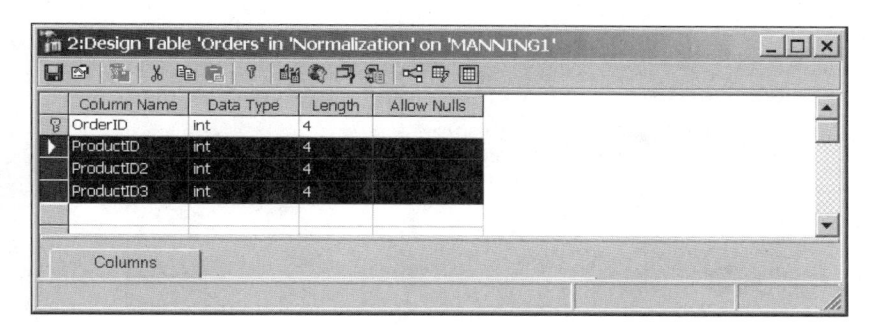

Column Name	Data Type	Length	Allow Nulls
OrderID	int	4	
ProductID	int	4	
ProductID2	int	4	
ProductID3	int	4	

The first rule states that we must not duplicate data within a single table row. A more technical term for this practice is called achieving atomicity. Tables that do not duplicate data within the same row are atomic in nature. Here, we have an Orders table that lists the order ID and the products purchased on the order.

In order to satisfy our second condition, we need an identifier (or primary key) that will identify the each row in the table as unique. A more effective design would be to eliminate the redundant fields, as demonstrated in Orders1NF.

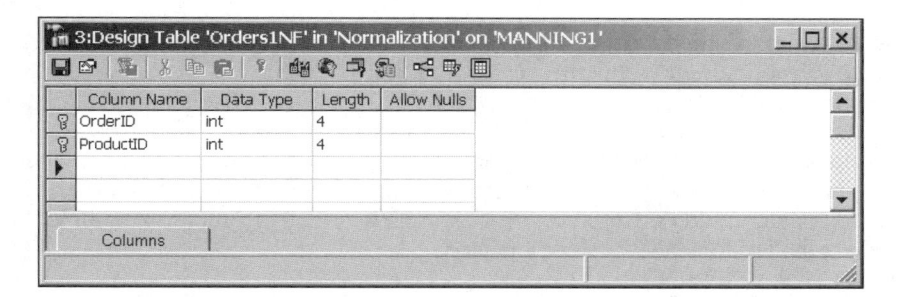

Column Name	Data Type	Length	Allow Nulls
OrderID	int	4	
ProductID	int	4	

Redundancy is now eliminated and each row has a unique identifier, so 1NF is satisfied. 1NF, however easy to achieve, is often not accomplished during a database design.

109

Second Normal Form

Second Normal Form (2NF) improves on 1NF by adding additional requirements to the database design. 2NF has the following requirements:

- Remove like columns of data and separate them into a single row
- Create relationships and link the new rows to the existing data via foreign key relationships

Here is an example of a typical customers table. Each column represents information about the customer.

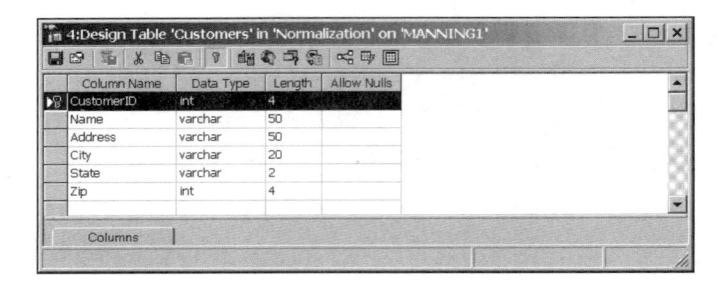

Column Name	Data Type	Length	Allow Nulls
CustomerID	int	4	
Name	varchar	50	
Address	varchar	50	
City	varchar	20	
State	varchar	2	
Zip	int	4	

The information stored in the Customers table could look like the following:

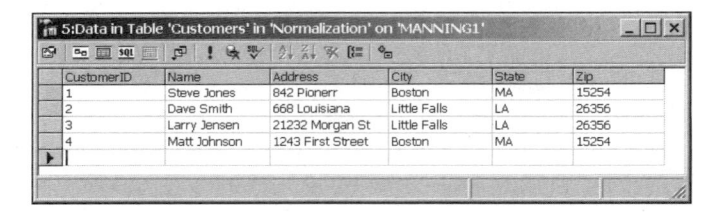

CustomerID	Name	Address	City	State	Zip
1	Steve Jones	842 Pionerr	Boston	MA	15254
2	Dave Smith	668 Louisiana	Little Falls	LA	26356
3	Larry Jensen	21232 Morgan St	Little Falls	LA	26356
4	Matt Johnson	1243 First Street	Boston	MA	15254

As the customer base grows, we begin to maintain similar information that is a candidate for normalization. In particular, we notice that the City, State, and Zip fields contain duplicate information. If we assume the city and state are dependent on the zip, then we can abstract out the information into a ZipCodes table. Notice that in real-world situations a zip code can extend into multiple cities or across states. If that is the case, the additional ZipCodes table would contain a unique identifier and the unique identifier would be stored in the Customers table. For simplicity, assume that a zip code is limited to a city/state combination.

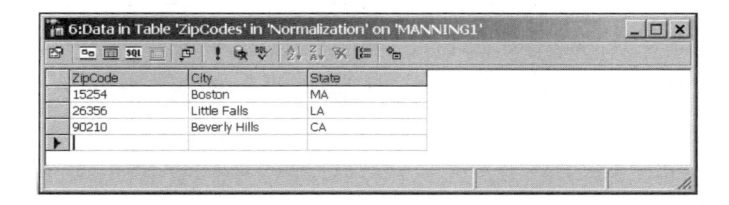

ZipCode	City	State
15254	Boston	MA
26356	Little Falls	LA
90210	Beverly Hills	CA

The `Customers` table would be simplified to `Customers2NF`:

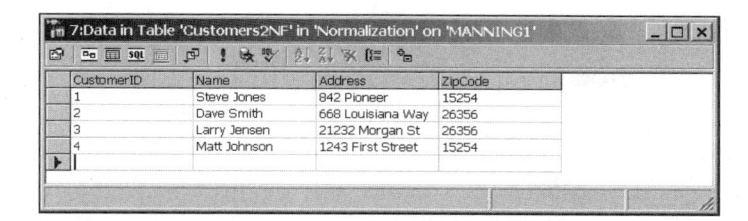

CustomerID	Name	Address	ZipCode
1	Steve Jones	842 Pioneer	15254
2	Dave Smith	668 Louisiana Way	26356
3	Larry Jensen	21232 Morgan St	26356
4	Matt Johnson	1243 First Street	15254

Now that we have successfully separated subsets of data into their own rows, the first premise of 2NF is covered. In order for us to satisfy 2NF completely, we create a foreign key relationship between the `Customers2NF` and `ZipCodes` tables. The foreign key relationship ensures that all zip codes used in the `Customers2NF` table are already present in the zip codes table.

Third Normal Form

Achieving the first two forms of normalization, in theory, is quite simple and straightforward. The third normal form extends the first two forms by adding an additional requirement to the data structure:

❏ Remove columns that are not dependent upon the primary key

Quite often, when saving data, calculated fields are saved into database tables. These calculated values can be unnecessary and consume space that could be used elsewhere. As far as solid database design is concerned, 3NF requires us to remove these values as they are unnecessary. As we will see shortly, keeping aggregate or calculated values could help improve performance depending on the application's purpose. First, let's examine an `OrderDetails` table that is not in third normal form:

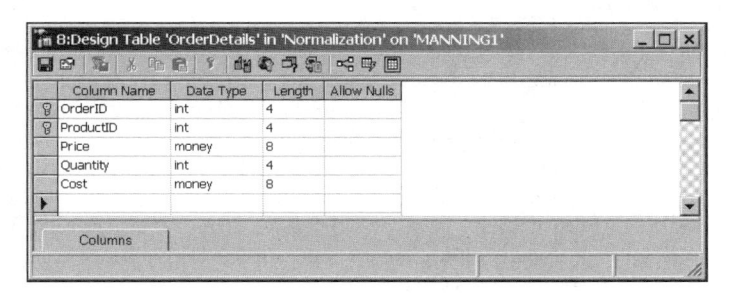

Column Name	Data Type	Length	Allow Nulls
OrderID	int	4	
ProductID	int	4	
Price	money	8	
Quantity	int	4	
Cost	money	8	

111

The `OrderDetails` table would contain data similar to the following:

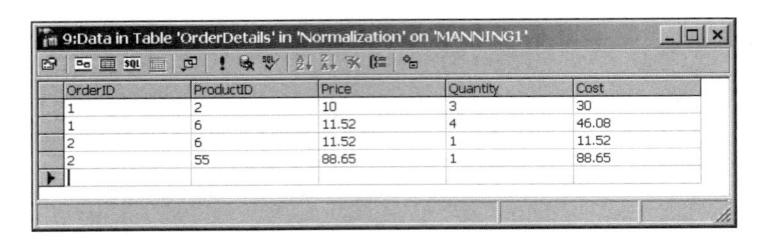

OrderID	ProductID	Price	Quantity	Cost
1	2	10	3	30
1	6	11.52	4	46.08
2	6	11.52	1	11.52
2	55	88.65	1	88.65

Figure 9: Data in Table 'OrderDetails' in 'Normalization' on 'MANNING1'

According to the rules specified by 3NF, the `Cost` column is not dependent on the primary key. `Price` and `Quantity` are unique to the record because the price and quantity differ between records. We could charge each customer different prices if they buy products in tandem or purchase on a discount. The `Quantity` field is dependent for each order/product as well. Different orders for the same product can have different quantities, so `Quantity` is dependent on the primary key.

`Cost` is not dependent on the primary key since the cost is dependent on the price and quantity. Satisfying 3NF, we remove the `Cost` field to have the following in `OrderDetails3NF`:

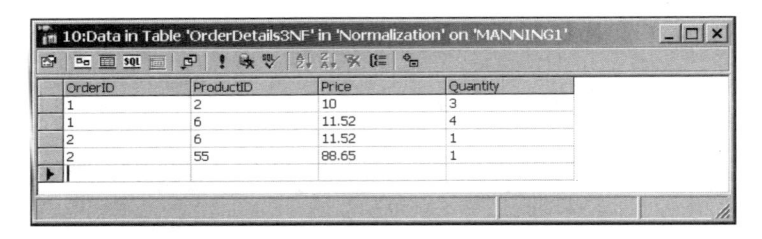

OrderID	ProductID	Price	Quantity
1	2	10	3
1	6	11.52	4
2	6	11.52	1
2	55	88.65	1

Figure 10: Data in Table 'OrderDetails3NF' in 'Normalization' on 'MANNING1'

Normalization and Scalability

Now that we have refreshed our minds with the forms of normalization, it becomes important to note what happens as the degree of normalization increases. Generally, as we create a highly normalized structure, the number of tables and their relationships increase. The queries used to retrieve data must similarly become more involved. Creating more tables generally means creating more `JOIN` queries. Joins can be very resource intensive to execute, especially if the indexes are not set appropriately (we discuss indexes shortly). Improperly designed databases decrease scalability by requiring complex joins between multiple tables. Complex joins hinder scalability by requiring vast amount of resources to issue queries.

As we have previously mentioned, there are times when we want to highly normalize our databases and times when we would like to keep aggregate and redundant data to avoid recalculation. Typically, databases fall into two categories: Online Analytical Processing (OLAP) and Online Transaction Processing (OLTP). OLAP and OLTP have different, but related purposes and normalization requirements.

Database Design

OLTP

Online Transaction Processing systems are typically created to handle customer transactions. For example, in an online retail scenario, a customer's order information would be created within an OLTP environment. OLTP databases are typically highly normalized since they are updated quite frequently. Storing redundant or aggregate information in OLTP system slows the insert and update processes. OLTP systems have the following characteristics:

- Best for entering data quickly, safely, and efficiently
- Fast retrieval and updating of single records
- Not suited for delivering meaningful analysis (ad hoc reports could take days)

OLAP

Online Analytical Processing systems are typically created to handle data analysis and decision making. OLAP systems are optimized for read-only SELECT queries. Speeding SELECT queries generally means creating fewer joins and having a flatter, denormalized structure. Often aggregate data is kept to avoid recalculation when the queries are executed. Sacrificing normalization in OLAP systems can vastly improve performance. Characteristics of an OLAP system include:

- It is an interface between decision makers and the database
- It enables queries for complex analysis
- It can retrieve multiple records or reports quickly
- Its records are updated in the background

Many large systems keep both types of databases. OLTP databases are kept for the daily transaction processing and OLAP systems are kept for summarization and reporting capabilities. Separating the databases improves scalability because the resources can be divided. The data in the OLTP system is more immediate and can be purged from time to time into the OLAP system. If you have the resources (machines, disk space, etc.), one approach is to have both a highly normalized database and an additional non-normalized data store for quick reporting and analysis purposes.

For example, the normalized database would be responsible for taking new orders and interacting with the user interface. At regular intervals (typically off peak hours) the data is queried, translated, and saved into a separate OLAP database for reporting capabilities. The reporting database would sacrifice on normalization in favor of better performance.

If the reporting and "offline" data queries are heavily used in the enterprise, creating such periodic snapshots in a separate OLAP data store frees the transactional, real-time OLTP database from needing to work overtime creating internal queries so it can dedicate itself to servicing the main application.

Chapter 3: The Data Tier

Stored Procedures

Once the database design is constructed, we need the ability to retrieve data. Programmatically, we could use ADO.NET to create SQL statements and issue them against the database. Although a common practice, this limits the application from a scalability standpoint. Stored procedures are the preferred method for data access and manipulation and offer the following benefits over dynamic SQL statements:

- They typically improve performance, because the database can optimize the data access plan used by the procedure and cache it for subsequent reuse. Since issuing SQL calls can be one of the most time consuming activities, squeezing all the performance we can from the database is essential to a high-performing system.

- They provide an additional level of security and can be restricted. For example, we could restrict a user from having access to the data tables, but allow them access to the data through a stored procedure. Such a practice increases security by forcing users to interact with the data only via our permitted stored procedures.

- They result in easier maintenance as they do not need to be compiled by the programmer, which means if a defect correction, improvement, or change is necessary, the text can be edited directly and take effect immediately without need for manual recompile. Conversely, dynamic SQL is compiled into the middle tier application and a SQL statement change requires a recompile and redeploy.

- They add an extra level of abstraction from the underlying database schema beyond that offered by dynamic SQL. If the database schema needs change, perhaps because we wish to restructure the tables for improved performance, then the stored procedure can be altered to reflect this change and effectively hide the changes from the code calling the stored procedure. The client of the stored procedure is isolated from the underlying schema.

Stored Procedure Lifecycle

We briefly mentioned that one of the benefits of using stored procedures is the ability to cache execution plans. Let's discuss the lifecycle of the stored procedure to point out the efficiencies they provide.

Step 1: Parse

When the SQL call is issued against the database, the command parser must check the call for proper syntax and translate the call into SQL Server's internal format to be compiled. The internal format used by SQL is called a query tree, and prepares the statement for the compiler to compile.

Database Design

Step 2: Compile

Once the query tree is parsed by the parser, the compiler generates a plan for executing the query. The execution plan is the detailed sequence of commands necessary to perform in order to fulfill the query. Checks are entered in the execution plan for constraints and any necessary triggers that may exist.

Step 3: Execute

After the compiler has created the execution plan, the plan is executed and the results are returned to the caller. SQL Server will keep the execution plan in memory so the next time the procedure is executed (provided the procedure wasn't changed or the plan didn't expire from memory), the execution plan is reused. It is not necessary to perform the parse and compile steps again.

Step 4: Recompile When Necessary

If the database schema changes (via an ALTER TABLE statement), indexes are added/removed, multiple rows are altered, the execution plan is dropped from memory, statistics on the tables are updated, or the procedure is told to recompile, the execution plan will be recompiled.

Stored Procedures and Scalability

Perhaps the most important benefit of stored procedures from a scalability standpoint is the ability to provide a layer of abstraction between the physical data and the data layer. Data is a sensitive issue and if security is of high concern, we can limit access to the database by denying all users direct access to the data tables. This gives us the ability to control access, provide data validation, and monitor security closely when data is accessed.

Abstraction also separates the data tier from the underlying database platform. Different database platforms differ in the SQL statements that they allow. For example, if the business was moving from SQL Server to Oracle, the SQL statements would most likely need to be altered to conform to Oracle's SQL syntax. If our data access layer accesses the database, then the amount of data access code that would need to be changed during the migration would be drastically reduced.

Likewise, if we add databases to our architecture to offload parts of our database to alternative servers, the stored procedures can contain logic to access the alternative databases. Transferring the SQL processing and querying performance across multiple servers allows the data tier's scalability to increase.

Stored Procedures and ADO.NET

As we will see shortly, ADO.NET has the ability to keep an in-memory copy of a relational set of tables. Having the ability to keep hierarchical data and enforce constraints on that data makes us think carefully about how we create stored procedures.

With the ability to keep multiple tables in a single `DataSet`, we could return multiple result sets with one stored procedure and create relationships between the tables from within the middle tier to enforce data integrity. Having one stored procedure that returns multiple result sets can reduce the number of stored procedures that we need to create and can improve our performance by reducing the network call traffic.

Having the ability to store related tables can also alter the logic our application uses to update data. For example, relationships can be enforced before the stored procedures are called. Enforcing the relationships eliminates the need for stored procedures to be called if the data is invalid. Understanding ADO.NET and the `DataSet` forces us to think carefully about how we should create our stored procedures to take advantage of what the `DataSet` has to offer.

Indexes

When SQL is executed, the query processor is responsible for locating the data relevant to the query. Indexes allow the query to execute faster by telling the query processor where the relevant data is located. Indexes in SQL server are similar to the index at the end of this book. If you are told to search for "Stored Procedure" within the text, you can either page through the book, page by page, looking for the words "Stored Procedure" or you could look in the book's index and turn to the relevant pages listed. Indexes for a database are similar; they allow fast access to data.

Indexes in SQL Server are important for increasing query performance and should be evaluated when developing the data-tier design. Indexes especially shine in large databases where the amount of data potentially relevant to a SQL query is large. There are two types of indexes that can be created on tables: clustered and nonclustered.

Clustered Indexes

Clustered indexes keep data physically structured to match the index key. For example, if you have a set of data with an `ID` value from `1` to `100`, inserting the `ID` of `50` will mean the record is inserted immediately after `ID` `49` and before `51` in the set of data. When querying using the clustered index, the index actually returns the data since the data is stored corresponding to the index. Take the following query:

```
SELECT * FROM MyTable WHERE ID > 40 AND ID < 50
```

Since `ID` is the clustered index, once the index is searched, the query processor does not need to go any further since the data is contained in the order of the index. A clustered index in SQL Server is similar to turning to the index of this book and not only finding the item being searched for, but also the actual data. At this point you would have the information and the search is over.

The data can only be physically arranged in one way, so there is a limit of one clustered index per table. The query optimizer strongly favors using a clustered index since it does not need to find the data once it searches through the index.

Nonclustered Indexes

A nonclustered index is actually similar to the index in the back of this text. Once the nonclustered index is searched, it tells the query processor where to find the relevant data. The index data pages contain a pointer to the actual location of data. The query processor, once it finds the data location from the nonclustered index, must then retrieve the data from the location to pointed. It is because of this extra step the query processor favors clustered indexes over nonclustered indexes.

Even though nonclustered indexes are a bit more resource intensive than clustered indexes, they are generally much quicker than a full table scan (equivalent to flipping through the book, page by page). As we will see in the performance tips for index creation, it becomes important to make nonclustered indexes highly selective to increase their effectiveness.

Index Performance Tuning Tips

Creating useful indexes is one of the most critical tasks you need to do to increase performance. Indexes dramatically speed data retrieval and collection. In order to use indexes effectively, the following points must be considered:

- Indexes actually decrease performance when inserting, updating, and deleting
- Nearly every table should have a clustered index
- Index on WHERE or JOIN clause search fields
- Make nonclustered indexes highly selective to increase their effectiveness
- Design indexes around database (and table) function

Design Indexes to Database Function

When data is inserted, updated, and deleted the indexes need to re-adjust themselves to continue to report correct results to the query processor. In OLTP systems, where the frequency of data change is high, the number of indexes should be kept low.

With OLAP systems, which are almost purely used for selecting data, table could reasonably have ten to twelve nonclustered indexes to increase performance. Indexes benefit OLAP systems tremendously since they improve speed when reading data and the OLAP system is overwhelmingly read-only.

Consider the type of database being used to determine the number of indexes and which fields should be indexed. Be careful that you do not create too many indexes on frequently updated, or "hot", data as this will reduce the performance of the system. Likewise, databases used primarily for selecting data are candidates for heavy indexing.

Index on Search Fields

We still haven't addressed the question "Which fields should I index?" The answer depends on the fields being used in queries. Fields used in the WHERE and JOIN clauses of SQL queries are good candidates for indexes because they must be analyzed by the query processor. For example, examine the following queries:

```
SELECT * FROM Users WHERE LastName = 'Johnson' OR FirstName = 'Emily'

SELECT * FROM Users WHERE LastName like 'jack%'

SELECT * FROM Orders JOIN Users ON Orders.CustID = Users.ID
   WHERE Users.ID = 10
```

The LastName field is a prime candidate for a nonclustered index. Chances are the CustID field is the primary key field and is responsible for many queries in the application. Keeping CustID as the clustered index is most likely a good idea. We are interested in the SELECT statements for determining indexes. Here, we will want to examine the LastName and FirstName as candidates for nonclustered indexes.

It is often difficult to determine performance when the application is under development. If performance slows after the application goes into production, we need a way to examine the current traffic coming into a system and analyze it for possible performance improvements. SQL Server offers us the SQL Profiler for examining and monitoring the current database traffic.

Once we have the data, we must manually iterate through the gathered statements looking for common patterns and begin to determine a strategy for creating indexes. Since the process of query analysis is repetitive, tools have been created to ease the process. SQL Server comes with a tool called the Index Tuning Wizard that analyzes the output generated by the profiler and recommends indexes it thinks can benefit performance. Generally, taking what we know about indexes and the results from the Index Tuning Wizard, we are armed with enough information to re-examine our index design.

Using the SQL Profiler

The SQL Profiler offers the ability to examine many interesting events related to transactions, SQL statements, stored procedure recompilations, and many others. The SQL Profiler can run from any machine on the network and point to the database instance of interest. It listens to the traffic generated by the SQL Server engine and stores the messages for later analysis. The purpose of the SQL Profiler is self explanatory and the effectiveness of the tool has been well documented. The following screenshot is a snapshot of the SQL Profiler in action.

Database Design

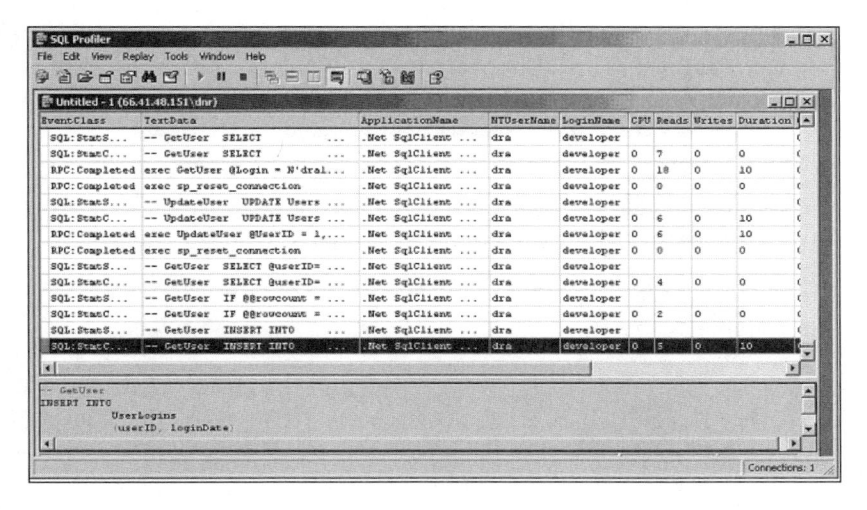

[Screenshot of SQL Profiler window showing event class trace data with columns EventClass, TextData, ApplicationName, NTUserName, LoginName, CPU, Reads, Writes, Duration]

The SQL Profiler gives us powerful information for making scalability decisions. By quantifying performance, we can determine which parts of the application would benefit the most from extra tuning. For example, if a large portion of the application's usage surrounds a particular set of search queries, it might be possible to move the search data and queries to a separate system or consider indexing the table more efficiently. Having the SQL Profiler data opens up ideas to improving system scalability.

Index Tuning Wizard

Once we have the database performance data from the SQL Profiler, it is time to examine the data to determine which tables and columns we should index. The Index Tuning Wizard in SQL Server gives us an automated approach to help generate ideas. Regardless of whether the application is just being developed or has been in production for some time, modifying indexes with the Index Tuning Wizard can benefit the application.

The Index Tuning Wizard takes the output from the SQL Profiler (called a trace), examines the data for patterns, and makes index recommendations. Often these indexes are fairly useful and many systems could simply implement the indexes the Index Tuning Wizard recommended.

For those developers who demand more control over the performance of the system, the Index Tuning Wizard assists them by guiding them into the direction they should consider when manually iterating through the SQL Profiler output.

Very briefly, here is a sample of the Index Tuning Wizard in action. If you have not used the SQL Profiler and the Index Tuning Wizard at the data-tier level, you could be missing on potential scalability improvements not easily recognized by normal operation. Even speeding up one slow but critical query could make the system perform much more efficiently.

119

Chapter 3: The Data Tier

When started, the Index Tuning Wizard (this example is shown from SQL Server 2000) asks for the workload file.

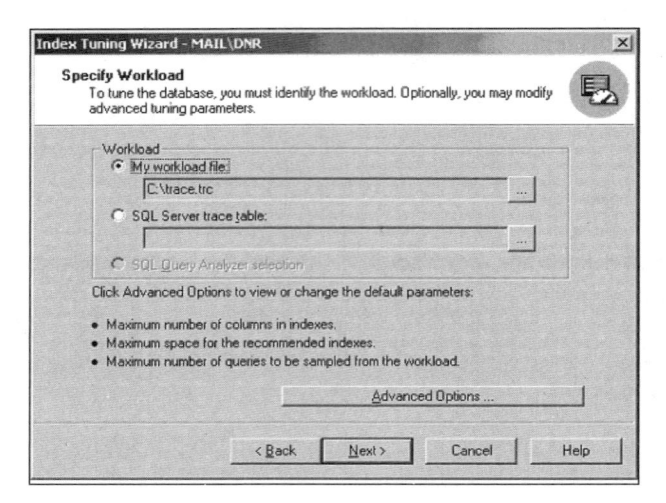

Once the file has been obtained, it analyzes it for a list of the rows that could be affected by the indexes. Generally, the more projected and actual rows, the more improvements an index can provide. Select the tables you are interested in having the Index Tuning Wizard analyze.

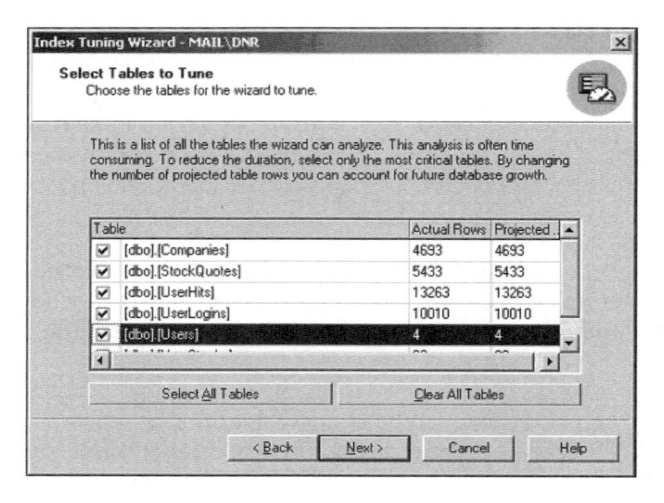

Once the tables have been selected, the Index Tuning Wizard will report the indexes it recommends implementing. You can then have the Wizard apply the selected indexes. The process of analyzing the data tier with the tools is relatively painless and highly effective. Keep in mind when running the index tuning wizard on your database that the output being analyzed for tuning should be a snapshot of live production usage. Live production data gives the Index Tuning Wizard the most relevant data from which it will make the most relevant suggestions.

120

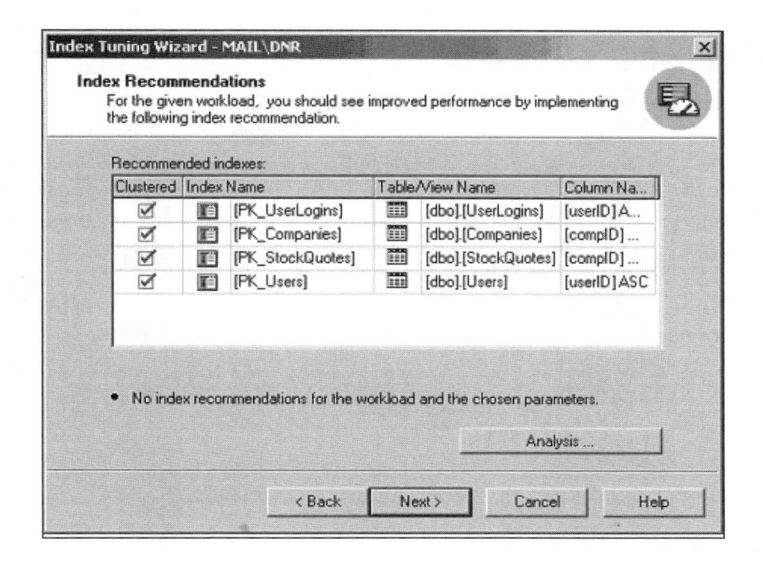

ADO.NET

Once we have a solid database design established, it's time to interact with the database and the data within it. One of the most exciting improvements for the data tier is the introduction of ADO.NET, which improves upon ADO by offering, among other things, a dedicated SQL Server access library, an XML-friendly data storage mechanism, and an easy-to-learn object model.

In the pages that follow, we will turn our attention directly to the data access layer and ADO.NET. It is important to understand the ADO.NET object model and the functionality the model exposes to us.

We will examine ADO.NET in detail, including:

- Describing data providers and their advantages over previous models
- Creating and using `DataSet` objects and examining their impact on scalability
- Creating and using `DataReader` objects and examining their performance benefits
- Executing stored procedures from ADO.NET using the highly efficient SQL Managed Provider
- Using the XML functionality built into ADO.NET and its implications on scalability
- Designing the data tier for high performance and scalability

121

ADO.NET at a Glance

There are many database platforms, all with different underlying architectures and communication mechanisms. Despite the differences between database platforms, ADO.NET provides a common data access object model and encapsulates the intricacies of the different platforms in the implementation of each provider. For example, the SQL Server .NET Data Provider allows connectivity to SQL Server, while the OLEDB or ODBC .NET Data Providers allow connectivity to virtually any data store conforming to the relevant standard. If OLEDB or ODBC .NET Data Providers are not fast enough for your data platform, you could write your own managed provider to provide customized and efficient connectivity to your underlying platform.

Microsoft has identified three major design goals with ADO.NET:

- Familiar programming model
- Better support for n-tier programming than ADO
- Integrated XML support

Familiar Programming Model

ADO was very simple and effective to use. When developing ADO.NET, Microsoft kept many of the same features and objects used in traditional ADO. ADO can interoperate with ADO.NET; however, the benefits of ADO.NET and its managed classes over ADO warrant the upgrade.

In order to improve the ADO.NET model over ADO, changes had to be made to the object model. However, when making changes, Microsoft has attempted to preserve objects such as the `Connection` and `Command` objects that will be familiar for ADO developers.

Support for N-Tier Programming Model

A principle of scalable systems design is the ability to separate the application into logical tiers. Logical tiers, if under heavy load, can be scaled into their own physical tier.

In ADO programming, a disconnected `Recordset` was often used to transfer data between tiers. With ADO.NET, the data access layer objects work in a completely disconnected fashion. For example, the `DataSet` object, which is at the center of the ADO.NET programming model, is completely disconnected from the data store. Disconnecting the data from the data source allows the data to be transferred across tiers without concern for holding connection-oriented resources open.

The `DataSet` object itself can act as a relational data model, complete with constraints and relationships between `DataTable` objects. We can use the built-in relationships to increase the performance of our data tier by returning a greater portion of the object model with one SQL call or avoiding expensive looping to obtain a subset of data in a child table. Using these n-tier improvements, ADO.NET allows us to perform logic when the data is being updated rather than needing to make calls to our data store.

Native XML Support

The benefits of XML as a data format are far reaching. Tools and libraries for creating and manipulating XML have been developed for the vast majority of the popular platforms. ADO.NET has the ability to consume, read, and create XML that is capable of being transferred across tiers or between application platforms.

ADO.NET and the XML libraries in the .NET Framework have a close relationship. ADO.NET interacts with the XML libraries to both accept and send data between the libraries. XML that is being consumed in the XML library set can be transferred to a `DataSet` and vice versa. For example, the XML library set has an `XmlDataDocument` class capable of accepting an ADO.NET `DataSet` object, which populates the `XmlDataDocument` in as little as two lines of code:

```
Dim ds As DataSet = New DataSet()
Dim xd As XmlDataDocument = New XmlDataDocument(ds)
```

XML integration gives our system the capability of potentially scaling to include different system architectures or platforms that can accept, parse, and create XML documents. From an interoperability perspective, XML is an ideal solution. XML support is built into the vast majority of development platforms and is thus an ideal format for transporting data between .NET and non .NET applications.

Unfortunately the flexibility of XML comes at a cost. XML is verbose and transferring verbose information between application tiers is expensive in terms of performance and scalability when compared to more compact native .NET data formats. If you have .NET at both ends of the call, transferring data in .NET's native binary format will show ample performance gains. In the next chapter, we will discuss the performance and scalability differences between XML (SOAP) and binary RPC calls between application tiers.

ADO.NET Object Model

ADO, for the most part, was a connection-based architecture. A `Recordset` could be disconnected from the database, however the default nature of ADO was connection-based.

ADO.NET separates the database connection objects from the data storage and manipulation objects. The `DataSet` object is the focal point for the data storage object model, and the selected .NET data provider is responsible for database communication. Having a separated object model means we can work with and pass data using only the data storage engine and use the database connection piece only when required.

Having a completely separated object model allows our application to scale well since we can keep all our connection-oriented code closer to our data store where the persistence happens and keep our data manipulation code closer to where the data manipulation happens.

Chapter 3: The Data Tier

Graphically, the ADO.NET object model looks like Figure 1. The .NET data provider is responsible for communicating with the database and contains classes for the communication. The `DataSet` and set of child classes have no knowledge of where the data physically comes from.

Figure 1

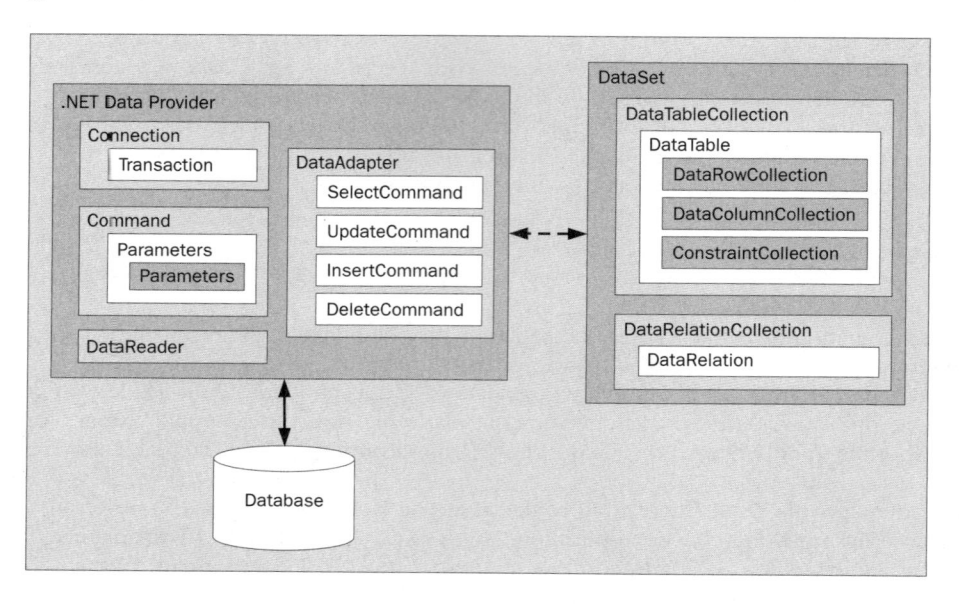

```
┌─────────────────────────────────────────────────────┬──────────────────────────────────────┐
│ .NET Data Provider                                  │ DataSet                              │
│  ┌──────────────────┐  ┌──────────────────┐         │  ┌─────────────────────────────┐     │
│  │ Connection       │  │ DataAdapter      │         │  │ DataTableCollection         │     │
│  │  ┌────────────┐  │  │  SelectCommand   │         │  │  ┌───────────────────────┐  │     │
│  │  │Transaction │  │  │  UpdateCommand   │◄ - - ►  │  │  │ DataTable             │  │     │
│  │  └────────────┘  │  │  InsertCommand   │         │  │  │  DataRowCollection    │  │     │
│  └──────────────────┘  │  DeleteCommand   │         │  │  │  DataColumnCollection │  │     │
│  ┌──────────────────┐  └──────────────────┘         │  │  │  ConstraintCollection │  │     │
│  │ Command          │                               │  │  └───────────────────────┘  │     │
│  │  Parameters      │                               │  └─────────────────────────────┘     │
│  │   Parameters     │                               │  ┌─────────────────────────────┐     │
│  └──────────────────┘                               │  │ DataRelationCollection      │     │
│  ┌──────────────────┐                               │  │  DataRelation               │     │
│  │ DataReader       │                               │  └─────────────────────────────┘     │
│  └──────────────────┘                               │                                      │
│           ▲                                         │                                      │
│           ▼                                         │                                      │
│       ┌────────┐                                    │                                      │
│       │Database│                                    │                                      │
│       └────────┘                                    │                                      │
└─────────────────────────────────────────────────────┴──────────────────────────────────────┘
```

.NET Data Providers

A .NET data provider is used for database connectivity. If the data provider is used to retrieve data, it can be stored into a `DataSet` object. There are four main objects that together make up the heart of the .NET data provider:

- `Connection` – Connects to data source and so provides transaction ability
- `Command` – Executes a command (stored procedure) against the data source
- `DataReader` – A fast read-only, forward-only data result set
- `DataAdapter` – Used to populate a `DataSet` object and provide updates from a `DataSet` object to the data source

In order to communicate with data sources in previous technologies, data source vendors agreed on a common interface to standardize communication. ODBC and OLEDB were created to simply access to data sources by providing a common set of interfaces that various database implementations adhered to. As long as the provider could communicate via OLEDB or ODBC, a data access technology (like ADO) could access the data source.

While the standard communication mechanism promoted interoperability, the extra abstraction layer caused slower performance. With .NET, Microsoft has created the data access layer general enough for any database vendor to create a managed .NET-ready provider. Oracle, DB2, or any other database vendor is able to create a .NET data provider to bypass the OLEDB and ODBC layers and execute commands directly to the native data store format.

Microsoft's SQL Server .NET Data Provider is contained within the `System.Data.SqlClient` namespace. It is optimized to access SQL Server databases directly.

Using the SQL Server .NET Data Provider

Without code, it is difficult to explain how the .NET data provider objects interact. The following code describes the interaction between the objects. Keep in mind that the SQL Server .NET Data Provider and the OLEDB .NET Data Provider offer the same set of functionality. The object model is common across all providers, making the data-tier code similar across different data providers. Let's start with an example called `DataProvider.vb`:

```
'****************************************************************
' DataProvider.vb
'
' Compile with:
' vbc DataProvider.vb /r:System.dll,System.Data.dll,System.Xml.dll
'****************************************************************
Imports System
Imports System.Data
Imports System.Data.SqlClient

Module DataProvider

  Sub Main()
    Dim cn As New SqlConnection("Data Source=(local);" & _
        "Initial Catalog=MyInvestmentWatch;User ID=sa;Password=;")
    cn.Open()

    Dim cm As New SqlCommand("GetUser", cn)
    cm.CommandType = CommandType.StoredProcedure
    cm.Parameters.Add("@Login", "dralogin")
    Dim dr As SqlDataReader = cm.ExecuteReader()
    PrintReader(dr)

    'Release the data reader to free the connection
    dr.Close()

    Console.WriteLine()

    'Use SqlDataAdapter object to populate DataSet object.
    Dim da As New SqlDataAdapter("SELECT * FROM USERS", cn)
    Dim ds As New DataSet("Users")
    da.Fill(ds)
```

125

Chapter 3: The Data Tier

```vb
      ds.Tables(0).TableName = "Users"
      PrintDataSet(ds)
   End Sub

   Public Sub PrintReader(ByVal dr As SqlDataReader)
      Dim i As Integer
      While dr.Read()
         Console.WriteLine("--- NEW ROW ----------")
         For i = 0 To dr.FieldCount - 1
            Console.WriteLine("Field " & i & ":" & dr(i))
         Next
         Console.WriteLine("--- END OF ROW -------")
      End While
   End Sub

   Public Sub PrintDataSet(ByVal ds As DataSet)
      Dim dt As DataTable
      Dim dr As DataRow
      Dim dc As DataColumn
      For Each dt In ds.Tables
         Console.WriteLine("--- PRINTING TABLE: " & _
                           dt.TableName.ToUpper() & " --")
         For Each dr In dt.Rows
            Console.WriteLine("------ NEW ROW -------")
            For Each dc In dt.Columns
               Console.WriteLine(dc.ColumnName & ":" & dr(dc.ColumnName))
            Next
            Console.WriteLine("------ END OF ROW ----")
         Next
         Console.WriteLine("--- END TABLE: " & _
                           dt.TableName.ToUpper() & " -------")
      Next
   End Sub
End Module
```

Let's focus directly on the SQL data provider object code and leave the `DataSet` object printing functions aside for the time being. The `SqlConnection` object is responsible for creating the connection to the data source. The `SqlCommand` object executes the stored procedure. Since the stored procedure returns a `SqlDataReader`, the `ExecuteReader()` method is called, returning the reader object. Because the `SqlDataReader` object is connection-based, there can only be one `SqlDataReader` attached to a `SqlConnection` object at one time. The `SqlDataAdapter` object is used to populate the `DataSet` object. In those few lines of code, we have shown the primary function of each of the four main data provider objects.

As you can see, once we have the `DataSet` object, we can iterate through the object model hierarchy, printing out the contents of the objects. When printing the `SqlDataReader`, we get the first section in the following screenshot. Keep in mind the stored procedure executed returns one row. Notice that we used SELECT * FROM within our SQL call, which was mentioned as a technique not to be performed from within a scalable application. Our small example is simply meant to provide an interaction between the .NET data provider objects.

126

ADO.NET

The `DataSet` object was populated with an ad hoc SQL query for illustration. In a production environment, a stored procedure is beneficial. Printing out the `DataSet` returns the second section of the following output.

```
C:\Scalability\Chapter 3\ADO.NET>DataProvider
--- NEW ROW ---------
Field 0:1
Field 1:Damon Allison
Field 2:dralogin
Field 3:drapass
--- END OF ROW -------

--- PRINTING TABLE: USERS ---
------ NEW ROW -------
userID:1
name:Damon Allison
login:dralogin
password:drapass
------ END OF ROW ----
------ NEW ROW -------
userID:2
name:Ben Hyrman
login:benlogin
password:benpass
------ END OF ROW ----
------ NEW ROW -------
userID:3
name:Nick Manning
login:nicklogin
password:nickpass
------ END OF ROW ----
--- END TABLE: USERS -------

C:\Scalability\Chapter 3\ADO.NET>
```

Using the native SQL Server .NET Managed Provider allows our application to speak in native SQL Server TDS (Tabular Data Stream) format. Speaking in a TDS format allows our application to bypass OLEDB and ODBC interfaces and results in performance gains for our application. While exact performance gains vary between systems, Microsoft has seen performance gains up to 200% using a managed provider over a non-managed OLEDB provider.

Connection Pooling with the SQL Server .NET Data Provider

Pooling connections is a great source of scalability since it offers a more efficient usage of connection resources. By default, the SQL Server .NET Data Provider provides connection pooling. You also have the ability to control connection pooling via connection string modifiers.

When connections are created, the provider starts a new pool using the connection string as an identifier. By default, multiple connection objects are created until the minimum of the connection pool is reached. If another connection is opened with the same connection string, the pool is consulted for available connections. If a connection is in the pool, it is returned to the caller. If not, a new connection is created. If a different connection string is used, a new pool is created. If the pool limit is reached, connection requests are queued for the next available connection. If a connection object's lifetime has expired then the connection is removed from the pool. Likewise, if database connectivity is broken, any connection objects in the pool are removed.

Connection pooling is established via connection string parameters. The following connection string creates a connection pool:

```
Dim cn As New SqlConnection("Data Source=(local);" & _
    "Initial Catalog=MyInvestmentWatch;User ID=sa;Password=;")
    "Connection Lifetime=90;Min Pool Size=50;" & _
    "Max Pool Size=100;Pooling=true;")
cn.Open()
```

The parameters `Connection Lifetime`, `Min Pool Size`, `Max Pool Size`, and `Pooling` are responsible for setting up connection pooling. Note that if the parameters are omitted, the provider inserts defaults. Here are the values:

Parameter	Default	Description
Connection Lifetime	0	If the connection, when returned to the pool, has been open for longer than the Connection Lifetime parameter, it is destroyed.
Min Pool Size	0	Minimum number of connections to keep in the pool.
Max Pool Size	100	Maximum number of connections to keep in the pool.
Pooling	True	If True, the connection is pulled from the connection pool if appropriate. If there are no available connections in the pool, a new connection is created and added to the pool.

In order to take advantage of connection pooling, it is important to keep the connection strings similar. This book uses SQL Server Authentication for illustration. If we were to deploy into a production environment, we would use Windows security to authenticate.

Let's assume for argument that each user is assigned a unique login. In this scenario, we cannot take advantage of connection pooling since we must alter the `User ID` and `Password` connection string parameters. Since the connection strings become different, each connection is assigned to a new pool.

However, Windows authentication does offer our application the following benefits:

- Security is easier to manage since you work with a single security model rather than introducing the additional SQL Server model. There is no need for the user to maintain additional passwords for database access and no need for the administrator to maintain extra account information in SQL Server.

ADO.NET

- Security is improved since user names and passwords are not passed over the network in clear text as they are with SQL Server authentication.
- Logon security improves through password expiration periods, minimum lengths, and account lockout after multiple invalid logon requests, which are provided in the Windows authentication security model.

Windows authentication allows us to take advantage connection pooling since the connection string stays the same. Connection pooling is important to scalability since we can reuse the connection objects without requiring any complex code. Having hot connections within a pool allows us to save the initial connection creation and destruction processes.

In a web environment that could potentially have thousands of concurrent users, keeping connections open for the session lifetime is wasteful and a tremendously inefficient usage of resources. Connections are meant to be obtained late and released early, typically within the context of the same web form. With a tremendous amount of creation and destruction, having a pooled set of connections allows us to use a smaller working set of connection objects, increasing our scalability.

ADO.NET DataSet

The `DataSet` object is a completely connectionless object capable of storing, manipulating, adding, and deleting data. The `DataSet` is unaware of the underlying source of data, so as far as it is concerned, the data source could be an XML document, an Oracle database, a SQL Server database, a text file, or any other data storage medium.

The disconnected nature of the `DataSet` is excellent for passing data between tiers. In the example we will conclude this chapter with we pass the `DataSet` object from the data tier to the business logic tier. The `DataSet` object could just as easily be serialized and sent across a remoting channel, even passed as a serialized string via a web service. The disconnected nature of the `DataSet` allows a versatile data storage mechanism.

Having a flexible object model, like the `DataSet` that can be passed between tiers, promotes a scalable design. Passing `DataSet` objects between tiers is trivial in the .NET Framework. Using the `DataSet` enables us to focus on creating the application logic and not needing to create a persistence mechanism or data storage mechanism for each tier. Reducing the amount of work that is required for a multi-tiered design and providing a relational data structure for high performance makes it easier for our application to scale into multiple tiers.

Figure 2 illustrates the `DataSet` object hierarchy.

Chapter 3: The Data Tier

Figure 2

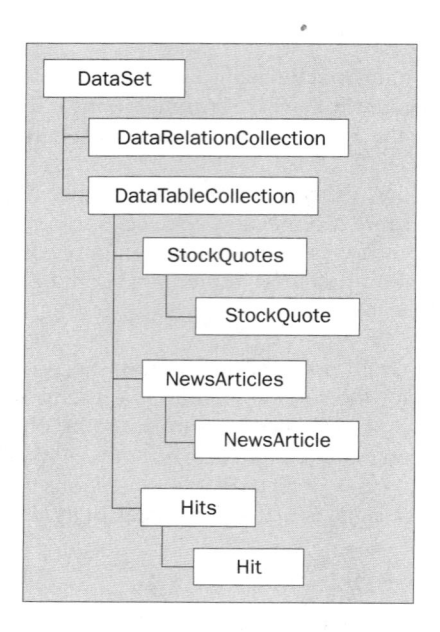

```
DataSet
├── DataRelationCollection
└── DataTableCollection
    ├── StockQuotes
    │   └── StockQuote
    ├── NewsArticles
    │   └── NewsArticle
    └── Hits
        └── Hit
```

Using DataRelations

Prior to ADO.NET, it was difficult to create a hierarchical set of data. In ADO, we could use the `SHAPE` SQL syntax with the `MSDataShape` data provider to create a hierarchical `Recordset`. The child tables were appended to the main `Recordset` as columns.

With ADO.NET, the ability to create relations between tables provides a much simpler, more straightforward approach to creating hierarchical sets of related data. The data table objects also provide a way for us to prevent looping through the entire child `DataTable` looking for rows that match criteria in the parent table.

Adding a `DataRelation` to a `DataSet` adds a `UniqueConstraint` to the parent table and a `ForeignKeyConstraint` to the child table. These constraints enforce the relationship and prevent rows from being added to the child table without a corresponding row in the parent table.

The `DataRelation` object allows us to create a relational data structure with methods providing simple access to return select rows representing only relevant data. Understanding how to use the `DataRelation` allows you to simplify a great deal of your data gathering code.

Let's take a look at an example of creating a `DataRelation` object. This example also illustrates the `ForeignKeyConstraint` that is established on the child table as a result of adding the `DataRelation`. When we try to add a record to the child `Orders` table that violates the constraint, an error occurs:

```vb
'******************************************************************
' DataRelations.vb
'
' Compile with:
' vbc DataRelations.vb /r:System.dll,System.Data.dll,System.Xml.dll
'******************************************************************
Imports System
Imports System.Data
Imports System.Data.SqlClient

Module DataRelations

  Sub Main()
    CreateDataSet()
  End Sub

  'Example to illustrate creating a hierarchical dataset from scratch
  Public Sub CreateDataSet()
    Dim ds As New DataSet("MyDataSet")

    'Step 1: Create Customers Table
    Dim custs As DataTable = ds.Tables.Add("Customers")
    Dim pk As DataColumn = _
        custs.Columns.Add("CustID", Type.GetType("System.Int32"))
    custs.Columns.Add("CustName", Type.GetType("System.String"))
    custs.Columns.Add("CustAddress", Type.GetType("System.String"))
    'Adds the CustID to the PK column collection of the datatable
    custs.PrimaryKey = New DataColumn() {pk}

    'Add data
    custs.Rows.Add(New Object() {1, "User1", "1234 First Street"})
    custs.Rows.Add(New Object() {2, "User2", "1 Madison Way"})
    custs.Rows.Add(New Object() {3, "User3", "1123 Sunset Strip"})

    'Step 2: Create child table
    Dim orders As DataTable = ds.Tables.Add("Orders")
    Dim opk As DataColumn = _
        orders.Columns.Add("OrderID", Type.GetType("System.Int32"))
    orders.Columns.Add("CustID", Type.GetType("System.Int32"))
    orders.Columns.Add("DateOrdered", Type.GetType("System.DateTime"))
    orders.PrimaryKey = New DataColumn() {opk}
    orders.Rows.Add(New Object() {1, 1, New DateTime(2003, 3, 4)})
    orders.Rows.Add(New Object() {2, 1, New DateTime(2003, 3, 6)})
    orders.Rows.Add(New Object() {3, 1, New DateTime(2003, 3, 7)})
    orders.Rows.Add(New Object() {4, 2, New DateTime(2003, 3, 8)})
    orders.Rows.Add(New Object() {5, 2, New DateTime(2003, 3, 9)})

    'Step 3: Add relation
    ds.Relations.Add("ChildOrders", _
                ds.Tables("Customers").Columns("CustID"), _
                ds.Tables("Orders").Columns("CustID"))
```

Chapter 3: The Data Tier

```
        'Illustrate ForeignKey relationship is created on the child table
        Try
          orders.Rows.Add(New Object() _
                          {6, 22, DateTime.Parse("10/10/2006")})
        Catch e As Exception
          Console.WriteLine("Exception: " & e.Message)
        End Try

        'Step 4: Use the relation
        Dim dr As DataRow
        Dim orderRow As DataRow
        For Each dr In ds.Tables("Customers").Rows
          Console.WriteLine("Orders for Customer ID: " & _
                            CStr(dr("CustID")))
          For Each orderRow In dr.GetChildRows("ChildOrders")
            Console.WriteLine("Order#: " & CStr(orderRow("OrderID")) & _
                              " Date: " & CStr(orderRow("DateOrdered")))
          Next
        Next
    End Sub
End Module
```

Once the tables are created and populated, the `DataRelation` object is created linking the two tables together:

```
        'Step 3: Add relation
        ds.Relations.Add("ChildOrders", _
                         ds.Tables("Customers").Columns("CustID"), _
                         ds.Tables("Orders").Columns("CustID"))
```

Once the `DataRelation` object is created, calling the `GetChildRows()` method on the `DataRow` of the parent table returns a `DataRowCollection` object containing only the rows from the child table that meet the relationship criteria.

Compiling and executing the example gives us the following results:

```
C:\Scalability\Chapter 3\ADO.NET>DataRelations
Exception: ForeignKeyConstraint ChildOrders requires the child key values (22) t
o exist in the parent table.
Orders for Customer ID: 1
Order#: 1  Date: 04/03/2003
Order#: 2  Date: 06/03/2003
Order#: 3  Date: 07/03/2003
Orders for Customer ID: 2
Order#: 4  Date: 08/03/2003
Order#: 5  Date: 09/03/2003
Orders for Customer ID: 3

C:\Scalability\Chapter 3\ADO.NET>
```

ADO.NET

Working with Constraints

In the previous example, we illustrated the implicit `ForeignKeyConstraint` object implemented when the `DataRelation` was added between the `Customers` and `Orders` tables. Constraints are used to maintain the integrity and validity of the data and are enforced when data is added, updated, or deleted. If the `EnforceConstraints` property of the `DataSet` is set to `True`, relations will be enforced. Setting this property to `False` would have prevented the error from being raised when attempting to add the row that did not have a corresponding row in the parent `Customers` table. Generally, we will want to enforce constraints in our application to help ensure data is valid.

There are two types of constraints in ADO.NET:

- `UniqueConstraint`
- `ForeignKeyConstraint`

UniqueConstraint

The `UniqueConstraint` object ensures that data in a specified column, or set of specified columns, is unique. You can set the constraint to monitor a single `DataColumn` object by setting the `Unique` property of the column to `True`. Likewise, you can set the `UniqueConstraint` constraint to monitor multiple columns. When we created the primary key fields in the previous example, a unique constraint was automatically added.

Determining constraints on a table object is a matter of examining the `Constraints` property of the `DataTable` object. We simply print out the table name and the constraint name for each constraint in the `Customers` and `Orders` tables. This is demonstrated in `DataRelations2.vb`:

```
'Step 4: Use the relation
Dim dr As DataRow
Dim orderRow As DataRow
For Each dr In ds.Tables("Customers").Rows
   Console.WriteLine("Orders for Customer ID: " & _
                CStr(dr("CustID")))
   For Each orderRow In dr.GetChildRows("ChildOrders")
      Console.WriteLine("Order#: " & CStr(orderRow("OrderID")) & _
                " Date: " & CStr(orderRow("DateOrdered")))
   Next
Next

   PrintConstraints(ds.Tables("Customers"))
   PrintConstraints(ds.Tables("Orders"))
End Sub

Public Sub PrintConstraints(ByVal dt As DataTable)
   Dim c As Constraint
   For Each c In dt.Constraints
      Console.WriteLine(c.Table.TableName & ":" & c.ConstraintName)
   Next
End Sub
```

Chapter 3: The Data Tier

We have three constraints between the two tables. Each table's primary key has a `UniqueConstraint` and the `DataRelation` object added a `ForeignKeyConstraint` on the `Orders` table to enforce the relationship. Running the updated code gives us the following screenshot.

```
Command Prompt
C:\Scalability\Chapter 3\ADO.NET>DataRelations2
Exception: ForeignKeyConstraint ChildOrders requires the child key values (22) t
o exist in the parent table.
Orders for Customer ID: 1
Order#: 1  Date: 04/03/2003
Order#: 2  Date: 06/03/2003
Order#: 3  Date: 07/03/2003
Orders for Customer ID: 2
Order#: 4  Date: 08/03/2003
Order#: 5  Date: 09/03/2003
Orders for Customer ID: 3
Customers:Constraint1
Orders:Constraint1
Orders:ChildOrders

C:\Scalability\Chapter 3\ADO.NET>
```

ForeignKeyConstraint

Similarly to how a foreign key works in SQL Server, the `ForeignKeyConstraint` enforces rules when data in the related tables changes. In our example, if the `CustID` column of the `Customers` table is altered, the `ForeignKeyConstraint` will determine what happens to the rows in the `Orders` table. By default, the `ForeignKeyConstraint` will cascade the changes made in `Customers` to the `Orders` table. If we delete a customer record, the related `Orders` rows are deleted. If we change the `CustID` column value, any related child `Orders` rows will be updated to reflect the change.

The developer can determine what they want to happen when the data in the `Customers` table is changed. The `UpdateRule` and `DeleteRule` properties of the `ForeignKeyConstraint` object can have the following values:

Action	Result
Cascade	Delete or update rows in child table; `Cascade` is the default action
SetNull	Set values in the child table to `DBNull`
SetDefault	Set values in child rows to the column's default value
None	No action is performed on child rows

Depending on how the `UpdateRule` and `DeleteRule` properties are set, exceptions could be thrown when the constraint is enforced. If we have set the `DeleteRule` to action `None`, an exception will be thrown if we attempt to delete a row in `Customers` with related records in `Orders`.

Determining the `UpdateRule` and `DeleteRule` on the `ForeignKeyConstraint` is rather straightforward. The following code examines the `ForeignKeyConstraint` between the `Customers` and `Orders` table. Since the code uses the default `Cascade` options for the `UpdateRule` and `DeleteRule` properties, we test the constraint by changing the `CustID` of the first row to 9. We expect to see similar changes in the `Orders` table after the constraint is enforced. Any row containing the `CustID` of 1 (the value before the update) will be updated to have a `CustID` of 9. We call this file `DataRelations3.vb`:

```vb
'Step 3.5: Test cascading nature of constraint
Dim fk As ForeignKeyConstraint = orders.Constraints("ChildOrders")
Console.WriteLine("Examining foreignKey 'ChildOrders'")
Console.WriteLine(fk.DeleteRule.ToString())
Console.WriteLine(fk.UpdateRule.ToString())
'Test Constraint
custs.Rows(0)("CustID") = 9

'Step 4: Use the relation
Dim dr As DataRow
Dim orderRow As DataRow
For Each dr In ds.Tables("Customers").Rows
   Console.WriteLine("Orders for Customer ID: " & dr("CustID"))
   For Each orderRow In dr.GetChildRows("ChildOrders")
      Console.WriteLine("Order#: " & CStr(orderRow("OrderID")) & _
                      "   Date: " & CStr(orderRow("DateOrdered")))
   Next
Next
Console.WriteLine("Constraints")
PrintConstraints(ds.Tables("Customers"))
PrintConstraints(ds.Tables("Orders"))
End Sub
```

Running the example proves that the `Cascade` action is true to its word. The change made to the `Customers` was cascaded to the `Orders` table when the `ForeignKeyConstraint` was enforced.

```
C:\Scalability\Chapter 3\ADO.NET>DataRelations3
Exception: ForeignKeyConstraint ChildOrders requires the child key values (22) t
o exist in the parent table.
Examining foreignKey 'ChildOrders'
DeleteRule ForeignKeyConstraint: Cascade
UpdateRule ForeignKeyConstraint: Cascade
Orders for Customer ID: 9
Order#: 1   Date: 04/03/2003
Order#: 2   Date: 06/03/2003
Order#: 3   Date: 07/03/2003
Orders for Customer ID: 2
Order#: 4   Date: 08/03/2003
Order#: 5   Date: 09/03/2003
Orders for Customer ID: 3
Constraints
Customers:Constraint1
Orders:Constraint1
Orders:ChildOrders

C:\Scalability\Chapter 3\ADO.NET>
```

If you are holding multiple related tables in the `DataSet` object, understanding and using the `ForeignKeyConstraint` gives you power to enforce actions to occur if a data change affects multiple tables. Both the `ForeignKeyConstraint` and the `UniqueConstraint` provide data validation for very little cost to the programmer.

DataRelations and Scalability

At first glance, creating relationships between data tables may not seem to provide a high degree of scalability. However, when you consider the ability to hold a set of related tables in memory, there are scalability improvements that relations allow. Having the ability to keep an entire set of data in memory allows you to make changes to the data without needing to issue SQL calls to the database until all changes have been made. In this respect, there is no need to create and destroy connection objects during every update. Since the relations force the data to be valid, we are less likely to have errors raised during the saving process, which decreases our resource usage.

ADO.NET DataView

The `DataView` object allows the developer to provide different views of the data stored within a `DataTable`. For example, a `DataView` allows you to create a view on the data containing a subset of data determined by a filtering expression.

In some respects, the `DataView` is similar to a view within SQL Server. The SQL Server view object allows you to create logical tables (often called virtual tables) based on a `SELECT` query written against any number of tables. A view is a filter to underlying tables where the data is physically stored. The `SELECT` statement that creates the view can include data from one or more underlying tables or other view objects.

Views in SQL Server are primarily meant for presentation or to provide a set of data for other queries. While modifications to the view are possible, they are limited to one base table. More often than not, the view objects are used for presentation or to provide logical representations of data stored in one table or perhaps from different tables.

The `DataView` allows you to return a subset of data from a single `DataTable` object. Unlike the SQL Server view object, the `DataView` cannot be treated as a table for use within other SQL statements. `DataView` objects are also limited since it is not possible to append columns that do not exist in the original source table.

Creating a DataView

The `DataTable` object has a `DefaultView` property that can be used to retrieve the default view from the `DataTable` object. For example:

```
Dim dv As DataView = New _
    DataView(myDataSet.Tables("Customers").DefaultView)
```

ADO.NET

The index for the `DataView` is built when the `DataView` object is initially created or when the `Sort`, `RowFilter`, or `RowStateFilter` properties are changed. In order for the `DataView` to apply the changes when the properties are changed, the index must be rebuilt. Since rebuilding the index incurs overhead, it is best to set default sort order and filtering criteria when creating the `DataView`. If the sort and filter properties are not set at creation time, the index must be built at least twice. The index is created at object creation and when the first sort or filter properties are set.

In the following example, we will create a view to return only the customer records with `CustID = 2` as the filtering criteria, `DataView1.vb`:

```vb
'****************************************************************
' DataView1.vb
'
' Compile with:
' vbc DataView1.vb /r:System.dll,System.Data.dll,System.Xml.dll
'****************************************************************
Imports System
Imports System.Data
Imports System.Data.SqlClient

Module DataView1

    Sub Main()
        CreateDataSet()
    End Sub

    'Example to illustrate creating a hierarchical dataset from scratch
    Public Sub CreateDataSet()
        Dim ds As New DataSet("MyDataSet")

        'Step 1: Create Customers Table
        Dim custs As DataTable = ds.Tables.Add("Customers")
        Dim pk As DataColumn = _
            custs.Columns.Add("CustID", Type.GetType("System.Int32"))
        custs.Columns.Add("CustName", Type.GetType("System.String"))
        custs.Columns.Add("CustAddress", Type.GetType("System.String"))
        'Adds the CustID to the PK column collection of the datatable
        custs.PrimaryKey = New DataColumn() {pk}

        'Add data
        custs.Rows.Add(New Object() {1, "User1", "1234 First Street"})
        custs.Rows.Add(New Object() {2, "User2", "1 Madison Way"})
        custs.Rows.Add(New Object() {3, "User3", "1123 Sunset Strip"})

        'Step 2: Create the view with initial sort order and filter
        Dim i As Integer
        Dim dv As DataView = New DataView(custs, "CustID = 2", _
            "CustID", DataViewRowState.CurrentRows)
        Dim drv As DataRowView
```

Chapter 3: The Data Tier

```
        'Step 3: Loop through the view
        For Each drv In dv
          For i = 0 To custs.Columns.Count - 1
            Console.WriteLine(custs.Columns(i).ColumnName.ToString() & _
                              ":" & CStr(drv(i)))
          Next
        Next
      End Sub
End Module
```

Running the example produces the following output. Notice that the filter has worked, and only the row for `CustID` equal to 2 is returned.

```
C:\Scalability\Chapter 3\ADO.NET>DataView1
CustID:2
CustName:User2
CustAddress:1 Madison Way

C:\Scalability\Chapter 3\ADO.NET>
```

Creating DataViews with Relationships

If we have multiple tables with relationships, we can create a `DataView` containing only related rows from the child table by using the `CreateChildView()` method of the `DataRowView` on a row of the parent table's view.

In the previous example, we created a view on the parent `Customers` table. When we have access to the `DataRowView` object representing a single row within the view, we can create a new view containing rows from the child `Orders` table that satisfy the relationship between the tables.

Since we are dealing with quite a few objects in the ADO.NET object hierarchy, it is quite simple to get the concepts confused. The following example will illustrate returning a view from the child `Orders` table that matches the row in the parent `DataView` and conforms to the relationship between the tables:

```
'****************************************************************
' DataView2.vb
'
' Compile with:
' vbc DataView2.vb /r:System.dll,System.Data.dll,System.Xml.dll
'****************************************************************
Imports System
Imports System.Data
Imports System.Data.SqlClient

Module DataView2

  Sub Main()
    CreateDataSet()
  End Sub
```

ADO.NET

```vb
'Example to illustrate creating a hierarchical dataset from scratch
Public Sub CreateDataSet()
    Dim ds As New DataSet("MyDataSet")

    'Step 1: Create Customers Table
    Dim custs As DataTable = ds.Tables.Add("Customers")
    Dim pk As DataColumn = _
        custs.Columns.Add("CustID", Type.GetType("System.Int32"))
    custs.Columns.Add("CustName", Type.GetType("System.String"))
    custs.Columns.Add("CustAddress", Type.GetType("System.String"))
    'Adds the CustID to the PK column collection of the datatable
    custs.PrimaryKey = New DataColumn() {pk}

    'Add data
    custs.Rows.Add(New Object() {1, "User1", "1234 First Street"})
    custs.Rows.Add(New Object() {2, "User2", "1 Madison Way"})
    custs.Rows.Add(New Object() {3, "User3", "1123 Sunset Strip"})

    'Step 2: Create child table
    Dim orders As DataTable = ds.Tables.Add("Orders")
    Dim opk As DataColumn = orders.Columns.Add("OrderID", _
      Type.GetType("System.Int32"))
    orders.Columns.Add("CustID", Type.GetType("System.Int32"))
    orders.Columns.Add("DateOrdered", Type.GetType("System.DateTime"))
    orders.PrimaryKey = New DataColumn() {opk}
    orders.Rows.Add(New Object() {1, 1, New DateTime(2002, 6, 2)})
    orders.Rows.Add(New Object() {2, 1, New DateTime(2002, 4, 4)})
    orders.Rows.Add(New Object() {3, 1, New DateTime(2002, 4, 6)})
    orders.Rows.Add(New Object() {4, 2, New DateTime(2002, 4, 7)})
    orders.Rows.Add(New Object() {5, 2, New DateTime(2002, 4, 8)})

    'Step 3: Add relation
    ds.Relations.Add("ChildOrders", _
        ds.Tables("Customers").Columns("CustID"), _
        ds.Tables("Orders").Columns("CustID"))

    Dim dv As New DataView(custs, "CustID = 2", _
        "CustID", DataViewRowState.CurrentRows)
    Dim dvChild As DataView
    Dim drv As DataRowView
    Dim drvChild As DataRowView
    Dim i As Integer

    'Step 4: Loop through the view
    'Loop through parent
    For Each drv In dv '
      'Create view of child (orders) table based on relationship
      dvChild = drv.CreateChildView("ChildOrders")
      'Loop through child view
      For Each drvChild In dvChild
        For i = 0 To orders.Columns.Count - 1
          Console.WriteLine(orders.Columns(i).ColumnName & ":" & _
                      drvChild(i).ToString())
```

```
            Next
        Next
    Next
    End Sub
End Module
```

Running the example illustrates that only the orders matching the `Customer` table's `DataView` and the relationship are returned.

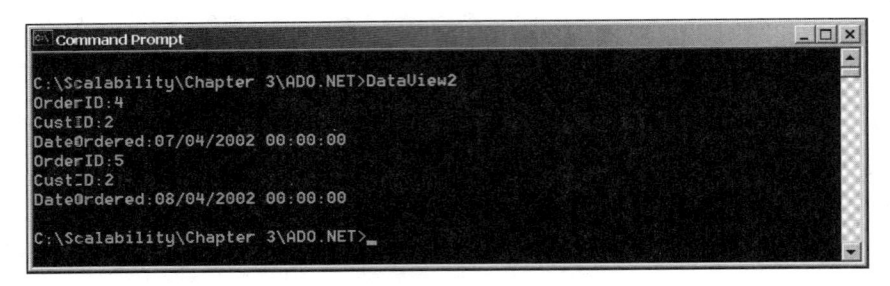

```
C:\Scalability\Chapter 3\ADO.NET>DataView2
OrderID:4
CustID:2
DateOrdered:07/04/2002 00:00:00
OrderID:5
CustID:2
DateOrdered:08/04/2002 00:00:00

C:\Scalability\Chapter 3\ADO.NET>
```

Updating a DataTable with the DataView

Typically, the `DataView` object is created to return a filtered set of data from a `DataTable`. The `DataView` is particularly useful for situations like user interface data presentation where you want to present only a subset or tailored set of data from a larger `DataTable` object.

It is possible to add, edit, and delete rows from the `DataView` object and synchronize the changes with the underlying `DataTable`. The `DataView` has `AllowNew`, `AllowEdit`, and `AllowDelete` properties that, when set to `True`, allow the `DataView` object to be updated and committed. Once changes have been made to the `DataRowView` object, the `EndEdit()` method is called and the changes are applied to the underlying `DataTable` object.

While it is possible to update data, the true power of the `DataView` object lies in the fact that multiple representations of a `DataTable` object can be created when the need arises. It is important to note that all these changes are occurring offline, without connecting to the data store. Creating views, applying filters, removing records, etc., has no impact on the database server.

DataView and Scalability

The `DataView` object excels in read-only scenarios, especially in user interface scenarios. Imagine we are holding a set of products in a `DataTable`. As the customers search for products, we create a view matching their query on the `DataTable` object and bind the `DataView` to an ASP.NET data repeater control for display. If the `DataTable` is held in memory or the ASP.NET cache (we discuss scalability benefits of ASP.NET caching in Chapter 5), the server requires minimal resources to create, bind, and display the `DataView`.

ADO.NET and Scalability

The discussion of the ADO.NET object model we just conducted provided a high-level introduction to the scalability benefits ADO.NET provides. ADO.NET is vastly more scalable than previous versions of ADO and other data access technologies, such as OLEDB and ODBC. As a recap, here are the important scalability features ADO.NET provides:

- ADO.NET separates data storage from data source communication. The connectionless nature of the `DataSet` allows us to consume expensive connection-oriented resources less often and for a shorter duration.

- SQL Server and other .NET-managed providers avoid the OLEDB and ODBC layers. The .NET-managed providers, with their data-store native communication protocols, are vastly more efficient than the standard OLEDB and ODBC connection layers.

- Connection pooling. Pooling allows us to reuse expensive connection objects with very little, if any, development effort.

- The `DataSet` object is excellent for passing state between tiers. In a scalable system, passing state between tiers (physical or logical) efficiently relieves stress on critical communication points. The `DataSet` has the ability to be serialized and sent between processes and tiers efficiently and without maintaining open connection resources.

- `DataRelations` provides fast access to related rows in different tables and save us from unnecessary looping and searching for important rows between multiple tables. By using the `ForeignKeyConstraint`, applying data relations provides a built-in mechanism for ensuring newly created data conforms to the requirements established by the `DataRelation` relationship.

- Constraints enforce integrity. The `ForeignKeyConstraint` and `UniqueConstraint` help us ensure data added has integrity with respect to the constraint rules. The constraints are especially helpful for ensuring data integrity on primary and foreign key fields. These constraints are not meant to replace, but rather enforce, constraints at the data-store level. The constraints also do not take the place of an application's data validation logic.

- `DataView` provides a lightweight snapshot of a `DataTable` object. The `DataView` allows us to create different configurations of a `DataTable` object for display or presentation purposes without requiring resources from the database.

Without question, the ADO.NET object model provides a great basis for creating a scalable data tier. However efficient and scalable, ADO.NET does not replace the need for an efficient and scalable design and implementation of the data tier.

We will now turn our attention to our sample application that we are following through the book to illustrate concerns when using ADO.NET and creating a data-access layer.

MyInvestmentWatch.com Data Tier

We have discussed the fundamentals of proper relational database design using the principles of normalization, the principles around ADO.NET, and the advantages the .NET platform offers us in the realm of database access. The concepts and object models discussed provide us with the tools necessary for creating a data layer.

The tools discussed are just that: tools. The design of the object model for the data-access layer is overwhelmingly the most important factor that impacts on the overall scalability and performance of the data-access layer.

At the end of Chapter 1 we discussed the scalability limitations of the VB6 version of MyInvestmentWatch.com. The application's scalability was limited within the data tier since expensive resources were being used far too liberally and wastefully. The SQL queries used to retrieve the data were written inline and did not take advantage of stored procedures.

In this section, we implement the design and .NET concepts presented in this chapter to create a more scalable data-access layer. The benefits of the updated data-access layer include:

- **Reuse**. Multiple applications, including web applications and Windows forms applications, should have the ability to use the same data-access layer for data needs.
- **Abstraction**. Free the application business logic from needing to concern itself with data-access code. The middle tier is not concerned with writing or maintaining SQL statements.
- **Insulation**. Insulate the application business logic from potential database schema changes or changes to ADO.NET.
- **Scaling**. Allow the data-access layer to reside on a separate physical tier if performance becomes a concern.
- **Testing**. Isolate the testing concerns for maintenance and troubleshooting reasons from the application logic. Creating a separate data layer allows us to unit-test our data-access procedures and stress-test the data portion of the application to locate and prevent bottlenecks.

In order to create a data-access layer with these characteristics, we will begin by examining the database design. We will look at the normalization of the database and the use of stored procedures for controlling access to the physical data tables.

Once we have created the database, we will discuss and illustrate the implementation of stored procedures and their importance to overall scalability.

After the stored procedures are developed and we have access points into the database, we discuss the Data-Access Layer (DAL) object model that is ultimately responsible for interacting with the database via ADO.NET.

Data-Access Layer: Goals

A **Data-Access Layer** (DAL) is responsible for providing data store connectivity and an intuitive interface for the other tiers of our application to use. Creating, Reading, Updating, and Deleting (CRUD) operations are generally very resource intensive and involved processes. The DAL takes the burden from the application middle tier logic by abstracting (or "black boxing") the database connectivity code into a separate tier of the application solely responsible for these operations. As far as our middle tier is concerned, the DAL provides all the necessary data.

Figure 3

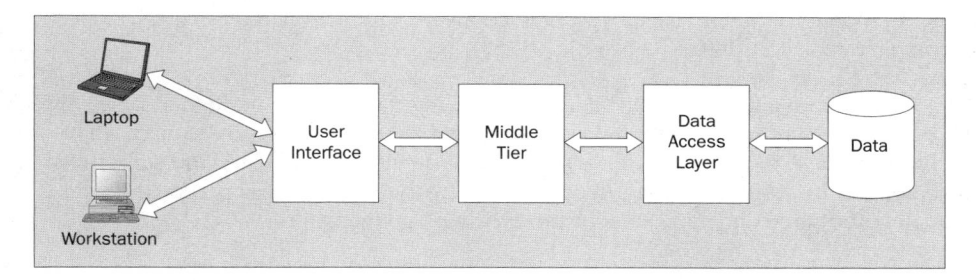

A DAL can come in many flavors. A design commonly used with smaller applications is to incorporate the business logic and the DAL layer directly into the user interface code. If you see web applications with SQL code interspersed with HTML or Windows forms controls, you are witnessing a two-tier logical design with the DAL included at the front end.

While not many truly enterprise systems rely on the presentation layer for performing logic and data access, many applications are designed with this architecture because it is typically the most straightforward and quickest to market. However, imagine changing the database schema in a two-tier logical design. You must then update the user interface code and business logic to reflect the changes. Since the application design does not have logical layers, implementing change requires retesting the entire application. With a tiered approach, testing can be more targeted and accurate.

An application utilizing a middle-tier application layer that provides data access and business functionality has taken a great step in scalability by separating the presentation from the logic. Often referred to as an n-tier model, this model incorporates the business and DAL layers into the same logical layer.

Creating a three-tier logical system positions the application to take advantage of multiple scalability improvements. However, having the business layer mixed with the DAL prevents the application from recognizing important scalability enhancements. By creating a separate DAL logical tier we can extend the application layout by splitting the business logic from data-access code.

Chapter 3: The Data Tier

A well written DAL provides great benefits in dealing with application scalability. When reading over the benefits, keep in mind the logical n-tier design as a reference point. A separate logical DAL tier improves on the three-tier model in a great number of ways. Let's examine each goal in closer detail to illustrate their importance for designing the DAL and separating it from the middle tier.

Reuse

Multiple applications use the same set of data. A financial institution will allow its customer to access their checking account transaction history in a read-only fashion. Internal employees access the same data via a Windows client application, but will also have the ability to perform CRUD operations on the data. Management will have the ability to monitor account activity and predict business trends via accessing calculation-intensive stored procedures.

While the underlying application functionalities, interfaces, and middle-tier logics differ, the data, and more importantly the access needed to that data, is very similar. All applications have the ability to read, some have the ability to update, and still others have abilities to perform privileged operations. Despite their access points, the data is ultimately the same and can benefit from sharing a common DAL.

Provide Abstraction

Providing abstraction is a common theme throughout the discussion of scalability. At the data tier, abstraction provides a simplified interface for the middle-tier logic to interact with. Any persistence code, whether it deals with a database, an XML formatted text file, or another data storage medium, is contained in the DAL.

Abstraction allows the business tier to focus on the business logic and forget data access. It is inevitable that the data-access technologies and database platform will change over time. The next version of ADO.NET or SQL Server will offer improvements we may like to take advantage of. Abstracting the DAL into a separate tier makes it easier to take advantages of these upgrades when upgrading our application. If the ADO.NET object model changes, for example, we could implement the changes in the DAL with little or no change necessary to the middle or user interface tiers.

Stateless Design

As applications need to scale up, they benefit from a stateless design. Holding state in the DAL would hinder our scalability potential by pegging resources to a particular machine or processor. As mentioned in Chapter 2, a stateless design improves scalability in a multiple server scenario. We are going to avoid holding state in our DAL implementation.

Improved Performance Testing

Database access code is complex and resource intensive, which makes it an ideal candidate for a through test plan. Systems with hundreds of stored procedures become unwieldy. When developing a test plan, the DAL needs to be tested by itself before the business logic is applied. Having separated the code allows the programmer to write isolated and detailed test cases during development that focus solely on testing the performance and logic of the DAL.

Testing does not stop when the product is delivered. When discussing scalable and enterprise systems with a large user base, testing and bug fixing will lead to increases in performance. More users generally tend to stress the system in unintended ways and find more bugs.

As the application ages and code changes are implemented, the possibility of introducing unintended side effects becomes very real. Segmenting the code into discrete testable code blocks allows you to concentrate on a smaller implementation and promotes effective testing. Performance monitoring and application testing with scalable systems will be covered in detail in Chapter 6.

Database Design

Knowing what we do about the principles of normalization, let's reevaluate our database design shown in the following screenshot for possible improvements.

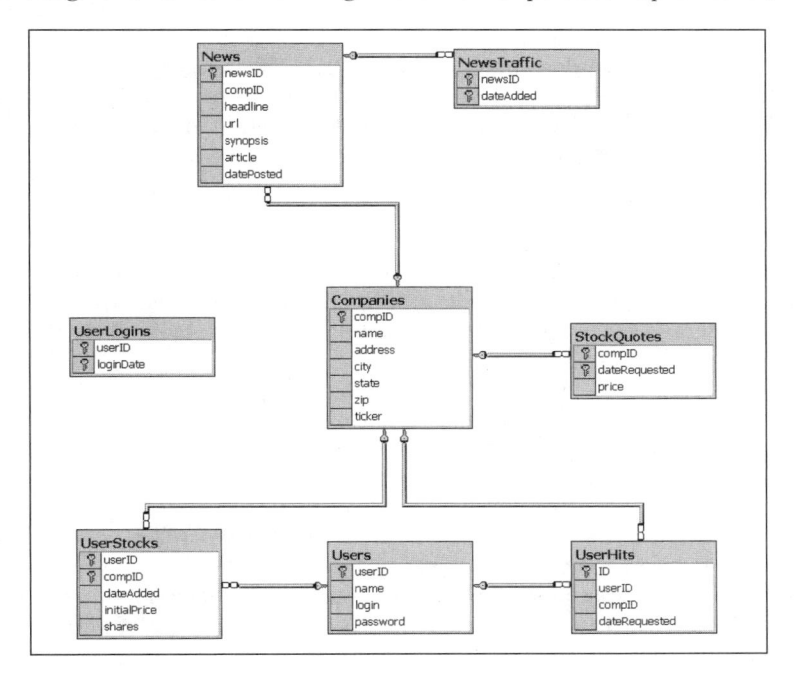

A more detailed explanation of the tables and their relationships can be found in Appendix A. Let's discuss the levels of normalization that we will be using in our database.

First Normal Form

- Duplicated columns are eliminated from the same table
- Separate tables are created that group related data and identify each row with a unique identifier

Our database contains no duplicated columns in a table. We have created separate tables with unique identifiers to handle all tables where required. For example, `userID` in the `Users` table, `compID` in the `Companies` table, and `newsID` in the `News` table are all auto-incrementing values.

It is safe to say that our database complies with 1NF.

Second Normal Form

- Remove like columns of data and separate them into a single row
- Create relationships and link the new rows to the existing data via foreign key relationships

By definition, our database does not conform to 2NF. The `Companies` table contains `city`, `state`, and `zip` fields that contain like data dependent on the `zip` field. To comply with the second degree of normalization, we could remove the `city` and `state` columns from the `Companies` table, putting them into a table dependent on Zip as the primary key.

Why do we not normalize the `Companies` table? Companies, on average, will not contain very high concentrations in a single Zip. If we have 20,000 companies with 8,000 unique `zip` fields, we felt the time associated to join the tables was more costly than the extra storage space required with storing duplicate `city` and `state` fields.

Here we have a classical deviation from the normalization requirements. When dealing with normalized databases, some aspects of a database design are best denormalized for performance reasons. In our case, our personal preference was to increase performance and sacrifice disk space.

If our database purpose was different, perhaps we might have a `Customers` table that could theoretically grow to contain millions of records. In this case, the space requirements to store duplicate data might be more expensive than the cost associated with the multi-table `JOIN` or `SELECT` statement. Since our database of public companies is limited in size, storage concerns are not as relevant, but they are definitely relevant.

Third Normal Form

❏   Remove columns that are not dependent upon the primary key

Our tables are dependent on their respective primary key. There is no redundant or calculated data that would break third normal form. In tables (such as `UserStocks`) with composite primary keys, the key represents a combination of both tables.

In the sense that our columns depend on the primary key, we are in compliance with the 3NF. Technically, however, since we are not compliant with 2NF, the accumulative nature of normalization prevents us from claiming complete compliance with 3NF or any higher form of normalization.

Our simple database design is relatively normalized without making any changes. The principles we used to examine the database are vastly more important, as they are application independent and capable of being applied to all database architectures.

Stored Procedures

One of the serious limitations in our previous application was the use of dynamic SQL. Understanding the performance benefits of cached query plans, security, and abstraction that stored procedures provide, we can access to our database through stored procedures and increase our application's scalability.

We have stored procedures in place to handle all select, insert, update, and delete statements. While most of the procedures contain simple SQL queries, we have a few stored procedures of particular interest.

Prior to using stored procedures we loaded all user hits, all quotes, and all news articles when the `User` object was loaded. We will see when we implement our business logic in Chapter 4 that not all objects will be initially loaded. For the stocks that we do wish to load, we restrict the amount of data being retrieved to improve throughput. We only want to retrieve, at most, the top 20 units for each item. Restricting the amount of data improves our load times and should be considered if the context of the application allows. We chose 20 because that will provide a relevant history for our domain area. In the example, the `GetHits` stored procedure is responsible for retrieving the latest requested stocks. The `GetQuotes` procedure returns the latest stock quotes for a particular stock. `GetNews` returns the most recent news articles for the company:

```
CREATE PROCEDURE GetHits
  @UserID int
AS
  SELECT TOP 20 * FROM UserHits
  WHERE UserID = @UserID
  ORDER BY ID DESC
GO
```

147

```
CREATE PROCEDURE GetQuotes
  @CompID int
AS
  SELECT TOP 20 * FROM StockQuotes
  WHERE CompID = @CompID
GO

CREATE PROCEDURE GetNews
  @CompID int
AS
  SELECT TOP 20 * FROM News
  WHERE CompID = @CompID
GO
```

Data-Access Layer: Application Logic

So far our application changes are extremely trivial and not very different from the best practices introduced in Windows DNA with VB6. As we move into the logical DAL application tier, we begin to leave the VB6 and COM world behind in favor of .NET.

One of the goals of a DAL is to provide insulation for our application logic and user interfaces from changes made at the database level. We want our application to be able to readily adapt to data-access and data-store upgrades without needing to affect the entire application.

In many large systems, completely changing database platforms is not a practicable option. However, as systems grow and merge, having a single DAL with the ability to access multiple data stores allows us to implement multiple data stores under the same DAL logic. If our application needs to access legacy data stored within the file system or within an additional data store, the DAL can provide the logic to the middle tier without the middle tier knowing or caring where the data originates. A separate DAL can improve migration as well. If pieces of the application are being migrated to a more scalable platform, the DAL reduces the complexity required when changing the code to access the new database.

DAL Object Model

As we will describe shortly, the DAL object model uses an Abstract Factory design pattern to control object creation. The middle tier will use the factory to create individual persistence objects that all implement a respective interface. By returning interfaces to the middle tier, we enforce all objects that are being returned to have the interfaces as described in their respective interface definition. Our class design is shown graphically in Figure 4:

Figure 4

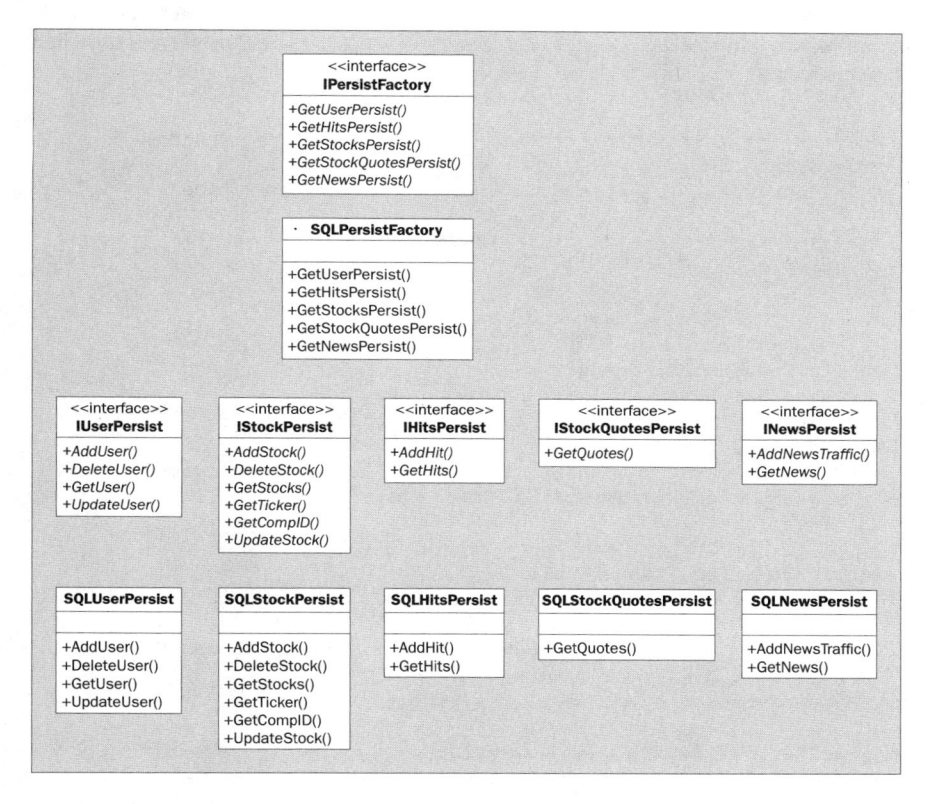

```
                        <<interface>>
                        IPersistFactory
                    +GetUserPersist()
                    +GetHitsPersist()
                    +GetStocksPersist()
                    +GetStockQuotesPersist()
                    +GetNewsPersist()

                        SQLPersistFactory

                    +GetUserPersist()
                    +GetHitsPersist()
                    +GetStocksPersist()
                    +GetStockQuotesPersist()
                    +GetNewsPersist()
```

<<interface>> IUserPersist	<<interface>> IStockPersist	<<interface>> IHitsPersist	<<interface>> IStockQuotesPersist	<<interface>> INewsPersist
+AddUser() +DeleteUser() +GetUser() +UpdateUser()	+AddStock() +DeleteStock() +GetStocks() +GetTicker() +GetCompID() +UpdateStock()	+AddHit() +GetHits()	+GetQuotes()	+AddNewsTraffic() +GetNews()

SQLUserPersist	SQLStockPersist	SQLHitsPersist	SQLStockQuotesPersist	SQLNewsPersist
+AddUser() +DeleteUser() +GetUser() +UpdateUser()	+AddStock() +DeleteStock() +GetStocks() +GetTicker() +GetCompID() +UpdateStock()	+AddHit() +GetHits()	+GetQuotes()	+AddNewsTraffic() +GetNews()

The `SQLPersistFactory` is solely meant to provide methods for creating the other persistence objects (`SQLUserPersist`, `SQLStockPersist`, `SQLHitsPersist`, etc.) that adhere to their respective interfaces. If you are having trouble following the class layout, no need to panic. We'll discuss each object in greater detail in the remainder of the chapter.

Creating the Interfaces

In order to create an effective DAL we expose a set of consistent interfaces to the middle tier. The middle tier is guaranteed to be returned an object that implements the contract of the interface. This predictability gives the middle tier the ability to call the interfaces' methods to persist an object to the data source. The middle tier does not need to know how the interfaces are implemented; it simply needs to understand that the functionality will be performed correctly.

Chapter 3: The Data Tier

The interfaces are presented below. Notice the interface structure for each object corresponds to the typical functions that can be preformed on the object in question. For example, we can update, delete, add, or retrieve (get) a user; however, the client is not allowed to add, update, or delete a stock quote:

```
'*************************************************************
' PersistInterfaces.vb
' Any concrete DAL classes must implement these interfaces.
'
'*************************************************************
Imports System.Data

Namespace com.myinvestmentwatch.data

  Public Interface IPersistFactory
    Function GetUserPersist() As IUserPersist
    Function GetHitsPersist() As IHitsPersist
    Function GetStocksPersist() As IStockPersist
    Function GetStockQuotesPersist() As IStockQuotesPersist
    Function GetNewsPersist() As INewsPersist
  End Interface

  Public Interface IUserPersist
    Function AddUser(ByVal Name As String, _
              ByVal Login As String, _
              ByVal Password As String) As Integer

    Sub DeleteUser(ByVal UserID As Integer)

    Sub GetUser(ByVal Login As String, _
          ByRef UserID As Integer, _
          ByRef Name As String, _
          ByRef Password As String)

    Sub UpdateUser(ByVal UserID As Integer, _
          ByVal Name As String, _
          ByVal Login As String, _
          ByVal Password As String)
  End Interface

  Public Interface IHitsPersist
    Sub AddHit(ByVal UserID As Integer, ByVal CompID As Integer)
    Function GetHits(ByVal UserID As Integer) As DataSet
  End Interface

  Public Interface IStockPersist
    Sub AddStock(ByVal UserID As Integer, _
           ByVal CompID As Integer, _
           ByVal InitialPrice As Single, _
           ByVal Shares As Integer)

    Sub DeleteStock(ByVal UserID As Integer, ByVal CompID As Integer)
```

150

```vb
        Function GetStocks(ByVal UserID As Integer) As DataSet

        Function GetTicker(ByVal CompID As Integer) As String

        Function GetCompID(ByVal Ticker As String) As Integer

        Sub UpdateStock(ByVal UserID As Integer, _
                    ByVal CompID As Integer, _
                    ByVal InitialPrice As Single, _
                    ByVal Shares As Integer)
    End Interface

    Public Interface IStockQuotesPersist
        Function GetQuotes(ByVal CompID As Integer) As DataSet
    End Interface

    Public Interface INewsPersist
       Sub AddNewsTraffic(ByVal NewsID As Integer)
       Function GetNews(ByVal CompID As Integer) As DataSet
    End Interface
End Namespace
```

This code requires explanation. The `IPersistFactory` interface represents the function declarations necessary to return concrete data classes. `IPersistFactory` is an example of a common design pattern called an abstract factory. We will discuss more about the factory pattern very shortly.

The other interfaces, `IUserPersist`, `IHitsPersist`, `IStockPersist`, `IStockQuotesPersist`, and `INewsPersist`, are interfaces that concrete classes will implement to execute methods to perform data persistence on their respective data tables. For example, if we have a class called `OracleNewsPersist` that implements `INewsPersist`, we are guaranteed that the `OracleNewsPersist` object will have methods to `AddNewsTraffic()` to and `GetNews()` from an Oracle database. These methods will add a news hit for the `NewsID` being inquired about, and retrieve all the news for a particular ID, respectively.

Each method on the interfaces is implemented by concrete classes to get or set data. For example, let's examine the most straightforward interface, `IStockQuotesPersist`. It has one method, `GetQuotes()`, which is meant to return stock quote data for a given company ID. Anyone implementing this interface is required to provide a `GetQuotes()` method to access the data source and return the quote information in a `DataSet` object. The `DataSet` is a data-store-independent structure capable of holding data from any data store. As long as the developer of the middle tier understands the structure of the `DataSet` they are able to consume it.

The interfaces only provide the structure for what the real 'working', or concrete classes, are going to implement. A class that implements the interface is considered the concrete class because it provides the concrete functionality that the interface expects. The interface defines the functionality; the concrete class implements the functionality. Now that we have the interfaces designed, we need to provide an implementation for our concrete classes to adhere to these interfaces.

Implementing the Interfaces

Since our data source is SQL Server, we will implement a set of concrete classes able to persist to the SQL Server data source. Let's look at the classes in succession to allow for a more detailed discussion of each object.

Implementing IPersistFactory

The following code implements `IPersistFactory`. Notice how this class is simply a set of functions that return objects. The `SQLPersistFactory` follows the Factory design pattern since its purpose is solely to create objects. As a computer factory produces computers, so an object factory produces objects. In our case, the `SQLPersistFactory` has the capability of creating any of the specific concrete objects:

```
'**************************************************************
' SQLPersist.vb
' SQL Concrete implementation of IPersistFactory Interfaces.
' If there were an oracle, access, or alternate storage
' implementation, it would follow this design pattern.
'**************************************************************
Imports System.Data
Imports System.Data.SqlClient

Namespace com.myinvestmentwatch.data

   Public Class SQLPersistFactory
      Implements IPersistFactory

      Public Function GetUserPersist() As IUserPersist _
            Implements IPersistFactory.GetUserPersist
         GetUserPersist = New SQLUserPersist()
      End Function

      Public Function GetHitsPersist() As IHitsPersist _
            Implements IPersistFactory.GetHitsPersist
         GetHitsPersist = New SQLHitsPersist()
      End Function

      Public Function GetStocksPersist() As IStockPersist _
            Implements IPersistFactory.GetStocksPersist
         GetStocksPersist = New SQLStockPersist()
      End Function
```

```
    Public Function GetStockQuotesPersist() As IStockQuotesPersist _
        Implements IPersistFactory.GetStockQuotesPersist
      GetStockQuotesPersist = New SQLStockQuotesPersist()
    End Function

    Public Function GetNewsPersist() As INewsPersist _
        Implements IPersistFactory.GetNewsPersist
      GetNewsPersist = New SQLNewsPersist()
    End Function
  End Class
```

It may seem strange that we are using a class solely to return instances of the different `SQL...Persist` objects. The sharp thinker is wondering why we don't just create instances of the `SQL...Persist` objects directly, perhaps with the following code:

```
'Return persistence object without use of factory.
Dim np as INewsPersist = New SQLNewsPersist()
```

In contrast, by using the factory to control access to the objects, we are required to write the following code to create an instance of the `SQLNewsPersist` object:

```
'Create the factory to obtain object instances
Dim persistFactory As IPersistFactory = new SQLPersistFactory()
'Use factory to create persistence object.
Dim np As INewsPersist = persistFactory.GetNewsPersist()
```

The reason we use the factory is to make the code more generic. If we implement another set of objects to persist to or from another data store, for example, we need to change the first code to return a new `OracleNewsPersist()` object. Likewise, we would need to change all the calls to `SQLStockPersist`, `SQLStockQuotesPersist`, and `SQLHitsPersist` to their Oracle equivalents as well.

In contrast, using the factory only requires us to change the factory from `SQLPersistFactory` to `OraclePersistFactory` and we are finished. The factory helps us to reach our goal of scaling our application to additional data stores when appropriate.

Relying on the factory object to control what objects are created allows us to create an instance of the factory and have the factory be responsible for delegating the right persistence object back to the caller. All we need to do is make sure our middle tier creates the right factory.

Creating the right factory presents a problem. While using the factory to create objects is preferable, it still ties the middle tier to one instance of the factory. In our example, we would need to recompile our middle tier to utilize an additional data source. Say we write a new SQL Server access DAL providers to attach to a different data store (perhaps to target a new version of SQL Server), we could pull the provider class from a configuration file, which we could change on the fly:

Chapter 3: The Data Tier

```
Dim type As Type = _Type.GetType( _
    Configuration.ConfigurationSettings.AppSettings( _
    "CurrentProvider"))
Dim persistFactory As New IPersistFactory = _
    Activator.CreateInstance(type, Nothing)
```

Here the actual name of the factory we want to create is retrieved from the CurrentProvider application configuration setting. We can then code the name of the factory class we want to create in the configuration file. The code will dynamically create the correct factory using the information in the configuration file:

```
<configuration>
  <appSettings>
    <add key="CurrentProvider" value="AdvancedSQLPersistFactory" />
  </appSettings>
</configuration>
```

Changing the DAL provider is now a matter of changing the application's configuration file and the code will not need to undergo any changes or recompiles.

Implementing IUserPersist

To this point, we have not actually performed any data persistence code. What we have done is set the stage for the persistence objects to be created in a dynamic fashion via a factory object. The interfaces have been put in place to provide the middle tier a generic, expected set of functionality regardless of what data source the concrete classes persist to.

Before we create the implementation classes, we need to establish a common connection string that all our persistence classes will use for accessing the SQL Server. In order to take advantage of object pooling we use a static connection string. For simplicity, we created a small CONSTS class that is responsible for holding our database connection and perhaps any other common variables that may be needed in the DAL in the future:

```
Public Class CONSTS
    Public Const CONNSTR As String = "Data Source=ServerName;" & _
        "user id=developer;password=developer;" & _
        "Initial Catalog=myinvestmentwatch"
End Class
```

Now it's time to provide the actual implementation and see the persistence code for a set of concrete classes. The SQLUserPersist is the concrete class that will implement IUserPersist functions for interacting with the User object. It contains methods, all of which execute Command objects to provide their data access:

```vb
Public Class SQLUserPersist
  Implements IUserPersist

  Friend Sub New()
  End Sub

  Public Function AddUser(ByVal Name As String, _
                    ByVal Login As String, _
                    ByVal Password As String) As Integer _
                    Implements IUserPersist.AddUser

    Dim id As Integer
    Dim cn As New SqlConnection(CONSTS.CONNSTR)
    Dim cm As New SqlCommand("AddUser", cn)
    cm.CommandType = CommandType.StoredProcedure
    cm.Parameters.Add("@Name", Name)
    cm.Parameters.Add("@Login", Login)
    cm.Parameters.Add("@Password", Password)
    Dim p As New SqlParameter("@UserID", SqlDbType.Int)
    p.Direction = ParameterDirection.Output
    cm.Parameters.Add(p)
    Try
      cn.Open()
      cm.ExecuteNonQuery()
      AddUser = p.Value
    Finally
      cm.Dispose()
      cn.Dispose()
    End Try
  End Function

  Public Sub DeleteUser(ByVal UserID As Integer) _
        Implements IUserPersist.DeleteUser

    Dim cn As New SqlConnection(CONSTS.CONNSTR)
    Dim cm As New SqlCommand("DeleteUser", cn)
    cm.CommandType = CommandType.StoredProcedure
    cm.Parameters.Add("@UserID", UserID)
    Try
      cn.Open()
      cm.ExecuteNonQuery()
    Finally
      cm.Dispose()
      cn.Dispose()
    End Try
  End Sub

  Public Sub GetUser(ByVal Login As String, _
                ByRef UserID As Integer, _
                ByRef Name As String, _
                ByRef Password As String) _
                Implements IUserPersist.GetUser
```

```vbnet
        Dim cn As New SqlConnection(CONSTS.CONNSTR)
        Dim cm As New SqlCommand("GetUser", cn)
        Dim dr As SqlDataReader
        cm.CommandType = CommandType.StoredProcedure
        cm.Parameters.Add("@Login", Login)
        Try
          cn.Open()
          dr = cm.ExecuteReader(CommandBehavior.CloseConnection)
          If Not dr.Read() Then Throw New ArgumentException( _
              "Login '" & Login & "' does not exist", UserID)
          UserID = CInt(dr("UserID"))
          Name = CStr(dr("Name"))
          Password = CStr(dr("Password"))
        Finally
          cm.Dispose()
          cn.Dispose()
        End Try
    End Sub

    Public Sub UpdateUser(ByVal UserID As Integer, _
                    ByVal Name As String, _
                    ByVal Login As String, _
                    ByVal Password As String) _
                    Implements IUserPersist.UpdateUser

        Dim cn As New SqlConnection(CONSTS.CONNSTR)
        Dim cm As New SqlCommand("UpdateUser", cn)
        cm.CommandType = CommandType.StoredProcedure
        cm.Parameters.Add("@UserID", UserID)
        cm.Parameters.Add("@Name", Name)
        cm.Parameters.Add("@Login", Login)
        cm.Parameters.Add("@Password", Password)
        Try
          cn.Open()
          cm.ExecuteNonQuery()
        Finally
          cm.Dispose()
          cn.Dispose()
        End Try
    End Sub
End Class
```

The implementation of `SQLUserPersist` is very straightforward and easy to follow. The `Command` objects are created and executed. In the case of the `GetUser()` method, the values are set to the `ByRef` parameters, so the calling code will have access to the return variables.

The `UpdateUser()`, `DeleteUser()`, and `AddUser()` methods simply call into their respective stored procedures, which update the `Users` table.

Since this is the SQL persistence set of objects, we are using the SQL Server .NET managed provider because of the performance gains offered by the .NET managed provider. If we were to implement functionality to access an additional data store, we would check to see if the data-store vendor had a managed provider.

One interesting thing to note is that the constructor is created with the `Friend` keyword. We are essentially limiting class creation to the assembly level to prevent the middle tier from creating direct persistence object instances. Remember, all persistence objects are meant to be created by the factory class. By limiting the persistence object creation to the assembly level, we force the issue by offering no other alternative for the caller.

All persistence objects, `SQLPersistFactory` aside, will contain constructors with the `Friend` keyword to limit instantiation to the factory object.

Implementing IHitsPersist

Following the lead of `IUserPersist`, the rest of the persistence objects are implemented in a similar fashion. `IHitsPersist` is responsible for logging 'hits' when a user selects a company to retrieve a quote for. Maintaining a list of stock hits allows us to tailor the interface for the user. We could present the most 'recent' companies the user selected or present news for the last companies quoted:

```
Public Class SQLHitsPersist
  Implements IHitsPersist

  Friend Sub New()
  End Sub

  Public Sub AddHit(ByVal UserID As Integer, _
                    ByVal CompID As Integer) _
            Implements IHitsPersist.AddHit

    Dim cn As New SqlConnection(CONSTS.CONNSTR)
    Dim cm As New SqlCommand("AddHit", cn)
    cm.CommandType = CommandType.StoredProcedure
    cm.Parameters.Add("@UserID", UserID)
    cm.Parameters.Add("@CompID", CompID)
    Try
       cn.Open()
       cm.ExecuteNonQuery()
    Finally
       cm.Dispose()
       cn.Dispose()
    End Try
  End Sub

  Public Function GetHits(ByVal UserID As Integer) As DataSet _
           Implements IHitsPersist.GetHits
```

Chapter 3: The Data Tier

```
            Dim cn As New SqlConnection(CONSTS.CONNSTR)
            Dim cm As New SqlCommand("GetHits", cn)
            Dim da As New SqlDataAdapter(cm)
            cm.CommandType = CommandType.StoredProcedure
            cm.Parameters.Add("@UserID", UserID)
            Try
              cn.Open()
              Dim ds As New DataSet()
              da.Fill(ds)
              GetHits = ds
            Finally
              cm.Dispose()
              da.Dispose()
              cn.Dispose()
            End Try
        End Function
    End Class
```

Implementing IStockPersist

SQLStockPersist allows the user to interact with their current portfolio of maintained stocks. A stock object can be added, deleted, or updated. Again, to return an arbitrary number of stock objects, we return the objects wrapped in the DataSet data structure since the DataSet is generic:

```
    Public Class SQLStockPersist
        Implements IStockPersist

        Friend Sub New()
        End Sub

        Public Sub AddStock(ByVal UserID As Integer, _
                            ByVal CompID As Integer, _
                            ByVal InitialPrice As Single, _
                            ByVal Shares As Integer) _
                            Implements IStockPersist.AddStock

            Dim cn As New SqlConnection(CONSTS.CONNSTR)
            Dim cm As New SqlCommand("AddStock", cn)
            cm.CommandType = CommandType.StoredProcedure
            cm.Parameters.Add("@UserID", UserID)
            cm.Parameters.Add("@CompID", CompID)
            cm.Parameters.Add("@InitialPrice", InitialPrice)
            cm.Parameters.Add("@Shares", Shares)
            Try
              cn.Open()
              cm.ExecuteNonQuery()
            Finally
              cm.Dispose()
              cn.Dispose()
            End Try
        End Sub
```

MyInvestmentWatch.com Data Tier

```vb
Public Sub DeleteStock(ByVal UserID As Integer, _
                ByVal CompID As Integer) _
                    Implements IStockPersist.DeleteStock

   Dim cn As New SqlConnection(CONSTS.CONNSTR)
   Dim cm As New SqlCommand("DeleteStock", cn)
   cm.CommandType = CommandType.StoredProcedure
   cm.Parameters.Add("@UserID", UserID)
   cm.Parameters.Add("@CompID", CompID)
   Try
      cn.Open()
      cm.ExecuteNonQuery()
   Finally
      cm.Dispose()
      cn.Dispose()
   End Try
End Sub

Public Function GetStocks(ByVal UserID As Integer) As DataSet _
        Implements IStockPersist.GetStocks

   Dim cn As New SqlConnection(CONSTS.CONNSTR)
   Dim cm As New SqlCommand("GetStocks", cn)
   Dim da As New SqlDataAdapter(cm)
   cm.CommandType = CommandType.StoredProcedure
   cm.Parameters.Add("@UserID", UserID)
   Try
      cn.Open()
      Dim ds As New DataSet()
      da.Fill(ds)
      GetStocks = ds
   Finally
      cm.Dispose()
      da.Dispose()
      cn.Dispose()
   End Try
End Function

Public Function GetTicker(ByVal CompID As Integer) As String _
        Implements IStockPersist.GetTicker

   Dim cn As New SqlConnection(CONSTS.CONNSTR)
   Dim cm As New SqlCommand("GetTicker", cn)
   cm.CommandType = CommandType.StoredProcedure
   cm.Parameters.Add("@CompID", CompID)
   Dim p As New SqlParameter("@Ticker", SqlDbType.VarChar, 4)
   p.Direction = ParameterDirection.Output
   cm.Parameters.Add(p)
   Try
      cn.Open()
      cm.ExecuteNonQuery()
      GetTicker = CStr(p.Value)
   Finally
```

Chapter 3: The Data Tier

```
         cm.Dispose()
         cn.Dispose()
      End Try
   End Function

   Public Function GetCompID(ByVal Ticker As String) As Integer _
         Implements IStockPersist.GetCompID

      Dim cn As New SqlConnection(CONSTS.CONNSTR)
      Dim cm As New SqlCommand("GetCompID", cn)
      cm.CommandType = CommandType.StoredProcedure
      cm.Parameters.Add("@Ticker", Ticker)
      Dim p As New SqlParameter("@CompID", SqlDbType.Int)
      p.Direction = ParameterDirection.Output
      cm.Parameters.Add(p)
      Try
         cn.Open()
         cm.ExecuteNonQuery()
         GetCompID = CInt(p.Value)
      Finally
         cm.Dispose()
         cn.Dispose()
      End Try
   End Function

   Public Sub UpdateStock(ByVal UserID As Integer, _
                  ByVal CompID As Integer, _
                  ByVal InitialPrice As Single, _
                  ByVal Shares As Integer) _
                  Implements IStockPersist.UpdateStock

      Dim cn As New SqlConnection(CONSTS.CONNSTR)
      Dim cm As New SqlCommand("UpdateStock", cn)
      cm.CommandType = CommandType.StoredProcedure
      cm.Parameters.Add("@UserID", UserID)
      cm.Parameters.Add("@CompID", CompID)
      cm.Parameters.Add("@InitialPrice", InitialPrice)
      cm.Parameters.Add("@Shares", Shares)
      Try
         cn.Open()
         cm.ExecuteNonQuery()
      Finally
         cm.Dispose()
         cn.Dispose()
      End Try
   End Sub
End Class
```

Implementing IStockQuotesPersist

As much as the user would like, they are not allowed to add, delete, or change the price of a stock. Thus, stock quotes can only be read, not altered. `GetQuotes()` simply returns a `DataSet` of records pertaining to the stock in question:

160

```vbnet
Public Class SQLStockQuotesPersist
   Implements IStockQuotesPersist

   Friend Sub New()
   End Sub

   Public Function GetQuotes(ByVal CompID As Integer) As DataSet _
         Implements IStockQuotesPersist.GetQuotes

      Dim cn As New SqlConnection(CONSTS.CONNSTR)
      Dim cm As New SqlCommand("GetQuotes", cn)
      Dim da As New SqlDataAdapter(cm)
      cm.CommandType = CommandType.StoredProcedure
      cm.Parameters.Add("@CompID", CompID)
      Try
         cn.Open()
         Dim ds As New DataSet()
         da.Fill(ds)
         GetQuotes = ds
      Finally
         cm.Dispose()
         da.Dispose()
         cn.Dispose()
      End Try
   End Function
End Class
```

Implementing INewsPersist

SQLNewsPersist allows the middle tier to get the current news articles for a given company and add a hit to the news article when a user reads it:

```vbnet
Public Class SQLNewsPersist
   Implements INewsPersist

   Friend Sub New()
   End Sub

   Public Function GetNews(ByVal CompID As Integer) As DataSet _
         Implements INewsPersist.GetNews

      Dim cn As New SqlConnection(CONSTS.CONNSTR)
      Dim cm As New SqlCommand("GetNews", cn)
      Dim da As New SqlDataAdapter(cm)
      cm.CommandType = CommandType.StoredProcedure
      cm.Parameters.Add("@CompID", CompID)
      Try
         cn.Open()
         Dim ds As New DataSet()
         da.Fill(ds)
         GetNews = ds
      Finally
         cm.Dispose()
```

Chapter 3: The Data Tier

```
            da.Dispose()
            cn.Dispose()
         End Try
      End Function

      Public Sub AddNewsTraffic(ByVal NewsID As Integer) _
            Implements INewsPersist.AddNewsTraffic

         Dim cn As New SqlConnection(CONSTS.CONNSTR)
         Dim cm As New SqlCommand("AddNewsTraffic", cn)
         cm.CommandType = CommandType.StoredProcedure
         cm.Parameters.Add("@NewsID", NewsID)
         Try
            cn.Open()
            cm.ExecuteNonQuery()
         Finally
            cm.Dispose()
            cn.Dispose()
         End Try
      End Sub
   End Class
End Namespace
```

Data Access Layer: Highlights

Our DAL implementation has the following benefits:

- ❑ It provides the ability to implement multiple data stores with little to no impact on the middle tier
- ❑ It separates the DAL layer from the middle tier
- ❑ It takes advantage of stored procedures rather than inline SQL
- ❑ It creates an efficient, stateless model that is relatively easy to separate into a separate physical middle tier
- ❑ `Connection` objects utilize default .NET Managed Provider connection pooling

We have created a DAL with the capability for multiple persistence mechanisms. Using the interfaces, we could create another set of persistence objects. Assuming we want to create an Oracle provider, the following would need to be performed:

- ❑ Create a properly normalized Oracle database complete with stored procedures, indexes, and any Oracle-specific performance enhancements.
- ❑ Create `OraclePersistFactory`, implementing `IPersistFactory`
- ❑ Create `Oracle<object>Persist`, where `<object>` is each of the concrete persistence classes including `User`, `Stock`, `StockQuote`, `Hits`, and `News`.
- ❑ Configure the middle tier to create instances of `OraclePersistFactory` rather than `SQLPersistFactory`

Data Access Layer: Possible Improvements

Our application was fairly simple and could benefit from a common stored procedure execution method. We could create a generic method that accepts the name of the stored procedure to execute and the names and values for its parameters. The method would be responsible for executing the stored procedure and return any output to the caller. Such a method would save the repetition of opening/closing objects and executing `SQLCommand` objects found in the concrete classes.

If we use a configuration file to determine which persistence object instance to create, the application is highly dynamic. In ASP.NET scenarios, the need for such dynamic code is potential not necessary. Chances are we won't need to convert to a new data store on a daily basis. Perhaps hard-coding `SQLPersistFactory` as the factory object would be plenty dynamic enough. If a new data store needs implementing, that sort of code change would not require much time at all.

Obviously one DAL implementation is not suitable for multiple applications. With proper planning and design techniques and understanding the pieces involved in creating a DAL, we can begin to piece together a DAL customized to the application's needs. For truly scalable systems capable of changing in size and scope, a separate logical DAL provides ample benefits at a relatively low development cost.

Summary

Data-access layers are designed in many flavors. Smaller, two-tier applications implement data-access code directly into the user interface code. Three-tier sites abstract the business application logic and the data-access layer together into the middle-tier layer. We can go one step further and abstract the data-access layer into its own logical (and possibly physical) tier. Separating the middle tier provides multiple benefits:

- **Reuse** – the ability to reuse the data layer across applications
- **Abstraction** – this frees the middle-tier code to concentrate on logic, not data-access code
- **Insulation** – the DAL insulates the middle and user interface tiers from database and DAL technology changes (ADO.NET for example)
- **Scalability** – a DAL provides the ability to implement a separate physical tier capable of scaling up and out if required
- **Testing** – a logically separate DAL enables the application developer to test the database and data-access tier separately from the other application layers before integration and overall application testing

The foundation for the data tier begins with the database design. To design a well structured database, we must consider the concepts of normalization. Designing a normalized database helps us eliminate redundancy and ensure data integrity via table relationships.

Chapter 3: The Data Tier

SQL Server provides features to increase scalability and improve performance. Implementing stored procedures and the correct indexes within SQL Server increases performance by caching compiled query plans and provides faster access to data. SQL Server includes a query profiler and an index tuning wizard application for assisting the developer with database performance analysis.

Most modern relational databases, including SQL Server, provide additional functionality to enhance the scalability and performance of the database. Proper use of stored procedures and indexes in particular allow us to squeeze even more performance from our application. The benefits and usage scenarios of these technologies help us create a more flexible middle tier.

After the database is created, ADO.NET is used to provide access to the database. ADO.NET is built with scalability in mind by separating the connection and storage functionality into two distinct pieces. The `DataSet`, the heart of data storage, is connectionless and able to be passed (serialized) between tiers. A connectionless storage mechanism allows us to efficiently use our expensive connection instances to the fullest by providing capabilities for relationships and constraints between tables.

Since there is not a single data access layer architecture that is right for every application, it is important to consider different alternatives to implementing a DAL. The implementation we saw provides the ability to add additional data sources and implementation with little or no changes required to the middle-tier code. The DAL's stateless nature allows it to be separated logically or physically from the middle-tier logic.

By implementing an abstract factory pattern, the middle-tier code is capable of creating any concrete factory classes we choose to implement. In the example, we implemented a `SQLPersistFactory` and set of related objects for providing data access to SQL Server. A similar set of classes could be written to take advantage of additional data stores. Such stores include other relational databases, such as Oracle, or non-relational data stores including XML or flat text files.

Now that the application's foundation is in place, we can focus on developing the middle tier. As we will see, .NET includes multiple interesting and useful technologies at the middle-tier level. Having a DAL in place allows us to concentrate on the design of these components without worrying about the logic of accessing the data store.

VB.NET

Scalability

Handbook

4

4

The Middle Tier

The middle tier is where the vast majority of an application's logic will be performed. In order to create a highly scalable middle tier, we must understand the technologies that .NET has built into the Framework. This chapter provides high-level introductions to the concepts behind the middle tier, as well as a first look into the technologies that .NET provides for middle-tier development.

With the OO-focused nature of .NET, developing objects becomes a native skill set for developing on the platform. In previous versions, the Visual Basic language was not as OO-focused as .NET, which allowed developers to sacrifice the middle tier in favor of implementing logic at other application tiers, particularly the user interface (UI). In many cases, it was possible to create entire applications without creating object instances.

Developing a middle tier also provides our application with ample benefits realized at the UI tier. Reuse, for example, is particularly important within an application, and allows us to use the same middle-tier logic across a wide variety of client applications. For example, the ASP.NET UI is responsible for interacting with the middle tier to present the user with information. The same middle tier could also be responsible for providing information to a Windows forms UI for our internal staff. Along the same lines, a web services interface could be created to allow third-party vendors to communicate programmatically with our middle-tier logic.

This chapter takes a look at the two characteristics that all middle tiers possess: a logical and a physical architecture.

Chapter 4: The Middle Tier

The logical middle tier is the object model and set of functionality that our middle tier exposes. This is where the heart of the application is typically coded. Designing the middle tier is not simply a process of defining the objects necessary and beginning to code. We must consider how to design our middle-tier interfaces in such a fashion that changing the objects that implement them will not break our UIs depending on the middle-tier. We must also make sure the logical design is intuitive and presents a set of consistent and understandable interfaces.

The physical middle tier is the hardware architecture on which the middle tier is deployed. A middle tier can reside on the same physical machine as other tiers in our application or be deployed to a separate machine or set of machines. In applications with multiple clients depending on middle-tier logic, creating a physical middle tier gives us many benefits, including simplified deployment, integration, and upgradeability.

Creating a separate physical middle tier with DCOM was a daunting and complicated task limited by DCOM's network complications. .NET introduces the concept of **Remoting** to provide cross-process code invocation and the framework necessary for implementing our own custom communication channels and formatters.

In this chapter, we will implement a fully functional remoting server and client. We illustrate the concepts behind Remoting including channels, formatters, `MarshalByRefObjects`, and serializable objects. Our Remoting example illustrates the use of dynamically loading configuration information via configuration files. The concepts of `SingleCall` and `Singleton` objects are discussed in relation to object creation.

Web services, based upon a set of open technologies including SOAP, WSDL, and XML, have provided a promising mechanism for remote procedure invocation. We take a look at extending our remoting object into a web service and illustrate the built-in functionality .NET and IIS provide for creating web services. We also design a client to consume the web service and illustrate the tools necessary to create a client proxy object from reading the web service's WSDL contract.

We continue the ongoing application started in Chapter 3 by creating a middle tier for the MyInvestmentWatch.com web application. We create an object model capable of interacting with the Data Access Layer (DAL). The object model illustrates how to implement strongly-typed collections to hold our object state as well as design considerations for adding, updating, and deleting data in our data store by using the DAL persistence objects for persistence. We also create a sample application for simulating a UI interaction to test the application.

The middle tier, from a logic perspective, is the most interesting part of the application. With proper design techniques and the understanding of the base functionality that .NET provides, we are able to create a highly functional middle tier capable of being reused via multiple client applications both with a GUI (ASP.NET and Windows Forms) and without (remoting and web services).

Middle-Tier Definition

The middle tier is the logical layer in a distributed (commonly called n-tier) system residing between the UI (client) and the DAL. Typically, the middle tier contains the functionality and logic necessary to define the purpose and workings of the system. The middle tier is commonly a collection of rules, objects, and functions that generate and operate on data to accomplish the system's goals.

The middle tier is typically where the heart of the application logic is performed. Since all systems are logically different, the scope of the middle tier can vary widely. In a system that is meant to push and pull data to and from a database, the middle tier can be very simple. In heavy calculation-intensive applications, the middle tier is typically responsible for performing the calculations and applying application logic. Having so many different middle tier architectures provides developers with a tremendous opportunity for creative system design and planning. It is this opportunity that interests developers as they are able to stretch their imagination.

Middle-Tier Benefits

A common theme in n-tier architecture is the ability for a tier to provide abstraction for the tier above it. For example, the data tier encapsulated the data access logic into a set of objects responsible for communicating with the data store. With the DAL in place, the middle tier developer is freed from the responsibility of understanding how to implement code to interact with the database. In fact, the middle tier developer does not need to understand the architecture of the database in a detailed manner.

Developing a middle tier provides this abstraction for developers working on the UI. Just as we don't want to require middle-tier developers to understand the database logic, we don't want to require UI developers to deal with the application logic. UI developers should only need to concern themselves with the middle-tier API.

Creating a middle tier has numerous benefits when compared to implementing an application with the logic built into the UI. Let's take a closer look at the benefits a middle tier provides.

Scalability

Developing a middle tier allows our application to scale better than if the code was pushed down to each user. Imagine we have a Windows forms application where the middle tier is deployed on each client PC. If the middle tier is logic intensive, perhaps the client PC will not have the horsepower to handle the logic in a timely manner. However, if the middle tier was physically separated, we gain the ability to scale out the middle tier for faster response times.

A common middle tier also improves scalability by taking advantage of shared resources. Having one middle tier allows the middle tier to service numerous clients. There are many positive externalities that result from a single contact point. For example, we could implement data caching, object pooling, and connection pooling to reduce the resources necessary for the application to service clients.

Separating the middle tier physically from the client application allows us to scale up, out, or down depending on the changing application landscape.

Reusability

Developing a tiered system promotes reuse at each tier. At the middle-tier level, we separate the logic from the UI code. The abstraction allows us to implement multiple front-end clients on the same set of middle-tier logic.

Reuse is also possible from within the same UI. If we have a set of code used frequently, separating it into middle-tier logic allows us to reuse it at different parts of the application.

Reuse is often underestimated. When developing an application, developers tend to rule out how the system could be reused in other applications. If the project is to implement a web system, consideration is often not given to administrative front ends, reporting clients, or Windows-based applications. Perhaps other front ends will not be implemented, but having the logic in place in case requirements change is worth the development effort.

One of the reasons reuse is underestimated is because there is a perception that reuse involves higher costs. However, if components are designed with a generic purpose, reuse can be quite inexpensive. For example, if we design a search component for searching our database, any application needing to search the database can use the component. The reason we are able to reuse the search component is because it has a clearly defined purpose and does not tie itself into other parts of the application.

In contrast, if we integrate the search component into the application, we cannot reuse it from outside the application. Designing with reuse in mind generally means that we factor our application into sets of components with a specific purpose.

Integration

Systems that integrate with multiple legacy or external systems will benefit from having a common middle tier. Assume we have a connection to an Oracle data store with a limited set of connections. Implementing the middle tier allows our middle tier to pool connection objects to service clients. We could pool 10 connections that might satisfy 100 clients. Had the middle-tier logic been implemented at the client level, each client would require their own connection object.

Middle-Tier Definition

A common middle tier provides a common interface to disparate systems. If we would like to consume our logic from another application running on another platform, we could expose our middle-tier logic via a web service and allow those systems to interact with us using SOAP. The common API we expose is only possible if the middle-tier logic is separated from the application code.

In some situations, the physical network design may prevent the clients from accessing internal systems. Servers and resources are typically segmented differently from the general user base. For security purposes firewalls are established to provide physical barriers to reaching servers. Accessing the system from the physical middle tier allows us to control access to these systems and prevents the need for us to open the network to all clients.

Deployment

Middle-tier applications typically use the services of additional resources that require deployment. If our middle-tier code interacts with a data store, the client machine must be configured with the appropriate drivers. If the application code is altered, it must be redeployed. Requiring ODBC or OLEDB connections to be established complicates the deployment and administration process by needing to administer the application for each client. If the code requires system files or certain versions of libraries, those must also be deployed as well.

One of the strengths of .NET is the ability to have multiple versions of assemblies executing side by side and instruct the application to use a particular version by using a configuration file. Using .NET's versioning does not replace the need for a middle tier; it simply gives us more options for upgrading and versioning the client. We'll discuss .NET versioning in more detail later in this chapter.

Benefits Summary

By now it is clear how a middle tier can benefit an application. Scalability, reuse, abstraction, system integration, upgradeability, and deployment prove to be excellent reasons for creating a middle tier.

The benefits of the middle tier are well documented within the industry and ubiquitous with enterprise application architectures. We have not done justice to the amount of benefit middle-tier separation has on the overall design architecture of the system. We could spend the entire chapter discussing the benefits in detail, but a cursory introduction is ample to highlight the necessity of the middle tier.

Middle-Tier Drawbacks

From the previous section you may have thought that a middle tier only provides benefits. However, there are some drawbacks and we'll briefly discuss them now.

Performance

Implementing a physical middle tier suffers from performance degradation since the application must cross physical processes, and perhaps the network, to execute. We'll discuss the concerns associated with performance and the middle tier in the discussion of the physical middle tier.

Configuration

Whenever we deploy code to a physical server, the calling server or application must be configured to execute the code. If our machine name, IP, or port changes, then the client configuration must be reconfigured to recognize the change.

Middle-Tier Design

Now that we understand the benefits and drawbacks, we can turn our attention to the design decisions involved when creating a middle tier. Before we open Visual Studio .NET and write object models, there are important design considerations we should take into consideration, including planning and designing our logical and physical middle-tier architectures.

All middle-tier implementations have both a logical and physical representation. The logical middle tier defines the set of functionality and objects that make up the middle tier. The physical portion of the middle tier is the physical architecture (processes and/or servers) where the logical middle code executes. Let's take a detailed look at both the logical and physical middle-tier design considerations.

Logical Middle Tier

The logical middle tier is the set of objects and code that is separated from the data access and UI layers into a discrete set of components and object models. Typically, middle tier functionality can include:

- **Data Validation** – code required to ensure high data integrity
- **Actions & Events** – the ability to interact with the UI code via events and asynchronous communication
- **Application Logic** – a set of functionality or algorithms particular to your application domain

Managing Interfaces

Developing a logical middle tier means understanding how the interfaces between the UI and middle-tier components are established. As in COM, interface versioning is a crucial part of application development. Whenever class interfaces are changed, they have potential to break any code dependent on the class.

In COM, as well as Java and .NET, developing a robust set of interfaces allows the code to version gracefully. In COM, versioning was complicated by the fact that you could not have different versions of the same component. The problem became so far reaching for developers that the term "DLL Hell" was created to describe the problem.

.NET versioning is vastly improved over its COM predecessor. However great the versioning support, we must continue to develop a set of interfaces that will be unchanged over time while allowing for the application's functionality to change.

There are many OO design patterns and logical architecture designs developed to assist us with interface versioning. However, we do not need to be an expert on design patterns to understand the importance of managing interfaces.

Interface Design Example

When determining the interface exposure, we must first determine to what extent the UI will interact with our middle tier.

To illustrate interface design considerations, let's assume we are in charge of developing a middle tier for an order-entry system. Once the order items have been selected, the order must be run through a set of validations. For example, when an order is placed for overseas delivery, add a handling charge. Or if the order weighs over 100 pounds do not allow overnight shipping. Once the order is verified, the user must interact with a credit card billing system.

The first logical step might be to create three components to host within the middle tier:

- `Order` – maintains order state including products, user information, discounts, and order totals
- `Verification` – performs `Order` object verification
- `Billing` – prepares, processes, and stores credit card and billing information and interacts with a third-party credit vendor

The UI interacts with all three components. Graphically, the UI would resemble that shown in Figure 1.

173

Figure 1.

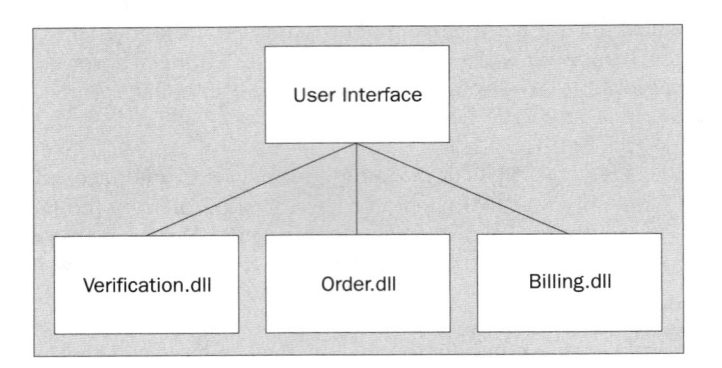

```
                    ┌──────────────┐
                    │ User Interface│
                    └──────────────┘
                    ╱       │       ╲
                   ╱        │        ╲
      ┌──────────────┐ ┌──────────┐ ┌──────────┐
      │Verification.dll│ │ Order.dll│ │Billing.dll│
      └──────────────┘ └──────────┘ └──────────┘
```

In this logical middle-tier design scenario, the UI is responsible for interacting with three components directly. If any of these components change interfaces, we must upgrade our UI code. Example pseudocode might look like the following:

```
'Build Order
Dim _order as New Order()
Dim _billing As New Billing()
_order.AddItem("123D33", 1, 32.22)
_order.AddItem("443D333, 3, 9.09)
_order.CardNumber = "1234567890"

Dim _val As Validation(_order)
Dim rules As BrokenRules = _val.ValidateOrder

If rules.Count > 0 Then
   'List validation errors
Else
   _billing.Approve(_order.CardNumber, _order.TotalAmount)
   If _billing.Accepted Then
      'Approved, completed
   Else
      'Declined, list declined
   End If
End If
```

If we look at this middle-tier design in terms of interaction between the UI layer and the middle-tier layer, we see that the UI is dependent on the `Order`, `Billing`, and `Validate` object model interfaces. If at any time these interfaces change in a way that breaks compatibility, then we will be required to change the UI code to take into account that change.

Middle-Tier Design

Instead of having the UI dependent on all three objects, we could implement the `Order` object model to expose access points (methods) on the class to handle the validation and billing functions. The UI is then dependent on only the `Order` object model. We would have the logical middle-tier architecture shown in Figure 2.

Figure 2.

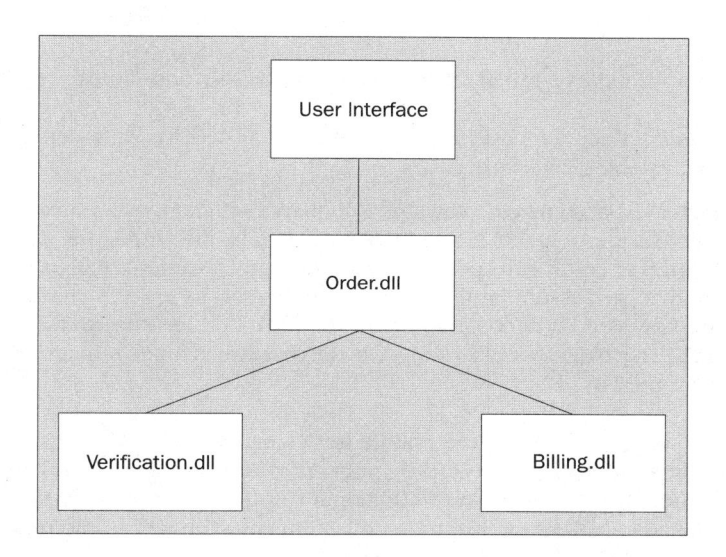

[Diagram: User Interface connects to Order.dll, which connects to Verification.dll and Billing.dll]

New pseudocode shows that the UI is now only dependent on the `Order` object model. In some places we can use common functionality. For example, we could create a general `Errors` object to represent errors created in the `Billing` and/or `Validation` object:

```
'Build Order
Dim _order as New Order()
Dim _rule As BrokenRule
_order.AddItem("123D33", 1, 32.22)
_order.AddItem("443D333", 3, 9.09)

If Not _order.IsValid Then
   For Each _rule in _order.BrokenRules
      'List
Else
   If order.Approve Then
      'Approved, Complete
   Else
      'Declined
   End If
End If
```

Both examples are drastically simplified versions of true production systems, but we can start to see the design decisions involved with creating a logical middle tier. In the second example, we decided to encapsulate the functionality of `Billing` and `Verification` within the `Order` object. The `Order` object will use the services of the `Billing` and `Verification` objects when processing; however, the UI is completely freed from understanding what is needed to provide this functionality. It does not need to issue calls directly to these services, only interact with the `Order` object model.

We have accomplished two things between the first and second logical designs:

- Less interface dependence between layers. The UI is only dependent on the `Order` object interface.

- Increased abstraction allows us to enhance. If changes are made to the `Billing` and `Verification` object models, the UI code is unaffected. A change in credit card processing vendors, for example, would not require UI changes (assuming the information needed to process credit cards with the new vendor is consistent with the old). Perhaps the interface with the `Billing` object would change; however, the changes remain unnoticed from the UI.

In more cases than not, changing the middle-tier object model is easier than changing the UI. Typically a different group of programmers is responsible for the UI from those for the middle tier. Needing to involve additional resources may be difficult. In Windows Forms applications, where the application is distributed to multiple clients, changing a common middle tier saves on deployment.

Understanding the benefits of encapsulating objects and providing a smaller interface to the next logical tier (UI), you may incorrectly assume the best design is that which provides the most encapsulation and exposes the smallest interface possible. However, there are drawbacks to this approach:

Encapsulation has a tendency to increase logical layers, or depth, in the object model. It may not seem readily apparent with our small object model, but in general as object models grow and provide more functionality per call, objects start to gain dependencies on each other where they were once not needed. For example, the `Order` object is now dependent on the `Billing` and `Validation` objects. In effect what we have done is moved the burden of change from the UI to the other logical layers of the middle tier. Instead of changing the UI code to comply with the `Verification` and `Billing` changes, we are required to change the `Order` object.

Encapsulation also increases the complexity of the `Order` object by requiring more functionality from it. The `Order` object is now responsible for maintaining state or exposing methods that interact with the `Billing` and `Validation` objects. The `Order` object becomes littered with state that is not meant for the `Order` object's true purpose of holding state for an order.

Middle-Tier Design

So, where do we draw the line between encapsulating functionality into a compact interface and exposing a larger object model to prevent objects from becoming cluttered? The answer involves both good and bad news.

The bad news is there is no right answer for every application. In a web application scenario, it may not be difficult to change the UI of the application since the ASP.NET application is only deployed to one or a set of servers. However, in a Windows Forms application where the UI is deployed to multiple clients, changing the UI may require a huge deployment effort and creating a smaller interface would be preferable. The application dictates the logical middle-tier design choices.

The good news is we can plan for change. By understanding the physical architecture and the deployment base of the UI, we can design the application appropriately.

Interfaces and Physical Tiers

Obviously there are important design decisions to consider before implementing a logical middle tier. Designing proper interfaces with respect to the physical middle tier is a staple of good design in a multi-tiered system. Understanding the physical architecture can help determine what direction the logical layout should go.

As we look into the middle-tier functionality provided by .NET, we see that the importance of interfaces is compounded by the new technologies offered. For example, when we examine Remoting, we will see that both the client and the server must maintain copies of the remoted object's interface. Obviously, once a remote object is deployed, we are bound to the interface contract. Breaking the interface would require all clients of the remoted object to be updated with the new interface. While this is not ultimately too complex, it throws another wrinkle into the upgrade process.

Interfaces are extremely important in web services architecture as well, especially if the service consumers are customers or third-party users. Much like remoting, if we need to alter the interface of a web service, all the clients using the web service must be altered. If the service's consumers are customers or off site users, every change will require their programmers to alter their systems. Obviously web service interfaces, once deployed, aren't altered drastically, if at all.

In many cases, it may be easier to keep the current web service running and implement an upgraded service to run in parallel until users can all be converted to the new implementation. While this would require extra code and more planning, it would provide a more gradual upgrade cycle for clients.

Physical Middle Tier

In conjunction with designing the logical middle tier, we must plan for the physical implementation. With the .NET Framework, we are exposed to multiple configurations and options for hosting the middle tier in different operating system processes. Remoting and web services, for example, provide the ability to consume functionality executing on another physical machine or set of machines.

Technically speaking, if two pieces of the middle-tier logic are executing in different physical processes, they are physically separated regardless of whether they are executing on the same physical computer. For example, a middle-tier process could be dedicated to execute on a different processor from the web server on the same physical machine. .NET, like COM+ before it, has made it trivial for parts of applications to execute in different processes.

Once the middle tier is physically separated from the UI or data-access tier, we can scale up or down to meet demand placed on the middle tier. For example, if we placed each logical tier on a physical tier, our network would look like the Figure 3.

Figure 3.

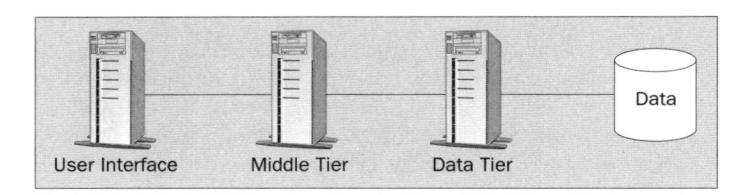

Once the middle tier is physically separated, it can be scaled out to meet demands. We could load-balance or run as a cluster, increasing the performance of the middle tier, as shown in Figure 4.

Figure 4.

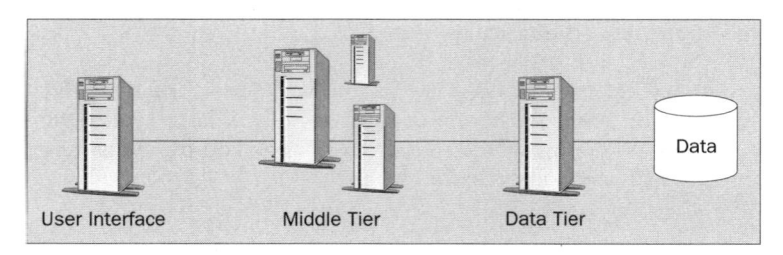

Before we implement the separate physical middle tier architecture, we must carefully consider if our application will benefit from the design. In many cases, having the separate physical middle tier is more costly in terms of performance than if the resources were spent upgrading the UI tier.

Performance in a Physical Middle Tier

There is a natural tendency is to associate a separate physical middle tier with performance advantages. The idea is the separated physical architecture tends to improve performance because the middle tier can be optimized to execute the middle-tier code and gains the benefits associated with shared resources.

Shared resources and middle-tier optimizations indeed make for perhaps huge performance improvements. But these benefits do not come for free. In order for the UI to communicate with the middle tier, the data must be marshaled between the UI and middle tier. If this is not done correctly, the expense of marshaling can negate the performance improvements of the middle tier.

In order for a UI to communicate with a separate physical middle tier, the following must happen with each communication:

- ❑ Client packages the data to be sent to the middle tier. In .NET, this process is often known as serialization.
- ❑ Client sends the data across the network.
- ❑ Server rehydrates the value or objects.
- ❑ Server executes the request.
- ❑ Server packages the response for transfer to the client.
- ❑ Server sends the response across the network.
- ❑ Client deserializes the response and rehydrates object (if necessary).

The two main drawbacks for a separate physical middle tier are network latency and the process of packaging (or serializing) the data. The question we must determine is whether these two drawbacks are enough of a liability that implementing the separate physical middle tier would actually slow performance. Both network latency and serialization are closely related to .NET Remoting and will be explained later in this chapter.

The only way to truly determine the performance costs associated with the physical middle tier is to performance-test different scenarios. Chapter 6 will give a detailed look at performance monitoring with .NET.

When we are developing an application, we can take design measures to minimize the drawbacks. As discussed in Chapter 2, creating "chunky" interfaces allows us to minimize the number of calls across the network. The alternative interface, the "chatty" interface, incurs a huge amount of overhead since each communication call is subject to network latency and serialization.

Determining the UI

Like many other aspects of design, a single architecture does not fit all. There are parts of the application where we want to execute middle-tier logic directly on the client. Other times we want the client to call into a designated server. Our goal as architects is to understand what costs are associated with each design and how to design with the least cost.

Understanding the UI and the client architecture of our application can help determine an appropriate architecture. With .NET, there are two primary client design architectures: Windows Forms (Winforms) and ASP.NET. Web services can also be considered a system interface to other applications since they are ultimately programmatic interfaces. However, we will focus on the differences between Winforms and ASP.NET when discussing reasons for architecting around the physical tier.

ASP.NET and Winforms applications benefit from middle architectures in many ways. In the ASP.NET scenario, the middle tier 'client' is actually a set of servers running ASP.NET. UI deployment scenarios are not difficult in ASP.NET when compared to Winforms. We simply update the ASP.NET servers and deployment is done. We do not need to manually update each user's client machine.

Understanding the client will help determine the scope of the middle tier. Some points of interest are:

- How geographically close are the clients? The more distributed in nature, the greater the deployment effort.

- How does the client access the middle tier? A LAN and dial-up client connection will have vastly different network latency.

- How frequently will the client interact with our middle tier? If the client requires constant interaction with the middle tier, it might be more efficient to place the middle-tier logic on the client application to avoid network latency.

.NET Middle Tier

Now that we have defined aspects of the middle tier, it's time to switch gears and focus entirely on .NET and the features exposed by the Framework that we can use to help build our middle tier.

In today's application development landscape, a shift is taking place away from proprietary protocols and data formats towards standard protocols and data formats such as HTTP and XML. Traditional client applications suffer from deployment, configuration, and maintenance nightmares that are both time consuming and expensive. Browser-based clients, while actually more limited in their functionality than Windows client applications, are attractive because the client is easy to maintain. Developers and IT professionals will trade limited functionality for simplified deployment.

Another reason for a shift towards browser-based clients is caused by the limitations imposed by DCOM and the middle-tier architectures. Configuring DCOM to work with the client application was no trivial task. Having each client PC communicating with DCOM was not simple. Browser-based clients allow only the web servers to interact with DCOM, eliminating the need for configuration and deployment.

The way to avoid DCOM and the related configuration nightmare is to use HTTP as the communications protocol between the client and server. HTTP is ideal because client machines that have a web browser installed are able to communicate via HTTP. On the server side, most network firewalls are configured to allow HTTP traffic, meaning no network changes are required.

Since DCOM does not communicate natively over HTTP, alternatives are needed. Microsoft .NET Remoting and web services provide the capabilities to expose our middle-tier architectures to clients using standard protocols.

In many respects, .NET Remoting and web services allow us to expose our middle tier architectures without the nightmares that DCOM imposed. Remoting and web services are similar in that they allow programmatic access into our application from the UI tier or perhaps another middle tier within the network or outside of the network.

.NET Remoting

Whenever we implement a separate physical middle tier, running in a different process or different computer, we must have the facilities for communication between the processes. At a very high-level, we need:

- A 'server' or listener prepared to handle the incoming traffic
- An agreed upon protocol for communication
- An agreed upon data format for passing data
- A client capable of invoking the server process

Within the .NET Framework, Remoting is the technology based upon which cross-process communication becomes possible. The remoting framework, also called .NET Remoting or just Remoting, provides a surprisingly easy set of classes and tools to make cross-process communication possible.

The topic of .NET Remoting is broad. We could discuss implementing security, creating custom transport mechanisms, custom data compressions for faster transmission, or even using remoting over SMTP or a POP3 channel. It is interesting to note that with DCOM and its proprietary transport protocol, it was difficult, if not impossible, for a developer to tap deeply into the DCOM processes. In contrast, remoting allows us to implement our own transport channels or data formatters if the pre-built stacks don't provide the functionality we are looking for.

Chapter 4: The Middle Tier

Just because we can tap into the remoting processes, doesn't mean we need to. Microsoft has provided default protocol and data formatting stacks that provide a great solution that will meet the vast majority of our needs.

Implementing a remoting scenario is rather straightforward; however, since we need to create both a client and a server application, there are a fair number of failure points we need to watch closely. In particular, we must ensure we have the proper configuration at both ends. If we watch these parts closely, we will have no problems creating a remoting application. Figure 5 illustrates the lines of communication and the different aspects that are needed in a .NET remoting scenario. It is a rather simplified diagram and illustrates the remoting pieces at a high level. We'll discuss each of the pieces in more detail shortly.

Figure 5.

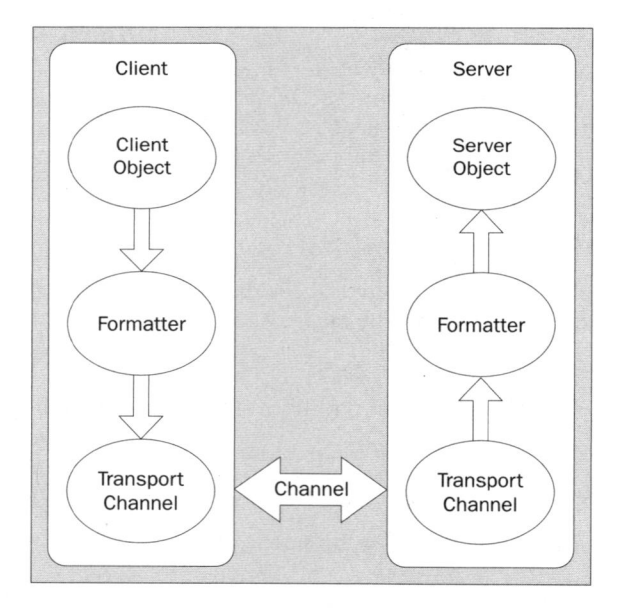

The client has an object called a proxy that is actually a pointer to an object existing within the server process. The client thinks the object is local; however, when calls are made to the object, the remoting framework is responsible for making sure the call is passed to the server for execution. In order for the remoting call to be made, the remoting framework is responsible for formatting the request into a data format that the server understands. Once the call is formatted, it is handed to the transport channel that sends the call to the server machine.

.NET Middle Tier

Since remoting comes with a complete default channel and formatter stack, we are able to create a simple remoting client and server from scratch in very little time. The following example will create a very simple client and server application to provide a detailed introduction to remoting. While reading the example, start thinking in terms of how you could implement remoting in the context of your application to host your middle-tier components within their own physical middle tier.

Terminology

With the introduction of new technologies, we get new terminology related to those technologies. In the previous paragraphs, for example, we introduce data formatting and channels. Let's take a look at a few common terms related to .NET remoting.

MarshalByRefObject

Before we jump into writing code, we must understand there are two ways for a client to interact with objects hosted on the server. First, we could pass the client a reference to an object running on the server. The client would call against this reference as if it were a local object. However, when the calls are issued, the reference would actually relay the calls ahead to the server process, execute the call there, and marshal the result back to the client. Objects that are exposed via remoting as `MarshalByRefObject` execute on the server; no work is done on the client side.

What we have described is a scenario where the client has a proxy object that is responsible for interacting with the server. The object on the server derives from `System.MarshalByRefObject`, which is the base class for allowing the client to interact with proxy objects. We will take a look at an example implementing a `MarshalByRefObject` shortly.

Serializable (ByValue)

In contrast to a `MarshalByRefObject`, we could implement an object that once created is passed back to the client. The client would ask the server for an object, the server would then create the object, serialize it into a string or binary representation, and pass it completely over to the client. Once the client had the object in hand, there would be no further relationship between the client and server. All calls made against the object would be executed on the client as if the client had originally created the object. Serializable objects are commonly referred to as "Marshal-by-Value" objects to denote that the entire object itself is marshaled to the client, not just the reference to the object.

In .NET, providing the `<Serializable>` attribute at the class level is all we need to do to make our objects pass by value from the server to the client. The remoting framework takes care of packaging the object, sending it to the client, and recreating it in the client's space.

183

Formatter

When data is transferred between processes via Remoting or web services, it must be sent in a format that both the client and server understand. You could, for example, create your own formatter that specifies what data is coming over, what type that data is in, etc. The stack used on the server for packaging that data would be the same stack used on the client for unpackaging it.

Creating a formatter and plugging it into the remoting framework actually wouldn't be too difficult since the framework offers base classes that we can use to provide the structure for how the formatter would need to be implemented. Still, creating a custom formatter would be out of scope for most projects.

In addition to providing the ability to create your own formatter, the remoting framework offers two pre-built formatters, the binary and SOAP formatters.

The binary formatter is very efficient because it can serialize the object into a very small byte stream. All objects serialized with the binary formatter must also be deserialized with it, so it is the ideal solution if you have .NET on both ends of the wire.

However, the binary formatter's efficiency comes at a price; its output stream is not human readable and is limited to those platforms that have the binary formatter installed. At the time of writing, the binary formatter is only implemented on the .NET platform, so using the binary formatter requires that you send from a .NET server to a .NET client and vise versa.

The SOAP formatter transfers data in the form of SOAP messages. The SOAP messages are more verbose than their binary counterparts, making them less efficient than the binary formatted message.

However, the SOAP formatter is vastly more powerful than the binary formatter in terms of providing portability and interoperability to your messages. Perhaps the most interesting usage of SOAP is the ability for SOAP messages to be parsed and interpreted by any platform that has the ability to understand SOAP. This flexibility allows us to implement the server and client under different platforms, most notably, but not limited to, .NET and Java. A Java client can receive a SOAP message from a .NET server, and vise versa. What we are discussing here is the basis for web services. The only missing requirement to enabling the cross-platform communication is transmitting the SOAP message over the same protocol, or channel.

Channel

Similar to how the client and server must agree on a message format, they must also agree on a communication mechanism, or channel, to provide the data transfer. Channels are transport mechanisms on which the messages are sent. For example, the World Wide Web uses HTTP as the agreed upon channel for communication. If the client computer can send an HTTP request to a server, the server can respond with the HTTP response and the communication is successful. If the client computer issued a request using an SMTP channel and received the data in HTTP format, the communication will fail. Similar to the web, remoting clients and servers must also agree on the communication channel.

.NET Middle Tier

Similarly to how we can create our own formatter in .NET Remoting, we can also create our own channel. Creating a channel would be a matter of implementing a set of identifiers that both the client and server could agree on. For example, we could implement the SMTP channel and send messages in SMTP format.

The .NET Framework comes with two pre-installed channels called the TCP and HTTP channels. The TCP channel communicates in raw TCP and is very efficient. The HTTP channel communicates messages in the HTTP protocol, a higher-level protocol that resides on TCP/IP.

Similar to the binary formatter, the TCP channel is limited to those platforms that can communicate in raw TCP. This typically means that like the binary formatter, both sides of the communication must be .NET clients.

The HTTP channel communicates messages in the HTTP protocol. As long as the client and server processes can communicate via the HTTP channel, the communication will succeed. Since HTTP resides on top of TCP, the HTTP channel is not as efficient as communicating in direct TCP. However, since the HTTP protocol is vastly popular and implemented on many platforms, the HTTP channel is more flexible.

Channel/Formatter Guidelines

The channel/formatter combination is an important decision and needs to be considered during development. When we create our Remoting and web services examples, you will notice that the use of configuration files allows us to dynamically change the formatter and channel after deployment. Even with the flexibility of allowing the formatter and channel to be changed, we should consider the proper configuration while the application is in development. While not a hard and fast rule, the following provides guidelines for choosing a formatter.

Channel	Formatter	Characteristics
TCP	Binary	The fastest channel/formatter combination. The combination of the efficient TCP channel and the terse binary format makes this the ideal choice for speed. Ideal when both clients are using .NET.
TCP	SOAP	Not typically used. If you specify the TCP channel, you are limited to those platforms that can communicate in native TCP. At the time of this writing, using the TCP channel requires .NET, in which case the binary formatter should be used.
HTTP	Binary	Not typically used. The binary formatter is only implemented in .NET. With a .NET client on each end, the TCP and Binary formatter provides the best performance.

Table continued on following page

Chapter 4: The Middle Tier

Channel	Formatter	Characteristics
HTTP	SOAP	Ideal for standardized communication between .NET and non-.NET clients. The performance is not as good as the TCP/Binary combination. However, the flexibility offered by this combination is ideal for allowing anyone with an HTTP and SOAP stack to communicate. This is the basis for web services.

Creating a Remoting-Accessible Object

In this remoting example, we are going to create an object to be instantiated on the server and called by the clients over the HTTP channel using the HTTP channel's default formatter, the SOAP formatter. Since this example has .NET on both ends of the communication, we could have just as easily used the TCP channel and binary formatter.

The goal of this example is to show the basis for calling into another server via a remoting call. The example will illustrate how we could use Remoting to host our middle tier in a separate physical middle tier from the client application. In our example, we will create an object with a simple calculation method and show the execution running on the server machine. We will create an object to be remoted, a server to host the remoting object, and a client to consume the remoted object. Graphically, we will create the scenario shown in Figure 6.

Figure 6.

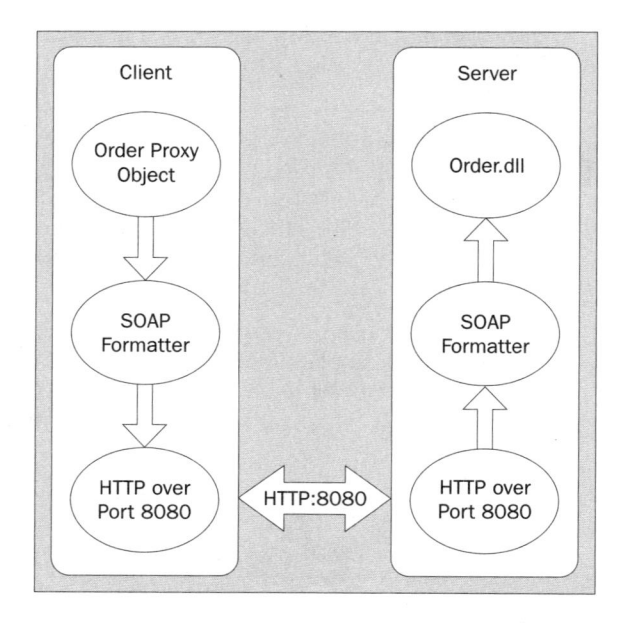

.NET Middle Tier

The client will create an `Order` object, which it thinks is local to the client process. However, as the `Order` object is used, the remoting framework will package up the call into a SOAP message and transfer it over HTTP port 8080 to the server. The server will unpack the SOAP message, execute the method, and package up the message in a return SOAP message to the client. The client will unpack the return call and retrieve the result from the method call.

Before we implement the remoting server and client, we need to create an object or set of objects capable of being called via remoting. In order to expose our class, we need to determine whether to implement a `MarshalByRefObject` or create a serializable object. Since we want the logic of our object to execute on the server, we are going to create a `MarshalByRefObject`.

The following code provides the basic object that we will expose via remoting:

```
'*************************************************************
' Order.vb
' Implementation of the object to be exposed via remoting
'
' Compile with:
' vbc /t:library Order.vb
'*************************************************************
Imports System

Public Class Order
  Inherits MarshalByRefObject

  Private _creation As DateTime

  Public Sub New()
    _creation = DateTime.Now
  End Sub

  Public ReadOnly Property GetMachineName() As String
    Get
      Console.WriteLine("Order.GetMachineName() called")
      GetMachineName = "Order object created at: " & _
                _creation.ToLongTimeString() & " on " & _
                Environment.MachineName
    End Get
  End Property

  Public Function CalculateItem(ByVal Cost As Single, _
                  ByVal TaxCode As Integer) As Single
    Console.WriteLine("Order.CalculateItem() called")
    Select Case TaxCode
      Case 0
        CalculateItem = Cost
      Case 1
```

187

```
            CalculateItem = Cost * 1.06
        Case 2
            CalculateItem = Cost * 1.12
    End Select
  End Function
End Class
```

Compile the class with the following command line instruction:

```
> vbc /t:library Order.vb
```

Notice that the logic of the object is not altered because we are planning to expose this object via remoting. The only difference between this and a standard object is that it inherits from `MarshalByRefObject`, making it available to be remoted.

We are keeping the object's creation time to help determine when the object was created. The `GetMachineName` property will return the machine name under which the object's code is executing. This machine name will prove the object actually executes within a server process. The `CalculateItem()` method is a small example of business logic that could be found within the `Order` class. Obviously, for demonstration purposes we are creating a simple function. If this example were a true `Order` object, the methods would be much more involved, perhaps the `CalculateItem()` method would return an XML document defining an entire purchase order.

A good rule of thumb when creating a remoting object is to make it stateless. Since remoted objects are going to be called from multiple client applications, we will not want to hold instances open for each user. Keeping state in the middle tier for a client increases resource usage and decreases our potential to scale the middle tier.

Creating the Server

Now that we have the object created, we need to publish the object on our server. The remoting object needs a server that exposes the object, via a port, to clients. Each remoted object needs to be published via a server host. The host could be IIS, a Windows service, or a custom-implemented host (we will discuss using IIS briefly when we discuss web services). For simplicity, we will create our own host to publish this remoting object:

```
'***************************************************************
' Server.vb
' Hosts remoting object objects specified in 'server.exe.config'
'
' Compile with:
' vbc /r:Order.dll Server.vb
'***************************************************************
Imports System
Imports System.Runtime.Remoting
```

.NET Middle Tier

```vb
Module ServerHost
  Sub Main()
    Console.WriteLine("ServerHost.Main(): Server Started")
    RemotingConfiguration.Configure("server.exe.config")
    Console.WriteLine("Server is running, Press <return> to exit.")
    Console.ReadLine()
  End Sub
End Module
```

Compile this application via the command line (`Order.dll` must be in same directory as `Server.vb`):

```
> vbc /r:Order.dll Server.vb
```

Before we can execute the server, we need to specify how the remoting objects will be published. The remoting framework allows us to read the configuration via the application configuration file. We could have hard-coded the configuration into the application, but a configuration change would require a recompile of `Server.vb`. Configuration files offer much more flexibility than hard-coding the configuration into the server host.

Once the configuration file is created, we tell the remoting runtime to retrieve its configuration via the file with the line:

```
RemotingConfiguration.Configure("server.exe.config")
```

The file `server.exe.config` file looks like the following:

```xml
<configuration>
  <system.runtime.remoting>
    <application>
      <channels>
        <channel ref="http" port="8080" />
      </channels>
      <service>
        <wellknown mode="Singleton"
                   type="Order, Order"
                   objectUri="Order.soap" />
      </service>
    </application>
  </system.runtime.remoting>
</configuration>
```

The remoting framework reads the `<system.runtime.remoting>` node and configures the remoting runtime with its contents. This configuration file must be placed in the same directory as `server.exe`.

We tell the runtime the channel we wish to expose the object. Since we wish to use the HTTP channel, we create the following `channel` tag:

```
<channel ref="http" port="8080" />
```

We must also expose the object and there are two object creation types, `wellknown` and `activated`. Similar to COM objects, `activated` objects can be stateful and the client maintains the lifetime. `wellknown` objects are created under the server process and the server maintains the lifetime for which they are available.

The two modes of `wellknown` objects are `Singleton` and `Singlecall`. Under the `Singleton` mode, one object is created to handle all requests. The object is kept alive between client requests. `Singlecall` objects are created for every call issued by each client. Every time a client call comes in, a new object is created, the client is serviced, and the object is destroyed. The `Singleton` object is excellent if you would like to share common data between client requests. `Singlecall` objects leave a small footprint since all objects are created and destroyed when the call terminates.

Here, we illustrate the use of a `Singleton` object:

```
<wellknown mode="Singleton"
           type="Order, Order"
           objectUri="Order.soap" />
```

The `type` property tells the remoting runtime which object we are going to be publishing, and is declared in the `<type>, <assembly>` format. Here the `type` property states that we are going to be publishing the `Order` object from the `Order.dll` assembly. In order for this to work properly, the `Order.dll` assembly must be located where the runtime can reach it. We install the `Order.dll` in the same physical directory as the `Server.exe`. Notice that the assembly's `.dll` extension is not appended.

The `objectUri` property is the identifier for which our object will be published. Since multiple objects can be called over the same channel and port, we must give each object a specific identifier to distinguish it from others. We give it the `.soap` extension to make it clear that this object is going to use the SOAP formatter. Since the SOAP formatter is the default formatter for the HTTP channel, we do not need to specify a formatter in this configuration file.

Now that we have the server compiled and the configuration file in place, we can execute `Server.exe` from a command prompt and the server will be ready to accept incoming requests. Here is an example of what the server process will look like when it begins execution.

.NET Middle Tier

```
Command Prompt - Server
C:\Scalability\Chapter 4\Remoting>Server
ServerHost.Main(): Server Started
Server is running. Press <return> to exit.
```

Creating the Client

Now that the server is established, we need to create the client. Creating the `Order` object is the same process as creating a local object, except that the remoting runtime will intercept the object creation call and return a proxy object that the client will actually use. From the development standpoint, the developer can treat the proxy object in the same fashion as a normal object instance:

```
'****************************************************************
' Client.vb
' Client uses the 'Order' object as specified in 'client.exe.config'
'
' Compile with:
' vbc /r:Order.dll Client.vb
'****************************************************************
Imports System
Imports System.Runtime.Remoting

Module Test
  Sub Main()
    Console.WriteLine("Client.Main() created at " & _
                    DateTime.Now.ToLongTimeString() & " on " & _
                    Environment.MachineName)

    RemotingConfiguration.Configure("client.exe.config")
    Dim o As New Order()    ' Created as proxy

    Console.WriteLine(o.GetMachineName)
    Console.WriteLine("Total cost: " & o.CalculateItem(22.32, 2))
  End Sub
End Module
```

In order to compile this application, we must reference the remoting runtime object and the `Order.dll`. It may seem odd that we need to reference the `Order.dll` since the object is ultimately executing on the server. The client needs the metadata from the remoting object to be able to call into the server object. Without the metadata, the compiler and runtime have no idea what the remoting object looks like. We could retrieve the metadata from the `soapsuds.exe` tool as well. For brevity we will keep an instance of `Order.dll` on our client. For more information on metadata issues, refer to the .NET SDK documentation for the `soapsuds.exe` command-line tool. The command line to compile the application is:

```
> vbc /r:Order.dll Client.vb
```

191

Chapter 4: The Middle Tier

Our application simply prints out the current time and machine name so we can compare the values of our client application to those returned by the server application.

In the same fashion as on the server, the client implements a configuration file to retrieve its remoting object configuration. The file is called `client.exe.config` and is kept in the same directory as our client application:

```
<configuration>
  <system.runtime.remoting>
    <application>
      <client>
        <wellknown type="Order, Order"
                   url="http://ServerName:8080/Order.soap" />
      </client>
    </application>
  </system.runtime.remoting>
</configuration>
```

Now that we have the server running and the client built, we can start the client application. The client application will produce the following output (execution time and server names will vary). Note that the server machine this example was named DOTNET and the client was named BOSTON.

```
C:\Scalability\Chapter 4\Remoting>client
Client.Main() created at 19:12:37 on BOSTON
Order object created at: 19:12:38 on DOTNET
Total cost: 24.9984

C:\Scalability\Chapter 4\Remoting>client
Client.Main() created at 19:12:45 on BOSTON
Order object created at: 19:12:38 on DOTNET
Total cost: 24.9984

C:\Scalability\Chapter 4\Remoting>
```

We executed the client twice to illustrate the fact that the same `Singleton` object is being used for both requests. Notice that the client execution time was 8 seconds apart and the `Order` object creation time remained the same. This illustrates that the same `Order` object is being used for both client requests.

The most interesting point about the results is the fact that we have achieved inter-process communication in very little development time. The `Order` object is created and executed within the server process, while our client application runs within a process on our client machine. The entire process of formatting, sending, receiving, and deformatting the message is completely handled by the remoting runtime.

Within our server application, we wrote a line to the console when the methods were executed. To verify that the server process was executing, we look at the console output from our server application.

```
Command Prompt - Server
C:\Scalability\Chapter 4\Remoting>Server
ServerHost.Main(): Server Started
Server is running. Press <return> to exit.
Order.GetMachineName() called
Order.CalculateItem() called
Order.GetMachineName() called
Order.CalculateItem() called
```

This example just begins to scratch the surface of remoting. For a more detailed description of remoting, refer to *Visual Basic .NET Remoting Handbook*, ISBN 1-86100-740-X.

Remoting and the Middle Tier

Remoting is powerful since the framework handles the vast majority of the work required to make inter-process communication happen. When exposing our middle tier, we need to determine just how to expose our object model via remoting for the best scalability.

If we were creating our middle tier, we could expose one or some of our middle-tier objects directly to the remoting framework. In a `MarshalByRefObject` scenario, this means we need to derive from `System.MarshalByRefObject`, effectively killing our ability to derive the object from a different base class.

A more flexible approach would be to create a remoting object capable of calling into our middle tier object model and returning the results over the wire. In effect, we would wrap our middle tier object model with a dedicated remoting object. This would allow us to develop our middle tier independently of the remoting framework, which allows us to concentrate on the logic when developing the middle tier, not how the object will be exposed via remoting (or web services).

Web Services

When web services were introduced, they generated a great deal of popular press and industry buzz. Web services were exciting because they promised to deliver what proprietary RPC mechanisms like DCOM couldn't: standardized protocols and data formats.

Web services are very similar to implementing a remoting object using the HTTP channel and SOAP formatter. Both the HTTP and SOAP protocols/specifications are ubiquitous and implemented in a wide variety of platforms. As long as the middleware running has implemented a web server or custom listener to listen for HTTP requests and has facilities for reading and writing SOAP messages, it has the ability to communicate via web services. The vast majority of the major development platforms including the various .NET and Java platforms have ample facilities available for communicating via web services.

Web Services Defined

There is a great deal of misinformation in circulation around what defines a web service. There are lofty claims being promoted of how web services are poised to revolutionize the computing industry. While there is no doubt that web services have the potential to drastically change the way systems interact, we must understand what web services are and how they propose to make life easy for developers before we make lofty claims and read the glossy marketing sheets.

On the surface, a web service is an API that is accessible over HTTP via a HTTP GET, HTTP POST, or SOAP message. Applications that know the interface of the API can invoke it via one of these methods. The most straightforward web service interaction is the HTTP GET.

Despite the hype around web services, implementing a web service is trivial. In fact, we could implement a web service with a traditional ASP page. All we would need to do is specify the input parameters and their format and return the data in a specified format (perhaps a comma-delimited string). For example, assume we create an ASP page that accepts the stock ticker we would like to invoke as a parameter. To invoke the service, a client would issue the HTTP GET request with the following URL and wait for the response:

```
http://services.company.com/getstockquote.asp?ticker=ABC
```

The service would process the request and perhaps return the following data:

```
ABC,44.02,42.02
```

The client would accept the results, parse the necessary information, and continue processing. In order to read the information, the client must understand the API exposed by the service. This particular service might return the ticker sent in, the current price, and the last day's closing price, which allows the client to determine the performance for the current day.

While this is a fully functioning web service, we can see the potential for a much richer interaction between the client and server. For example, perhaps the client would like to send us a set of product ID's they would like priced. Our middle-tier web service accepts the request and returns to them a complete XML representation of the possible purchase order.

In order to provide the rich interaction between the client and server, the following must happen:

- The server must establish an API for the client to understand
- The client must send data to the web service in a format it expects
- The data must be encoded in a format that both sides, regardless of what development framework they execute on, can manipulate

Figure 7 illustrates the interaction between the various parts of a web service:

Figure 7.

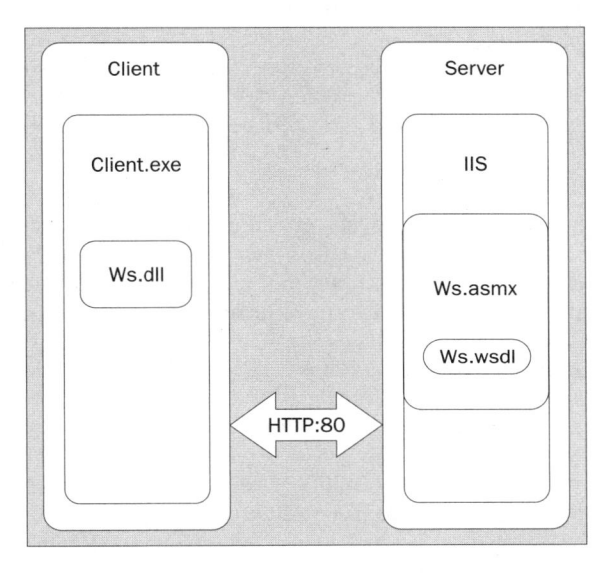

[Diagram showing Client side with Client.exe containing Ws.dll, connected via HTTP:80 to Server side with IIS containing Ws.asmx and Ws.wsdl]

From the server perspective, a web service is created within the IIS process. The server exposes the WSDL contract that the client reads to understand what methods are exposed by the web service. On the client side, the client consumes the WSDL contract. In the context of this diagram, the WSDL functions are compiled into a DLL that the `client.exe` application uses to make the calls to the web service. Let's take a look at the pieces of the web service in detail.

Web Services Description Language

In order for a client to invoke a web service, it must understand that web service's interface. It needs to know what parameters to send to the function and what it can expect in return. In order to make this happen, the web service developer might write a document or specification and hand it to the client's developer. The client developer can then implement the web service.

However, this type of interaction is resource intensive and not productive. What happens when additional web services are published or we want to version the application? The web service and client developer must interact to communicate the changes. Also, if multiple companies are exposing web services they may all choose to communicate or document their services differently, causing confusion.

What is needed is a standard description language for web services. To solve this problem, the W3C introduced the Web Services Description Language (WSDL) that defines a standard grammar for describing web services.

195

Chapter 4: The Middle Tier

Advanced tools like Visual Studio .NET and the .NET Framework allow WSDL to be automatically generated. When we develop our simple web service, we will briefly examine the structure of the WSDL created to illustrate how the built-in tools can facilitate writing the WSDL without any code being written by us.

WSDL can also be read by IDE's to give developer-friendly features such as IntelliSense to provide a more user friendly interface when developing. In the background, the IDE has a copy of the WSDL document and can produce the IntelliSense based on that WSDL.

Simple Object Access Protocol

In order to invoke a web service, the web service must be able to understand the format of the incoming message. In DCOM or Java's RMI protocols, the data transfer formats were different. A DCOM client could not talk to a Java RMI server or vice versa because they couldn't understand how to transfer messages between each other.

The Simple Object Access Protocol (SOAP) is a defined data description standard that clients and servers agree upon to transfer data. With the industry agreeing on the standard, SOAP messages can be sent to any SOAP listener and can be processed.

What does a SOAP message actually look like? Let's assume our web service client exposes an Add() method responsible for adding two integers:

```
Public Function Add(Num1 as integer, Num2 as integer)
    Add = Num1 + Num2
End Function
```

In order for the client to invoke the web service, it would require a message to be passed to the server in a similar form to the following:

```
<Add>
  <Num1>100</Num1>
  <Num2>400</Num2>
</Add>
```

This message is no different from any other XML string that can be passed into the server. In order for the server to understand that the message is meant to be processed as a SOAP message, we must provide more information to the SOAP server in order for the server to understand our intensions. For example, how do we know which object's Add() method to call? How does the SOAP listener know the message coming in is a SOAP message meant to be handled? How do we know what data type 100 and 400 are? String or integer? In order to provide more information to the SOAP listener, the client sends well formed SOAP messages such as the following:

```
<SOAP:Envelope xmlns:SOAP="http://schemas.xmlsoap.org/soap/envelope/"
    SOAP:encodingStyle="http://schemas.xmlsoap.org/soap/encoding/"
    xmlns:xsi="http://www.w3.org/2001/XMLSchema-instance"
```

.NET Middle Tier

```
      xmlns:xsd="http://www.w3.org/2001/XMLSchema">
  <SOAP:Body>
    <m:Add xmlns:m="http://services.company.com/">
      <Num1 xsi:type="xsd:int">100</Num1>
      <Num2 xsi:type="xsd:int">400</Num2>
    </m:Add>
  </SOAP:Body>
</SOAP:Envelope>
```

This message tells the SOAP listener that a SOAP envelope (or message) is being sent in. The additional namespaces are used to further document the `Add()` call for the SOAP listener.

Now that we have a standard format defined for data transfer, the next task we need to do is package and unpackage the SOAP calls. Fortunately the .NET Framework handles packaging the SOAP message and transferring it from the client to the server.

XML

In order for SOAP and web services to work, the format of SOAP and the tools for parsing the messages must be built on a set of standards. SOAP, as you can tell by the previous message, is XML-based and is capable of being parsed by a number of XML parsers available.

One of the notorious shortcomings of XML is its size. XML, with its verbose syntax is very bloated. Receiving an XML message, parsing it into an object model, and reading the data is by no means a trivial task. It is expensive when compared to using remoting's binary formatter where the data is more compact.

However, what web services lack in efficiency, they more than make up for by being flexible. By implementing the XML standard for data description, we are able to access it via any client that is capable of sending and receiving XML.

Web Service Example

Web services have the ability to provide an external, industry-standard programmatic interface for clients located within or outside the company. Designing a web service's interface is a matter of creating the interface required to access the underlying middle tier object model.

Web service's interfaces should be separated from the actual middle-tier object model. The interface exposed for the web service will most likely look quite different from the middle-tier object model used by the client applications. Since web services are rather time consuming to call, especially from distributed networks, our interfaces should be compact and provide as much functionality as possible without the client needing to issue multiple calls.

197

Chapter 4: The Middle Tier

Implementing web services in the .NET Framework is trivial, so the challenge from a design perspective is to determine the set of middle-tier functionality that needs to be exposed and how it should be exposed. Let's take a look at a simple example to illustrate the simplicity involved in creating web services with .NET.

Creating the Web Service

Web services are exposed via IIS and are created as files with .asmx extensions. The IIS runtime maps the .asmx extension for the ASP.NET application to the aspnet_isapi.dll, which is responsible for handling the web service request. In our example, we will create a virtual directory in IIS called webservice to host our service.

Creating a simple web service is similar to creating a class. The difference between a class and a web service is that the web service methods must be attributed with the WebServiceAttribute. WebServiceAttribute tells the runtime to expose this method as part of the service. Without the attribute, the method will not be exposed.

Sticking with the same class for simplicity, we create an .asmx file to expose the Order class. The WebService directive tells the framework to expose the class as a web service. Deriving our object from WebService is optional and gives our class access to the intrinsic ASP.NET object model, including the Application and Session objects:

```vb
<%@ WebService Language="VB" Class="Order" %>
Imports System
Imports System.Web.Services

Public Class Order
   Inherits WebService

   'Returns Machine name where object is executing
   <WebMethod()> Public Function GetMachineName() As String

      Console.WriteLine("Order.GetMachineName() called")
      GetMachineName = "Order object created on: " & _
                        Environment.MachineName
   End Function

   <WebMethod() >Public Function CalculateItem(ByVal Cost As Single, _
      ByVal TaxCode As Integer) As Single

      Console.WriteLine("Order.CalculateItem() called")
      Select Case TaxCode
         Case 0
            CalculateItem = Cost
         Case 1
            CalculateItem = Cost * 1.06
         Case 2
            CalculateItem = Cost * 1.12
      End Select
   End Function
End Class
```

.NET Middle Tier

Like ASP.NET pages, the ASP.NET runtime will automatically compile the web service with the first request. Subsequent requests for the service use the compiled object.

To test the web service, we point our browser to the service and see the default .NET help page describing the service.

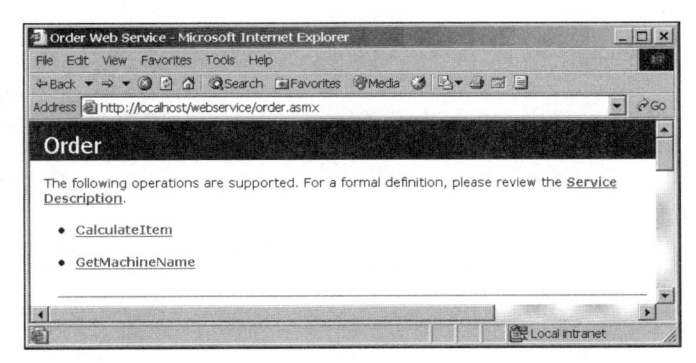

By clicking on the CalculateItem link, we can test the method.

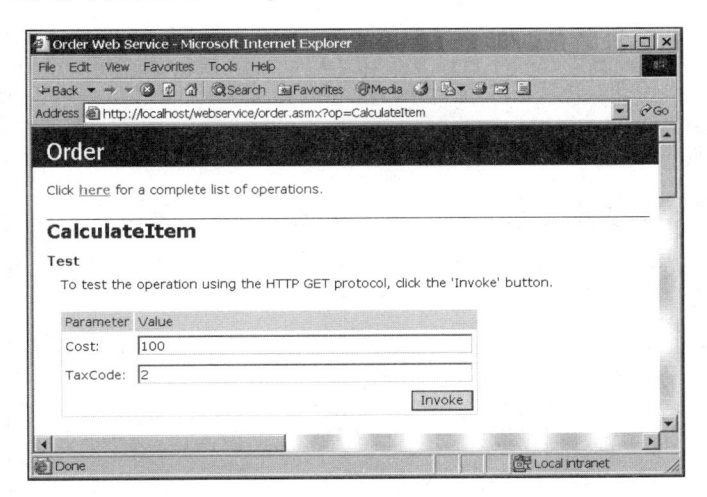

When we click the Invoke button, we can examine the response from the service. Notice that the response is passed back in well formed XML format.

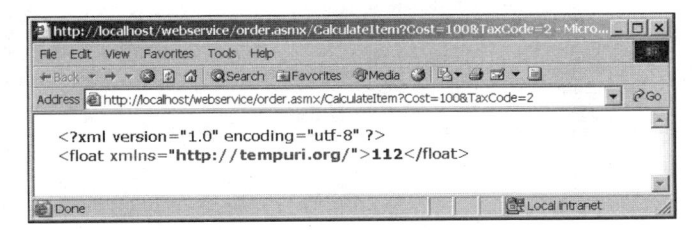

Chapter 4: The Middle Tier

Creating the Client

The browser interface is useful for testing purposes only and is nice because it allows us to test the web service using the HTTP GET only. In order to invoke the service programmatically using SOAP, we need to create a client capable of invoking the web service.

In a similar fashion to how a remoting client needs metadata to use the server's object, a web services client must also obtain the service's metadata. In the remoting example, we could take for granted that the client application could have the entire `Order.dll` assembly copied into the client application. In the remoting example, the client could have been executing on a web server. In this case, the client is physically within the same environment.

With web services, we cannot afford, nor would we want, to distribute the object assembly to each client. Web services are exposed over the web, so anyone connected to the Internet could potentially invoke the service. Sending every possible customer a copy of the assembly would be expensive and allow the assembly holder to read the contents of the assembly with an IL disassembler.

When a service is published, the WSDL service description file is created automatically by the .NET runtime. We can browse the WSDL by invoking our service with the `WSDL` querystring parameter. This indicates that we would like to view the WSDL description file. The following screenshot shows the first portion of the WSDL file. The WSDL file is XML-compliant and follows the standards of the WSDL specification.

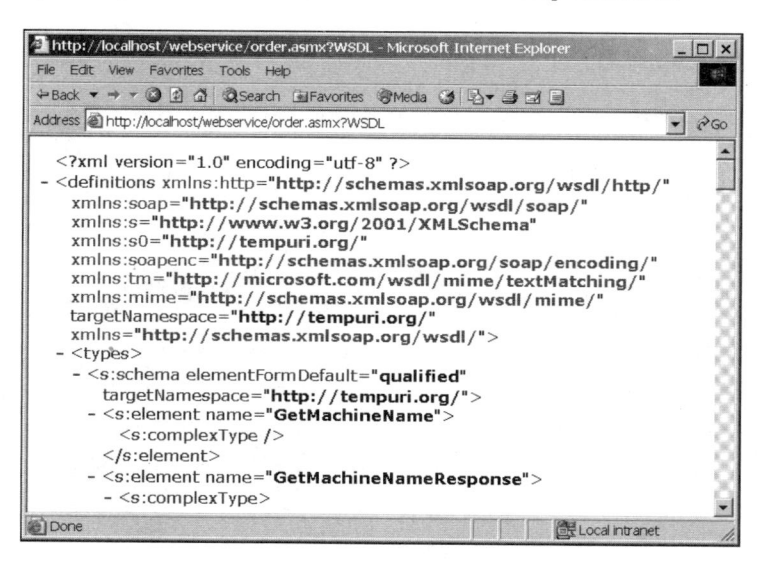

```xml
<?xml version="1.0" encoding="utf-8" ?>
- <definitions xmlns:http="http://schemas.xmlsoap.org/wsdl/http/"
    xmlns:soap="http://schemas.xmlsoap.org/wsdl/soap/"
    xmlns:s="http://www.w3.org/2001/XMLSchema"
    xmlns:s0="http://tempuri.org/"
    xmlns:soapenc="http://schemas.xmlsoap.org/soap/encoding/"
    xmlns:tm="http://microsoft.com/wsdl/mime/textMatching/"
    xmlns:mime="http://schemas.xmlsoap.org/wsdl/mime/"
    targetNamespace="http://tempuri.org/"
    xmlns="http://schemas.xmlsoap.org/wsdl/">
  - <types>
    - <s:schema elementFormDefault="qualified"
        targetNamespace="http://tempuri.org/">
      - <s:element name="GetMachineName">
          <s:complexType />
        </s:element>
      - <s:element name="GetMachineNameResponse">
        - <s:complexType>
```

200

In order to consume the service, we must have the ability to invoke it. The .NET Framework includes a command-line tool to automatically generate a proxy class derived from the WSDL file. The `wsdl.exe` tool generates proxy classes for the web methods exposed on the web service. The proxy class is similar to the actual class, except all calls made to the proxy class are relayed to the web service. Once we have the proxy class, we can compile our code with the proxy class included.

In order to create the proxy class, we invoke `wsdl.exe` with the following command line (all one line):

```
> wsdl /language:vb /namespace:OrderService
  http://ServerName/webservice/order.asmx
```

The `wsdl.exe` tool will create the proxy object in a file named `Order.vb` by default unless we specify a different name using the `/out:` switch. We specify we want the class output to be in Visual Basic .NET and the namespace of the class to be `OrderService`.

Once we have the proxy object, we will compile it into a `.dll` file independently of our client application, which allows us to reuse the `.dll` in other client applications. Compiling the proxy into its own `.dll` file requires the following command line:

```
> vbc /t:library /r:System.dll,System.xml.dll,System.Web.Services.dll
  order.vb
```

Now that we have the proxy objects created, we are able to create the actual client application, `Client.vb`:

```vb
'****************************************************************
' Client.vb
' Used to invoke the Order web service.
'
' Compile with
' vbc /r:Order.dll,System.dll,System.Web.Services.dll Client.vb
'****************************************************************
Imports System
Imports OrderService

Module TestClient
  Sub Main()
    Dim _order As New Order
    Console.WriteLine("Order client started")
    Console.WriteLine(_order.GetMachineName())
    Console.WriteLine(_order.CalculateItem(90.21, 2))
    Console.WriteLine("Order client finished")
  End Sub
End Module
```

The `OrderService` namespace was imported because that is the namespace we specified when creating the proxy object. Once we have the proxy object, we can treat the object as if it were local to our application. As far as our code is concerned, we need to know nothing of where the `Order` object is created.

Compile the client with the following command line:

```
> vbc /r:Order.dll,System.dll,System.Web.Services.dll Client.vb
```

Running the client shows us that the `Order` object is invoked and the methods are executed from the web service.

```
C:\Scalability\Chapter 4\WSClient>Client
Order client started
Order object created on: MANNING1
101.0352
Order client finished

C:\Scalability\Chapter 4\WSClient>
```

Web Services and the Middle Tier

Web services, in their basic form, are very similar to remoting objects using the SOAP formatter and the HTTP channel. The .NET Framework allows us to publish web services dynamically by creating .asmx pages and classes optionally inheriting from `System.Web.Services.WebService`. We need no special configuration and the compilation of the service is provided to us automatically by the ASP.NET runtime.

In the remoting section, we said that developing the middle tier apart from the remoting objects allowed us to reuse functionality. The same case holds true for web services. Having a logically separated middle-tier object model allows us to create web service interfaces that use the object model's functionality. Had we created the object model to expose itself via remoting and inheriting from `MarshalByRefObject`, we could not create a service with the same class inheriting from `System.Web.Services.WebService`.

Logically separating the object model from the remoting and web services interfaces allows us to reuse the object model in both remoting and web service scenarios, as well as any other front end we would like to use on top of the object model. Ultimately, the web service is another user interface on top of our middle-tier object model. What separates the web service user interface from the more traditional user interfaces, such as ASP.NET and Winforms, is that the interface is programmatic rather than graphical.

Web services allow us to expose our object model to any client capable of invoking web services. Since web service support is included in many popular development environments, web services allow us to expose our logic to a wide range of clients running code on diverse platforms.

Additional Web Services Concerns

Many of the concerns around web services have not been addressed in this simple example. Of the highest priority is security. Since web services are hosted in IIS, we can require the users of the service authenticate with IIS before having the ability to invoke our service.

This example is the most basic introduction to web services available and is meant to provide only a cursory overview to illustrate the potential for using web services for cross process communication and method invocation at the middle-tier layer. Web services are still an infant technology capable of growing immensely. For additional information on web service development, refer to *Professional ASP.NET 1.0 Web Services with VB.NET*, ISBN 1-86100-775-2.

MyInvestmentWatch.com Middle Tier

We have taken a look into the fundamentals associated with creating a middle tier and some of the exciting advances .NET makes over its predecessors for taking advantage of cross-process communication. The groundwork has been laid for creating a middle tier; however, no logic has been written.

The following will illustrate a sample implementation of a middle tier for our continuing application, MyInvestmentWatch.com. Our design goal was to make the chapter as independent from the other chapters as possible; however, it builds on the DAL developed in Chapter 3 and assumes you have a reference to the code when compiling the middle-tier application.

Determining the Middle-Tier Environment

The most important determination to make before beginning our middle tier is to determine the UIs that could potentially interact with our middle-tier system. From the client perspective, we have an ASP.NET front end that will be responsible for the vast majority of the usage. We may also have a Windows forms administrative client for the staff to enter news and stock quote updates. In order to get our stock quotes updated, we may have an interface that is responsible for communicating with the stock exchange. This application will most likely act as a link between our database and the stock exchange and not require much logic from our middle tier. If all the systems are implemented, the application would have the physical architecture shown in Figure 8.

Figure 8.

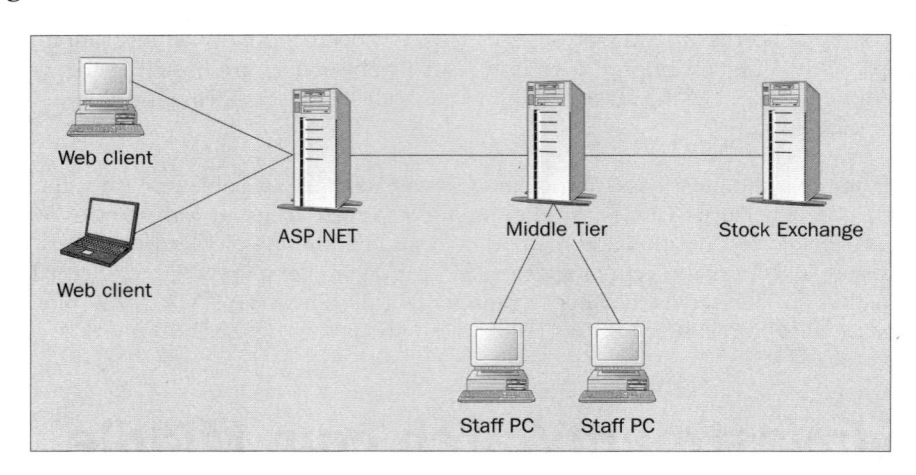

In order to limit scope of the example, we are going to focus on creating the middle tier solely for the ASP.NET front-end application. We will pay particular attention to creating the objects necessary for providing the middle-tier logic.

Since we are creating our middle tier for an ASP.NET front end, we will not be able to recognize many of the benefits of creating a physical middle tier. For example, if we had multiple clients interacting with the middle tier, we could benefit from caching and connection pooling within the physical middle tier. Since we have only the ASP.NET client, we can maintain these benefits by caching and using object pooling within the ASP.NET process. The performance improvements associated with having the middle tier execute locally are more beneficial to the application than having a separate physical middle tier.

Even though we are foregoing the physical middle tier, we retain scalability benefits in the ASP.NET tier. If the application needs scalability, more resources can be implemented at the ASP.NET tier to provide scaling.

With our logical middle-tier design, one of our goals is to recognize that at some point the application will benefit from a physical middle tier. At that point, having a design that can be used from within a remoting object or web service would be important to avoid logic redesign.

Our application will have the physical architecture shown in Figure 9:

Figure 9.

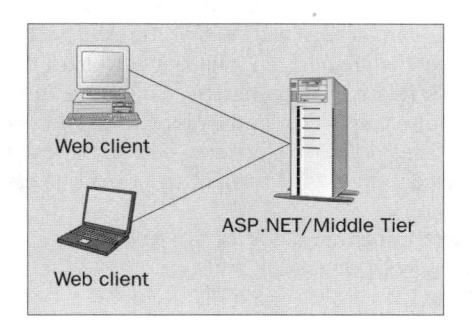

Creating the Object Model

Now that we have the architecture completed, we can design the middle-tier object model. Our object model has the following hierarchy and will be explained in detail shortly. The object model represents a user object model capable of retrieving and saving data related to the user.

Figure 10.

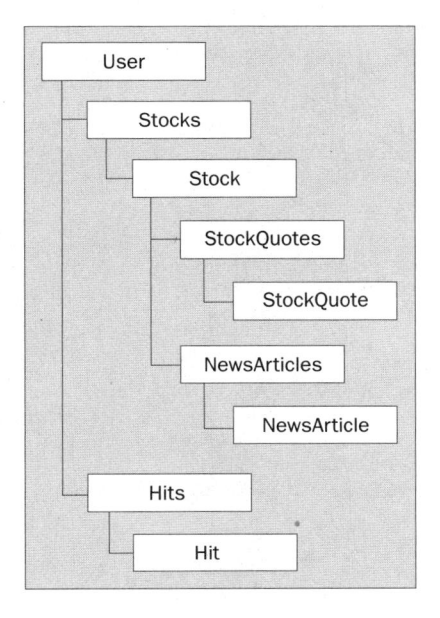

Chapter 4: The Middle Tier

The object model is typical of OO designed object models. We implement strongly-typed collection objects to hold each of our individual object instances. The root of the object model, `User`, is the main object with which the ASP.NET application will interact. When a `User` object is created, we will begin to load the rest of the object model. Some objects, those related to companies, can be created directly by ASP.NET. `NewsArticles`, for example, can be created as long as we know the company ID for which to retrieve news articles. Other collections, like `Hits`, can't be created from outside the object model since they require a valid `User` object be created to validate the user.

Now let's take a look at the implementation of the objects by looking at the model from the top down, starting with `User`.

User

The `User` object provides functionality for users of the system to log in and provides access to the underlying `Hits` and `Stocks` collection that the user has entered into their profile:

```vb
'**************************************************
' User.vb
'**************************************************
Imports System
Imports com.myinvestmentwatch.data

Namespace com.myinvestmentwatch.middle
  Public Class User

    'OK to leave _userPersist open throughout object lifetime.
    Private _userID As Integer
    Private _name As String
    Private _login As String
    Private _password As String
    Private _userPersist As IUserPersist
    Private _preferredStocks As Stocks
    Private _hits As Hits

    'Object control variables
    Private _childrenLoaded As Boolean
    Private _isDirty As Boolean

    'User cannot set UserID
    Public ReadOnly Property UserID() As Integer
      Get
        UserID = _userID
      End Get
    End Property

    'Password can be set only.
    '(Improvement: require previous password for verification)
```

206

```vb
Public WriteOnly Property Password() As String
  Set(ByVal Value As String)
    _password = Value
    _isDirty = True
  End Set
End Property

Public Property Name() As String
  Get
    Name = _name
  End Get
  Set(ByVal Value As String)
    _name = Value
    _isDirty = True
  End Set
End Property

Public Property Login() As String
  Get
    Login = _login
  End Get
  Set(ByVal Value As String)
    _login = Value
    _isDirty = True
  End Set
End Property

Public ReadOnly Property PreferredStocks() As Stocks
  Get
    If Not _childrenLoaded Then LoadChildren()
    PreferredStocks = _preferredStocks
  End Get
End Property

Public ReadOnly Property Hits() As Hits
  Get
    If Not _childrenLoaded Then LoadChildren()
    Hits = _hits
  End Get
End Property

'To Create a new User
Public Shared Sub CreateNew(ByVal Login As String, _
                            ByVal Password As String, _
                            ByVal Name As String)

  Dim persistFactory As IPersistFactory = New SQLPersistFactory()
  Dim uPersist As IUserPersist = persistFactory.GetUserPersist()
  uPersist.AddUser(Name, Login, Password)
End Sub
```

Chapter 4: The Middle Tier

```vb
          'LoadAll = true will automatically create children.
          Public Sub New(ByVal Login As String, _
                        ByVal Password As String, _
                        ByVal LoadAll As Boolean)

             Dim persistFactory As IPersistFactory = New SQLPersistFactory()
             _userPersist = persistFactory.GetUserPersist()
             'Fails if Login does not exist
             _userPersist.GetUser(Login, _userID, _name, _password)
             If Password <> _password Then
                Throw New ArgumentException("Password is not valid")
             End If
             _login = Login
             If LoadAll Then LoadChildren()
          End Sub

          Public Sub Save(ByVal WithChildren As Boolean)
             If _isDirty Then
                _userPersist.UpdateUser(_userID, _name, _login, _password)
                _isDirty = False
             End If
             If WithChildren Then
                _preferredStocks.Save()
             End If
          End Sub

          Public Shared Sub DeleteUser(ByVal UserID As Integer)
             Dim persistFactory As IPersistFactory = New SQLPersistFactory()
             Dim userPersist As IUserPersist = _
                 persistFactory.GetUserPersist()
             userPersist.DeleteUser(UserID)
          End Sub

          Private Sub LoadChildren()
             If Not _childrenLoaded Then
                _preferredStocks = New Stocks(_userID)
                _hits = New Hits(_userID)
                _childrenLoaded = True
             End If
          End Sub
       End Class
    End Namespace
```

The implementation of User is interesting because we have provided a few performance improvements that will help our application become more scalable. In particular, the User object has implemented a technique called **lazy loading**. Lazy loading is a technique that is used to defer state creation until absolutely necessary. In the User object, we don't want to load the PreferredStocks or Hits objects until they are requested. We could have also loaded the Hits and PreferredStocks objects independently of each other to further lazy-load the data.

The constructor implements a `LoadAll` parameter that when `False` defers loading the child objects until they are first requested. Lazy loading is best used when objects are expensive to create, not needed during initial creation, or are seldom used.

It's also interesting to note that the `User` object keeps an instance of `IUserPersist` open for the lifetime of the object. Since the DAL is stateless, only an object pointer is kept open while the object is alive. There are no database connections or expensive resources being held open, meaning there is no performance hit when keeping the `IUserPersist` reference alive for the entire object lifetime.

Stocks

When users add, update, or delete stocks from their personal list, our application internally uses the `Stocks` collection. The `Stocks` collection allows the UI to retrieve information about a particular company, search through the user's collection for a given stock, or add, delete, update, and retrieve `Stock` objects for the user.

The `Stocks` object represents our first look into a strongly-typed collection object. The purpose of a strongly-typed collection is to provide a container object for child objects of a specific type. In case of `Stocks`, the type being held is the `Stock` object:

```vb
'***********************************************
' Stocks.vb
'***********************************************
Imports System
Imports System.Data
Imports System.Collections
Imports com.myinvestmentwatch.data

Namespace com.myinvestmentwatch.middle

    Public Class Stocks
        Inherits CollectionBase
        'Based off CompID
        Private _userID As Integer
        Private _stockPersist As IStockPersist

        Public Shared Function GetStock(ByVal CompID As Integer) As Stock
            GetStock = New Stock(CompID)
        End Function

        Public Shared Function GetStock(ByVal Ticker As String) As Stock
            Dim _sharedFactory As IPersistFactory = New SQLPersistFactory()
            Dim _sharedPersist As IStockPersist = _
                _sharedFactory.GetStocksPersist()
            GetStock = New Stock(_sharedPersist.GetCompID(Ticker))
        End Function
```

```vb
Public Function Add(ByVal CompID As Integer) As Stock
  If Contains(CompID) Then
    Throw New ArgumentException("Company " & CompID & _
                                " already exists")
  End If
  Dim s As Stock
  s = New Stock(_userID, CompID)
  InnerList.Add(s)
  Add = s
End Function

Public Shadows Sub Clear()
  Dim s As Stock
  For Each s In Me.List
    s.Delete()
  Next
End Sub

Public Function Contains(ByVal CompID As Integer) As Boolean
  Dim s As Stock
  For Each s In List
    If s.CompID = CompID Then Return True
  Next
  Return False
End Function

Public Function Contains(ByVal Ticker As String) As Boolean
  Dim s As Stock
  For Each s In List
    If s.Ticker.Trim.ToUpper() = Ticker.Trim().ToUpper() Then
      Return True
    End If
  Next
  Return False
End Function

Default Public ReadOnly Property Item(ByVal CompID As Integer) _
        As Stock
  Get
    Item = CType(InnerList.Item(IndexOf(CompID)), Stock)
  End Get
End Property

Public ReadOnly Property IndexOf(ByVal CompID As Integer) _
        As Integer
  Get
    Dim i As Integer
    If Not Contains(CompID) Then
      Throw New ArgumentException("Company " & CompID & _
                                  " does not exist")
    End If
```

```vb
      For i = 0 To List.Count - 1
        If CType(InnerList(i), Stock).CompID = CompID Then Return i
      Next
    End Get
  End Property

  'If compID does not exist, exit silently
  Public Sub Remove(ByVal CompID As Integer)
    If Contains(CompID) Then
      RemoveAt(IndexOf(CompID))
    End If
  End Sub

  Public Shadows Sub RemoveAt(ByVal Index As Integer)
    If Index >= 0 And Index < InnerList.Count Then
      If CType(InnerList.Item(Index), Stock).IsNew Then
        InnerList.RemoveAt(Index)
      Else
        CType(InnerList.Item(Index), Stock).Delete()
      End If
    End If
  End Sub

  Sub New(ByVal UserID As Integer)
    Dim persistFactory As IPersistFactory = New SQLPersistFactory()
    Dim dr As DataRow
    _stockPersist = persistFactory.GetStocksPersist()
    Dim stocks As DataSet = _stockPersist.GetStocks(UserID)
    For Each dr In stocks.Tables(0).Rows
      InnerList.Add(New Stock(dr("UserID"), dr("CompID"), _
                    dr("DateAdded"), dr("InitialPrice"), _
                    dr("Shares"), dr("Ticker")))
    Next
    _userID = UserID
  End Sub

  Public Sub Save()
    Dim i As Integer
    Dim s As Stock
    For i = InnerList.Count - 1 To 0 Step -1
      s = CType(InnerList.Item(i), Stock)
      If s.IsDeleted Then
        _stockPersist.DeleteStock(s.UserID, s.CompID)
        InnerList.RemoveAt(IndexOf(s.CompID))
      ElseIf s.IsNew Then
        _stockPersist.AddStock(s.UserID, s.CompID, _
                               s.InitialPrice, s.Shares)
        s.IsNew = False
        s.IsDirty = False
      ElseIf s.IsDirty Then
```

Chapter 4: The Middle Tier

```
            _stockPersist.UpdateStock(s.UserID, s.CompID, _
                                  s.InitialPrice, s.Shares)
          s.IsDirty = False
       End If
    Next
  End Sub
 End Class
End Namespace
```

We use the .NET Framework's `CollectionBase` class as our collection's base class. `CollectionBase` provides a default set of methods and is meant to be inherited from to create strongly-typed collections. Of important note, the underlying data structure of `CollectionBase` is the `ArrayList` object. `ArrayList` is a managed version of a C-like array. The `ArrayList` object allows you to add objects to or remove objects from the list. If objects are added to the list and the number of elements exceeds the internal capacity of the `ArrayList`, the `ArrayList` will increase the size and reallocate the variables to the increased array list.

For our objects, the collection size will remain small (under 20 elements). If the collection was to become large, we would want to set the `Capacity` property on the `ArrayList` object to the default size to avoid the expensive reallocation.

Another point of concern is the search algorithm code found in the `IndexOf` property:

```
        Public ReadOnly Property IndexOf(ByVal CompID As Integer) _
                As Integer
          Get
            Dim i As Integer
            If Not Contains(CompID) Then
              Throw New ArgumentException("Company " & CompID & _
                                   " does not exist")
            End If
            For i = 0 To List.Count - 1
              If CType(InnerList(i), Stock).CompID = CompID Then Return i
            Next
          End Get
        End Property
```

Notice here that we use a brute force linear search technique to find the element. Since our internal data storage structure is the `ArrayList`, we are limited to retrieving elements by ordinal. In a large collection, the search for the correct index would become grossly inefficient and kill our performance. Implementing a binary tree algorithm or using a pre-built object such as the `Hashtable` would be more efficient. For our small collections the performance will not be drastically affected by using the `ArrayList`.

Benefits of the DAL

It is in the middle tier that we recognize the benefits of the DAL. Notice how simple the persistence code is since we have encapsulated it within the DAL. We need to know nothing about our data store, SQL queries, or stored procedures at this point. We are free to concentrate on implementing the logic of the middle tier.

Looking at the constructor, we see calling the `IUserPersist` object's `GetStocks()` method is all the persistence code needed to retrieve the information:

```
Sub New(ByVal UserID As Integer)
    Dim persistFactory As IPersistFactory = New SQLPersistFactory()
    Dim dr As DataRow
    _stockPersist = persistFactory.GetStocksPersist()
    Dim stocks As DataSet = _stockPersist.GetStocks(UserID)
    For Each dr In stocks.Tables(0).Rows
        InnerList.Add(New Stock(dr("UserID"), dr("CompID"), _
                    dr("DateAdded"), dr("InitialPrice"), _
                    dr("Shares"), dr("Ticker")))
    Next
    _userID = UserID
End Sub
```

Stock

The `Stock` object represents an individual stock within a user portfolio, and allows the user to enter the number of shares owned, the initial price, and the date added. The UI could use this information to present the percentage of raw gain/loss information or simply just present the values to the user.

When the user interacts with their stock profile, we want that user to have the ability to roll back their changes before they commit them. For example, if the user is editing their profile and they delete a stock accidentally, we want to give them the ability to cancel their changes. In order to provide this functionality, we implement state variables that indicate the object's current state. The properties `IsNew`, `IsDirty`, and `IsDeleted` can be set by the collection object when the user makes changes to their stock portfolio. Once the changes have been confirmed, the UI will call the `Stocks` object's `Save()` method and the changes will be applied. The `Stocks` object's `Save()` method uses these state properties to determine what action to take when persisting the object to the data store:

```
'*****************************************************
' Stock.vb
'*****************************************************
Imports System
Imports System.Data
Imports System.Collections
Imports com.myinvestmentwatch.data

Namespace com.myinvestmentwatch.middle
```

213

```
Public Class Stock

  Private _userID As Integer
  Private _compID As Integer
  Private _dateAdded As DateTime
  Private _initialPrice As Single
  Private _shares As Integer
  Private _ticker As String

  Private _stockQuotes As StockQuotes
  Private _newsArticles As NewsArticles

  'Control variables
  Private _isDirty As Boolean
  Private _isDeleted As Boolean
  Private _isNew As Boolean

  Public ReadOnly Property Gain() As Double
    Get
      Gain = _shares * _
             (StockQuotes.LatestQuote.Price - _initialPrice)
    End Get
  End Property

  Public ReadOnly Property UserID() As Integer
    Get
      UserID = _userID
    End Get
  End Property

  Public ReadOnly Property CompID() As Integer
    Get
      CompID = _compID
    End Get
  End Property

  Public ReadOnly Property StockQuotes() As StockQuotes
    Get
      If _stockQuotes Is Nothing Then _stockQuotes = _
          New StockQuotes(_compID)
      StockQuotes = _stockQuotes
    End Get
  End Property

  Public ReadOnly Property NewsArticles() As NewsArticles
    Get
      If _newsArticles Is Nothing Then _newsArticles = _
          New NewsArticles(_compID)
      NewsArticles = _newsArticles
    End Get
  End Property
```

```vb
Public Property DateAdded() As DateTime
  Get
    DateAdded = _dateAdded
  End Get
  Set(ByVal Value As DateTime)
    _dateAdded = Value
    _isDirty = True
  End Set
End Property

Public Property InitialPrice() As Single
  Get
    InitialPrice = _initialPrice
  End Get
  Set(ByVal Value As Single)
    _initialPrice = Value
    _isDirty = True
  End Set
End Property

Public Property Shares() As Integer
  Get
    Shares = _shares
  End Get
  Set(ByVal Value As Integer)
    _shares = Value
    _isDirty = True
  End Set
End Property

Public ReadOnly Property Ticker() As String
  Get
    Dim persistFactory As IPersistFactory = _
        New SQLPersistFactory()
    Dim stockPersist As IStockPersist = _
        persistFactory.GetStocksPersist()
    If _ticker Is Nothing Then
      _ticker = stockPersist.GetTicker(_compID)
    End If
    Ticker = _ticker
  End Get
End Property

Friend Sub Delete()
  _isDeleted = True
End Sub

Friend Property IsDirty() As Boolean
  Get
    IsDirty = _isDirty
  End Get
  Set(ByVal Value As Boolean)
```

Chapter 4: The Middle Tier

```vb
            _isDirty = Value
        End Set
    End Property
    Friend ReadOnly Property IsDeleted() As Boolean
        Get
            IsDeleted = _isDeleted
        End Get
    End Property

    Friend Property IsNew() As Boolean
        Get
            IsNew = _isNew
        End Get
        Set(ByVal Value As Boolean)
            _isNew = Value
        End Set
    End Property

    'Called only when loaded from database
    Friend Sub New(ByVal UserID As Integer, _
                   ByVal CompID As Integer, _
                   ByVal DateAdded As DateTime, _
                   ByVal InitialPrice As Single, _
                   ByVal Shares As Integer, _
                   ByVal Ticker As String)

        Me.New(UserID, CompID)
        _dateAdded = DateAdded
        _initialPrice = InitialPrice
        _shares = Shares
        _ticker = Ticker
        _isNew = False
    End Sub

    Friend Sub New(ByVal UserID As Integer, ByVal CompID As Integer)
        _userID = UserID
        _compID = CompID
        _isNew = True
    End Sub

    Public Sub New(ByVal CompID As Integer)
        _compID = CompID
    End Sub
  End Class
End Namespace
```

Each `Stock` object has child `StockQuotes` and `NewsArticles` collections that correspond to the stock. Both the child collection objects are lazy-loaded when first requested.

From an object creation perspective, we only allow one public constructor accepting a `CompID` parameter. The other constructors that are linked to a user cannot be created publicly (they are declared with `Friend`). In order to create `Stock` objects related to the user, the `User` object must be populated. This technique forces the user interface to create user objects before they can create stock objects. We want all stock object creation to be attached only to the current `User` object. There is no need for the user interface to create `Stock` objects without having an associated `User` object.

StockQuotes

`StockQuotes` is a collection of `StockQuote` objects. Like `Stocks`, `StockQuotes` is a strongly-typed collection. However, since `StockQuote` objects are read only, the implementation of `StockQuotes` is quite simple. Since we only need to allow the UI to read the contents, we do not implement the ability to add, update, or delete `StockQuote` objects:

```vb
'*****************************************************
' StockQuotes.vb
'*****************************************************
Imports System
Imports System.Data
Imports System.Collections
Imports com.myinvestmentwatch.data

Namespace com.myinvestmentwatch.middle

  Public Class StockQuotes
    Inherits ReadOnlyCollectionBase
    'User cannot add/update/delete quotes via object model

    Public ReadOnly Property LatestQuote() As StockQuote
      Get
        If InnerList.Count < 1 Then
          Throw New InvalidOperationException( _
              "There are no quotes available")
        End If
        LatestQuote = CType(InnerList.Item(0), StockQuote)
      End Get
    End Property

    Public Sub New(ByVal CompID As Integer)
      Dim stockQuotesPersist As IStockQuotesPersist

      Dim persistFactory As IPersistFactory = New SQLPersistFactory()
      Dim dr As DataRow
      stockQuotesPersist = persistFactory.GetStockQuotesPersist()
      Dim stocks As DataSet = stockQuotesPersist.GetQuotes(CompID)
      For Each dr In stocks.Tables(0).Rows
        InnerList.Add(New StockQuote(dr("DateRequested"), _
                  dr("Price")))
```

217

Chapter 4: The Middle Tier

```
        Next
    End Sub
  End Class
End Namespace
```

The .NET Framework exposes a ReadOnlyCollectionBase abstract (MustInherit in VB.NET) object tailored to creating read-only collections. By implementing ReadOnlyCollectionBase, we are given a pre-built version of a collection's methods. The only thing we must implement is the custom code that is necessary for our particular collection.

Our class implements a single custom property called LatestQuote, which returns the most current stock price for a given stock. We also implement a custom constructor to retrieve the StockQuote objects from our data store.

StockQuote

StockQuote is a read-only object that simply contains Price and DateRequested properties to determine the price and when the price was retrieved for the StockQuote. Note again that we limit instantiation to the assembly level since we do not want the UI to have the ability to create its own stock prices:

```
'*******************************************************
' StockQuote.vb
'*******************************************************
Imports System
Imports System.Data
Imports System.Collections
Imports com.myinvestmentwatch.data

Namespace com.myinvestmentwatch.middle

  Public Class StockQuote
    Private _dateRequested As DateTime
    Private _price As Single

    Public ReadOnly Property DateRequested() As DateTime
      Get
        DateRequested = _dateRequested
      End Get
    End Property

    Public ReadOnly Property Price() As Single
      Get
        Price = _price
      End Get
    End Property
```

MyInvestmentWatch.com Middle Tier

```
    Friend Sub New(ByVal DateRequested As DateTime, _
                   ByVal Price As Single)
      _dateRequested = DateRequested
      _price = Price
    End Sub
  End Class
End Namespace
```

NewsArticles

Each stock has the ability to have news associated with it. The `Stock` object has a `NewsArticles` collection that contains the news elements for the company. Like `StockQuotes`, `NewsArticles` inherits from `ReadOnlyCollectionBase` which provides much of the default collection functionality. We simply implement a `LatestNews` property to return the latest news headline and an `Add()` method that the UI will call to indicate the news article was viewed:

```
'*****************************************************
' NewsArticles.vb
'*****************************************************
Imports System
Imports System.Data
Imports System.Collections
Imports com.myinvestmentwatch.data

Namespace com.myinvestmentwatch.middle

  Public Class NewsArticles
    Inherits ReadOnlyCollectionBase
    'User cannot add/update/delete quotes via object model
    Private _newsArticlesPersist As INewsPersist

    Public ReadOnly Property LatestNews() As NewsArticle
      Get
        If InnerList.Count < 1 Then
          Throw New InvalidOperationException( _
             "There is no news available")
        End If
        LatestNews = CType(InnerList.Item(0), NewsArticle)
      End Get
    End Property

    Public Sub Add(ByVal NewsID As Integer)
      _newsArticlesPersist.AddNewsTraffic(NewsID)
    End Sub

    Public Sub New(ByVal CompID As Integer)
      Dim persistFactory As IPersistFactory = New SQLPersistFactory()
      Dim dr As DataRow
      _newsArticlesPersist = persistFactory.GetNewsPersist()
```

219

```
            Dim stocks As DataSet = _newsArticlesPersist.GetNews(CompID)
            For Each dr In stocks.Tables(0).Rows
                InnerList.Add(New NewsArticle(dr("NewsID"), dr("CompID"), _
                        dr("Headline"), dr("Url"), dr("Synopsis"), _
                        dr("Article"), dr("DatePosted")))
            Next
        End Sub
    End Class
End Namespace
```

NewsArticle

`NewsArticle` is a read-only object that can only be created by the `NewsArticles` collection. Like `StockQuotes`, we definitely don't want the UI to have the ability to create its own news about a company:

```
'*****************************************************
' NewsArticle.vb
'*****************************************************
Imports System
Imports System.Data
Imports System.Collections
Imports com.myinvestmentwatch.data

Namespace com.myinvestmentwatch.middle

    Public Class NewsArticle
        Private _newsID As Integer
        Private _compID As Integer
        Private _headline As String
        Private _url As String
        Private _synopsis As String
        Private _article As String
        Private _datePosted As DateTime

        Public ReadOnly Property NewsID() As Integer
          Get
             NewsID = _newsID
          End Get
        End Property

        Public ReadOnly Property CompID() As Integer
          Get
             CompID = _compID
          End Get
        End Property

        Public ReadOnly Property HeadLine() As String
          Get
             HeadLine = _headline
```

```
            End Get
        End Property

        Public ReadOnly Property Url() As String
            Get
                Url = _url
            End Get
        End Property

        Public ReadOnly Property Synopsis() As String
            Get
                Synopsis = _synopsis
            End Get
        End Property

        Public ReadOnly Property Article() As String
            Get
                Article = _article
            End Get
        End Property

        Public ReadOnly Property DatePosted() As DateTime
            Get
                DatePosted = _datePosted
            End Get
        End Property

        Friend Sub New(ByVal NewsID As Integer, _
                       ByVal CompID As Integer, _
                       ByVal Headline As String, _
                       ByVal Url As String, _
                       ByVal Synopsis As String, _
                       ByVal Article As String, _
                       ByVal DatePosted As DateTime)

            _newsID = NewsID
            _compID = CompID
            _headline = Headline
            _url = Url
            _synopsis = Synopsis
            _article = Article
            _datePosted = DatePosted
        End Sub
    End Class
End Namespace
```

Hits

When a user asks to retrieve information on a particular company, we want to record their usage. Keeping a history of their activity allows us to personalize a listing of stocks that they have recently viewed. Whenever the user enters a valid stock ticker, for example, we will record that company into their `Hits` object:

```vb
'*****************************************************
' Hits.vb
'*****************************************************
Imports System
Imports System.Data
Imports System.Collections
Imports com.myinvestmentwatch.data

Namespace com.myinvestmentwatch.middle

  Public Class Hits
    Inherits CollectionBase
    'Based off CompID
    Private _userID As Integer
    Private _hitPersist As IHitsPersist

    Public Function Add(ByVal CompID As Integer) As Hit
      Dim h As Hit
      If Not Contains(CompID) Then
        _hitPersist.AddHit(_userID, CompID)
        h = New Hit(_userID, CompID, DateTime.Now)
        InnerList.Insert(0, h)   'insert at front
        Add = h
      Else
        Add = Item(CompID)
      End If
    End Function

    Public Function Contains(ByVal CompID As Integer) As Boolean
      Dim h As Hit
      For Each h In InnerList
        If h.CompID = CompID Then Return True
      Next
      Return False
    End Function

    Default Public ReadOnly Property Item(ByVal CompID As Integer) _
          As Hit
      Get
        Item = CType(InnerList.Item(IndexOf(CompID)), Hit)
      End Get
    End Property

    'Returns first (most current) index of CompID. Same hit
    ' could be entered multiple times.
    Public ReadOnly Property IndexOf(ByVal CompID As Integer) _
          As Integer
      Get
        Dim i As Integer
        If Not Contains(CompID) Then
          Throw New ArgumentException("Company " & CompID & _
                                  " does not exist")
```

```vbnet
            End If
            For i = 0 To InnerList.Count - 1
                If CType(InnerList(i), Hit).CompID = CompID Then Return i
            Next
        End Get
    End Property

    Friend Sub New(ByVal UserID As Integer)
        Dim persistFactory As IPersistFactory = New SQLPersistFactory()
        Dim dr As DataRow
        _hitPersist = persistFactory.GetHitsPersist()
        Dim Hits As DataSet = _hitPersist.GetHits(UserID)
        For Each dr In Hits.Tables(0).Rows
            InnerList.Add(New Hit(dr("UserID"), dr("CompID"), _
                        dr("DateRequested")))
        Next
        _userID = UserID
    End Sub
  End Class
End Namespace
```

The `Hits` object is a strongly-typed collection with very similar functionality to the other strongly-typed collections implemented. The `Hits` object contains an `Add()` method that is responsible for inserting the hit into the database, if it doesn't already exist in the collection. Keeping redundant hits is not necessary.

Hit

The last object in our logical middle tier is the `Hit` object. The `Hit` object is a read-only object used to store the stock request information:

```vbnet
'*******************************************************
' Hit.vb
'*******************************************************
Imports System
Imports System.Data
Imports System.Collections
Imports com.myinvestmentwatch.data

Namespace com.myinvestmentwatch.middle
  Public Class Hit
    Private _userID As Integer
    Private _compID As Integer
    Private _dateRequested As DateTime

    Public ReadOnly Property UserID() As Integer
      Get
        UserID = _userID
      End Get
    End Property
```

```vbnet
        Public ReadOnly Property CompID() As Integer
          Get
            CompID = _compID
          End Get
        End Property

        Public Function GetStock() As Stock
          Return Stocks.GetStock(_compID)
        End Function

        Public ReadOnly Property DateRequested() As DateTime
          Get
            DateRequested = _dateRequested
          End Get
        End Property

        Friend Sub New(ByVal UserID As Integer, _
                       ByVal CompID As Integer, _
                       ByVal DateRequested As DateTime)

          _userID = UserID
          _compID = CompID
          _dateRequested = DateRequested
        End Sub
      End Class
    End Namespace
```

One interesting point about the Hit object is the ability to turn the Hit into an actual Stock object via the GetStock() function. GetStock() converts the Hit into a Stock object, which can then be used to retrieve quote prices and latest news about the company.

Using the Logical Middle Tier

Now that the logical middle-tier object model is created, we can write tests simulating the expected UI code. For our tests, we will first create a User object and add some data to the object model:

```vbnet
    Sub Main()
      Dim _user As New User("test", "test", False)
      'Simulate user querying for stocks
      _user.Hits.Add(2)
      _user.Hits.Add(18)
      _user.Hits.Add(298)

      'Simulate user adding preferred stocks
      Dim stock As Stock = _user.PreferredStocks.Add(2)
      stock.InitialPrice = "32.90"
      stock.Shares = "21"
      stock.DateAdded = DateTime.Parse("1/5/1999")
```

```
stock = _user.PreferredStocks.Add(18)
stock.InitialPrice = "4.02"
stock.Shares = 539
stock.DateAdded = DateTime.Parse("5/5/1992")

'Save user profile additions
_user.Save(True)

End Sub
```

This adds a few company hits to resemble the user asking for quotes for a few companies. It also simulates a user adding stocks to their portfolio. The company ID is generated when a company is inserted into the database. For testing purposes, test companies can be entered into the database.

Now that we have the object model persisted to the database, let's simulate a user interacting with the object model:

```
Sub Main()
    'Do not load children immediately
    Dim _user As New User("test", "test", False)
    Dim _stock As Stock
    Dim _hit As Hit
    Dim _stockQuote As StockQuote

    Console.WriteLine("User stock Info for: " & _user.Name)
    For Each _stock In _user.PreferredStocks
        Console.WriteLine(vbCrLf & _stock.Ticker & _
                          vbTab & _stock.Shares & vbTab & _
                          _stock.InitialPrice)
        Console.WriteLine(vbTab & "Latest price: " & _
                          _stock.StockQuotes.LatestQuote.Price)
        If (_stock.NewsArticles.Count > 0) Then
            Console.WriteLine(vbTab & "LatestNews Headline posted " & _
                _stock.NewsArticles.LatestNews.DatePosted.ToShortDateString)
            If (_stock.NewsArticles.LatestNews.HeadLine.Length > 80) Then
                Console.WriteLine(vbTab & _
                    _stock.NewsArticles.LatestNews.HeadLine.Substring( _
                    0, 50) & "...")
            Else
                Console.WriteLine(vbTab & _
                                  _stock.NewsArticles.LatestNews.HeadLine)
            End If
        End If
    Next
```

```
        Console.WriteLine(vbCrLf & "User hit info")
        For Each _hit In _user.Hits
            Console.WriteLine(_hit.GetStock().Ticker & _
                            " Requested: " & _hit.DateRequested)
        Next

    End Sub
```

This code reads from the object model. Notice we have the ability to use the `For Each` construct for iterating through our strongly-typed collections. The collection enumerators are provided by the `CollectionBase` and `ReadOnlyCollectionBase` abstract classes in the .NET Framework that our collections inherit from.

The following console shows the output from our UI simulation test.

```
Command Prompt - TestApplication.exe

C:\Damon\TestApplication\bin>TestApplication.exe
User stock Info for: Test User Account

MSFT    21      32.9
        Latest price: 44.41
        LatestNews Headline posted 08/08/2002
        Microsoft Network Security Hotfix Take Advantage o...

T       539     4.02
        Latest price: 8.8

User hit info
KO Requested: 18/09/2002 15:44:25
T Requested: 18/09/2002 15:44:25
MSFT Requested: 18/09/2002 15:44:25
```

Possible Improvements

The object model presented is meant to provide insight into creating a logical middle tier capable of being implemented into a physical middle tier at some future point. For example, we could create a remoting server or web service to expose the functionality on the server. The client application would then call into the web service or use Remoting to access the object model on the physical middle tier.

In order to provide the logical model within the scope of a single chapter, some very important functionality and code design practices were sacrificed for brevity. To truly develop an enterprise-ready middle tier, we could spend entire books describing proper OO design techniques and detailed instructions for implementing a remoting or web services interface on top of our middle tier.

The following middle-tier design points were intentionally omitted from the application and should be added before the code could be implemented.

Error Handling

Error handling is an element that should obviously be included in every application. In our application, we would recommend wrapping all calls to the DAL within an error handler.

We also raise exceptions within the application if the parameters or logic is incorrect. For example, the `IndexOf` type members often check to ensure the parameter is not out of the array bounds. If it is, exceptions are raised so we should handle those exceptions within our code.

Searching/Sorting Techniques

When we added stocks to our test user's profile, we noticed that we needed the company ID to create the entry. The user will not and should not need to know our internal company ID when they are using our site. Instead, we should provide an additional object model that will allow the user to search for a company based on ticker symbol, company name, or any other metrics that would identify the company.

The model we created is used to provide only the necessary functionality for a user to interact with their profile. We could provide searching functionality to give the user more intuitive capabilities for searching for stock tickers. Perhaps we could allow them to search based on industry, company name, or location. Since the search is not related to the `User` object model, such a search object would be best implemented in a separate component dedicated to searching.

As previously mentioned, our internal data storage structure is the `ArrayList`. The `ArrayList` offers only ordinal-based search criteria. The .NET Framework provides collections that allow the items to be retrieved via a name criterion.

The most noticeable of the pre-built collection classes is the `Hashtable`, where we can store data with a key and retrieve items from the collection based on the key. Implementing the `Hashtable` with our objects would require that our individual object instances like `Hit`, `Stock`, `StockQuote`, and `NewsArticle` override the `System.Object`'s `GetHashCode` and `Equals` type members since these are used internally by the `Hashtable` when determining where in the binary tree the item should be stored.

Implementing the `Hashtable` with a small collection does not offer noticeable performance improvements since the `Hashtable` requires overhead to properly store and retrieve values within its internal bucket-based data structure. When adding items to the `Hashtable`, it must determine and reorder objects into buckets as they are being inserted. Once they are in the proper buckets, the search would be exponentially faster than our linear search technique. However, since the collections are small, we will not see huge performance gains.

Additional Functionality

There is a great deal of missing functionality to this application. Besides the searching functionality, we do not implement the ability to display company information, or provide an internal UI for which internal staff can update or edit company information. Also, we have no interface for retrieving stock quotes from a third-party vendor source. All such functionality is outside the realm of the user-focused object model and should be included in the middle-tier functionality depending on how large of a scope is required for the application.

In order for us to retrieve relevant stock ticker information, we would have some sort of connection mechanism to a stock quote database or service that we could use to gain current stock prices. Attaching to the stock quote database would best be implemented from within the data layer or as a separate application capable of interacting with our system. As far as our middle tier presented here is concerned, the middle tier can rely on this component or application to retrieve the current data and does not need to concern itself with functionality to access the external source.

Summary

The middle tier is where the vast majority of an application's logic will be performed. In order to create a highly scalable middle tier, we must understand the technologies that .NET has built in to the Framework. This chapter provided high-level introductions to the concepts behind the middle tier; as well as a first look into the technologies that .NET provides for middle tier development.

Developing a middle tier provides ample scalability benefits to applications at a very little cost to the developer. With the OO-focused nature of .NET, developing objects becomes a native skill set for developing on the platform. In previous versions, the Visual Basic language was not as OO-focused as .NET, which allowed developers to sacrifice the middle tier in favor of implementing logic at other application tiers, particularly the user interface (UI).

Developing a middle tier provides the following benefits:

- **Reusability** – The same middle-tier logic can be used from multiple UI, remoting, or web service clients.

- **Scalability** – When developing an application with multiple clients, providing a middle tier allows the clients to take advantage of shared resources. The most important resources include using a shared data cache and connections to data sources.

- **Integration** – Developing a middle tier gives us one access point into third-party systems. Having a single point of contact allows us to simplify network design as well as reap the scalability benefits of using shared resources to connect to the system.

Summary

- **Upgradeability** – Having a single middle tier allows us to focus on the logic of our application and test for improvements within the code. If the middle-tier logic was dispersed throughout a UI, it would become difficult to monitor performance and spot trends with the time-sensitive code.

- **Deployment** – Making changes in an application with multiple clients involves deploying the code to each client. The move towards browser-based applications confirms the fact that avoiding deployment is an important design concept. Designing a physical middle tier for applications with multiple clients allows us to deploy changes to the middle-tier server without the clients needing to be affected.

Every middle tier has two characteristics: a logical design and a physical design. Creating the logical design is the process of defining the inter-workings of the object model and how the user will interact with our middle tier. When defining the middle tier, we must consider the different alternatives and design patterns around creating interfaces. Interfaces are important since changes to interfaces break clients depending on that interface. With proper design, we can encapsulate the logic to minimize the number of interfaces that need to be broken when code changes.

In applications with multiple clients depending on middle-tier logic, creating a physical middle tier allows us to recognize many middle-tier benefits including simplified deployment, integration, and upgradeability.

Creating a separate physical middle tier with DCOM was a daunting and complicated task limited by DCOM's network complications. .NET introduces the concept of Remoting to provide cross-process code invocation and the framework necessary to implement our own custom communication channels and formatters.

In our example of .NET Remoting, we took an introductory look at how to publish and consume an object via .NET Remoting. The entry-level example illustrated the flexibility of configuration files and creating a simple remoting client and host. The application illustrated the basics necessary to enable our middle-tier object models to be exposed via remoting.

.NET provides ample support for developing web services. The attraction to web services is they are built upon a set of common standards and can be created or consumed by any server or client capable of communicating via HTTP and SOAP.

To continue with our ongoing example, we illustrated an example of creating a middle tier for our sample application: MyInvestmentWatch.com. The middle tier illustrated the concepts involved in creating a logical middle tier capable of interacting with a user's profile.

The important concepts of the example included creating sample collections and designing simple objects to update, add to, and delete from the data source. In order to build our strongly-typed collections, we inherited the vast majority of our functionality from `CollectionBase` and `ReadOnlyCollectionBase`. We also implemented a small set of functionality to provide persistence and some simple object conversion to simplify the UI. The example, while small, allows us to see an example of creating a middle tier.

VB.NET

Scalability

Handbook

5

The Presentation Tier

While the middle tier will house the majority of the application's business logic, the role of the presentation tier is largely to act as the external face of the application. The presentation tier is expected to manage and respond to user requests and must be capable of scaling to support the expected number of average and peak concurrent users in a timely manner. A poorly developed presentation tier, especially in a web-based environment, will not only fail to scale, but will also place an incredible strain on the middle tier. A well-developed presentation tier will actually work to decrease the load on the middle tier.

Increasingly, presentation tiers have become web-based. Therefore, this chapter will focus on ASP.NET and the .NET Framework's improvements for building highly scalable presentation tiers.

Rationale for a Web-Based UI

A web-based, or thin, client interface brings with it several advantages and disadvantages compared to a traditional Windows-based, or thick, client interface. Obviously, for MyInvestmentWatch.com, a web-based front end is a given. However, there are reasons for creating web application for internal systems as well.

Advantages of a Web-Based UI

A web-based presentation tier provides several benefits, both for internal-facing applications and for partner-facing applications. Of course, these benefits must be weighed against the disadvantages as well.

Fewer Deployment Targets

Suppose a typical business-facing application must support a hundred users. Obviously, with a web-based solution, the ratio of web servers to users will be quite low. By only deploying to web servers, the number of target machines is greatly reduced. There is also greater control over these servers, which will make verifying deployments simpler.

Consistent Deployment Platform

If our hypothetical application had to be deployed to hundreds of separate desktops, all with slightly different software, we would likely run into many different problems. Deployment, especially when software conflicts may arise, is not a trivial task. However, with web-based deployment, a best practice would be to configure every web server identically, which will greatly improve the application's deployability. While problems may still arise, the solution is repeatable across all servers in the farm.

Easier Collaboration with External Partners

Nowadays companies are increasingly relying on leveraging computer systems across partners. Due to many issues, such as firewalls within your company as well as within your partner's infrastructure, thick client deployments are not feasible, or at least present large obstacles from an environment and standards viewpoint. Web-based applications are generally easily deployed with minimal impact on these existing measures.

.NET Remoting and web services are making this type of scenario less of an issue. However, many companies will still be reticent to relinquish control in their environments. This would be necessary if the .NET option were used, as it will require the .NET Framework on each client machine.

As web services mature, they will present an appealing alternative in this arena. Of course, web services will still require a front end to function, but at least the choice in clients is virtually limitless.

Easier Support for Multiple Clients

One of the strongest arguments for web-based applications is that they can be easily targeted towards multiple devices. A page can be targeted to a browser on a PC, a handheld device, or a wireless phone, without regard to who makes the device. The methods to describe presentation to the client, such as HTML and WML, are industry standards that are fairly portable across devices with minimal effort. Functionality could be lost, depending on the client and the richness of the output, but it is still possible to deliver working applications across clients. Of course, there is still a large challenge to formatting pages for various screen sizes, but the underlying output is extremely portable.

Disadvantages of a Web-Based UI

Despite its many advantages, this approach is not without its drawbacks, so let's examine them now.

Less Functionality

Generally speaking, web-based applications do not have all of the niceties of Windows-based applications. Granted, it is possible to achieve much of the same functionality with DHTML controls; but then the cross-device support is lost, or solutions for each device must be created, and the amount of effort to build a rich web-based control is as great as for a Windows-based control. ASP.NET does ease packaging and targeting the output through the built-in controls and the ability to create custom controls. However, it is still not possible to have absolute control over the look, feel, and functionality of the front end on every possible client.

Slower Response Times (Perceived and Actual)

In many scenarios, processing data locally will be much faster than sending information over the network and processing it remotely on a web server. Rendering a client-side screen is also typically much faster than fetching HTML and waiting for a browser to render it. Additionally, certain concepts, such as lazy initialization, are much easier to implement in a traditional client-server model.

Client Processing Power Not Leveraged

Windows doesn't require a 2 GHz computer to function. Well, at least not yet. However, a web-based application is not able to make use of this spare processing power. This means that most computational tasks will be confined to the web tier rather than distributed across each client. Subsequently, more stress will be placed on the server farm. We will cover various methods in this chapter to reduce the strain on these servers and decrease the need to rapidly grow the web tier.

Of course, since our application happens to be a web site, the decision on which technology to utilize was rather a no-brainer. However, it is important to understand the rationale behind each approach if you happen to be in the business of creating scalable applications for businesses.

ASP.NET Scalability

The .NET Framework takes a large stride forward when building highly scalable Visual Basic applications. These advances are most apparent when looking at the transition from ASP to ASP.NET.

With regards solely to scalability, ASP.NET has introduced the following features as part of the base Framework:

- Compiled code
- Caching
- Session management in a web farm

233

Compiled Code

ASP was purely an interpreted language. Every time a page with the `.asp` extension was requested, the server had to send the file through the ASP scripting engine to look for `<%` and `%>` tags, process the associated code, and then send the results to the browser.

Contrast this with ASP.NET. The first time a page is requested from the server, it is compiled and the results are then sent to the client. Every subsequent page request will be answered by the compiled version. This improves the time to execute a page by quite a bit, which, subsequently, will allow more users through in a given time.

Caching

Caching is an integral concept when building scalable applications. The goal is to reduce the load on expensive resources. While caching can be utilized with great success at any tier, we will discuss caching only as it relates to ASP.NET in this chapter. In a sense, this is where some of the biggest gains can be made, as caching on the web tier will reduce the need for a round-trip across all tiers in the system.

ASP only had support for caching at the client. Of course, this method will only work if the client supports caching. To achieve caching on the web server the solutions ranged from building custom functionality to purchasing third-party products and implementing specialized hardware.

ASP.NET now has excellent support for caching built in. As you will see, the .NET caching model is robust, useful, and, most importantly, easy to use. While specialized caching servers will certainly still play a part in building large and highly scalable systems, ASP.NET now provides a wonderful alternative right from the start.

Session Management in a Web Farm

By far the most compelling argument for migrating from ASP to ASP.NET is in the built-in ability of ASP.NET to manage sessions in a web farm. One of the biggest headaches with ASP applications was that session state was maintained on the server that first processed a user request. This meant that a custom solution had to be implemented to store state in a central location.

Even worse, a solution had to be implemented so that it always sent the user back to the server that responded to their first request. This pinned all requests to the original server, which impacted on the user experience in two very real ways. Firstly, user load was not fully distributed across all servers. Secondly, because users were pinned to a specific server, if that server crashed then session data was lost for all users on that server.

By now you've probably noticed a trend here in what ASP.NET has addressed. Of course, the trend continues for session management as well. ASP.NET now offers multiple ways to manage user session state. In this chapter we will cover the various ways to manage state in a web farm.

The .NET Framework offers many improvements over traditional VB/ASP, and pure ASP, applications. As importantly, ASP has been revolutionized as ASP.NET. It is now possible to create robust applications in ASP.NET with little intervention from the developer. These improvements do not call for extraordinary code overhauls to implement. As you will see in the remainder of the chapter, these features are easy to implement at the start. However, they're also simple to implement after the fact, if needed.

Where do We Go from Here?

In this chapter we will touch on the facets of ASP.NET outlined above. It is important to understand that this chapter is not an introduction to ASP.NET. Rather, we will only discuss the portions of the Framework that contribute most towards building highly scalable systems.

In this chapter we will cover:

- Our existing application
- Caching
- State management
- The revised application

As with the other chapters in this book, we will be covering the metamorphosis of MyInvestmentWatch.com from a poorly designed system into a highly scalable one.

Our User Interface

Throughout the chapter we will be overhauling the entire application and we will be making some fairly significant changes to a few sections.

Page Flow

First, let's step through the various page flows within the current user interface. This will allow you to quickly see where the changes are being made in our final code.

User Login

At the top of every page is a check to verify whether the user is logged in or not. If they have not yet logged in then they are redirected to `Default.asp`. After successfully logging in, the `User` object is stored in the session and the user is redirected to the `Home.asp` page. `Home.asp` then loops through each preferred stock and stock hit in the `User` object and displays the stock data back to the user.

235

Chapter 5: The Presentation Tier

Figure 1

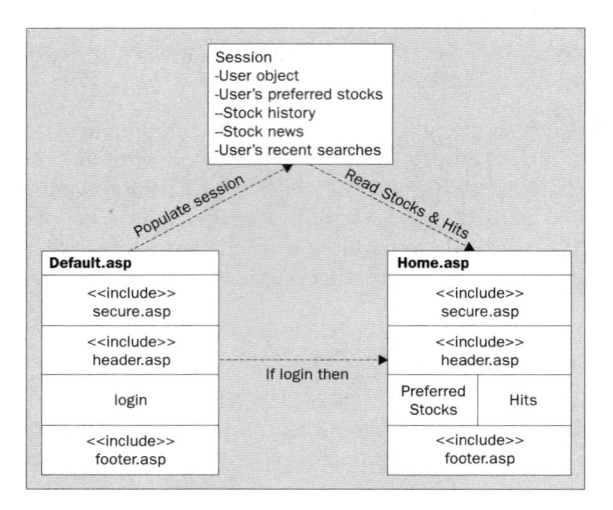

View Individual Stock

From `Home.asp` a user can click on an individual stock and a history of stock quotes for that ticker. Any news related to the company will also be displayed. When `Individual.asp` is called, the ticker requested is added to the recent `Hits` collection in the `User` object.

Figure 2

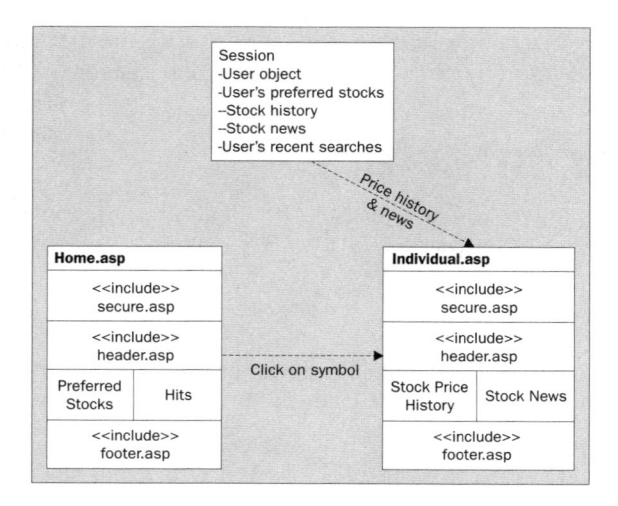

Our User Interface

Code Highlights

The first page, `Default.asp`, is very similar in layout to the other pages we will be discussing. Therefore, `Default.asp` will suffice for an overview of our page layout:

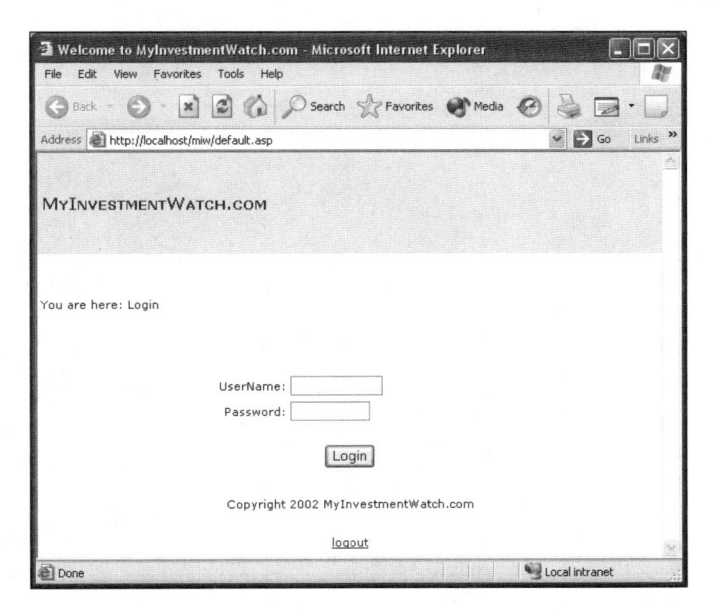

[screenshot of Welcome to MyInvestmentWatch.com page in Internet Explorer, showing MYINVESTMENTWATCH.COM banner, "You are here: Login", UserName and Password fields, a Login button, and footer "Copyright 2002 MyInvestmentWatch.com" with a logout link]

At the top of every page is a simple banner, the content goes in the middle of the page, and every page has a footer. While this isn't the most complex web site ever created, it will highlight several important scalability concepts. After all, less is more and simpler is better, right?

Again, the page layout for `Default.asp` is similar for `Home.asp` and `Individual.asp`, the other two pages we will discuss. The code structure is similar as well. Examine `Default.asp`:

```
<!-- #include file="includes/secure.asp" -->
<%
dim u, message
if len(request("username")) > 0 or len(request("password")) > 0 then
   Set u = server.CreateObject("StocksComponent.User")
   on error resume next
   u.Load request("username"), request("password")
   if err.number <> 0 then message = "Username or password is invalid"
   on error goto 0
   Set Session("user") = u     'Hold user object in session
   response.Redirect("home.asp")
end if
%>
```

237

Chapter 5: The Presentation Tier

```
<html>
<head>
  <title>Welcome to MyInvestmentWatch.com</title>
</head>

<body LEFTMARGIN="0" TOPMARGIN="0" MARGINWIDTH="0" MARGINHEIGHT="0">
<!-- #include file="includes/header.asp" -->

<table height="100" align="center" width="100%">
  <tr><td><div>You are here: Login</div></td></tr>
</table>

<p align="center"><%=message%></p>

<form action="default.asp" method="post" ID="Form1">
  <table width="100%" align="center" cellpadding="1" border="0">
    <tr>
      <td align="right" width="40%">
        <span>UserName:</span>
      </td>
      <td align="left" width="60%">
        <input type="text" name="username" maxlength="10" size="12"
               value="<%=request("username")%>">
      </td>
    </tr>
    <tr>
      <td align="right" width="40%">
        <span>Password:</span>
      </td>
      <td align="left" width="60%">
        <input type="password" name="password" maxlength="8"
               size="10" value="<%=request("password")%>">
      </td>
    </tr>
    <tr>
      <td colspan="2" align="center" width="100%">
        <br><input type="submit" value="Login">
      </td>
    </tr>
  </table>
</form>

<!-- #include file="includes/footer.asp"-->
</body>
</html>
```

The purpose of Default.asp is to verify the user and load a rather large object model with all data related to the user, the stocks in their portfolio, the previous stocks they've searched for, and any news related to those stocks. Once the user object is populated, it is stored in the session for later use:

```
<%
dim u, message
if len(request("username")) > 0 or len(request("password")) > 0 then
   Set u = server.CreateObject("StocksComponent.User")
   on error resume next
   u.Load request("username"), request("password")
   if err.number <> 0 then message = "Username or password is invalid"
   on error goto 0
   Set Session("user") = u     'Hold user object in session
   response.Redirect("home.asp")
end if
%>
```

In a sense, this accomplishes one of the goals of building a scalable system. The user data is cached for use throughout the session lifetime. After the initial hit on the database, subsequent requests will be much more lenient on the backend. However, because we are loading so much user state, we impose a large spike on the middle tier. Also, because we are loading so much data, memory on the web server will be fully used very quickly.

While a useful step in designing highly scalable systems is to reduce load on the middle and database tier, the implementation in our sample application isn't exactly ideal. Now the web tier must manage a large amount of state for a user at any given time. Of course, as you've seen, we've partially remedied this in the middle tier by allowing for lazy loading and deferring loading child objects until the first request. We will carry this new object model to the ASP.NET version of our application.

After a user successfully logs in, they are redirected to Home.asp, which then references the User object stored in the session to loop through each preferred stock and previous search in the object:

```
<!-- #include file="includes/secure.asp" -->
<%
dim u, stk, hit
set u = Session("user")
%>
<html>
<head>
   <title>Homepage for: <%=u.Name%></title>
</head>

<body LEFTMARGIN="0" TOPMARGIN="0" MARGINWIDTH="0" MARGINHEIGHT="0">
<!-- #include file="includes/header.asp" -->

<table height="100" align="center" width="100%">
   <tr><td><div>You are here: login > home</div></td></tr>
</table>

<p align="center">
   <span class="warn"><%=Request("message")%></span>
</p>
```

239

Chapter 5: The Presentation Tier

```
<table width="100%" border="1" cellpadding="1" cellspacing="0">
  <tr bgcolor="#eeeee0">
    <td width="60%"><span>portfolio</span></td>
    <td width="20%" valign="top"><span>get quote</span></td>
    <td width="20%" valign="top" ><span>recent stocks</span></td>
  </tr>
  <tr>
  <td valign="top">
    <table width="100%" border="0" cellpadding="1" cellspacing="0">
      <tr bgcolor="#eeeed0">
        <td width="10%" align="center">ticker</td>
        <td width="30%" align="center">date added</td>
        <td width="10%" align="center">shares</td>
        <td width="20%" align="center">original</td>
        <td width="20%" align="center">current</td>
        <td width="10%" align="center">+/-</td>
      </tr>
      <%for each stk in u.PreferredStocks%>
      <tr>
        <td width="10%" align="center">
          <a href="individual.asp?ticker=<%=stk.Ticker%>">
          <%=stk.Ticker%></a>
        </td>
        <td width="30%" align="center">
          <%=FormatDateTime(stk.DateAdded, 2)%>
        </td>
        <td width="10%" align="center">
          <%=stk.Shares%>
        </td>
        <td width="20%" align="center">
          <%=FormatNumber(stk.InitialPrice, 2, 0)%>
        </td>
        <td width="20%" align="center">
          <%=FormatNumber(stk.StockQuotes.Item(1).Price)%>
        </td>
        <%if stk.StockQuotes(1).Price < stk.InitialPrice then   'loss%>
        <td width="10%" align="center">
          <%=formatNumber((stk.StockQuotes(1).Price -
          stk.InitialPrice) * stk.Shares, 2, false)%>
        </td>
        <%else 'gain%>
        <td width="10%" align="center">
          <%=formatNumber((stk.StockQuotes(1).Price -
          stk.InitialPrice) * stk.Shares, 2, false)%>
        </td>
        <%end if%>
      </tr>
      <%next%>
    </table>

    ...
```

```
<!-- #include file="includes/footer.asp"-->
</body>
</html>
```

When a user clicks on a given stock, they are sent to `Individual.asp`. The stock symbol is sent along as part of the querystring:

```
<!-- #include file="includes/secure.asp" -->
<%
dim u, stk, ticker, sq, na
ticker = Ucase(Trim(request("ticker")))
set u = Session("user")
on error resume next
Set stk = u.PreferredStocks.GetStock(ticker)
u.Hits.AddNew stk.CompID
if err.number > 0 then
  Response.Redirect("home.asp?message=" & _
      Server.URLEncode("Stock " & Request("ticker") & " is invalid"))
end if
on error goto 0
%>

    ...

<%for each sq in stk.StockQuotes%>
  <tr>
    <td width="10%" align="center">
    <%=FormatDateTime(sq.DateRequested, 0)%><br>
    <%=formatNumber(sq.Price, 2, false)%>
    </td>
  </tr>
<%next%>

    ...

<!-- #include file="includes/footer.asp"-->
</body>
</html>
```

Aesthetically, one of the most annoying things about ASP is that HTML and logic are severely intermixed. A side effect of this is that it leads to an application that is more difficult to maintain. ASP.NET, in contrast, provides a wonderful method for separating code from presentation. While we won't be focusing on that feature here, as it doesn't entirely relate to scalability, it is worth noting as this is the method we will be following in the .NET version of MyInvestmentWatch.com.

Notice a trend in these page layouts. Each page has several include files. There is a banner along the top:

```
<body LEFTMARGIN="0" TOPMARGIN="0" MARGINWIDTH="0" MARGINHEIGHT="0">
<!-- #include file="includes/header.asp" -->
```

and a footer:

```
<!-- #include file="includes/footer.asp"-->
</body>
</html>
```

This is the typical method of reusing code across multiple pages in ASP. Simply package the reusable code off into its own file and then included it on the main page where you would like the code to appear. This included ASP page must also be processed before being displayed, and, of course, there is no inherent method for caching this data. This means that these include files must be processed every time as well.

As you will see, ASP.NET provides a much more sophisticated method of bundling common code for use across pages. ASP.NET allows the creation of custom controls. These controls can be cached, which, as you will see, is a basis for a very powerful means of increasing scalability.

Design Goals

The design goals for the web tier of this application are:

- **Reduce load on the web server** – By reducing the load on web server, we are able to support more concurrent users with the same amount of hardware. Subsequently, as user load increases, the hardware growth curve will be a good bit flatter, and cheaper.

- **Enable the web tier to function optimally in a web farm** – If you recall, one of the key concepts of growing an environment for scalability is to scale out a single tier. This is most apparent in the web tier, which will bear the brunt of user load and must, typically, manage state for every user. We will modify MyInvestmentWatch.com to work in a web farm, where any given request will not necessarily go to the same machine as any previous request from the same user.

- **Program against the new application model** – While it would be possible to develop ASP.NET against the existing VB COM object, we will be updating to program against the new VB.NET assembly as well.

We will accomplish these design goals in the following sections. While each section is directly related to scalability, there are other benefits as well. For instance, while a server farm will assist in scalability it will also greatly increase application availability. This is because a given server in a web farm can be down and the application still has plenty of servers available for processing. Of course, proper state management is necessary for both scalability and availability.

Caching

Caching is a key concept in building scalable systems. Certain operations, such as reading from a database, are expensive. The goal of caching is to keep data closer to the portion of the application that requires the information. This greatly reduces the number of round-trips required to retrieve information for display.

Caching is ideal in situations where the data is fairly static. The true power of caching comes in when the cached data can be used across multiple clients. A good example of this in our application would be the company news section on the stock details page. This data, while dynamically loaded from the database, does not change often. In addition, the data is not specific to a single client. Rather, any client requesting the same company information can use the cached version.

Conversely, the portion of the page that shows the stocks that the user has recently searched is not a good candidate for caching. This is because the data is totally dynamic; it must change every time the user performs a new search. In addition, this information is specific to each client.

To illustrate the benefit of caching, suppose we have a list of news articles on the MyInvestmentWatch.com. As this information seldom changes, it is a good candidate for caching. Without caching at some tier, every time the news page is loaded an entire roundtrip to the database is incurred. Hypothetically, suppose this page receives 3,000 page views in an hour. By caching the data for just 20 minutes, we reduce the number of hits on the database from 3,000 an hour to just 3 an hour. A 99.9% saving in the number of roundtrips to the server is certainly a large benefit to scalability. After all, the application database is now under much less load than before.

Caching has long been an integral part of web pages, at least for static pages. However, obviously, static pages do not allow for the dynamic nature of ASP. This led to many workarounds and third-party solutions.

A common method for caching in ASP is to store values at the application level. However, this has several drawbacks. Perhaps the largest downfall of this approach is that, if you will recall, VB COM objects cannot be stored within the `Application` object, only within the `Session` object. This means that an alternative must be found if you wish to store a strongly-typed VB collection. Application-level caching is best suited for single values or recordsets of data that change infrequently.

An alternative has been to attempt to mix the ease of caching static content with the abilities of dynamic pages. A common practice was to save the output of these dynamic pages as static pages for future use. The pages would be refreshed either by a simple timed batch job or a more involved solution that requires a good bit of logic to determine if a page, or multiple pages, should be recreated. This solution was best suited to large sets of data, such as a product catalog, or perhaps a list of companies and their associated ticker symbols.

Chapter 5: The Presentation Tier

As necessary as caching is for building highly scalable web sites, there was no single solution in ASP. Of course, as you're probably guessing, this all changed with the introduction of ASP.NET. Developers now have a consistent way to cache data. In addition, ASP.NET supports more than just caching entire pages. In fact, you now have three basic options for caching data:

- **Output Caching** – This is also often referred to as page-level caching. The concept is that you store an entire page for ready retrieval. Of course, things wouldn't be very dynamic if .NET assumed that all requests for the same page would receive the same output. We'll cover how ASP.NET provides varied means of differentiating content per request.

- **Partial Page Output Caching** – This is also often referred to as fragment caching. Sometimes, it is not practical to cache an entire page. For instance, our stock ticker on MyInvestmentWatch.com would be a poor candidate for caching the entire page, as some of the elements on the page will change frequently. However, on that same page, the header is ideal for caching as it changes very infrequently. ASP.NET supports fragment caching by allowing user controls to be cached separately from the output page.

- **Programmatic Caching** – Output caching and fragment caching are perfect solutions for caching the rendered page. However, it is also useful to cache information that will be shared across pages but displayed differently each time. For example, a site may want to display a list of countries. This information might be stored in a database and read at application startup. Obviously, with this data, the cache timeout can be set for a fairly long time. The benefit is that data can still be treated as being dynamic. However, as it is cached, it reduces the load on the database considerably.

Each of these caching methods will come into play when creating scalable systems. In this section, we will highlight the differences, advantages, and best practices for each method.

Where the Cache Fits

Traditionally, in ASP, a common method to store transient application-level information was via the `Application` object. A developer would simply add code to populate information into the application through the `Application_OnStart` method of `Global.asa`. This solution was adequate but somewhat lacking.

In ASP it would be common to read in information, such as the footer at the bottom of the page, or perhaps a menu on the sidebar, and store it in the `Application` object. This information is now, essentially, cached and ready for retrieval without reading back in the original file. However, what if the file changes? The desired course of action would be to read the information again to ensure that the changes were reflected in this cached data. Unfortunately, the implementation was not nearly as straightforward.

Caching

The method described above exposed no ability for automated features such as item expiration and establishing dependencies between items. These requirements had to be manually created by the programmer or ignored. Of course, this has been remedied in ASP.NET. Instead of the general Swiss army knife that was the `Application` object that had to be wielded in ASP, a much more specific tool is now available, the `Cache` object.

The `Cache` object has the same visibility as the `Application` object. That is, the `Cache` object is accessible across the entire web application but must be maintained on each server in a web farm. In the case of our example, the same `Cache` object would be available across the entire customer-facing MyInvestmentWatch.com web site. The `Cache` object exposes quite a bit if functionality as well:

- **Resource Management** – As we mentioned, one of the problems with using the `Application` object in ASP is that you must ensure that the cached item does not need to be refreshed. In ASP.NET, the `Cache` object will automatically remove items that have passed their expiration time. In addition, when memory resources become constrained, the `Cache` will automatically walk through all items in the cache and remove the items that are used the least. In this manner, the most frequently used items will almost always be cached and readily available.

- **Item Dependencies** – The cache allows items to be chained via dependencies. In this manner, it is possible to create a relationship between our fictitious footer control and the text file it reads its information from. When the text file is modified, the user control is invalidated and will be cached again on the next request.

- **Event-based Notification** – The `Cache` object has the ability to raise events when an item is removed from the cache. This event will be fired, for example, when an item decays and is automatically removed from the cache. Thus, with little effort, it is possible to be notified when a change to the text file causes the cached footer to be expired. It would further be possible to then programmatically re-add the footer to the cache before it is requested again.

It is this `Cache` object that provides the underlying functionality for page caching and fragment caching. Of course, as we will demonstrate, it is also possible to access this `Cache` object programmatically. Now, the question you may have is how cache, session, and application work together and when is the best time for each. As a general rule, the following will apply:

- **Session** – The `Session` object is used to store information related to a single user. Obviously, a good candidate for this in our application would be the `User` object. When using VB with ASP, a common practice was to load VB COM objects into the session whether they belonged there or not. Any of these objects that do not need to be tied to a specific user should be pulled out of session. This may include such information as lookup tables that were stored in session-level `Dictionary` objects in ASP.

Remember that each session will receive a copy of the data. Take care to be efficient with what is stored. Therefore, any data that will be useable by multiple clients should not be stored within the session.

❑ **Application** – In ASP, any fairly static information that was to be used by multiple clients was stored in the `Application` object. As `Application` could be updated by multiple sources, the lock and unlock methods always had to be explicitly performed. This carries through to ASP.NET.

Typically speaking, the `Application` object is now replaced by the `Cache` object. The `Application` object is still a preferable place to store settings and object references that apply to the entire web application. However, the `Application` should rarely be used for storing static or semi-static data that pertains to fulfilling client requests.

❑ **Cache** – The `Cache` should be used to store data that can be used by multiple clients and that is static, or semi-static in nature. `Cache` should also be used when dependencies between items must be established. Unlike `Application` objects, `Cache` objects implicitly perform the lock and unlock methods when updating data.

In ASP.NET, the `Cache` object serves to store either page output or other data that can be used to service multiple requests. This removes much of the burden that was previously placed on the `Session` and `Application` objects. In addition, as you will see, the `Cache` object provides many functions for controlling how data is stored.

Output Caching

The normal sequence for the first page request in ASP.NET is this:

1. Client requests a page.
2. The page is compiled to Intermediate Language (IL).
3. The page is run. The IL is Just-In-Time (JIT) compiled to machine code.
4. The results are sent to the client.

Each subsequent request for the page, until the page changes at least, will simply run the already compiled page. One thing to note is that the results, in a sense, are simply discarded by the server after each request. If client 'a' and client 'b' both request `Default.aspx` then the page will be rerun for each client. However, the page will only be compiled to Intermediate Language on the first request.

Caching

Subsequent requests then have this sequence:

1. Client requests a page.
2. The page is run. The IL generated at first request is simply JIT'ed and run.
3. The results are sent to the client.

For fairly static data, such as our `Default.aspx` page, which is, after all, just a login page that likely won't change often, this is horribly inefficient. If the page is performing complex, or multiple, functions, these functions must be run every time. While this may be desired sometimes, often it is not.

For example, a page that opens a connection to the database to retrieve daily sales information likely does not need the absolute newest information. After all, it's a daily report. A much better method would be to retrieve the data once and then store it for a certain period of time. Subsequent requests for this data, such as other clients or even the accidental page-refresh click, will then just read from this stored data. This reduces the strain on the database by greatly lessening user load.

In ASP, a custom solution would have to be devised. As with all things .NET, things are much better now. Microsoft has added the ability to save the results after the first request to respond to requests by other clients. This is accomplished via the `@OutputCache` page directive.

The @OutputCache Directive

Commands with a `<%@` go at the top of a page. These are referred to as page directives, or directives for short. One directive that is available, and that we will make extensive use of in this chapter, is the `@OutputCache` directive.

It is also possible to programmatically accomplish the same goal as this directive. We will touch on this, as well as a few techniques you can't currently accomplish with directives, later in the chapter. For now, we'll just discuss the caching directive as it is likely that it will be powerful enough to meet the majority of your needs, and it is exposed in a very clean and simple-to-use manner.

The `@OutputCache` directive has the following format:

```
<%@ OutputCache Duration="#ofseconds"
                Location="Any | Client | Downstream | Server | None"
                VaryByParam="none | * | parameters"
                VaryByControl="controlname"
                VaryByHeader="headers"
                VaryByCustom="Browser | customstring" %>
```

Let's look at each of the attributes of the `@OutputCache` directive in turn.

Duration

The first attribute, `Duration`, is required and specifies the time, in seconds, for which the page or user control is cached. Once this time span has elapsed, then the cached item is invalidated. Consequently, the next time the item is requested after the cache has been invalidated, the item will be rerun, cached, and the results will then be sent to the server.

Location

The `Location` attribute specifies where the cached data will reside. The possible values and their associated locations are shown in the following table.

Value	Description
Any	The cached information can be stored at the client, downstream, or on the server. This is the default value.
Client	The cache is located on the client, if the client device supports it. This is the equivalent of setting the Cache-Control header.
Downstream	The cache is located on any HTTP 1.1 cache-capable device. This could include edge servers, proxy servers, and the client that made the request.
Server	The cache is located on the web server where the request was processed. The downside to this method is that the cache will need to be recreated on each server in a web farm.
None	The output cache is disabled.

When the location is set to `Server`, client downstream caching is disabled. This ensures that the newest version is always pulled from the server, or at least the server's cache. This is useful as it ensures that the client always has the newest cached information and will receive refreshed output once the cache duration has expired.

> **Caching is not cascading. That is, if the page disables caching by specifying a location of None, then a user control is still free to specify cache information.**

VaryByParam

`VaryByParam` is required for pages. It is also required for user controls that do not implement `VaryByControl`. `VaryByParam` is a semicolon-separated list of strings that allows the output cache to be varied by the query string in a `GET` statement or parameters in a `POST` statement. The valid options are None, *, or any valid parameter name.

Caching

Value	Description
None	All changes in the query string are ignored. This is particularly useful in a user control if the output will be the same no matter what the parameters passed to the main page are.
*	Each variation is treated as a new output. Each subsequent output is cached separately and expired separately. This option is useful when you have a limited number of variations and want a simple blanket method to maintain the cache.
A list of one or more valid parameters	Any change in the parameters specified will be treated as a new output. While this is identical in nature to specifying a wildcard for the parameter list, it allows for a much finer level of control over which parameters will cause a new entry in the cache. This option is useful when only certain parameters would necessitate a data refresh.

> Using `VaryByParam` in a user control will only work if the user control manages its own postbacks. If the postback from the user control is to the containing page, the user control will not necessarily be rerun and re-cached.

VaryByControl

`VaryByControl` is a semicolon-separated list of strings that allow the output cache for the page to be varied by a user control's properties. This is useful in instances where a user control may hold semi-static data. For instance, we may want a user control that houses states and cities within each state to vary by property so that each state is separately cached for use on the containing page.

VaryByHeader

`VaryByHeader` is a semicolon-separated list of strings that allows the output cache for the page to be varied by HTTP headers. With this attribute set, the output cache will contain a version of the document for each specified header. This is useful when the primary determinant of the output of a page is header information. For example, the referrer header may be used to cache different output depending on which partner site a user navigates from.

VaryByCustom

Lastly, the `VaryByCustom` attribute has two possible values. The first is simply the text string `Browser`. If the attribute is set to `Browser` then the cache entry is varied by browser name and version. This is useful if multiple versions of a document will be displayed depending on browser capabilities. For example, it might be necessary to have both an IE 5.0 and a Netscape 6.0 version of a page as each has a slightly different document object model for client-side scripts.

249

The other possible value for `VaryByCustom` is a custom string. This is useful when you want a more central location for expiring a cached item that may be used across multiple pages. To utilize this method, you must override the `HttpApplication.GetVaryByCustomString()` method in `Global.asax` and supply your custom string. However, as you will see, directly using the `Cache` object provides better control, so, we will not delve much into `VaryByCustom`.

Output Caching Sequence

Remember in a standard ASP.NET page lifecycle, the order of events is:

1. Client requests a page
2. The page is compiled
3. The page is run
4. The results are sent to the client

Each request that follows simply runs the page and sends the results to the client. When we throw output caching into the mix, the steps are slightly different:

1. Client requests a page
2. The page is compiled
3. The page is run
4. The results are stored in the cache
5. The results are sent to the client

When fulfilling each subsequent request, the server will verify if the output is in the cache before running the page:

1. Client requests a page
2. The cache is checked
3. If the result is still valid then the result is sent to the client
4. Otherwise the page is run
5. The results are stored in the cache
6. The results are sent to the client

As you will see, while IIS and ASP.NET are doing much more, the difficulty in implementing caching is minimal.

Using Output Caching

We've discussed each of the `@OutputCache` attributes so let's see them in action.

Duration

Firstly, let's examine the simplest method of caching data. That is to simply rely on the `Duration` attribute of the `@OutputCache` directive. Create a file named using duration.aspx and add the following code:

```
<% @Page language="vb" %>
<html>
<head>
  <script runat="server">
    Sub Page_Load()
        Dim currentTime As DateTime=DateTime.Now()
        TimeCreated.InnerHTML=currentTime.ToString("T")
    End Sub
  </script>
</head>
<body>
  <div>
    <span>Current Server Time:</span>
    <span id="TimeCreated" runat="server"></span>
  </div>
</body>
</html>
```

Without the directive in place, the page will show the newest time every time the page is refreshed. In fact, examine the following two screenshots of the file without the output cache specified:

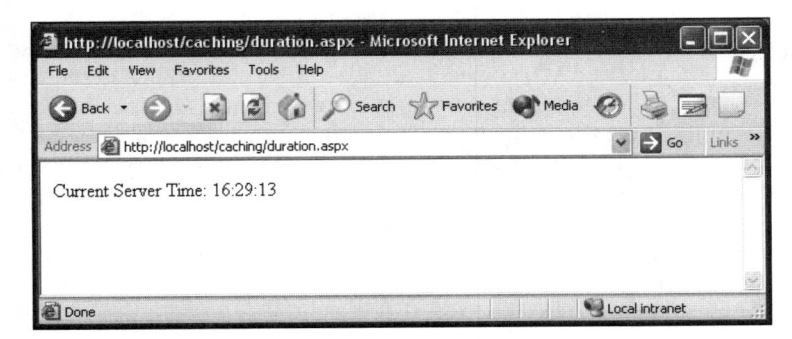

Pressing *F5* (refresh) yields a new time:

251

Chapter 5: The Presentation Tier

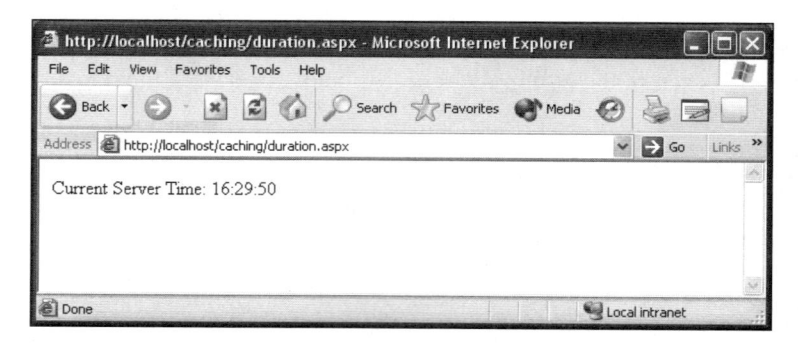

[Browser screenshot showing http://localhost/caching/duration.aspx with text "Current Server Time: 16:29:50"]

Now add the following line to the top of the duration.aspx page:

```
<% @Page language="vb" %>
<%@ OutputCache Duration="60" VaryByParam="None" %>
<html>
```

We're simply directing ASP.NET to cache the output of the page for sixty seconds and to ignore all parameter variations. This means that only one version of the output will be stored, and it will be invalidated after a minute. Reloading our page with the Duraticn in place will give us a new time on the page. However, pressing *F5* this time shows us that the page is still reading from the cached information because the time remains the same.

While the example here may be a bit contrived, it demonstrates both the usefulness and the danger of caching. Firstly, for the usefulness; suppose MyInvestmentWatch.com had a quote of the minute control. This control reads a random bit of sage advice from a database and displays it at the top of the web page.

If MyInvestmentWatch.com gets 500 page views a minute, then this code is accessed 500 times in a single minute, or 30,000 times in an hour. If we cached this quote of the minute as we have in the sample above, then the cached data is supplied fresh every minute. More importantly, the cached data is supplied rather than forcing a hit on the database for every request. This effectively reduces our load from 30,000 hits to 60 hits (from 500 a minute to one a minute).

However, you can also easily see the potential problems that can come into play with the output cache. In the above example the time, a rather dynamic entity, does not change at all between page refreshes. Yes, that is right, you heard it here first. Thanks to the power of Microsoft we've managed to make time stand still.

Seriously though, the problem with caching data, at least with blindly caching data as we've done above, is that we have to rely solely on the cache to expire data. If it is critical that data be as up to date as possible, then caching of this nature is not an acceptable solution.

Caching

VaryByParam

Expanding on our previous ..example, let's now make it vary by parameter values. This method might be ideal in a few distinctly different scenarios. Firstly, for highly customized data that is accessed a lot, such as the user portfolio on MyInvestmentWatch.com on heavy trading days, this will cache data for each user. While this may be a waste of resources on the web tier in some instances, it makes sense if you have users constantly accessing custom data that doesn't change much.

Another great fit for varying cache information by parameter might be with displaying data that is not customized by user, but rather changes fairly infrequently and could be expensive to look up. Suppose you have two listboxes. The first displays the states of the US. The second displays the cities after a state is selected. This is ideal for caching as the cache can be used to store each state and its associated cities. In this scenario, the data is common to all users. By fetching and caching as often as possible for this data, we greatly reduce load across the system.

The following code is saved in `varybyparam.aspx`:

```
<% @Page language="vb" %>
<%@ OutputCache Duration="60" VaryByParam="FirstName" %>
<html>
<head>
  <Script runat="server">
    Sub Page_Load()
       Dim currentTime As DateTime=DateTime.Now()
       TimeCreated.InnerHTML = currentTime.ToString("T")
       nameInnerHTML = Request("FirstName")
    End Sub
  </Script>
</head>
<body>
  <div>
    <span>Personal Page of:</span>
    <span id="name" runat="server"></span>
  </div>
  <div>
    <span>Current Server Time:</span>
    <span id="TimeCreated" runat="server"></span>
  </div>
</body>
</html>
```

Notice the `@OutputCache` directive; we are no longer instructing the runtime to ignore all parameters with regards to caching as in our last example. Rather, the directive is now to pay attention to a specific parameter, the `FirstName` parameter:

```
<%@ OutputCache Duration="60" VaryByParam="FirstName" %>
```

253

Chapter 5: The Presentation Tier

If `FirstName` is present in either the query string of an HTTP `GET` or the parameters of an HTTP `POST`, then a cache entry will be made for each unique value. Actually, if no `FirstName` parameter is specified then an entry will be made for the blank version as well. It is also important to note that the values are case sensitive. Therefore:

```
http://localhost/varybyparam.aspx?firstname=Ben
```

is not equal to:

```
http://localhost/varybyparam.aspx?firstname=ben
```

A cache entry will be created for each variation, as Ben does not equal ben. This can be a slight disadvantage. However, it should generally not be a problem, especially if most values are populated from the various server components.

To demonstrate, the output from the above code is:

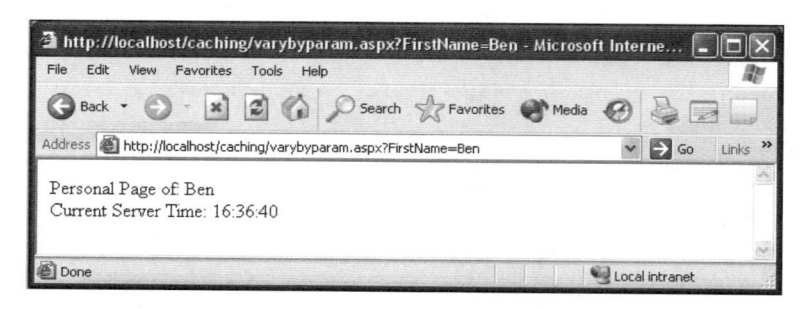

```
Personal Page of Ben
Current Server Time: 16:36:40
```

Refreshing will yield the same result. However, changing the `FirstName` parameter will result in another page being added to the cache:

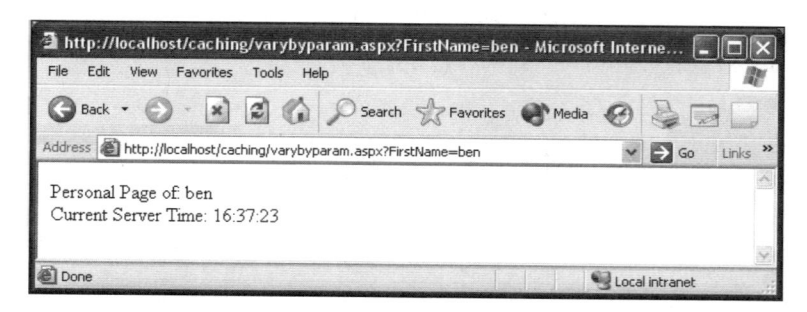

```
Personal Page of ben
Current Server Time: 16:37:23
```

`VaryByParam` will be very useful in our revised application. Recall that `Individual.asp` is sent the ticker symbol and then displays quite a bit of information about that ticker. By implementing `VaryByParam`, with a reasonable timeout so as not to miss any late-breaking news, we have a cached page for each symbol requested. This ensures that requested symbols are readily available. Furthermore, it ensures that the symbols that are never requested do not take up unneeded room in the cache.

Of course, the cache has a bit of intelligence built into it as well. While we will explore this further in the programmatic control of the cache, it's worth noting here. Items that are cached and then not requested within a certain period of time will eventually decay and be cleaned out of the cache. Also, as the cache fills, items that are less frequently used or have a lower cache priority, will be removed to make room for frequently used items. This ensures that the most often requested stocks are always in the cache, are optimally placed in the cache, and are able to quickly respond to use requests.

VaryByControl

There are two caveats with this option. Firstly, it cannot work with a page; it is only a valid option inside a user control (.ascx). Secondly, the containing page cannot programmatically manipulate an output-cached user control, and any attempt to do so will result in an error.

VaryByControl allows you to vary cached output based on the value of a specific control. For example, you might want to specify three logo styles in a dropdown and then cache the corresponding look and feel after a given value has been selected.

VaryByControl will most often be used as a subset of a caching scheme for fragment caching. However, it is worth demonstrating here so that you may compare and contrast to the methods mentioned earlier. First, examine the code for varybycontrol.ascx:

```
<Script runat="server">
Public Sub Page_Load()
  Dim currentTime As DateTime=DateTime.Now()
  TimeCreated.InnerHTML = currentTime.ToString("T")
End Sub

Public Sub Button_Click(Sender as Object, Args as EventArgs)
  Selection.InnerHTML = Food.Value
End Sub
</Script>

<div>
  <span>Current Server Time:</span>
  <span id="TimeCreated" runat="server"></span>
</div>
<div>
  <span>Selection:</span>
  <span id="selection" runat="server"></span>
</div>
<div>
  <form id="testForm" runat="server">
    <select id="food" runat="server">
      <option value="">Select a food</option>
      <option value="Pizza">Pizza</option>
      <option value="caffeinated Beverage">
        Caffeinated Beverage
      </option>
```

Chapter 5: The Presentation Tier

```
            <option value="Coffee">Coffee</option>
        </select>
        <input type="submit" value="Select" onserverclick="Button_Click"
                runat="server"/>
    </form>
</div>
```

We will then reference this control in `varybycontrol.aspx`:

```
<%@ Page Language="vb" %>
<%@ Register TagPrefix="MIW" TagName="varybycontrol"
            src="varybycontrol.ascx" %>

<MIW:varybycontrol id="vbcDemo" runat="server"/>
```

Notice at this point that we are not using the `@OutputCache` directive at all. This is simply to demonstrate the page without caching enabled. Here is our default page:

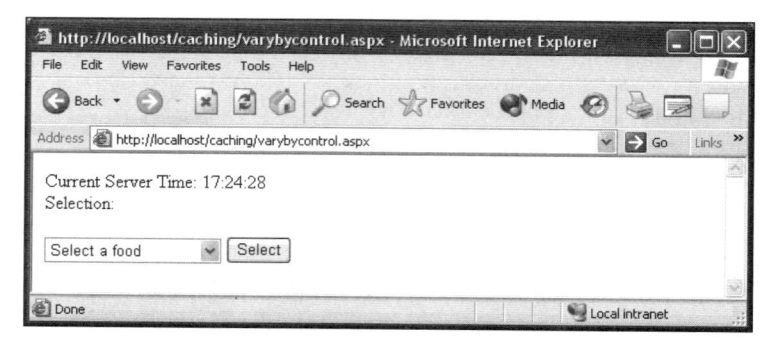

After selecting a new food from the dropdown and pressing select, you can clearly see that the current server time has updated:

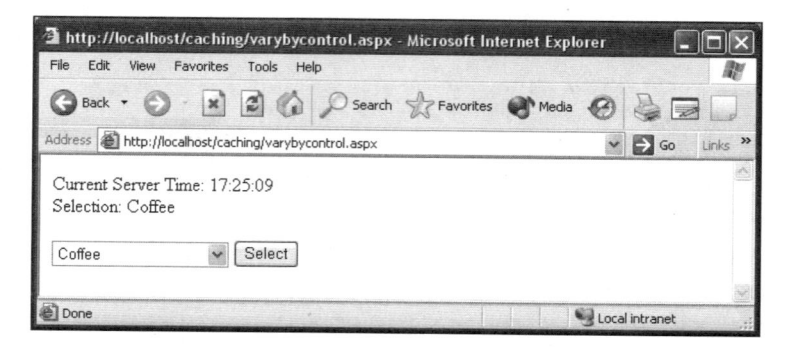

Caching

Now, let's get into `VaryByControl`. The basic structure is the same as the other parameters. The difference here is that you specify an ASP or HTML control to vary the cache by. In this example, we will be varying the cache by the dropdown control within the user control. This means that, for every new selection in the dropdown, a new entry will be made in the cache.

The format for the `VaryByControl` is as follows:

```
<%@ OutputCache Duration="#ofseconds" VaryByParam="none|*|paramlist"
                VaryByControl="controlname" %>
```

Note that the `VaryByParam` value is required. For this example we will set `VaryByParam` to None. This means that only the value of the control changing will affect the cache, not any parameters that are passed in. The `controlname` value for `VaryByControl` is simply the ID value of the control.

Our new `varybycontrol.ascx` code is:

```
<%@ OutputCache Duration="120" VaryByParam="none"
                VaryByControl="food" %>
<Script runat="server">
Public Sub Page_Load()
    Dim currentTime As DateTime = DateTime.Now()
    TimeCreated.InnerHTML = currentTime.ToString("T")
End Sub
...
```

Running our new code via `varybycontrol.aspx`, we can see the control is now cached for each unique value of the 'food' dropdown. Selecting **Coffee** from the food dropdown (hey, when you're a programmer, coffee *is* a valid food) places the control in the cache:

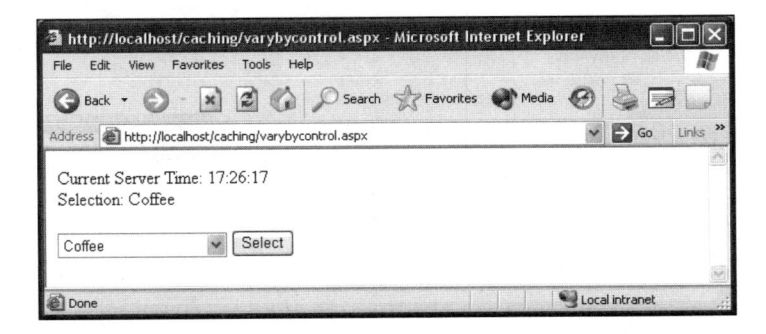

Reselecting **Coffee**, or pressing *F5* and clicking the **Retry** button, shows that the control is reading directly from the cache. Changing the selection to pizza and clicking the select button clearly changes the cache time:

257

Chapter 5: The Presentation Tier

[Browser screenshot: http://localhost/caching/varybycontrol.aspx showing "Current Server Time: 17:27:18", "Selection: Pizza", a dropdown with "Pizza" selected and a Select button.]

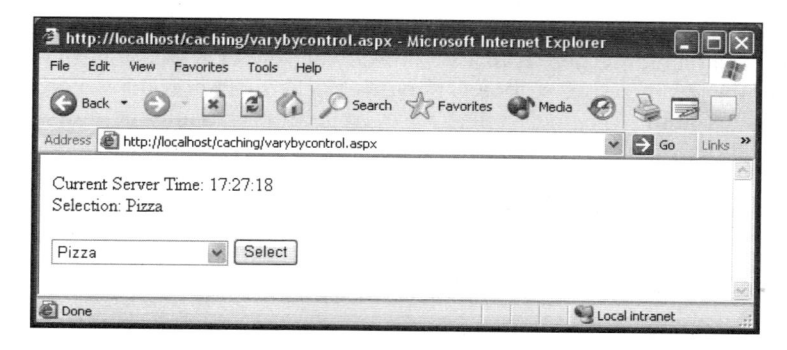

In some situations, varying a cache by control value is useful. If a control is used to populate a form based on the value selected, then it is a good candidate for caching. For example, a hosting company might have several hosting packages. Depending on which hosting package was selected, a different list of available features might be shown. As these features do not often change, and each output is varied by the selected package, this would be a strong candidate for `VaryByControl`.

VaryByHeader

It is possible to vary the cache entry by one or more header values. For instance, we may want to cache a particular menu for visitors from our partner site, www.WatchMyInvestments.com, and another menu for users directly accessing our site. This method is outlined below in `varybyheader.aspx`:

```
<% @Page language="vb" %>
<%@ OutputCache Duration="60" VaryByParam="None"
                VaryByHeader="referer" %>
<html>
<head>
  <Script runat="server">
    Sub Page_Load()
      Dim currentTime As DateTime=DateTime.Now()
      TimeCreated.InnerHTML = currentTime.ToString("T")
      referrer.InnerHTML = Request.Headers("referer")
    End Sub
  </Script>
</head>
<body>
  <div>
    <span>Referred By:</span>
    <span id="referrer" runat="server"></span>
  </div>
  <div>
    <span>Current Server Time:</span>
    <span id="TimeCreated" runat="server"></span>
  </div>
</body>
</html>
```

Caching

Within the @OutputCache directive, we are specifying to ignore the parameters and instead cache content based on the value of the referrer HTTP header. Programmatically, you could get this value through `Request.Headers("referer")`. However, we are allowing the directive to manage that reference behind the scenes:

```
<%@ OutputCache Duration="60" VaryByParam="None"
                VaryByHeader="referer" %>
```

We can verify that the output is cached for a blank referral, or presumably someone who has directly navigated to the page in question:

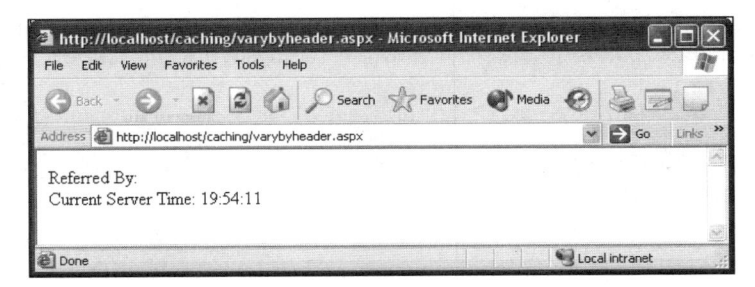

However, we must also populate the referrer header field. The simplest method to accomplish this is to create a page that the user clicks through to the varybyheader.aspx page. The code for testvarybyheader.aspx is rather simple. The goal is simply to get something into the referrer field to demonstrate how this caching method works.

The code:

```
<a href="varybyheader.aspx">Click</a>
```

The page:

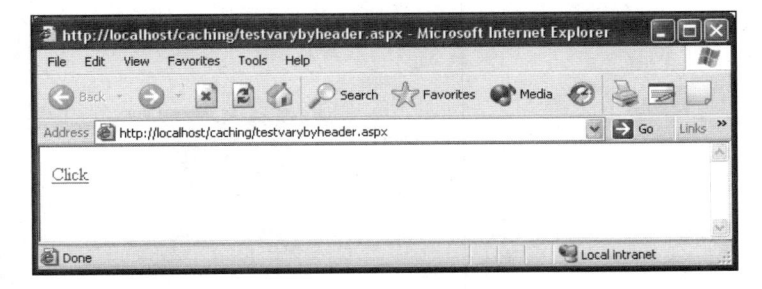

Following the link will bring you back to the varybyheader.aspx page. Here you can see that the referrer information has been populated. This means that another output result has been added to the cache.

259

Chapter 5: The Presentation Tier

> **http://localhost/caching/varybyheader.aspx - Microsoft Internet Explorer**
>
> Referred By: http://localhost/caching/testvarybyheader.aspx
> Current Server Time: 19:54:54

To verify, simply open IE in a new window and reload the `varybyheader.aspx` page. As you can see, the time is clearly before the entry with the referrer. In fact, it's identical to the first request to the page, which is the desired result of the test.

The `VaryByHeader` attribute can be useful in situations where header information is the factor differentiating the most between various request types. Another potential value for the `VaryByHeader` attribute is `Accept-Language`, which will cache pages according to the client's languages settings.

VaryByCustom

There is yet one more method for determining a caching strategy. That is the `VaryByCustom` option. While this method is by no means challenging, it is the most difficult method of the five covered here. At this point, a strong alterative may be to examine the programming method for dealing with the cache directly.

In `Global.asax`, we've added the following:

```
<%@ Import namespace="System.Web" %>
<%@ Import namespace="System.Web.SessionState" %>

<Script runat="Server">
Public Class Global
  Inherits System.Web.HttpApplication

  Sub Application_Start(ByVal sender As Object, ByVal e As EventArgs)
    Application("RecycleTimestamp") = DateTime.Now()
  End Sub

  Public Overrides Function GetVaryByCustomString( _
      ByVal context As HttpContext, ByVal arg As String) As String

    If (arg = "RecycleTimestamp") Then
      Return CStr(Context.Application("RecycleTimestamp"))
    End If
  End Function

End Class
</Script>
```

Caching

At the top of any page that we then want to be reliant on this custom string, we would specify our output cache directive as:

```
<%@ OutputCache Duration="#ofseconds" VaryByParam="none"
                VaryByCustom="RecycleTimestamp"%>
```

The code for `varybycustom.aspx` is as follows:

```
<% @Page language="vb" %>
<%@ OutputCache Duration="60" VaryByParam="None"
                VaryByCustom="RecycleTimestamp" %>
<html>
<head>
  <Script runat="server">
    Sub Page_Load()
      Dim currentTime As DateTime=DateTime.Now()
      TimeCreated.InnerHTML = currentTime.ToString("T")
      Timestamp.InnerHTML = Context.Application("RecycleTimestamp")
    End Sub
  </Script>
</head>
<body>
  <div>
    <span>Recycle Timestamp:</span>
    <span id="Timestamp" runat="server"></span>
  </div>
  <div>
    <span>Current Server Time:</span>
    <span id="TimeCreated" runat="server"></span>
  </div>
</body>
</html>
```

Now, here's where it gets really hard. OK, so it's actually quite straightforward. In order to expire the cache, we simply need to force the value for `RecycleTimestamp` to change. For this example, create a new page with a meaningful name, such as `triggerrecycle.aspx`. In the page, add the following code:

```
<Script runat="server">
  Sub Page_Load()
    Application.Lock()
    Application("RecycleTimestamp") = DateTime.Now()
    Application.Unlock()
  End Sub
</Script>
```

When `triggerrecycle.aspx` is called, it will force the value of `RecycleTimestamp` to change. In turn, the cache will invalidate for each page that has `VaryByCustom="RecycleTimestamp"` in the output cache directive.

261

Chapter 5: The Presentation Tier

Now reload `triggerrecycle.aspx`:

![Screenshot of Internet Explorer showing http://localhost/caching/triggerrecycle.aspx with a blank page]

We can revisit `varybycustom.aspx` and see that the output, as promised, has indeed changed:

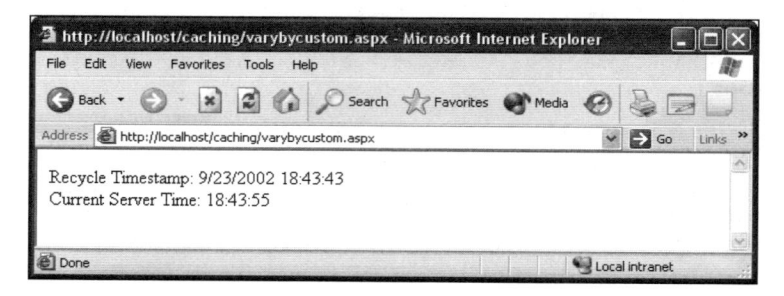

![Screenshot of Internet Explorer showing http://localhost/caching/varybycustom.aspx with:
Recycle Timestamp: 9/23/2002 18:43:43
Current Server Time: 18:43:55]

It should be pointed out that the reason for the time difference is that we triggered the cache flush on `triggerrecycle.aspx` by changing the application variable's value. However, the cache wasn't refreshed until the first request after the purge. Because the navigation back to `varybycustom.aspx` wasn't instantaneous, there is a few seconds difference.

Next, we will examine partial page caching. This next technique is another take on output caching. Partial page caching, or fragment caching, is quite important to scalability as it allows for more of a spot focus on caching.

Partial Page Caching

Sometimes caching an entire page is impractical. When a user selects a ticker, we want to display to them the most up-to-date price information. However, in this scenario, it is likely that we would still want to display other static information on the page. In our MyInvestmentWatch.com example, we would likely still want to cache certain static data, such as the banner and page footer, so that they are not dynamically rendered each time.

Caching

Microsoft supports this need very well in ASP.NET through a concept of partial page, or fragment, caching. Partial page caching simply involves applying what we've discussed above with regards to the `@OutputCache` directive to user controls. The syntax is the same and the options are the same, with the exception that a user control supports the additional `VaryByControl` parameter and does not support the `Location` parameter. You must use a user control to enable partial page caching.

We will detail the interaction between the container page and the cached control. First, it is important to understand the control will share the cache timeout of the container if the container's timeout is longer and if both simply have `VaryByParam` set. To demonstrate, create a control, `CachedControl.ascx` and add the following code:

```
<%@ OutputCache Duration="10" VaryByParam="none" %>
<Script runat="server">
  Public Sub Page_Load()
    Dim currentTime As DateTime = DateTime.Now()
    TimeCreated.InnerHTML = currentTime.ToString("T")
  End Sub
</Script>

<div>
  <span>Current Control Time:</span>
  <span id="TimeCreated" runat="server"></span>
</div>
```

Now, create a page, `CachedContainer.aspx`, and add the following code:

```
<%@ Page Language="vb" %>
<%@ Register TagPrefix="MIW" TagName="CachedControl"
            src="CachedControl.ascx" %>

<%@ OutputCache Duration="60" Location="Server" VaryByParam="none" %>
<Script runat="server">
  Sub Page_Load()
    Dim currentTime As DateTime = DateTime.Now()
    TimeCreated.InnerHTML = currentTime.ToString("T")
  End Sub
</Script>
<div>
  <span>Current Container Time:</span>
  <span id="TimeCreated" runat="server"></span>
</div>

<MIW:CachedControl id="nccDemo" runat="server"/>
```

As you can see, we are specifying that the page should be cached, and specifying a shorter output cache duration for the control. An initial visit to the page compiles the page and places it in the cache:

263

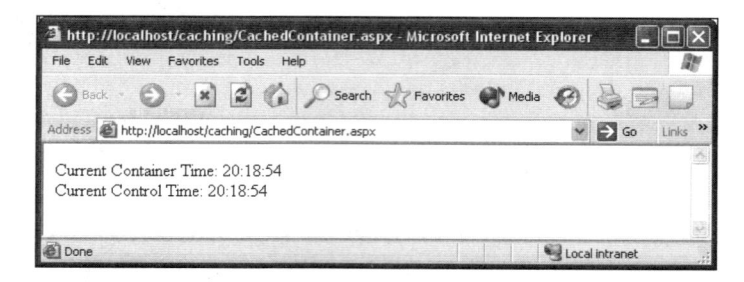

Chapter 5: The Presentation Tier

> Current Container Time: 20:18:54
> Current Control Time: 20:18:54

Refreshing will indicate that the page is still reading from the cache for both the container page and the control.

Now, modify the code so that the duration is shorter on the container page than the control. In `CachedControl.ascx`:

```
<%@ OutputCache Duration="120" VaryByParam="none" %>
```

and in `CachedContainer.aspx`:

```
<%@ OutputCache Duration="10" VaryByParam="none" %>
```

Now, a visit to the page clearly shows that the control is being cached longer than the container page. The first load synchronizes the load time for both container and control:

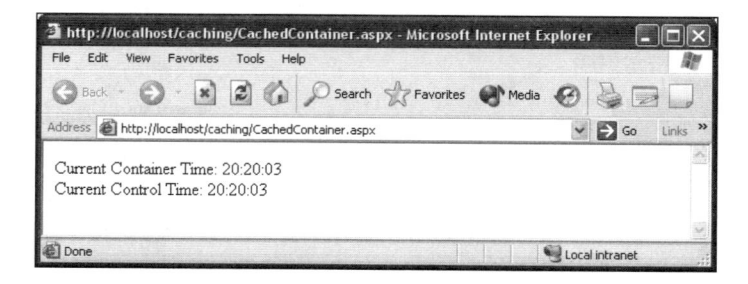

> Current Container Time: 20:20:03
> Current Control Time: 20:20:03

and a subsequent refresh indicates that the control is being cached long after the container page refreshes.

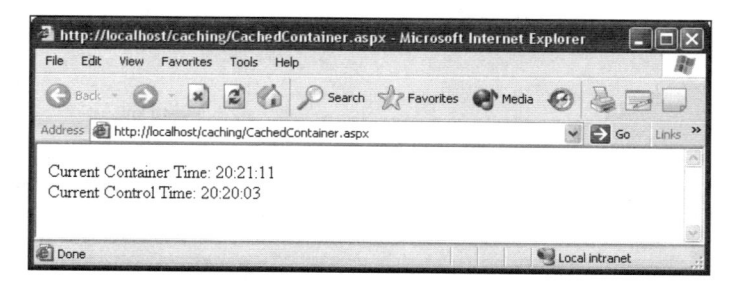

> Current Container Time: 20:21:11
> Current Control Time: 20:20:03

There are a few points worth noting with regards to caching controls. Firstly, a new copy of the control is cached for each page that includes that control. That is, if `myFirstPage.aspx` and `mySecondPage.aspx` both include `myCalendar.ascx` then `myCalendar.ascx` will be cached twice. Secondly, a cached control cannot be programmatically modified by the container, so you wouldn't want to put things in a control that need to be programmatically modified.

Next, we will explore how to programmatically add your own data to the cache. The output caching serves a very useful purpose in that it allows us to save already generated pages for reuse by multiple clients. However, it is also quite useful to programmatically access the cache to store fairly static data that will be used in generating multiple pages.

Programmatic Caching

The `Cache` object in ASP.NET is very powerful. Fortunately, it is also very easy to use. The cache is quite useful as a storage point for data that is somewhat static. Ideally, this data is expensive to create and usable by multiple pages. As a rule, much of information that was stored in the ASP `Application` object, apart from application configuration information, will now be stored in the ASP.NET cache.

The `Cache` object supports these key features:

- Dependencies between items
- Dependencies between an item and a file
- Expiration policies for items
- Priorities for items
- Event-based notification as items are added and removed

There are two basic ways to access the cache. Either implicitly, much as the `Application` and `Session` objects were accessed in ASP, or explicitly, which better exposes the functionality of the cache:

Implicit Access

```
Dim GreetingText As String
GreetingText = "Welcome to MyInvestmentWatch.com"
Cache("Greeting") = GreetingText
```

Explicit Access

```
Dim GreetingText As String
GreetingText = "Welcome to MyInvestmentWatch.com"
Cache.Insert("Greeting", GreetingText)
```

Throughout this chapter we will be utilizing the explicit method of accessing the cache.

Cache Item Dependencies

One of the greatest features of the cache is that it allows dependencies to be set on items. This alleviates much of the burden of manually managing items within the cache. For example, if our footer is generated from a text file then we can simply create a dependency between the cached footer and the text file. When the file that the footer draws information from changes then the footer control will be expired and subsequently regenerated and cached on the next request. This is obviously a much better way of updating the underlying control than implementing some manual process to determine if the file has changed and then finding and expiring the appropriate cache element.

Time-Based Dependency

Aside from simply adding the cache element as we did above, one of the simplest methods of controlling a cached item is to create a time-based dependency. The `Cache` object actually supports expiring data based on two different time-based methods; an absolute timespan or a sliding timespan.

Absolute Timespan

This sets a hard expiration for the cached item. For example, our stock detail page is always delayed by twenty minutes. This would be an ideal candidate for an absolute timeout of twenty minutes.

The signature for this method of updating the cache is:

```
Cache.Insert(ItemName As String,
             ItemToCache As Object,
             Dependency As CacheDependency,
             TimeToExpire As DateTime,
             TimespanToLive As TimeSpan)
```

The code would be as follows:

```
Cache.Insert("Greeting", "Welcome to MyInvestmentWatch.com", _
             nothing, new TimeSpan(0,20,0), nothing)
```

This will cause the value of the `Greeting` key to expire every twenty minutes. This method is preferable when data must be refreshed on a known periodic interval.

Sliding Timespan

Another very useful method of caching is to set up a sliding time-based dependency on an item. We will use the same signature as the absolute expiration, but the parameters are slightly different:

```
Cache.Insert("Greeting", "Welcome to MyInvestmentWatch.com", _
             nothing, nothing, new TimeSpan(0,10,0))
```

The above code will set the cached item to expire after it has not been requested for the set timespan, or ten minutes in this case. In this situation, the item expiration time is reset on each request. That is, if the cached item is 9:59 minutes old and is requested again, then the expiration countdown is reset.

This method is most useful in responding to requests where the cached item does not need to be expired at a set time. In this case, it cannot be guaranteed when the cached item will be disposed of. Rather, it can only be guaranteed that the item will eventually be recreated and cached at some point. This would be useful for instances where data is expensive to create, but fairly static, and needs to be resynchronized when the application is idle.

File-Based Dependency

It may also be desirable to expire an item based on when a file is updated. For instance, we may wish to force the header control to expire when the page logo is updated.

The signature for this method of updating the cache is:

```
Cache.Insert(ItemName As String,
             ItemToCache As Object,
             Dependency As CacheDependency)
```

The corresponding code would be:

```
Cache.Insert("Header", headerControl, New CacheDependency("logo.gif"))
```

Or, we may wish to update the footer when an underlying XML file is updated:

```
<%@ Import Namespace="System.Xml" %>
<%@ Import Namespace="System.Web.Cache" %>

<Script language="vb" runat="server">
  Public Sub Page_Load(sender as Object, e as EventArgs)
    Dim footerDOM as new XmlDocument()
    footerDOM.Load("footer.xml")
    Cache.Insert("footer", footerDOM, _
                 new CacheDependency("footer.xml"))
  End Sub
</Script>
```

Now, when the underlying file is modified, the cached item is expired. This type of automatic expiration is very useful. As demonstrated above, we do not need to perform any manual work at all to expire the currently loaded footer and regenerate it from the changed XML file. Of course, there are instances where it would be useful to extend the above concept to establish relationships between cached values.

Key-Based Dependency

Another useful type of dependency is key-based dependency. Using this, you could have one item expire when an associated item expires. For instance, it may be useful to expire our company news when the current stock is expired. While this may prevent late-breaking news from being displayed, it would ensure that news is at least as current as the stock price.

In our example below, we're actually establishing a key-based and file-based dependency for the footer. If the header is modified, or if the `footer.xml` file is modified, then the footer will be expired:

```
<%@ Import Namespace="System.Xml" %>
<%@ Import Namespace="System.Web.Cache" %>

<Script language="vb" runat="server">
  Public Sub Page_Load(sender as Object, e as EventArgs)
    Dim headerDOM as new XmlDocument()

    headerDOM.Load("header.xml")
    Cache.Insert("header", headerDOM, _
            new CacheDependency("header.xml"))

    Dim footerDOM as new XmlDocument()
    Dim dependencyKey(0) as string

    dependencyKey(0) = "header"
    footerDOM.Load("footer.xml")

    Cache.Insert("footer", footerDOM,new
    CacheDependency("footer.xml", dependencyKey))
  End Sub
</Script>
```

If we had wanted to establish a dependency only between the header and footer, where the footer will expire when the header expires, then we would modify the above code:

```
<%@ Import Namespace="System.Xml" %>
<%@ Import Namespace="System.Web.Cache" %>

<Script language="vb" runat="server">
  Public Sub Page_Load(sender as Object, e as EventArgs)
    Dim headerDOM as new XmlDocument()

    headerDOM.Load("header.xml")
    Cache.Insert("header, headerDOM, _
            new CacheDependency("header.xml"))

    Dim footerDOM as new XmlDocument()
    Dim dependencyKey(0) as string
```

```
        dependencyKey(0) = "header"
        footerDOM.Load("footer.xml")

        Cache.Insert("footer", footerDOM, _
                    new CacheDependency(nothing, dependencyKey))
    End Sub
</Script>
```

The benefit of establishing dependencies, in general, is that it removes the administrative overhead of expiring related cache items. As we have demonstrated above, it is even possible to create multiple dependencies between cache items. However, this is only a part of cache management. As you will see, there are a few other aspects to effectively using the cache when building highly scalable systems.

Cache Item Priorities

When resources become constrained, ASP.NET will remove items from the cache in order to free up resources. In many cases, it would be preferable to specify which items should be removed first. ASP.NET provides this functionality through the ability to set priorities for each cached item.

The ability to set an item's priority is exposed through one of the overloaded `Cache.Insert()` methods:

```
<%@ Page Language="vb" %>
<%@ Import Namespace="System.Web.Caching" %>

<Script language="vb" runat="server">
    Public Sub Page_Load(sender as Object, e as EventArgs)
        Cache.Insert("Footer", "This is a string", Nothing, _
                    NoAbsoluteExpiration, NoSlidingExpiration, _
                    CacheItemPriority.High, Nothing)
    End Sub
</Script>
```

The possible values for item priorities, as exposed by the `CacheItemPriority` enumeration are:

Value	Description
AboveNormal	Cached items with this priority are less likely to be removed during cache cleanup than items with a Normal priority.
Normal	This is the default cache item priority. Items with this priority will be removed after items with a Low or BelowNormal priority.
BelowNormal	Items with this priority are more likely to be removed than items with a Normal priority.

Table continued on following page

269

Chapter 5: The Presentation Tier

Value	Description
High	Items cached with a High priority are the least likely to be removed, next to items that are NotRemovable.
Low	Low priority items are the most likely to be removed from the cache as system memory is freed.
NotRemovable	Items with this priority will not be removed, even when memory becomes constrained. These items are still subject to being expired.

Care should be taken not to abuse this method of cache control. The majority of items should simply be inserted into the cache with the default priority of Normal. Items that are expensive to create, or that will otherwise provide the most benefit through being cached, should have a higher priority set. Items that are fairly inexpensive to recreate, should be assigned a lower priority. However, as a rule, items should be assigned the default priority and control should be handed to the cache to manage removing seldom-used items.

Cache Events

Another rather powerful feature of the Cache object is that it is capable of notifying a delegate when an item is removed from the cache. Using this notification, it is possible to programmatically add the regenerated item back to the cache once it has been expired. The alternative is that the cached item is reloaded on the next request, which may not be desirable when caching items that are, time-wise, expensive to create.

Setting up a callback when a cached item is removed is also rather simple. The Cache.Insert() method simply takes another parameter to set up:

```
Cache.Insert(ItemName As String,
             ItemToCache As Object,
             Dependency As CacheDependency,
             TimeToExpire As DateTime,
             TimespanToLive As TimeSpan,
             ItemPriority As CacheItemPriority,
             Callback as CacheItemRemovedCallback)
```

In the following example, cacheCallback.aspx, we reload the footer once it expires from the cache:

```
<Script language="vb" runat="server">
  Public Sub onRemoveCallBack(ByVal key As String, _
                              ByVal value As Object, _
                              ByVal reason As CacheItemRemovedReason)
    LoadFooter()
  End Sub
```

```
    Public Sub Page_Load(sender as Object, e as EventArgs)
      LoadFooter()
    End Sub

    Public Sub LoadFooter()
      Dim footerDOM as new XmlDocument()
      Dim onRemove As CacheItemRemovedCallback = Nothing

      footerDOM.Load("footer.xml")

      onRemove = New CacheItemRemovedCallback(AddressOf _
                                              Me.onRemoveCallBack)

      Cache.Insert("footer",footerDOM,_
                   new CacheDependency("footer.xml"), _
                   NoAbsoluteExpiration, NoSlidingExpiration, _
                   CacheItemPriority.Normal, onRemove)
    End Sub
</Script>
```

In the above example, we have better control over what should happen when ASP.NET determines that an item should be removed from the cache. In addition, ASP.NET indicates the reason that the item was removed. This is provided through the `CacheItemRemovedReason` enumeration. The possible values for this enumeration are shown in the following table.

Value	Description
DependencyChanged	An item with a dependency specified, such as adding the footer with a dependency on the underlying XML file, has expired, causing the chained expiration.
Expired	The item expired from the cache because an absolute or sliding timespan was reached.
Underused	The item was discarded when the system was freeing memory.
Removed	The `Cache.Remove("itemKey")` method was explicitly called.

Obviously, we would want to check the reason why an item was removed before we add it back to the cache. If the item was removed due to underutilization, then it likely should not immediately be added back to the cache.

Caching is powerful and, as we have seen, very easy to use in ASP.NET. The `Cache` object exposes many methods to provide a very granular level of control when needed. However, as with anything, there are potential repercussions of using the extended functionality of the cache. Care should be taken when setting up dependencies and when specifying cache priorities to ensure that the cache isn't forced to work against itself when managing resources and expiring cached items.

Caching Best Practices

Generally, caching is a very good thing. When used properly it will dramatically reduce user load across all tiers in an application. However, when it is used incorrectly you can actually cause an application to perform less well than if you had not used caching at all.

Start with No Caching at All

As a rule, a best practice with regards to performance testing is to determine a baseline before making improvements. If you are at the point of not knowing if a particular item will benefit from caching, then start by testing the system without these improvements first.

There will certainly be items that are obvious candidates for caching, such as dynamically generated menus that don't change often. However, there will also be items where the tradeoffs between the gains of caching and loss of dynamic, up-to-date data must be weighed. A solid baseline will assist in making these determinations.

Don't Cache Data that Must be Up-To-Date on Each View

This probably goes without saying, but information that must be up to date cannot be cached. Since the whole point of output caching is to save output for use by multiple clients, or at least across multiple views, then the data will be out of date.

Our examples above are actually a perfect example of what not to cache. The time shown on the page does not reflect the actual current time. If a user were accessing our site to see if it was time for lunch or not, they would likely be very upset to find out that our time was off by quite a bit.

Don't Try to Cache Everything

It is easy to go cache happy, if you will, and attempt to cache everything. However, this will place unneeded load on server resources. Additional memory will be eaten and the cache will have to work harder to constantly remove decayed items.

Don't Cache Items that will Expire Quickly

In one of our examples above, we set the cache to time out every ten seconds. Don't do this' It is a bad practice to cache items that will expire quickly.

Don't Cache Rarely Used Data

The point of caching is, generally, to ensure data that must be accessed frequently will be readily available. If data is rarely used, then it does not make sense to add a strain on the cache to manage this data. The data will either decay or take up space long before it is useful.

Cache Items that are Expensive to Create

If a resource is expensive to create, and doesn't change often, then it is a good candidate for caching. For example, suppose we had a complex page structure that would show the ten most viewed stocks over the last 20 minutes in the order of popularity. Displaying this page might normally involve a lengthy operation against the middle tier and database. Caching this page and causing it to expire every 20 minutes will accomplish the same goal without the need for dynamic creation on every page view.

Cache Items that Can be Used by Multiple Clients

As a general rule, items that are specific to a single client should not be stored in the cache. The cache is intended as a shared storage point for multiple clients. For example, it would be foolish to cache a user control that displayed the user's name. It's highly likely that multiple users won't be using this data. Data of this nature can be stored within the session if some manner of storing data after the initial fetch is required.

Don't Use VaryByParam="*"

As a general rule, never allow the cache to vary by any parameter. It is likely that there are truly only a few parameters that will cause the output to vary. Varying by all parameters allows your code to accidentally be cached multiple times, by each parameter variation, whether it was supposed to be or not.

Following these guidelines will greatly assist in using the cache properly. As with many best practices, these will not fit all specific needs. However, as a good rule of thumb, start by following these guidelines and then modifying specific implementations as needed.

Caching is only part of the puzzle with building highly scalable web tiers. Properly managing user interactions with the system, such as entering data into forms and tracking user-specific information also play very large roles in the scalability of a system. What we're going to touch on next is how to perform this user state management in a scalable environment.

State Management

State management is vital to any application. It is further compounded in a web-based application where users and the application are disconnected from each other. ASP addressed this through the use of `Application` and `Session` objects. The `Application` object is a unique data store for each ASP application while a new `Session` object is created for each user.

However, the ASP solution still wasn't ideal. Specifically, there was no inherent support for managing session information in a web farm. This often led to implementing commercial third-party solutions or developing custom solutions, all with varying degrees of sophistication.

273

There were also less obvious shortcomings with ASP state management. There was no universal method to persist control state when working with a form. That is, once a user had filled in a form and pressed submit, the data was pushed into the `Response` object and lost from the form. If the user needed to modify any values, the developer would need to manually re-add all of the previously entered values.

ASP.NET addresses user state management needs through several very rich session management options. ASP.NET also addresses persisting form values through multiple postbacks through the use of ViewState. However, both ViewState and session management can adversely affect performance.

In this section we will discuss the multiple methods for session management as the advantages and disadvantages of each option. We will also discuss controlling the ViewState and best practices around when and how to use the ViewState.

Session Management

When we talk about session management, we're referring to the information in the `Session` object. This information is specific to each user. Of course, the more users you have, the more critical session management becomes. This problem is even further compounded once you have to add a second web server.

In ASP, it was common to place VB COM components that should otherwise live in the `Application` object into the `Session`. Workarounds such as this were necessary because of the apartment-threaded nature of the VB component did not lend itself well to supporting multiple requests simultaneously. Of course, this limitation is removed now in Visual Basic .NET and care should be taken to reevaluate instances of this in any current applications that are being migrated.

In ASP.NET, the `Session` should be confined to only storing information that is specific to a given user. Information that can be utilized by multiple clients should be placed within the cache. Objects that directly support the web application should be loaded into the `Application` object.

Within ASP.NET, there are three general means of storing user session information:

- In-process
- Out-of-process in a State Server
- Out-of-process in a SQL Server

We will discuss the advantages and disadvantages of each of these methods in the following section as well as the best practices for implementing scalability. We will be working with `machine.config` throughout this section. These changes could also be made to the `web.config` file for each web application if you do not want the changes to be universal. We will be modifying the `sessionState` settings:

State Management

```
<configuration>
  <system.web>
    <sessionState
      mode="InProc"
      stateConnectionString="tcpip=127.0.0.1:42424"
      stateNetworkTimeout="10"
      sqlConnectionstring="data source=machine;user id=sa;password="
      cookieless="false"
      timeout="20"
    />
  </system.web>"
</configuration>
```

The attributes for `sessionState` are shown in the following table:

Attribute	Description
mode	The possible settings are off, InProc, StateServer, and SQLServer. The InProc option causes the ASP.NET session to act identically to the behavior of the ASP session.
stateConnectionstring	This option specifies the use of an out-of-process state server and gives the IP address and port of the server that will be used to provide state management services. The IP address must be configured if the mode is set to StateServer.
stateNetworkTimeout	This is the timeout, in seconds, to be used when attempting to connect to an out-of-process session data store.
sqlConnectionString	Another option for state management is to utilize SQL Server. This setting will specify the location and connection options to access the database that will house the session data. The IP address and security credentials must be configured if the mode is set to SQLServer.
cookieless	ASP.NET has excellent built-in support for storing session information without requiring the user to have cookies enabled. Whether cookies will be used or the session ID will be stored in the URL is determined by this setting. The default is false. We will not discuss this in detail as it does not directly relate to scalability.
timeout	This specifies the lifetime, in minutes, of the user's session object and is a sliding value. The Session.Timeout will be set to the current time plus this value. The default is 20 minutes.

275

It is important to understand each option and its impact on scalability.

No State

While we did mention that there are three options for storing state, there is actually a fourth option with regards to user state. This option is to not store state on the server at all. This option will not work well on MyInvestmentWatch.com as we need to persist user information between transactions. However, in some instances, such as a site that largely delivers non-personalized content to users, the option to not store user state may be the best option of all.

To set up a server to not store user sessions, modify the `sessionState` as follows:

```
<configuration>
  <system.web>
    <sessionState
      mode="off"
    />
  </system.web>"
</configuration>
```

Obviously, one of the biggest challenges will now be on how to store user state. This setting should not be used unless you only need to store very small amounts of information. A cookie on the client could be used for most storage needs, such as a user's preferred page layout, or perhaps the user's postal code if you were delivering local news.

Pros

This is the most scalable option. As no user state must be stored, resources on the server are certainly not constrained. Also, as it doesn't matter which server in a farm responds the user's request, this option works exceptionally well in a web farm.

Cons

Well, obviously, the biggest disadvantage of this approach is that no user session state is stored. Many sites rely on the session to track information, such as personalization information, shopping carts, and profile data. It would be possible to load this information from backend components as needed but this places a large burden on the backend to constantly delivery data that is largely static in nature. Rather than accessing the backend on each page load to retrieve user information, it is preferable to load this information into the `Session` object.

In-process

This is the method that comes to mind when discussing session management in ASP. The same method carries over to ASP.NET as well. The sessions are created on the server that handles the original client request. In a web farm, the client must be routed back to the same server each time or else the session information will be 'lost' as it only exists on the originating server.

State Management

To set up a server to keep the user state in-process, modify the `sessionState` as follows:

```
<configuration>
  <system.web>
    <sessionState
      mode="InProc"
      cookieless="false"
      timeout="20"
    />
  </system.web>"
</configuration>
```

Keep in mind that this setting is the default option for ASP.NET. This method is perfect when only a single web server is involved. After that, things get a bit uncomfortable.

For each subsequent request, the user must be routed back to the server that handled their initial request. A common method to handle this was to affix the physical web server name to the URL for each request. In this situation, the user may request www.MyInvestmentWatch.com and be rerouted to www04.MyInvestmentWatch.com. Each URL, for that user, will then point to www04.MyInvestmentWatch.com.

Another option is that certain load-balancers can handle "pinning", or rerouting the client back to the same server. This removes the need to manually rewrite URLs on the page. However, it still brings with it the disadvantage of not properly balancing user load across all servers.

As you've by now likely noticed, changing from one mode to another requires little effort in configuring ASP.NET. A bit of set-up is required for the next two options, but changing over to utilize them is rather simple as well. So, determining a session management strategy that will last for the lifetime of the application is not required. Rather, session management can grow with the rest of the environment.

Pros

This is the fastest method of storing user state information. The state is on the same server, and in the same process, as the web pages that must access this state. No application boundaries must be crossed, no processor boundaries must be crossed, and most importantly, no network boundaries must be crossed.

Cons

From a scalability standpoint, the single biggest disadvantage to in-process session management is that it is tied to a single server. This method is also tied to the ASP.NET process. If this process fails due to rogue code, or if the application is unloaded, then session state will be lost on that server.

This method also prevents user load from being fully distributed across a web farm. Because a user must be rerouted to the same server each time, there is a good chance that some servers will have an inordinate amount user load while others will be underutilized.

Also, while not related directly to scalability, this method has a reliability problem. If the server goes down then all user session information being stored on that server is lost. This presents a single point of failure, which is a poor trait to have in any system.

State Server

A state server is simply a server dedicated to managing user sessions. This option allows all servers in a web farm to centralize user state. In turn, this makes it possible for a user's request to be fulfilled by any server, regardless of which server answered the initial request.

The state server will store all sessions in memory, much as server managing in-process sessions would. Thus, this option provides the same speed advantage of storing sessions in memory. Of course, there will be a performance penalty for crossing process and network boundaries. However, there is also a benefit in that the user state is not tied to the ASP.NET process.

To set up a web server to keep the user session on a separate state server, modify the sessionState as follows:

```
<configuration>
  <system.web>
    <sessionState
      mode="StateServer"
      stateConnectionString="tcpip=127.0.0.1:42424"
      stateNetworkTimeout="10"
      cookieless="false"
      timeout="20"
    />
  </system.web>"
</configuration>
```

When performance is important, this is the preferred option. However, this method still has a potentially significant disadvantage. The server cannot be failed over. This means that, if this server crashes, user state is lost. Keep in mind that this server is storing state for the entire web farm. That means that the crash is very global in nature. User state isn't wiped out for a single server, as it would be if the state were stored in-process. Rather, user state is lost for every single person on the site.

While the consequences if the state server goes down are rather dire, the fact is that this will be fairly reliable and a good option when performance is critical. As a precautionary method, a good practice is to implement a dedicated server as the state server. This server should not be managing state for every other server in addition to functioning as a web server. Rather, it should only manage state for the rest of the servers in the web farm. Our example shows the local computer being used as both a state server and web server, but the URL should be changed for a production environment.

State Management

Setup

A state server is nothing more than a server with the .NET Framework installed. To enable the state server, you simply need to start up a Windows Service. Specifically, the `aspnet_state` service needs to be running in order for session to be stored.

First, determine which machine will function as the state server. You can configure the service using the Services MMC snap-in, which is available from: Start | Settings | Control Panel | Administrative Tools | Services.

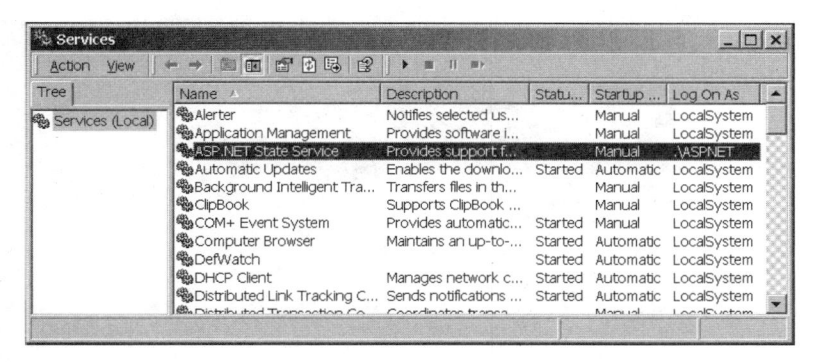

Locate the ASP.NET State Service in the right pane and right-click on it to open up a configuration menu. You will likely want to click to start the service automatically, so that you don't need to manually start the service every time the computer is restarted. This can be done by selecting Properties and using the Startup type dropdown box on the General tab. Then, start the service. That's all it takes to start up the state server.

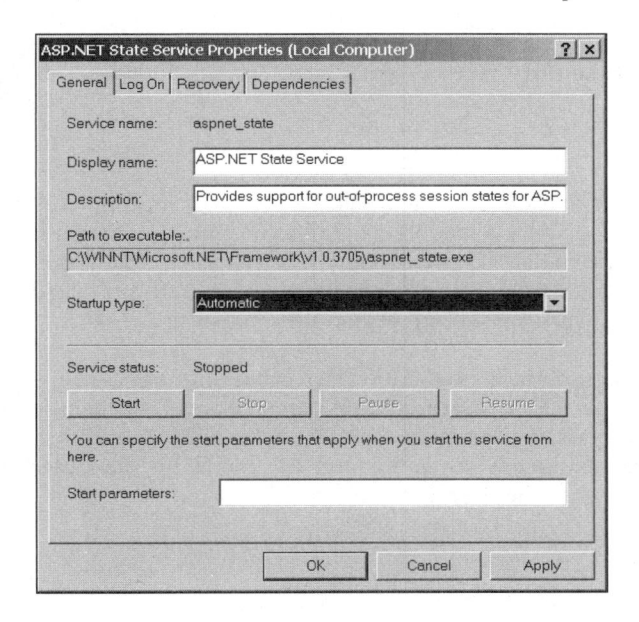

279

Chapter 5: The Presentation Tier

There is one more configuration change you will likely want to make. By default, the port that the state server will listen to is port `42424`. This may be acceptable, but for the sake of making things a bit more secure you may wish to change this port number.

To change the port number from the default, you will need to edit the registry. You'll also need to stop the `aspnet_state` service before making these changes. To configure the port, run `regedit.exe`, and then expand to HKEY_LOCAL_MACHINE | SYSTEM | CurrentControlSet | Services | aspnet_state | Parameters.

Within Parameters, open the `Port` value. This will allow us to configure the IP port that the `aspnet_state` service listens on.

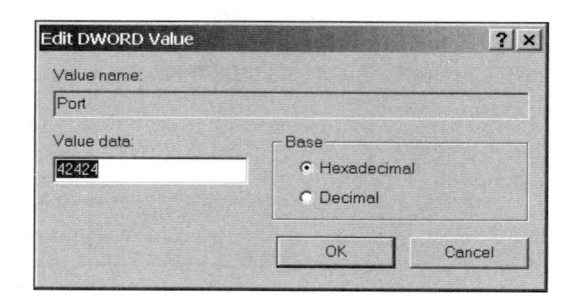

After changing the IP address and port, we must modify the `machine.config` to reflect the new settings:

```
mode="StateServer"
stateConnectionString="tcpip=192.168.0.2:42424"
```

We will need to make this change on each web server that we want to utilize this new state server.

Pros

The single biggest advantage of using a state server, over an in-process session manager, is that it functions very well in a web farm. Users no longer have to be bound to a single machine, which will allow requests to be balanced over all servers fairly equally. In addition, because session state is kept in memory, it is faster than the SQL Server option, which we will explore in the next section.

This method is also not bound to the ASP.NET process. If the ASP.NET process fails, session information is still persisted because the persistence mechanism, the `aspnet_state` service, is external to the ASP.NET process boundary. This adds a bit of reliability in that another server in the farm will simply handle a user's next request, with little interruption to the user.

State Management

Cons

The single biggest failing of this method is that it is bound to a single server. If this server crashes for any reason then state is lost for every single user currently on the web site. However, a properly configured and maintained server will have an extremely small unplanned outage percentage, and the speed increase might often be worth the perceived disadvantage.

Another disadvantage is that growth is largely tied to how much memory a single server can support. Realistically, the growth of a single server for session management will suffice for most applications. However, those applications that simply must support more sessions than can fit in memory will incur a heavy performance penalty when sessions are paged to disk.

SQL Server

The header probably makes this rather obvious. Setting the `sessionState` mode to `SQLServer` allows ASP.NET to utilize a SQL Server database for managing session state. This brings with it the same advantages as an out-of-process state server in that it is not bound to the ASP.NET process and it serves as a centralized session storage point for web farms.

The SQL Server mode is slower than a state server because it stores all sessions in a database, not in memory. However, this method can be much more reliable. With a single SQL Server, the database can still be persisted to an external storage device, such as a Storage Area Network. It can be made even more reliable than that by setting up a SQL Server cluster as the session manager. Thus, while this is a slightly slower option, it can provide a much higher guaranteed level of service.

To set up a web server to keep the user session on a separate SQL Server instance, modify `sessionState` as follows:

```
<configuration>
  <system.web>
    <sessionState
      mode="SQLServer"
      sqlConnectionstring="data source=machine; user id=user;
                          password=pwd"
      stateNetworkTimeout="10"
      cookieless="false"
      timeout="20"
    />
  </system.web>"
</configuration>
```

When reliability is important, this is the preferred option. However, to achieve a high level of reliability, you must install a clustered version of SQL Server. This means that a bit more cost will be involved, but if you are attempting to deliver a highly reliable solution then it is worth the price tag.

281

Setup

> A production environment should only use SQL Server. However, MSDE is a wonderful, and free, alternative to use during development.

Configuring SQL Server, or MSDE, to store session state is fairly straightforward. In fact, all it involves is running a T-SQL script that sets up the database and table structures. You can use a utility named `OSQL.EXE` to apply the script to our database server. However, you will need administrator-level access to the database to properly run the script.

The scripts are located in `\%WinDir%\Microsoft.NET\Framework\[version]\`, which in our case this translates to `C:\WINDOWS\Microsoft.NET\Framework\v1.0.3705`.

There, you will find two SQL scripts, `InstallSqlState.sql` and a corresponding `UninstallSqlState.sql`. If, for any reason, you need to uninstall the state server database from SQL Server then just follow the same process and run `UninstallSqlState.sql`.

To install the script, run the following from the above directory:

```
> OSQL -S machineName -U user -P password <InstallSqlState.sql
```

After configuring SQL Server, we must modify `machine.config` to add the following to the `sessionState` entry:

```
mode="SQLServer"
sqlConnectionstring="data source=MIWSQL ;user id=ASPNetSession;
                     password=Session1$$"
```

We will need to make this change on each web server we want to utilize this new SQL Server session manager.

Pros

The single biggest advantage of moving session state to SQL Server is that you can then implement a cluster to provide an extremely robust and reliable method of storing user sessions. While this isn't related directly to scalability, it can provide a deciding factor when choosing a method to utilize in a highly scaled system. That is, both a state server and a SQL Server provide a great method of state management in a highly scaled system. However, a state server should be used when performance is more important than reliability and SQL Server should be used when performance can be sacrificed in favor of greater reliability.

In addition to the added reliability, there is another, not so obvious benefit. Because a SQL Server database is largely only constrained by disk size, it can grow to accommodate a virtually limitless number of sessions. In addition, SQL Server can easily scale out, which will allow responding to requests for session data to be spread across multiple servers.

Cons

SQL Server for session management is slow. Rather, it is slow in comparison to the other methods detailed above. With it so simple to switch between session modes, it is possible to try SQL Server first and then determine the best fit for your needs.

Best Practices for Session Management

Session management is necessary, and useful, when building web-based applications. However, improper use of session state can lead to applications that do not scale well.

Only Use the Session if Required

You should only enable sessions for your web site if you absolutely need to store more than "small" amounts of user information while the user is on the site. If you only need to store certain information about a user, such as perhaps a site username and preferred layout, then consider persisting the data to cookies instead.

ASP.NET will create a new `Session` object for each user that does not already have a session and will fire the `Session_OnStart` and, later, the `Session_OnEnd` events. By removing session state completely, if it is not needed, then the overhead of creating, storing, and managing sessions is avoided.

Also, sessions do not disappear the minute a user leaves the site. Rather, sessions live on until the timeout period specified. The default for this is 20 minutes. Obviously, you don't want to set the timeout too short as the user will then lose their session data during lengthy think-time operations, such as filling out a form. The downside of this is that ASP.NET must manage session state for many users that are no longer on the web site.

Only Use the Session When Required

Turn off access to the session on pages that do not require any user state. To accomplish this, add the following directive to the top of the page:

```
<%@Page EnableSessionState="false" %>
```

Note that the session ID will still be sent to the client and that `Session_OnStart` will still fire if the page the user is first requesting a page with this directive. However, ASP.NET does not need to perform the normal session tracking that accompanies pages that must access session state.

283

Plan for SQL Server

In our opinion, SQL Server is the preferred method of state management for highly scalable web sites. SQL Server is the more reliable option and can be scaled out to support load across multiple servers:

- **Plan for a move to SQL Server** – You will need to implement a session manager as soon as you have more than one web server.

- **Determine the impact on the environment architecture** – Generally, you will want to have a dedicated session server in the same network layer as the web servers.

- **Don't start with SQL Server if it doesn't fit** – A move to SQL Server is not cheap. It can become more expensive if you plan to cluster SQL Server, which will require the Enterprise Edition. If needed, to start, you can designate a web server in the farm to act as a state server until you can transition to SQL Server.

Session management provides several challenges to building highly scalable systems. Sessions allow for a wonderful means of storing user state but at the cost of incurring an overhead to manage sessions across a user's lifetime. Following the above tips will help greatly in growing session management as the application environment increases.

While session management is a large part of state management, there is one more place where state management can pose an issue to scalability. That is with managing the state of controls on a form.

View State

In ASP, it was customary to use two or three pages to process a form. The first page displayed the form and redirected the output to a form handler. This form handler then worked with the data the user entered and possibly redirected the user back to the form page to correct errors or on to another view if the form was completed correctly. This method was cumbersome and resulted in fairly static forms.

ASP.NET is moving to a round-trip model where a form is posted back to itself in a manner that is almost invisible to the programmer. This allows a web form to appear to function much as a Windows-based form. However, the fact is that this new programming model is just that, appearance. The heart of this development model is still a stateless HTTP connection. There is no inherent ability for the server to remember values between requests.

The solution in ASP was to repopulate the form from the Request object. This was a rather involved process and prone to errors when dealing with lengthy or multi-page forms.

ASP.NET introduced the ViewState to tackle exactly this problem. The page will retain the ViewState for all controls between requests to the server. These values are stored as encoded key-value pairs through the use of a hidden form field.

State Management

Take a look at the code for showviewstate.aspx:

```
<%@ Page EnableViewState="true"%>

<html>
  <body MS_POSITIONING="GridLayout">
    <form id="showviewstate" method="post" runat="server">
      <input type="text" id="Name" runat="server">
    </form>
  </body>
</html>
```

This will yield the following output on the client:

```
<html>
  <body MS_POSITIONING="GridLayout">
    <form name="showviewstate" method="post"
          action="showviewstate.aspx" id="showviewstate">

      <input type="hidden" name="__VIEWSTATE"
             value="dDwxNzU2ODcxNTcyOzs+O3sS2H2Zc5PJs14ClQqs5KeoQ+w=" />

      <input name="Name" id="Name" type="text" />
    </form>
  </body>
</html>
```

By default, the ViewState is captured for each control on a form that is set to run on the server. Keep in mind that the ViewState shown above is actually for a single control, that can only hold a single value, and the control is empty. For a sizeable form, or even a form containing a treeview or grid control, the ViewState can quickly exceed 100k!

ViewState and Scalability

Poorly managed ViewState will adversely affect performance. Basically, ASP.NET must persist all of the state for all controls to the client. This will increase the work ASP.NET must do as well as increase network traffic. When the form is then posted back, the ViewState will be transmitted again, which will further affect network traffic.

However, there are several ways to manage ViewState as well. First, if an entire form does not require ViewState, then set the `EnableViewState` page directive to `false`:

```
<%@ Page EnableViewState="false"%>
```

This provides a method to turn off state across the page. Often, though, the preference is to simply turn off the ViewState for a single control. This is accomplished through a control property:

```
<ASP:Label ID="firstName" Runat="server" EnableViewState="false">
```

285

This method will be preferable for controls that will contain a large amount of data. An example of this would be a `DataGrid` that is displaying the results of a large database.

Best Practices

Viewstate can be a boon when interacting with users via postback forms. However, ViewState can also be a bane when used incorrectly. Poorly managed ViewState can impede both performance and scalability.

Use ViewState Sparingly

If ViewState isn't required, then be sure to switch it off. For example, we have a search form on MyInvestmentWatch.com. Viewstate isn't really required for this as it is a single textbox that we won't need the user to validate.

One problem is that we are, in essence, doubling the data that must be sent to the client. If we display a listbox to the client with the ViewState enabled, then we must transmit the encoded values of the listbox in the ViewState as well as the viewable version of the data to display to the user.

Don't Use ViewState if the Control Must be Recreated

On MyInvestmentWatch.com, we display a user's preferred stocks. This alone will produce a large ViewState. However, suppose we also wanted to give the user the option to sort by different fields. In this scenario, we will recreate the output of the control, and the subsequent ViewState, each time the user resorts the list.

Consider the ViewState for Caching "Expensive" Data

This may appear contrary to the other suggestions within this section, but if a control is fairly costly to populate and is static in nature, then consider using the ViewState to cache information to the client. This tip works best for controls that have a small amount of data but go through an expensive process to get that data.

To perform this function, populate the control during the page load and then don't repopulate the control on postback. The potential downside of this is that you then rely on the state of the ViewState for populating the control. The advantage of this is that it removes some burden from the cache.

Don't Use ViewState if the Output is Read-Only

The main benefit in using the ViewState is that you can persist user-entered form data between postbacks. Obviously, if this data does not change, then there is little reason to allow it to be stored in the ViewState.

The built-in support of ASP.NET to save control state across multiple postbacks provides a great benefit for improving the user's experience interacting with the application. However, persisting control data can tax a system's scalability and performance when used incorrectly. The above guides will help with determining when and where not to use the ViewState.

Now that we've covered several methods for improving scalability on the front end, let's implement these changes in our application. We will highly a few of the changes from the existing ASP implementation of MyInvestmentWatch.com to the new ASP.NET version.

Our Revised User Interface

Much of the architecture and page flow in our new application will stay the same. The main difference is that we have redesigned the ASP.NET version to take advantage of both the new features of the .NET Framework as well as the new MyInvestmentWatch.com middle tier.

Code Highlights

> We highly recommend using code-behind pages for development. This method allows a much cleaner separation between code and display. However, the code is much easier to illustrate here if it is embedded.

Let's start, as we did last time, by examining the default page:

```
<%@ Page Language="vb" EnableViewState="false"%>
<%@ OutputCache Duration="86400" VaryByParam="none" %>
<%@ Register TagPrefix="MIW" TagName="Header"
             Src="includes/_header.ascx" %>
<%@ Register TagPrefix="MIW" TagName="Footer"
             Src="includes/_footer.ascx" %>
<Script runat="server">
  Private Sub Page_Load()
    If Page.IsPostBack Then
      Try
        Session.Contents("user") = New User(username.Text, _
                                            password.Text, False)
        Response.Redirect("home.aspx")
      Catch exc As ArgumentException
        message.Text = "Username or password does not exist"
      Catch exc As Exception
        message.Text = "Check your username and password"
      End Try
    End If
  End Sub
</Script>
```

287

```html
<html>
<head>
  <title>Welcome to myinvestmentwatch.com</title>
</head>
<body LEFTMARGIN="0" TOPMARGIN="0" MARGINWIDTH="0" MARGINHEIGHT="0">
<MIW:Header runat="server" />

<table height="100" align="center" width="100%">
  <tr><td><div class="copy">You are here: Login</div></td></tr>
</table>

<form id="login" arunat="server">
<p align="center"><asp:Label ID="message" runat="server" /></p>
  <table width="100%" align="center">
    <tr>
      <td><span>UserName:</span></td>
      <td><asp:TextBox id="username" Runat="server"/></td>
    </tr>
    <tr>
      <td><span>Password:</span></td>
      <td>
         <asp:TextBox ID="password" Runat="server"
                      TextMode="Password" />
      </td>
    </tr>
    <tr>
      <td colspan="2"><input type="submit" value="Login"></td>
    </tr>
  </table>
</form>
<MIW:Footer runat="server" />
</body>
</html>
```

The most obvious scalability benefit comes in the first two lines:

```
<%@ Page Language="vb" EnableViewState="false" %>
<%@ OutputCache Duration="86400" VaryByParam="none" %>
```

Here we instruct ASP.NET to turn off the ViewState for the form on this page. State information will not be stored on the client, nor transmitted to the server, for the username or password fields. After all, there are only two fields and the user will likely type over what is there already if the page needs to be redisplayed.

More importantly, we are caching this page for a fairly long period of time. The login page is likely not going to change often. After all, it is not often that we will want to modify how we are asking the customer for a username and password. Because of this, we will cache the page for twenty-four hours at a time.

Our Revised User Interface

We've just cut the required ASP.NET processing down from once per page request to once per day! Imagine if this were a somewhat active site that received 100,000 visitors a day. As each visitor will need to access this page to log in, that is at least 100,000 page views per day. By adopting the above caching strategy, we have reduced our processing overhead from processing 100,000 times to just processing once, which is a pretty impressive reduction.

As a side note, the page must still process in order to validate the user and log them into the system. However, the work effort to generate the page is largely removed. While the server must still run the page and send the resulting output to the client, it is doing so from a cached version rather than running the page for each request.

Another slightly less obvious scalability improvement is that we have replaced our header and footer includes with user controls:

```
<%@ Register TagPrefix="MIW" TagName="Header"
             Src="includes/_header.ascx" %>
<%@ Register TagPrefix="MIW" TagName="Footer"
             Src="includes/_footer.ascx" %>

...

<body LEFTMARGIN="0" TOPMARGIN="0" MARGINWIDTH="0" MARGINHEIGHT="0">
<MIW:Header runat="server" />

...

<MIW:Footer runat="server" />
</body>
</html>
```

The header and footer controls are also fairly static. The following is the code for `footer.ascx`. The header is very similar, so we will just concentrate on the footer:

```
<%@ Control Language="vb"%>
<%@ OutputCache Duration="604800" Location="server" VaryByParam="none"
                VaryByCustom="RecycleIncludes"%>
<table colspan="1" width="100%">
  <tr>
    <td width="20%" align="left"> </td>
    <td width="60%" align="center">
      <span class="copy">Copyright 2002 MyInvestmentWatch.com</span>
    </td>
    <td width="20%" align="right"> </td>
  </tr>
  <tr>
    <td colspan="3" align="center">
      <a href="logout.aspx"><span class="copy">logout</span></a>
    </td>
  </tr>
</table>
```

Chapter 5: The Presentation Tier

Of note is that we are forcing the control to be cached on the server. This will help to ensure that, if the control does change, clients will get the newest version. To further help scalability, we are also caching the control for a week.

Keep in mind that the page cache duration dictates how long the control is cached for unless the control duration is set higher. In this instance, the footer will be cached for the full week while the default page will be cached for just a day. The footer is a good candidate for a lengthy cache lifetime as it will likely not change.

Also, if you will recall, a separate copy of the control output is cached for each page that is output cached. When a change arises, we may need to quickly expire these items across all pages. To accomplish this, we have added the `VaryByCustom` attribute to the `@OutputCache` directive. In order to enable this entirely, we must add the following code to our `Global.asax` file:

```
Sub Application_Start(ByVal sender As Object, ByVal e As EventArgs)
   Application("RecycleIncludes") = DateTime.Now()
End Sub

Public Overrides Function GetVaryByCustomString( _
      ByVal context As HttpContext, ByVal arg As String) As String

   If (arg = "RecycleIncludes") Then
      Return CStr(context.Application("RecycleIncludes"))
   End If
End Function
```

Now, if we need to expire the header and footer controls, they will expire across all pages, as we simply update the `RecycleIncludes` application variable. Note that it is possible to use any string; we simply choose to use a timestamp as it is readily available and you want to ensure that the new value is different from the old.

There is one more scalability enhancement that may look small, but is actually the most remarkable improvement in the rewrite. This code has to do with how the user is loaded:

```
Private Sub Page_Load()
   If Page.IsPostBack Then
      Try
         Session.Contents("user") = New User(username.Text, _
                                             password.Text, False)
...
```

If you will recall, back in Chapter 4, the overloaded method for fetching a user will allow us to retrieve enough information to log the user into the application without populating the entire object model. This helps greatly with regards to the `Session` object, as we are not immediately cramming the entire user object model into memory.

One last piece of code to highlight is the news control on the individual stock page. `Individual.aspx` is rather dynamic in that it shows all of the symbols a user has searched on as well as their individual stock portfolio. As such, this does not make a good candidate for caching.

However, the company news on the page certainly does make an excellent candidate for caching. In this instance, we will cache the output per company and set it to regenerate every fifteen minutes. While it should be assumed that this method of delayed updating will inevitably cause some news stories to be reported late, the maximum wait on this will only be a few minutes with the advantage being that every user does not incur a performance penalty for accessing the identical application data.

Of course, there is still something impeding scalability, and that is managing our session state. As you've likely noticed, we make liberal use of the session for storing the `User` object. In order to provide a working solution for a web farm, we have enabled session management on a single SQL Server machine with plans to introduce a second server for the sake of reliability.

From our `machine.config` configuration file, or `web.config` for a single web application:

```
<configuration>
  <system.web>
    <sessionState
      mode="SQLServer"
      sqlConnectionstring="data source=MIWSQLState; user id=aspState;
      password=&1StateServer5$"
      stateNetworkTimeout="10"
      cookieless="false"
      timeout="20"
    />
  </system.web>"
</configuration>
```

While this certainly did not provide an exhaustive look at the new code in MyInvestmentWatch.com, it provides an overview of implementing the concepts discussed throughout the chapter in our new, highly scalable system. A good next step would be to address potential scalability issues after thoroughly testing the system and identifying chokepoints in supporting user load.

Summary

ASP.NET provides for dramatic increases in performance, deployment, and usability over traditional ASP/VB applications. More importantly, at least from the standpoint of this book, ASP.NET greatly eases the work needed to create highly scalable systems.

Chapter 5: The Presentation Tier

With regards solely to scalability, ASP.NET has introduced the following features as part of the base Framework:

- **Compiled Code** – We didn't explicitly cover this, as it is not controllable by the programmer and actually makes up the basis for ASP.NET. However, the fact remains that ASP.NET is now compiled. The performance benefits of this over ASP are several-fold. While better performance doesn't necessarily equate to improved scalability, the less time a server has to spend on each page means the more pages an individual server can deliver.

- **Caching** – When used properly, caching provides a wonderful mechanism for increasing scalability. It allows the work to be saved, in a sense, for later use. This is especially useful when multiple clients can use a particular item or page.

With output caching, ASP.NET provides a wide range of options for caching the output of both pages and controls. Cached output can be sent to multiple clients without a need to refresh the page.

An old trick has been to save generated ASP output as HTML so that the cost of interpreting a page wouldn't be incurred for every page view. This is no longer needed as ASP.NET provides the same net benefit with much less effort. Simply set the output to expire after a sufficient period time.

In addition to output caching, ASP.NET provides a very useful method for caching items that will be used by multiple pages. This ability is provided through the new-to-.NET `Cache` object. The `Cache` object serves well to store data, or object references, previously stored within the ASP `Application` or `Session` objects.

The `Cache` object provides the ability to manage items at a very minute level of detail, if desired. There is also support for establishing dependencies between items as well as notifying the application when an item is removed from the cache, and why.

Caching is a cornerstone to building highly scalable systems. Therefore, it is important to understand the intricacies of working with the ASP.NET cache. However, caching is not the only requirement for building a highly scalable system. An eye must also be given to state management.

The necessity of managing state can tax any system. This problem is compounded in a web-based application where connections between the client and server are stateless. ASP.NET provides great support for state management in the several forms.

The bulk of the problem with state management is in supporting user state in a highly scaled web farm system. In this scenario, state must be maintained in a manner that will allow multiple servers in a web farm to access the same data. ASP.NET has several methods for storing session information in a web farm.

Summary

Due to the inherent scalability characteristics of SQL Server, the recommendation is to store state in a SQL Server database. However, as you have seen, switching between session storage modes is straightforward. As such, it is possible to start with a small solution and then scale to SQL Server when the need presents itself.

State management can now be applied to controls. One of the hurdles in ASP development was in maintaining form state across an entire user interaction. This is now addressed in ASP.NET through the use of the ViewState. The ViewState is germane to the new programming model of posting back to the same page to complete the bulk of form processing.

However, incorrect use of the ViewState presents scalability problems as well. If a page's ViewState is incorrectly used then too much data will be transmitted. This will negatively affect both performance and scalability, as the server must process this ViewState information.

Effective state management is often one of the most difficult challenges in building a highly scalable system. ASP.NET makes the process much easier, but a solid understanding of the ramifications is still a necessity.

The .NET Framework offers many improvements over traditional VB/ASP, and pure ASP, applications. As importantly, ASP has been revolutionized as ASP.NET. It is now possible to create robust applications in ASP.NET with little intervention from the developer. These improvements do not call for extraordinary code overhauls to implement. However, they do require an understanding of the effect of implementing each option as well as the best practices around these options.

VB.NET

Scalability

Handbook

6

Measuring Scalability

An important part throughout an application's lifecycle is determining how well the application will scale and having the ability to monitor its performance. In particular, every developer must be able to answer questions such as the following when developing scalable application:

- How many concurrent users and requests per second can the system handle?
- Which parts of the code can benefit from scaling and how can we write scalable code?
- Will additional memory, CPU, servers, or a combination of resources be the most effective in the scaling process?

Answering these questions involves understanding how to test, monitor, and instrument an application with scalability in mind.

Measuring for scalability is an ongoing process in the development cycle. In order to measure our code, we create a set of test cases that can be used to indicate how well an application is performing at its most basic level. Unit tests are sets of tests that developers create and use throughout the application's lifetime that help test the application for expected results, give us a set of test cases for which to measure performance, and ease regression testing efforts tremendously.

Stress testing is the process of simulating a user load on the system to determine the system's load limits and capacity. Stress testing can also be used to detect and prevent common factors that have traditionally limited scalability including bandwidth consumption, memory leaks, resource locking, and bottlenecks.

Understanding what tests to write and writing those tests is only the first part of the scalability measuring process. Once the tests have been executed, we need to understand the tools available for examining the data and providing us with execution metrics.

One powerful tool used in measuring performance is a code profiler. Code profilers allow us to view code-level statistics including method execution time, the number of times a method has executed, the method stack, and the time each line of code took to execute. Code profilers are excellent for detecting bottlenecks and can, for example, shed light on poorly performing algorithms.

While code profilers are meant for the detailed code level, performance monitoring also involves monitoring at the overall system level. Using Windows Performance Monitor, we have the ability to view operating system subsystem metrics for the current computer or any computer we have permission to monitor in our environment. Using these metrics, we can determine what system resources are under heavy system load and could thus limit our scalability.

A plethora of tools are available to assists us with executing stress tests. Microsoft Application Center Test (ACT) is a script generator and stress testing tool for testing web applications. By using ACT, we are able to write or generate scripts and execute the scripts to simulate a large concurrent user base. ACT has an underlying object model and is based on scripts that the developer can customize for more detailed control of the test cases.

A more advanced technique in scalability monitoring is building instrumentation within our code. Code instrumentation is a technique used to provide performance monitors with the necessary information as to how the code is executing. By writing trace statements and implementing custom `TraceListener` classes, we are able to create an application that outside tools can use to find out what is going on within our code. By inheriting from `TraceListener`, we are able to create our own trace listener to interact with Windows Performance Monitor or any other analysis tool we wish.

The goal of this chapter is to give you an overview of performance techniques and a look into a few common tools available to help measure an application's scalability. By having an understanding of the fundamentals regarding monitoring and performance, applications can be designed with measuring in mind. Designing an application that can be measured improves our ability to recommend system scalability changes.

Application Testing

Throughout this book, we have discussed the code techniques offered by .NET that can be used to help improve your application's scalability. For example, in the data-access tier we discussed the performance and scalability benefits of stored procedures, indexing, and abstracting the data-access layer from the middle tier of the application. At the middle-tier layer, we discussed how to implement .NET Remoting and web services, and provided an implementation of a middle tier. At the user interface layer, we discussed ASP.NET caching, session state mechanisms, and other tips for designing a scalable user interface.

Regardless of how many provisions we have made for designing a scalable system, how can we prove that our application will scale to our requirements or expectations? What is needed is a set of tests that we can throw at our system to test how our application performs under an increased user load or with additional resources.

Testing is an extremely complex process in the application lifecycle, especially in distributed systems. Testing brings us a wide range of benefits, the most important of which is that it helps us to determine if our application does what we intended it to do. Testing has numerous benefits including but not limited to:

- **Reducing costs**. Fixing a bug in the testing process saves money. Once applications are deployed, fixing defects becomes much more costly than if caught at during development or in testing. While this point seems rather obvious, it cannot be emphasized enough. Once the application is deployed, especially traditional shrink wrapped software, dispersing a bug fix is considerably more expensive than fixing it during the development cycle. Testing helps reduce costs by finding bugs earlier in the lifecycle.

- **Measuring functionality**. Testing ensures applications perform as described in the design document. As the application specification is passed from the business users to the project designers to the developers, the original intention of the application can be lost. Testing ensures that the application performs as desired.

- **Measuring performance**. It is quite obvious that scalability and performance have a strong correlation with one another. Testing allows us to benchmark, locate bottlenecks, and watch our application's performance under various circumstances. The vast majority of the material presented in this chapter is with relation to monitoring, designing for, and improving performance.

The benefits of a solid and complete testing plan are numerous, obvious, and well documented within the computer science industry. In order to create a testing plan, we must understand the different types of testing available and determine how to implement them into our application development lifecycle.

Unit Testing

All applications can be broken down into discrete pieces. Unit testing is the lowest form of testing in the software development lifecycle and is the process of separating the application into individual units and running tests on those units to ensure they behave as expected.

The most elementary unit test is at the method level. At its basic form, a method accepts inputs and produces outputs. Our goal as developers is to execute the method with all possible inputs and check for the expected outputs. We could write scripts or blocks of code that help automate unit testing by executing the method with dynamically generated inputs.

Chapter 6: Measuring Scalability

In OO languages, such as VB.NET, C#, or Java, a potential unit test involves testing a class. As a unit of development, the class is a prime candidate for a unit test since it typically encapsulates a set of functionality. What we want to do is create a test scenario around a class to ensure the class behaves as expected. As we issue method calls on the class to alter the internal class state, our tests will ensure the state of the class is changed accordingly and the class behaves as expected.

Unit Test Example

To many Visual Basic 6.0 developers, the concept of a unit test is perhaps relatively new. The Visual Basic environment did not have many options for creating unit tests, nor did the documentation stress the importance of unit testing and give examples of creating unit tests for applications. It's not that unit testing was difficult or impossible with Visual Basic 6 or earlier, rather the industry emphasis was placed on Visual Basic's RAD GUI tools.

Within the realm of .NET, there are tools available for assisting the unit testing effort that we will discuss shortly. Many popular unit testing tools for other OO languages, most notably Java, are being ported to .NET.

Let's take a look into an example of unit testing. The following example illustrates unit testing at the class level. The class is, in effect, our 'unit' that we need to test. In the example, we create a very simple class that maintains internal state. The `Account` class is similar to a checking account in that it accepts an initial balance and you can perform withdraws and deposits on the balance:

```
Public Class Account
   Private _initialBalance As Double
   Private _balance As Double

   Public Sub New(ByVal InitialBalance As Double)
      _balance = InitialBalance
      _initialBalance = InitialBalance
   End Sub

   Public Sub Withdraw(ByVal Amount As Double)
      If Amount > _balance Then
         Throw New ArgumentException( _
            "Withdraw amount cannot exceed current balance")
      End If
      _balance -= Amount
   End Sub

   Public Sub Deposit(ByVal Amount As Double)
      If Amount < 0 Then
         Throw New ArgumentException( _
            "Deposit not valid")
      End If
      _balance += Amount
   End Sub
```

```vb
    Public ReadOnly Property InitialBalance() As Double
      Get
         InitialBalance = _initialBalance
      End Get
    End Property

    Public ReadOnly Property Balance() As Double
      Get
         Balance = _balance
      End Get
    End Property

    Public ReadOnly Property Activity() As Double
      Get
         Activity = _balance - _initialBalance
      End Get
    End Property

End Class
```

Determining the Test

In order to test the class, we must know how the class is expected to perform and write tests that validate these expectations. For example, we know that if we create the class with an initial balance of $1,000, both `InitialBalance` and `Balance` should be $1,000. If we withdraw money, the `InitialBalance` should not change, but the `Balance` should be decremented by the withdrawal amount. If we deposit money, the `InitialBalance` should not change and the `Balance` should increase by the `Deposit` amount. Understanding the class functionality allows us to write the following test case:

```vb
Imports System
Imports System.Diagnostics

Module Module1

  Sub Main()
    Dim acct As New Account(1000)
    Debug.Assert(acct.InitialBalance = 1000)
    Debug.Assert(acct.Balance = 1000)
    Debug.Assert(acct.Activity = 0)

    acct.Withdraw(200)
    Debug.Assert(acct.InitialBalance = 1000)
    Debug.Assert(acct.Balance = 800)
    Debug.Assert(acct.Activity = -200)

    acct.Deposit(2000)
    Debug.Assert(acct.InitialBalance = 1000)
    Debug.Assert(acct.Balance = 2800)
    Debug.Assert(acct.Activity = 1700, _
                 "Deposit activity assertion failed, check deposit")
```

Chapter 6: Measuring Scalability

```
        End Sub
    End Module
```

Using the `Debug` class within the `System.Diagnostics` namespace we can conditionally compile in the debug statements by specifying the `/define:debug=true` command-line parameter. Putting the `Account` class and test module into the file `Account.vb`, we can compile the debug statements into the resulting executable by issuing the following command line:

```
> vbc /r:System.dll /define:debug=true Account.vb
```

Notice that we purposely made an error in the last assertion. With a withdrawal of 200 and a deposit of 2,000, we know the activity should be 1,800. The reason we made the assertion mistake was to illustrate what a failure would look like. When running with the `debug` variable set to `true`, we are prompted when the assertion fails.

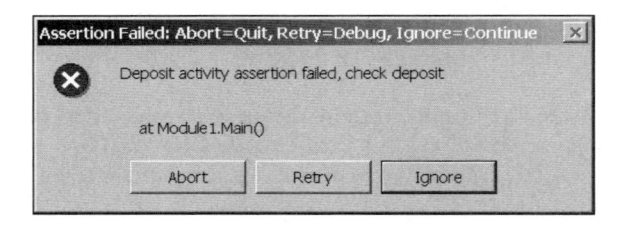

```
Assertion Failed: Abort=Quit, Retry=Debug, Ignore=Continue
    Deposit activity assertion failed, check deposit

        at Module1.Main()

        [ Abort ]    [ Retry ]    [ Ignore ]
```

The `Debug` class is unique in that the debug statements will only appear when the `debug` variable is set when compiling the application. If the `debug` variable was not defined during compilation, the assertion failure box would not have been raised because the compiler would not have compiled the statements into the resulting IL.

This functionality is ideal for testing since we can use the `Debug` class for testing and production builds. In Visual Studio .NET, the default build procedure includes this variable set to `true` by default. We can change this within the application's properties windows. For more about debugging your Visual Basic .NET applications see the Wrox Press book *Visual Basic .NET Debugging Handbook*, ISBN 1-86100-729-9.

Strengths of Unit Testing

At first glance it may appear that unit testing requires quite a bit of code. Indeed this is the case. However, writing unit tests is a powerful technique for helping us to find defects in our code by creating a set of tests that we expect to pass. In theory, writing tests may appear to take as much time as actually developing the software. In practice, however, writing the tests in conjunction with the class is efficient when compared to the time needed to tracking down the bugs resulting from poorly tested code.

When you are writing a class, you should be familiar with the functionality of that class and can create test cases quickly since the material is fresh in your mind. However, it is also beneficial if another developer can write tests against your code to provide additional testing you may have missed.

Regression

Perhaps the biggest strength of unit testing comes when system changes are made. For example, say the Account class interacted with a database and a stored procedure that performed calculations based on each transaction. If the stored procedure is changed and accidentally returns an incorrect return value to the Account class, our unit tests will catch the bug since the assertions checking the account balance will fail.

As a system is changed, regression testing becomes an extremely important, though time consuming task. Regression testing is the process of testing code changes to make sure the older programming still works with the new changes. Having an automated testing procedure in place saves countless hours in monotonous testing effort to ensure a change in functionality did not break other parts of the system.

Industry Support

Unit testing is popular across all languages and schools of development. Perhaps the most visible of unit testing efforts is an automated unit tested framework for the Java platform called JUnit (http://www.junit.org). JUnit is a unit testing framework that assists Java developers by providing a framework around writing test cases and sets of test cases.

The JUnit application has been ported to .NET and renamed NUnit (http://www.nunit.org). NUnit is written in C# and provides an extremely easy approach to set up suites of unit tests for applications and provides console and GUI tools for executing tests. NUnit is highly recommended for unit testing and is well worth the small amount of time required to learn how to use the tool.

Unit Testing, Performance, and Scalability

What does unit testing have to do with measuring application performance and more importantly how can it be used to measure scalability? As you have probably noticed, unit testing, by itself, only tests application logic for correctness, it does not provide performance metrics for us to examine.

While it may not seem readily apparent, unit tests provide a common unit of measurement for our application when testing for performance and scalability. In order to test our application in different environments or with different hardware, a common set of tests is necessary to illustrate how a change in system resources corresponds to a change in performance. Without a standard set of application tests, it becomes difficult to measure exactly how differently the application will perform given different environments. In many respects, having a set of unit tests available is the foundation for measuring and testing scalability and performance.

In order to measure performance, unit tests can be executed under the watchful eye of a code profiler to determine how efficiently the application is performing. As you will see later in this chapter, profilers are wonderful tools to have in your developer toolbox for monitoring performance and code execution metrics. We will discuss profilers when we discuss tools that are available to help us test and monitor performance and scalability.

Having unit tests available when the code profiler executes allows us to use the unit tests for both logical metrics and performance metrics.

Stress Testing

In order to determine how our application will perform in a production environment, we must test the system with a simulated user load above and beyond what is expected. Such testing is commonly referred to as stress testing. Needless to say, stress testing is very important to measure an application's scalability.

Stress testing is similar to, but not the same as, load testing. Load testing is the evaluation of application performance under normal conditions. Load testing occurs when we test the application from a few users to the maximum number of users supported by our application.

Stress testing takes load testing a step further by pushing the system beyond current and maximum user load by simulating a user load above and beyond what our application is known to handle. When stress testing, we push our system past its limits to see what parts of the system fail or become slow.

Stress testing builds on load testing. With unit testing, we looked at a very small piece of the application, a unit, and tested just that portion of the code in isolation from the rest of the application. While we can create unit tests that span multiple parts of the application or even create unit tests that test the entire application, they are individual tests that typically test one piece of functionality exactly once.

Stress testing is a system-wide effort that allows you to test the entire system. Typically, stress testing and unit testing are done independently of each other; however, there is no reason why stress tests cannot take advantage of unit tests when simulating a user load.

When discussing stress testing in the context of this chapter, we will be referring to it from a web application perspective. When we discuss tools related to performance monitoring and testing, we will implement a test to examine the scalability and performance of the MyInvestmentWatch.com web site created throughout the book.

Common Performance Limitations

What indicators should we look for when examining the performance and scalability of our application when performing stress tests? We'll take a look at some of the common areas related to how web applications typically suffer from performance limitations.

Application Testing

Keep these performance limitations in mind when stress testing an application. Later in this chapter we will discuss Microsoft's Application Center Test (ACT) tool used to perform stress testing and load testing.

Bandwidth Consumption

In order for a web site to function, the amount of bandwidth consumed by the application needs to be monitored. Typically, stress tests are executed within the confines of a LAN environment where bandwidth is prevalent. When the application is stress tested, bandwidth can be forgotten since the concentration is focused on the database, application, and web server performance.

As the application is moved to production and users enter the system, having an application that is limited in bandwidth can cause drastic performance degradation. There is a multitude of available applications created to monitor bandwidth consumption during stress testing intervals.

Memory Leaks

Memory leaks are often the source of bugs ranging from annoying to catastrophic. In environments such as C++ that do not rely on garbage collection to sweep up unused objects (unmanaged code), memory leaks create difficult-to-find bugs. On the annoying side, a memory leak could perhaps consume memory until the point it crashes and needs to re-spawn itself. While this is indeed a bug, it is not too detrimental as it will cause only a brief amount of downtime. On the catastrophic side, the component could use up more and more memory until the system becomes slow, unresponsive, or crashes.

Testing for memory leaks is often difficult since application tests only run for a certain period of time. Let's say we execute a test for 10 minutes. In that time we issue a series of tests against the system. If we had a slow memory leak, it would not be caught in the testing period. Creating a test plan for checking for memory leaks is time consuming and tedious. However, as long as we are aware of their existence, we can monitor our processes for increasing memory consumption.

While the .NET garbage collector solves many of the problems related to memory leaks, we still must be aware of their existence if we rely on third-party code not written in .NET. If your application relies on third-party code, you are exposed to memory leaks and should consider them when testing an application's performance.

Resource Locking

Another significant source of performance limitation involves resource contention or locking. As systems are developed, they are typically not tested with a high user load. As user load increases, users contend with each other for similar resources. If one user locks a resource, say a database, requests are queued up or denied for the duration of the resource lock.

Resource locking should be considered any time multiple users are using a similar resource. For some parts of the application, say the user interface in an ASP.NET scenario, each user will have a thread on which their code is executing. At the user interface level, it is relatively safe to assume that each user has their individual resources and the possibility for contention is relatively low.

However, if common resources such as a database or file are being used simultaneously by multiple users, contentions can occur. Perhaps one user is updating a database row being requested by another user. The updating user must lock the resource to perform its operation then release the resource to the next requestor.

Resource locking is a necessary evil. It would not be practical (or possible in many situations) to create an application without requiring resource locking. However, as long as we follow the 'obtain late and release early' philosophy when developing our application, we can minimize the possibility of contentions.

Resource locking becomes prevalent when stress testing since contentions generally increase with increases in user load. Stress testing can reveal resource locking problems as the same piece of code is executes many times.

Bottlenecks

A bottleneck is a rather generic term used to represent a piece of hardware or software within an application where the application flow is constrained. One interesting thing about bottlenecks is that the vast majority of applications developed have them. At some point when our application is being pushed to its limits, certain pieces will begin to slow the system. Stress testing is an excellent technique for identifying application bottlenecks. Knowing the locations of bottlenecks will allow system developers to plan for their existence and possibly rework the application late in its lifetime.

Bottlenecks can range from being a hardware limitation to a poorly written piece of code, making their scope potentially very broad. Bottlenecks can be caused on the hardware side by not having enough CPUs or memory (or fast enough CPUs), L2 cache, or by slow I/O. On the software side, they could be due to poor algorithms, inefficient sorting or searching techniques, poorly written SQL queries, or an improperly tuned database. Bottlenecks can occur at literally any part of the system.

More often than not, identifying a bottleneck isn't that difficult. A software component that isn't performing well will most likely take up a disproportionate amount of hardware resources. Such a component can be identified by watching the executing processes or the distribution of system resources as the application is executing.

After bottlenecks are found, however, determining the remedy can be quite difficult. If the most recent version of the application is being used, we must examine the component in question for possible remedies. At this point, having a set of unit tests will help us pinpoint the problem.

Bottlenecks can also be identified by developing the application to output performance metrics to the operating system or listening applications. At the end of this chapter, we will discuss the ability for our applications to provide hooks that listeners can use to monitor the frequency and performance of the application.

Importance of Tools in Testing

Measuring scalability involves executing a wide battery of consistent tests to see how they perform under different environmental conditions. As we alter resources, we must keep our tests uniform to base performance solely on the resource change. Keeping all testing variables the same will isolate the hardware and system changes and so allow us to attribute the change in performance solely to the hardware and system changes involved. It is measuring these test results that allows us to determine a system's potential scalability.

In developing scalable systems, testing is complicated by the distributed nature of the testing plan. Debugging or testing a particular piece of code is relatively straight forward. A challenge facing scalable systems is determining an effective set of tests that span across process, network, and geographic boundaries. Simply arranging a test environment to mimic the production environment, let alone writing the tests, is a project within itself.

Regardless of the effort involved, testing a scalable system is a necessity. In order to ease our troubles, we must understand the tools available to programmers to assist the testing effort. Knowing the different testing tools allows us to monitor our application without rewriting the plumbing code that is required to monitor the different application metrics.

It may seem that applications are wildly different, making a common tool difficult to write and even more impractical to use. What is interesting is that while all systems are different, they also have a great deal in common.

Applications contain executable code. OO languages, such as VB.NET and C#, contain objects. Objects contain interfaces, state, and accessors. All objects are collected by the CLR. All code executes within a process (or AppDomain in .NET).

At a higher level, applications that use database access use connection objects. Inter-process communication uses marshaling. Network traffic uses the same protocol infrastructure. File persistence and database access use the same I/O subsystem.

We can see that regardless of how different our application logic, the subsystems and underlying operating system are uniform across applications. It is in this uniformity that tools can be created to monitor the processes that applications having common.

In the following section, we will examine some very effective tools used to measure an application's performance and scalability. The tools presented here will be focused on the CLR; however, similar tools exist for almost all mainstream development platforms. Understanding the testing and monitoring tools allows us to reduce the development time needed to create test code. It will also allow us to create highly efficient code and troubleshoot the factors that limit our application's scalability.

Application Monitoring Tools

Now that we have discussed the theory behind testing, it is time to put the theory into practice. In the pages that follow, we will create a set of tests that we can use against the middle tier and data-access tier code written in the previous chapters. While this example uses the code written in this book, the concepts can be carried forward to your own applications. Great care has been taken to focus on generic topics and not to discuss the application in great detail.

> **The application code can be found at** http://www.wrox.com.

Our First Test

Before we can analyze the performance of the application, we must create a relevant test. Creating a test requires an understanding of exactly what we are testing. If we are testing an algorithm for scientific correctness, we will throw a wide variety of inputs at the test case to make sure that the algorithm produces the expected outputs. If we are stress testing an algorithm, we will throw perhaps a smaller set of inputs at the algorithm but execute it many times over. If we are testing an entire system, we will perhaps parse previous application log files and issue tests based on those results. Creating a relevant test includes (but is not limited to):

- ❏ Determining the goal and scope of the test
- ❏ Creating a set of inputs for which we know what outputs we expect
- ❏ Preparing and collecting a set of test results

Taking the MyInvestmentWatch.com as an example, we know the application is very light on the logic. Since the application is meant to illustrate creating a multi-tier scalable system, logic was sacrificed in favor of creating a tier structure relevant to a typical multi-tiered scalable system.

Application Monitoring Tools

In place of logic, we have a great deal of persistence code. When a user enters the application, we load their profile from a database. During their interaction with the object model, they are allowed to create, read, update, and delete various objects within the model. Without creating previous tests, we can feel confident creating testing functions that focus on the persistence of our object model will be an effective determinant of overall performance and scalability. At the very least, it will provide a nice starting point for the direction of our future test cases.

In order to test the persistence model, we will create a simple test to simulate a `User` being created, some `Stock` objects being added to the `User`, and then saving and eventually deleting the user. This set of tests allows us to hit the majority of the persistence code in our object model. Further tests can be written to test each function in depth. The following code illustrates our first simple test:

```vb
Imports System
Imports com.myinvestmentwatch.middle
Imports System.Data
Imports System.Data.SqlClient
Imports System.Diagnostics
Imports System.IO

Module TestExecutor

   Sub Main()
      Dim file As Stream = IO.File.Create("C:\Test.txt")
      Trace.Listeners.Add(New TextWriterTraceListener(file))

      Dim i As Integer
      Dim test As New TestCases()

      'Test case 1 - creating and destroying a user object
      test.TestUserCreation(100)

      'Test case 2 - stressing
      test.StressUserCreation(20)

      Trace.Flush()      'Flush output
   End Sub
End Module

Public Class TestCases

   'Tests creating and destroying a user object
   Public Sub TestUserCreation(ByVal ChildrenCount As Integer)
      Trace.WriteLine("TestUserCreation fired " & System.DateTime.Now())
      Dim u As User = Population.CreateUser(ChildrenCount)
      u.Save(True)
      User.DeleteUser(u.UserID)  'Cleanup
   End Sub
```

Chapter 6: Measuring Scalability

```vb
    Public Sub StressUserCreation(ByVal Count As Integer)
      Dim i As Integer
      For i = 0 To Count - 1
        TestUserCreation(i)
      Next
    End Sub
End Class

Public Class Population

    '*****************************************************************
    ' CreateUser - Create a user object with a set of children objects
    '*****************************************************************
    Public Shared Function CreateUser(ByVal ChildrenCount As Integer) _
        As User

      Dim u As User
      Dim cn As New SqlConnection("Data Source=Server;" & _
                  "user id=username; password=password;" & _
                  "Initial Catalog=myinvestmentwatch")
      cn.Open()

      Dim cm As New SqlCommand("SELECT TOP " & ChildrenCount & _
                  " * FROM Companies", cn)    'load x companies
      Dim dr As SqlDataReader = _
        cm.ExecuteReader(CommandBehavior.CloseConnection)

      Try
        User.CreateNew("testUser", "testUser", "Test User Name")
        u = New User("testUser", "testUser", True)
      Catch e As Exception 'User already exists
        Console.WriteLine(e.Message)
        User.DeleteUser(New User("testUser", "testUser", False).UserID)
        User.CreateNew("testUser", "testUser", False)
        u = New User("testUser", "testUser", True)
      End Try

      While dr.Read()
        u.PreferredStocks.Add(CType(dr("compID"), Integer))
        u.Hits.Add(CType(dr("compID"), Integer))
      End While

      dr.Close()
      cm.Dispose()
      cn.Dispose()
      CreateUser = u
    End Function
End Class
```

If you are compiling from a command line, the compilation command is (assuming the `MiddleTier.dll` and `DataAccessLayer.dll` components are in the current directory):

```
> vbc /r:System.dll /r:System.Data.dll /r:System.xml.dll
/r:MiddleTier.dll /r:DataAccessLayer.dll TestCases.vb
```

If we run the application we should see results similar to the following:

```
TestUserCreation fired 24/09/2002 09:42:08
TestUserCreation fired 24/09/2002 09:42:12
TestUserCreation fired 24/09/2002 09:42:12
TestUserCreation fired 24/09/2002 09:42:12
TestUserCreation fired 24/09/2002 09:42:12
TestUserCreation fired 24/09/2002 09:42:12
TestUserCreation fired 24/09/2002 09:42:12
TestUserCreation fired 24/09/2002 09:42:12
TestUserCreation fired 24/09/2002 09:42:12
TestUserCreation fired 24/09/2002 09:42:12
TestUserCreation fired 24/09/2002 09:42:12
TestUserCreation fired 24/09/2002 09:42:12
TestUserCreation fired 24/09/2002 09:42:12
TestUserCreation fired 24/09/2002 09:42:12
TestUserCreation fired 24/09/2002 09:42:12
TestUserCreation fired 24/09/2002 09:42:12
TestUserCreation fired 24/09/2002 09:42:12
TestUserCreation fired 24/09/2002 09:42:13
TestUserCreation fired 24/09/2002 09:42:13
TestUserCreation fired 24/09/2002 09:42:13
```

We structured the test around three blocks. The Sub Main() method is the controlling method responsible for issuing the tests. The TestCases class is exactly what the name describes: a set of test cases, each of which is meant to be atomic in nature. They are self contained and executing one case will not alter or destroy any object state dependent on another test case.

The Population class is a helper class responsible for populating our objects with data. For our small tests, creating a separate class dedicated to common User object population is potentially overkill. However, factoring out the common persistence code will most likely be nice to have if we were to extend our test cases beyond this small number.

The TestUserCreation() method is responsible for creating the User object populated with Stock objects, and then saving and deleting it to prevent the database from accumulating users. As a side note, make sure any tests you execute do not leave the database in an invalid state either intentionally or by accident. The second test, StressUserCreation(), is simply a wrapper for testing the population in succession.

Let's turn our attention to the output of the test. We sent our output to a text file for simplicity; however, we could have logged this information to a database or other means of storage if we see necessary. Regardless of how the data is stored, the important point is that we somehow collect it in a meaningful way for analysis.

Now that we have the data, we have the ability to analyze the results. Typically, at this point the development and management teams would compare the actual output with the expected or baseline output. Depending on how the actual results stack up against the expected results will determine the future course of action. If the actual results perform as or better than expected, we can be reasonably happy and perhaps move on to the next development step. If the tests perform worse than expected, we are left looking into the code for improvements. Hopefully in this case testing was done early and often so that serious development time was not sunk in creating the poorly performing code.

As developers, we understand that simply creating print statements at the outermost layers of a test case is not sufficient for performance metrics. What we would like is a detailed breakdown of each method's performance. In our example, we could create print statements or log when each method is beginning and ending.

Inserting print statements in our `CreateUser()` method allows us to determine exactly the amount of time taken to create, populate, and destroy the `User` object:

```
Public Shared Function CreateUser(ByVal ChildrenCount As Integer) _
    As User

    Dim u As User

    Console.WriteLine("Starting CreateUser with " & _
            ChildrenCount & " Children " & _
            DateTime.Now.Second() & ":" & DateTime.Now.Millisecond)

    Dim cn As New SqlConnection("Data Source=Server;" & _
                "user id=username; password=password;" & _
                "Initial Catalog=myinvestmentwatch")
    cn.Open()

    ...

    dr.Close()
    cm.Dispose()
    cn.Dispose()
    CreateUser = u

    Console.WriteLine("Ending CreateUser with " & _
            ChildrenCount & " Children " & _
            DateTime.Now.Second() & ":" & DateTime.Now.Millisecond)
End Function
```

As a side note, in order to increase the portability of our tests, we could have implemented a configuration file to host our connection string. A configuration file would be much more flexible, especially when running tests against different data stores. Running the test cases again gives us a more detailed output. The output shown here is with five iterations under the stress testing case for brevity.

Application Monitoring Tools

```
C:\Scalability\miwnet\TestApp\bin\TestApp.exe
Starting CreateUser with 100 Children 23:873
Ending CreateUser with 100 Children 27:658
Starting CreateUser with 0 Children 27:899
Ending CreateUser with 0 Children 27:919
Starting CreateUser with 1 Children 27:929
Ending CreateUser with 1 Children 27:939
Starting CreateUser with 2 Children 27:939
Ending CreateUser with 2 Children 27:959
Starting CreateUser with 3 Children 27:959
Ending CreateUser with 3 Children 28:9
Starting CreateUser with 4 Children 28:19
Ending CreateUser with 4 Children 28:29
```

Now we have a more interesting set of performance data. The results confirm what we would expect: adding more children to the user object slows creation. However, the results allow us to compare scenarios and test different scenarios.

We are still in need of more meaningful data to determine how the application is performing and to identify possible scalability limitations to our applications. In particular, we would like to know some of the following:

- What is a method's average execution time?
- Which methods do the current methods depend upon?
- How much of the execution time is being consumed by our code and how many resources does the testing framework take up?
- Which (if any) of the underlying methods consume the majority of the execution time?

At this point, we start to realize that our homegrown testing framework will not provide very detailed functionality without a dedicated effort to creating application monitoring code. Writing such code would involve intercepting the CLR events and capturing them into meaningful data. While this kind of tool would not be impossible to write, it definitely seems more efficient to use an automated solution.

Code Profiler

What we did in our last application is create a very rudimentary code profiler. By definition, a code profiler helps you tune the performance of the application by listening for an application's 'events'. Some typical events include recording when a method is being entered, when it is being exited, and how much memory the method consumes.

By accumulating these low-level events, the profiler is able to create a rather detailed summary of an application's historical execution path. The data accumulated can be analyzed by the developer and gives the ability to look for code "hotspots" or resource usage. Understanding where the application is spending time is a very effective technique for understanding an application's current execution, and allows the developer to focus on those spots for code improvement.

Chapter 6: Measuring Scalability

Code profilers are available for the vast majority of Windows and non-Windows programming languages. With the release of Visual Studio .NET, some tool providers have begun to create code profilers for profiling applications directly within the IDE. Many code profilers are available for the .NET runtime ranging from command-line to visual interfaces.

In the context of this example, we will use a profiler called the DevPartner Profiler Community Edition created by Compuware. Compuware distributes the Community Edition of their profiler with no charge. When loaded, DevPartner profiler is integrated into Visual Studio .NET and allows you to create code profiles from within the development environment. The DevPartner is available from Compuware and can be downloaded from their site at: http://www.compuware.com/.

Regardless of which profiler you choose, the lessons learned from this particular profiler can be carried forward to other profilers.

Profiling Test Cases

Using a profiler is our first true attempt at measuring our application's scalability. Let's identify some common performance metrics we may wish to gain when performance testing our application:

- Where are the application's bottlenecks?
- Which methods are particular resource-intensive?
- What resources are being used? (Examples include Memory, CPU, I/O)
- Where are the application 'hotspots' and how can they be alleviated?
- How much of the testing execution time is taken by the testing framework and how much is consumed by our application's code?

Before we establish the profiler, let's remove our first attempt at creating profiling code. We'll simply remove the output statements from our test cases since the profiler has the ability to capture more detailed information automatically. Also notice that we changed the `StressUserCreation()` call to an argument of 50 to provide higher amounts of stress in order to get more result data:

```
Module TestExecutor
  Sub Main()
    Dim test As New TestCases()
    'Test case 1 - creating and destroying a user object
    test.TestUserCreation(100)
    'Test case 2 - stressing
    test.StressUserCreation(50)
  End Sub
End Module
```

Application Monitoring Tools

Establishing the Profiler

Establishing the profiler to profile the test case execution will be dependent on the profiler itself. Each profiler will have a different configuration or set of requirements. The documentation will explain the individual profiler's usage. In our DevPartner profiler, establishing the application for profiling is a matter of enabling the profiler using the Tools | DevPartner Profiler | Enable DevPartner Profiler menu and running the application via the Debug | Start Without Debugging menu option. You do not want to run the profiler with debugging enabled since your debugging time would throw off your results. This profiler ensures you do not have it enabled.

As a side note, notice how this particular profiler integrates with the VS.NET IDE. In some respects, integration with the IDE is nice to have since it allows us to code and test without leaving the tool. Dependence on the IDE however, makes it difficult to script profiler tests and is difficult to use in automated situations. For our purposes here, however, it works fine.

Once the profiler is attached to the application, we are ready to begin execution. We click the Debug | Start Without Debugging (*Ctrl-F5*) and the test application executes.

Analyzing Results

Let's take a look at the profiler's output. When the code is executed, the profiler creates a separate node off the solution file dedicated to the DevPartner Profiler. Double clicking on a test run file brings up the profiler output.

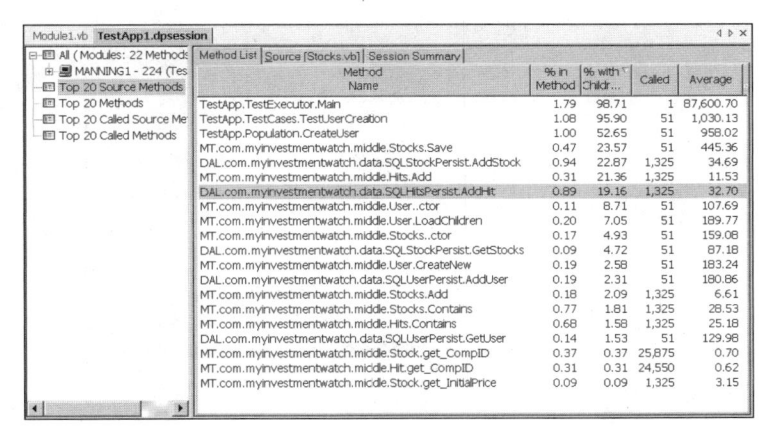

Method Name	% in Method	% with Childr...	Called	Average
TestApp.TestExecutor.Main	1.79	98.71	1	87,600.70
TestApp.TestCases.TestUserCreation	1.08	95.90	51	1,030.13
TestApp.Population.CreateUser	1.00	52.65	51	958.02
MT.com.myinvestmentwatch.middle.Stocks.Save	0.47	23.57	51	445.36
DAL.com.myinvestmentwatch.data.SQLStockPersist.AddStock	0.94	22.87	1,325	34.69
MT.com.myinvestmentwatch.middle.Hits.Add	0.31	21.36	1,325	11.53
DAL.com.myinvestmentwatch.data.SQLHitsPersist.AddHit	0.89	19.16	1,325	32.70
MT.com.myinvestmentwatch.middle.User..ctor	0.11	8.71	51	107.69
MT.com.myinvestmentwatch.middle.User.LoadChildren	0.20	7.05	51	189.77
MT.com.myinvestmentwatch.middle.Stocks..ctor	0.17	4.93	51	159.08
DAL.com.myinvestmentwatch.data.SQLStockPersist.GetStocks	0.09	4.72	51	87.18
MT.com.myinvestmentwatch.middle.User.CreateNew	0.19	2.58	51	183.24
DAL.com.myinvestmentwatch.data.SQLUserPersist.AddUser	0.19	2.31	51	180.86
MT.com.myinvestmentwatch.middle.Stocks.Add	0.18	2.09	1,325	6.61
MT.com.myinvestmentwatch.middle.Stocks.Contains	0.77	1.81	1,325	28.53
MT.com.myinvestmentwatch.middle.Hits.Contains	0.68	1.58	1,325	25.18
DAL.com.myinvestmentwatch.data.SQLUserPersist.GetUser	0.14	1.53	51	129.98
MT.com.myinvestmentwatch.middle.Stock.get_CompID	0.37	0.37	25,875	0.70
MT.com.myinvestmentwatch.middle.Hit.get_CompID	0.31	0.31	24,550	0.62
MT.com.myinvestmentwatch.middle.Stock.get_InitialPrice	0.09	0.09	1,325	3.15

While it is difficult to illustrate the output via screenshots, the single image tells us a great deal about what the profiler has done for us. The profiler keeps statistics on every method call. In particular, it keeps a trace of how long on average the method executes, how many times the method executes, what the average execution time was, and the percentage of time the method was called including the time spent within its children. The child methods are all methods that are called in the context of the method. On the left pane, we see that the profiler knows what our source methods are (our application) and can separate those from the system calls. This allows us to focus on only our code and keeps the ability to drill-down into the details.

313

Chapter 6: Measuring Scalability

In the main pane, we notice that as expected the `TestExectution.Main()` method consumes the vast amount of time (98.71% including children). Since this method controls the execution for our other tests, its children obviously contain the entire set of tests. We can disregard these methods since we expect the outermost methods to score high in the percentage with children category.

One of our goals in determining scalability is to determine how much code execution time is created by the testing code and what percentage is created by our executing code. Knowing that the `TestApp` methods are part of the testing framework, those counters can be disregarded in further analysis.

Further Analysis

Typically, profilers will allow you to drill-down into a method to obtain more performance detail. In our application, we notice that the `Stocks.Contains()` method is called 1,325 times and takes an average of 28.53 microseconds to execute. When we developed the application, we used a linear sort (from 1 to n) to determine if a stock object exists.

By double-clicking on the `Stocks.Contain()` method, we are presented with a breakdown of the method's execution detail.

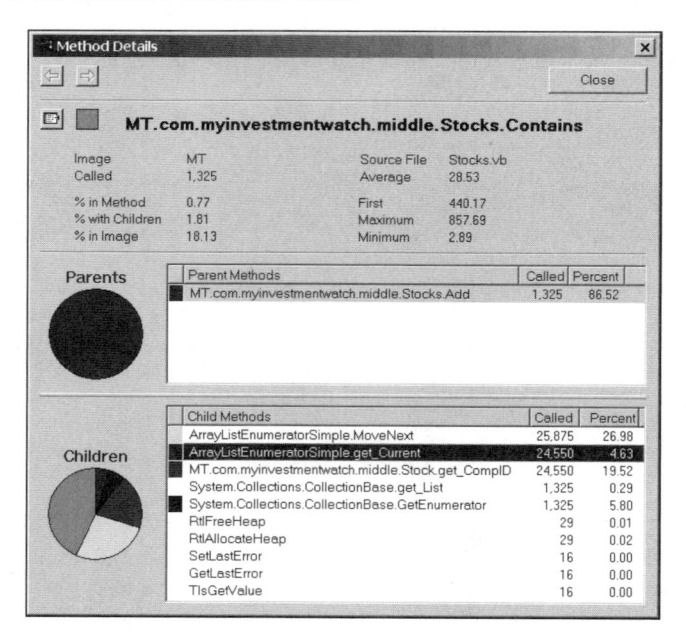

![Method Details window showing MT.com.myinvestmentwatch.middle.Stocks.Contains with Image: MT, Called: 1,325, % in Method: 0.77, % with Children: 1.81, % in Image: 18.13, Source File: Stocks.vb, Average: 28.53, First: 440.17, Maximum: 857.69, Minimum: 2.89. Parent Methods: MT.com.myinvestmentwatch.middle.Stocks.Add called 1,325 times (86.52%). Child Methods table showing ArrayListEnumeratorSimple.MoveNext 25,875 (26.98%), ArrayListEnumeratorSimple.get_Current 24,550 (4.63%), MT.com.myinvestmentwatch.middle.Stock.get_CompID 24,550 (19.52%), System.Collections.CollectionBase.get_List 1,325 (0.29%), System.Collections.CollectionBase.GetEnumerator 1,325 (5.80%), RtlFreeHeap 29 (0.01%), RtlAllocateHeap 29 (0.02%), SetLastError 16 (0.00%), GetLastError 16 (0.00%), TlsGetValue 16 (0.00%)]

Taking a look at the breakdown, we notice that the `ArrayList`'s enumerator is responsible for the overwhelmingly majority of the method's performance cost. We notice that the `get_Current` method (used in checking for equality) was executed nearly 25,000 times. Obviously, this means that the underlying sorting and searching algorithm (Linear sort) could be improved to a more efficient algorithm (b-tree perhaps).

Application Monitoring Tools

Back at the main window, there is one more interesting method we should consider, the `SQLHitsPersist.AddHit()` method, which is executed 1,325 times and taking up over 32% of the execution time (with children). We notice that this method occurs in the Data-access Layer. At this layer, we typically issue SQL calls. Calling SQL 1,325 times definitely warrants a more detailed look. Peering into the method we notice the following output:

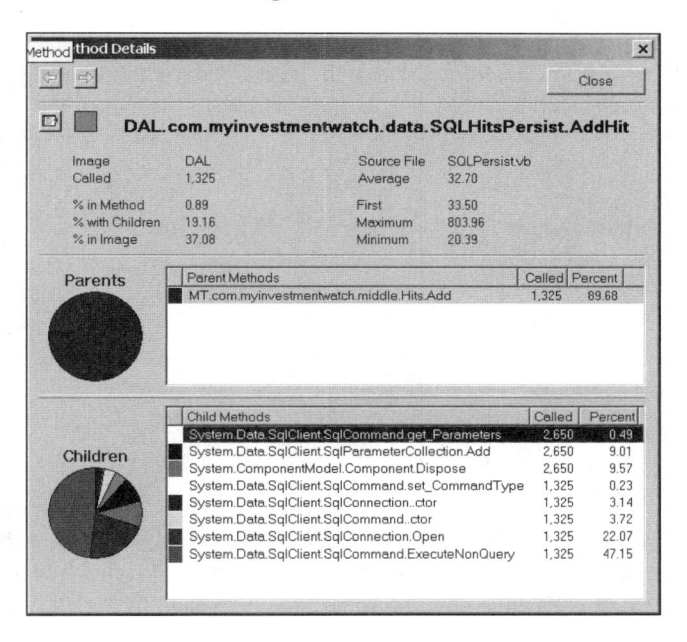

Method Details

DAL.com.myinvestmentwatch.data.SQLHitsPersist.AddHit

Image	DAL	Source File	SQLPersist.vb
Called	1,325	Average	32.70
% in Method	0.89	First	33.50
% with Children	19.16	Maximum	803.96
% in Image	37.08	Minimum	20.39

Parents

Parent Methods	Called	Percent
MT.com.myinvestmentwatch.middle.Hits.Add	1,325	89.68

Children

Child Methods	Called	Percent
System.Data.SqlClient.SqlCommand.get_Parameters	2,650	0.49
System.Data.SqlClient.SqlParameterCollection.Add	2,650	9.01
System.ComponentModel.Component.Dispose	2,650	9.57
System.Data.SqlClient.SqlCommand.set_CommandType	1,325	0.23
System.Data.SqlClient.SqlConnection..ctor	1,325	3.14
System.Data.SqlClient.SqlCommand..ctor	1,325	3.72
System.Data.SqlClient.SqlConnection.Open	1,325	22.07
System.Data.SqlClient.SqlCommand.ExecuteNonQuery	1,325	47.15

We notice that the `ExecuteNonQuery()` is taking up the majority of the execution time. From the main pane, we can right-click on the method name and select the option to view the method source. The source of `SQLHitsPersist.AddHit()` looks like the following:

Count	% with Children	Source
51	0.00	End Sub
1,325	0.00	Public Sub AddHit(ByVal UserID As Integer, ByVal Com
		Implements IHitsPersist.AddHit
1,325	0.91	Dim cn As New SqlConnection(CONSTS.CONNSTR)
1,325	0.83	Dim cm As New SqlCommand("AddHit", cn)
1,325	0.10	cm.CommandType = CommandType.StoredProcedure
1,325	1.39	cm.Parameters.Add("@UserID", UserID)
1,325	0.52	cm.Parameters.Add("@CompID", CompID)
1,325	0.00	Try
1,325	4.29	cn.Open()
1,325	9.17	cm.ExecuteNonQuery()
1,325	0.01	Finally
1,325	0.57	cm.Dispose()
1,325	1.34	cn.Dispose()
1,325	0.00	End Try
1,325	0.00	End Sub
51	0.00	Public Function GetHits(ByVal UserID As Integer) As

315

Having the ability to analyze the source is excellent not only for pinpointing the functions that are code hotspots, but also gives us the ability to examine the logic within the method for possible performance concerns. For example, if we had a rather extensive looping sequence, we would have the ability to see how many times the loop was executed and could re-factor our code to test alternative looping sequences. This technique is terrific for analyzing an application's true hotspots.

Even after looking over the code, we notice that our code itself is executing normally and our logic is sound. Noticing the vast majority of the performance occurs on the stored procedure execution, we need to go one last step further to examine the `AddHit` stored procedure:

```
CREATE PROCEDURE AddHit
   @UserID int,
   @CompID int
AS

INSERT INTO UserHits
   (UserID, CompID, dateRequested)
VALUES
   (@UserID, @CompID, GetDate())

GO
```

The `AddHit` stored procedure is responsible for adding a hit every time a stock is requested by the user. Gathering this information, we are able to tell which stocks are popular and what our busy times are for gathering stock quotes.

The original application intention was to record the times and stocks for each hit to give the business user enough metrics about which stocks were popular and what our peak times are for requesting stocks. Since our application was designed correctly, we must make a business decision whether to keep the code as designed or redesign for faster performance. Regardless of the decision made, we can rest assured we have accomplished our job of measuring our code's performance and have determined potential bottlenecks at the code level.

Keep in mind that there will typically be a piece of code that takes up the vast majority of the execution time or resources. In our case, we know our users will not be logging in and adding/deleting stocks from their profile 100+ times a minute and the performance of the test cases is not a problem. Even though our performance is satisfactory, it does not mean we should disregard profiling our code to understand the bottlenecks and code hotspots. Understanding our code limitations well is a cornerstone of measuring how well our code will scale under different environments.

Profiler Strengths

Profilers are excellent tools for developers to have in their toolbox, particularly when developing high performance, highly scalable systems. Code profilers allow us to accomplish many tasks including:

Application Monitoring Tools

- Locating code bottlenecks
- Analyzing performance at the method or line-of-code level
- Determining code hotspots

In our scenario, our code was written by the time we hooked the profiler to it. The profiler can be used at any time during the development cycle and is definitely not limited to working with finished code. Using a profiler throughout development allows you to get in the habit of building a piece of code, running it through the profiler, and tweaking it for performance. The sooner in the development cycle performance bottlenecks can be detected, the greater the percentages of success in creating a well performing and scalable application.

Profiler Limitations

Profilers can typically allow us to determine what sorts of resources are being used. We could follow the application's execution path down to the heart of the Windows operating system, examine the average time and number of calls executed against the system libraries, and get a good idea for the amount of system resources we are using.

For example, if we run across a method called `WriteToFile()` in the Windows system library commanding a high percentage of execution time, we can likely guess that our I/O system is under heavy load. It is also hard to determine how our CPU is performing during the test cases.

The code profiler is meant to do exactly as its name implies: profile code. In order to determine our resource usage during test execution, we need a tool that has the ability to monitor or capture events at the operating-system level. In the Windows operating system family, the tool we are looking for is the Performance Monitor.

Performance Monitor

Performance monitor is a familiar tool to the vast majority of Windows application developers and allows us to measure system events on our computer or other computers. It is a GUI-based MMC snap-in (also available in Administrative Tools) that allows us to configure listeners to listen for interesting system events including many low-level system events that could not be monitored from the code profiler.

Performance monitor is a great tool to use in conjunction with the code profiler. As we profile our code, we can add relevant application counters to our performance monitor to watch for interesting events. Using the tools in conjunction with one another allows us to follow both our code and system performance together. If we find high correlations of one piece of code triggering a high usage of system resources, we can examine the code for improvements. Likewise, if we find an unsuspected high system usage count, we can examine the code known to trigger that system counter. For example, if we notice that the application is spending a lot of time reading and writing to disk, we may choose to monitor Windows' I/O performance to find out if the I/O subsystem is performing poorly.

Performance Monitor and Distributed Applications

Performance monitor has the ability to monitor any machine that you have privileges to monitor. By default, administrative permissions are required. In a testing environment, permissions should not be a limiting factor in monitoring all systems in a distributed application while running your tests.

Having the ability to monitor multiple machines simultaneously gives us the opportunity to monitor many levels of the system from one tool and from one machine. When systems span boundaries, the Performance Monitor allows us to view and record events from differing systems, making analysis a simplified process.

When we finished the discussion on the code profiler, we noticed that a SQL stored procedure was being called numerous times to add user activity data to our database. Our code profiler got our analysis to the point of determining which stored procedure was being fired.

Now that we understand where a possible bottleneck could limit our scalability, we would like to get as much information about the bottleneck's cause as possible. What we want to do is configure Performance Monitor to listen to a few relevant counters.

The Windows environment offers performance counters for all of the interesting operating system subsystems. We can choose to monitor a wide variety of processes; the most significant are those dealing with our more critical resources: CPU usage, memory usage, I/O activity, network activity, SQL Server activity, IIS, and other systems our application relies on for its operation.

For our example, we noticed that the INSERT statement caused quite a bit of activity during our test run. What we'll do is setup the Performance Monitor on the SQL Server and pull out a few counters. The counters we want to examine include:

- Processor: % Processor Time. The percentage of processor activity. This counter is frequently used to measure overall CPU usage.

- Physical Disk: Disk Transfers/sec. This is the rate of read and write operations on the disk. If this counter is high, the I/O subsystem is working hard. This is highly correlated with the next counter.

- Physical Disk: % Disk Time. This is the percentage of elapsed time that the selected disk drive was busy servicing read or write requests. Having a high counter here means our I/O subsystem is not keeping up or is being pushed hard by our application.

- SQLServer.SQL Statistics: SQL Compilations/sec. Number of times a query is compiled. If low, this counter ensures our SQL Server is compiling our stored procedures correctly. Highly correlated with the next counter.

- SQLServer.SQL Statistics: SQL Re-Compilations/sec. Number of times a query is re-compiled. If this counter is low, we know our SQL Server is storing the SQL query execution plans correctly.

Application Monitoring Tools

These counters were not chosen at random, rather they were chosen because they are expected to tell us more about the nature of the problem at hand. In our case, we are working with an `INSERT` statement within a stored procedure. We monitor the processor to determine if the SQL Server's CPU is slowing down our queries. Since our `INSERT` is not processor-intensive (calculation or otherwise), we want to monitor the physical disk as well. Even though SQL was set up properly to handle query compilation, we include the SQL counters as a measure to ensure it is working as desired. We expect the SQL counters to remain relatively low.

If we set up the Performance Monitor with the following monitors and run our test scripts, we collect the following performance data.

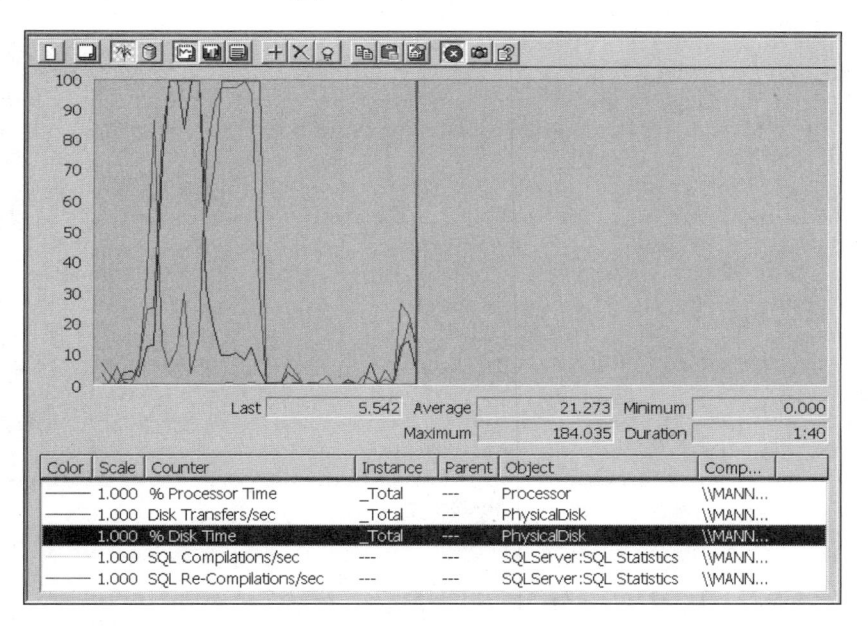

Color	Scale	Counter	Instance	Parent	Object	Comp...
	1.000	% Processor Time	_Total	---	Processor	\\MANN...
	1.000	Disk Transfers/sec	_Total	---	PhysicalDisk	\\MANN...
	1.000	% Disk Time	_Total	---	PhysicalDisk	\\MANN...
	1.000	SQL Compilations/sec	---	---	SQLServer:SQL Statistics	\\MANN...
	1.000	SQL Re-Compilations/sec	---	---	SQLServer:SQL Statistics	\\MANN...

Last: 5.542 Average: 21.273 Minimum: 0.000
Maximum: 184.035 Duration: 1:40

From the output, we notice a number of interesting things that help measure our scalability:

- ❑ SQL is compiling and using our query cache correctly. Notice that the SQL Server is not compiling or recompiling the stored procedure much, if at all, during the tests.

- ❑ I/O is our bottleneck with these tests. The % Disk Time counter hovers around 90% and the Disk transfers/sec counter exceeds our scale's limits of 100 or more transfers a second. Having the disk usage hover at 90% allows us to note that our disk subsystem is heavily used.

If these tests were system-wide stress tests, we could improve our performance and scalability by improving our physical disk system or altering the code to reduce the pressure being put on the I/O system.

The nice thing about Performance Monitor is that there are a wide variety of counters available to monitor different subsystems. In our example, we use the physical disk, SQL, and processor counter objects; however, .NET, IIS, and ASP.NET also implement their own sets of counters. Not only can you monitor the physical hardware resources, you can also monitor the applications (CLR, ASP.NET) upon which you write your code.

The code you are testing will determine the type of performance counters you require. The best results are obtained from Performance Monitor if you understand which subsystems your code is using, determining from the documentation which counters are relevant, and attaching the Performance Monitor accordingly. While this example is I/O intensive, others are perhaps memory, processor, or network intensive and would benefit from monitoring a different set of counters.

Providing an exhaustive list of even the relevant .NET performance counters would not be practical at this stage of the chapter. For a complete list of performance counters, refer to the .NET SDK, MSDN, and the documentation for the other applications that you wish to monitor, such as SQL Server.

Performance monitor is a generic tool that has the ability to listen for any source of events that are published from code – even our code. .NET has managed libraries written to allow developers to implement their own custom performance counters and manipulate the counters as their code requires.

In the previous example, perhaps we would like to raise an event when a user logs into the application or manipulates their portfolio. Monitoring these events in conjunction with system events gives the administrator and developer a better insight into where the applications are consuming resources. When we discuss code instrumentation later in this chapter, we will walk through an example of creating and writing to a custom performance counter.

Microsoft Application Center Test

As you have probably noticed, we have gone from very low-level code testing with the code profiler a to a higher operating-system level performance analysis tool. The goal is to lay the framework for measuring scalability and performance for all aspects of the application from the very low level to the entire application-scope level.

As we mentioned earlier, two of the most important tests to determine the level of scalability are the stress test and the load test. Stress tests help us to determine our application's limitations and bottlenecks from an overall system perspective.

In order to provide a load test, we could continue to write test scripts that mimic general usage. While writing system-level tests is entirely possible, there are ample pre-built tools that help us generate test scripts and provide us with the ability to create our own customizations to enhance the automatically generated output.

Application Monitoring Tools

Microsoft Application Test Centre (ACT, previously known as Web Application Stress tool or WAS) is a tool that assists us with running system tests and script generation for testing our ASP.NET web applications. Using the tool, we can configure how many connections and users we want the test to simulate. By simply changing configuration settings, we can run the test against our servers and determine what points of the application become overwhelmed first.

For a 120-day evaluation copy, see http://www.microsoft.com/applicationcenter/default.asp. For a more complete coverage than is possible here, see the Wrox Press book *Professional Application Center 2000*, ISBN 1-86100-447-8.

Configuring Application Center Test

At the heart of ACT is a script engine that executes script code to perform its functionality. In order to create the script, we could manually code the script or leverage the tool to record our user actions and dynamically create a script based on our user actions. Once the dynamic script is created, we could then alter the code to tailor the script to our needs. In the vast majority of the cases, the automatically generated script along with examining and perhaps fine tuning the script is sufficient to perform quality tests.

Dynamically Generated Script Creation

In order for ACT to dynamically produce the script file, it must record your actions through a browser session. When you are set to create a new test, you have the option to create the test manually by writing script or by recording your browser activities while you navigate through your site. The following wizard window shows the ability to create an empty test or have the tool record your browser window. Creating a new test in ACT will start the New Test Wizard:

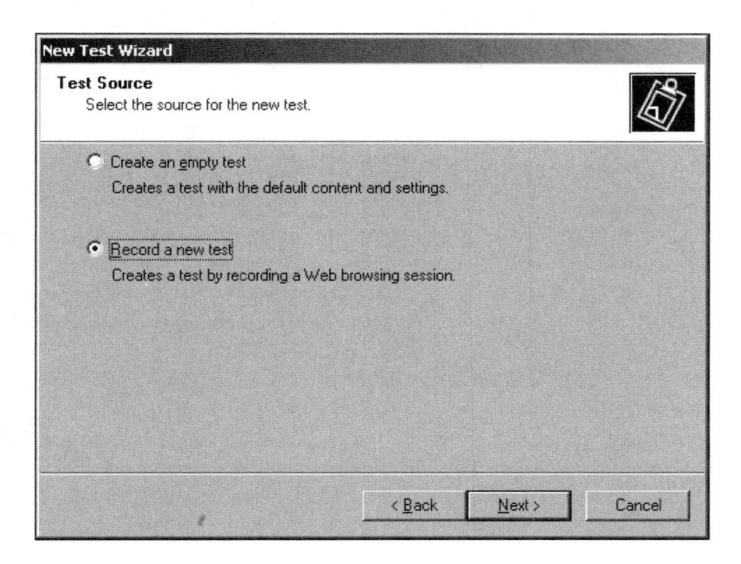

321

Once the test begins, a browser window opens and you are free to navigate your site with the tool recording your HTTP activity for later playback. When navigating your test, it is important to follow the normal course of action that a user would follow to simulate a true test. If you are dealing with a data-driven application, choose a path that will not cause conflicts once the path is followed in a stress scenario but still follows a typical user session as closely as possible.

In our application, we have the ability to add stocks to our user portfolio. If we attempt to add a stock twice to the portfolio, a trappable error occurs on the ASP.NET page and the stock is not added to the portfolio. If we add a stock to our portfolio, we should also delete the stock in order to avoid the error being created for every future test case using that portfolio. In general, try to leave the data in a test-friendly fashion between requests as much as possible.

Running the Test

Once the script is generated, we can configure the stress test and execute it. Notice from the following screenshot that the script has been generated and we are able to alter it if needed at this point.

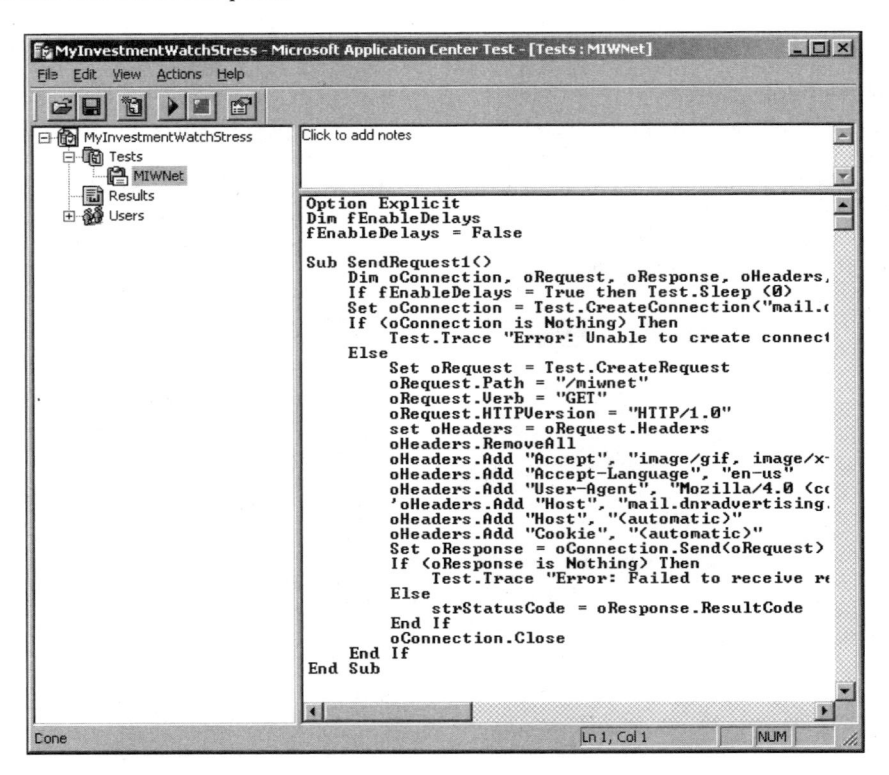

```
Option Explicit
Dim fEnableDelays
fEnableDelays = False

Sub SendRequest1()
    Dim oConnection, oRequest, oResponse, oHeaders,
    If fEnableDelays = True then Test.Sleep (0)
    Set oConnection = Test.CreateConnection("mail.c
    If (oConnection is Nothing) Then
        Test.Trace "Error: Unable to create connect
    Else
        Set oRequest = Test.CreateRequest
        oRequest.Path = "/miwnet"
        oRequest.Verb = "GET"
        oRequest.HTTPVersion = "HTTP/1.0"
        set oHeaders = oRequest.Headers
        oHeaders.RemoveAll
        oHeaders.Add "Accept", "image/gif, image/x-
        oHeaders.Add "Accept-Language", "en-us"
        oHeaders.Add "User-Agent", "Mozilla/4.0 (co
        'oHeaders.Add "Host", "mail.dnradvertising.
        oHeaders.Add "Host", "<automatic>"
        oHeaders.Add "Cookie", "<automatic>"
        Set oResponse = oConnection.Send(oRequest)
        If (oResponse is Nothing) Then
            Test.Trace "Error: Failed to receive re
        Else
            strStatusCode = oResponse.ResultCode
        End If
        oConnection.Close
    End If
End Sub
```

Application Monitoring Tools

Once the test is created, we are able to alter the stress level by changing the number of users and the number of connections used by the test. The number of users and the number of connections changes the stress level of the test. We will keep the default of one for our initial tests.

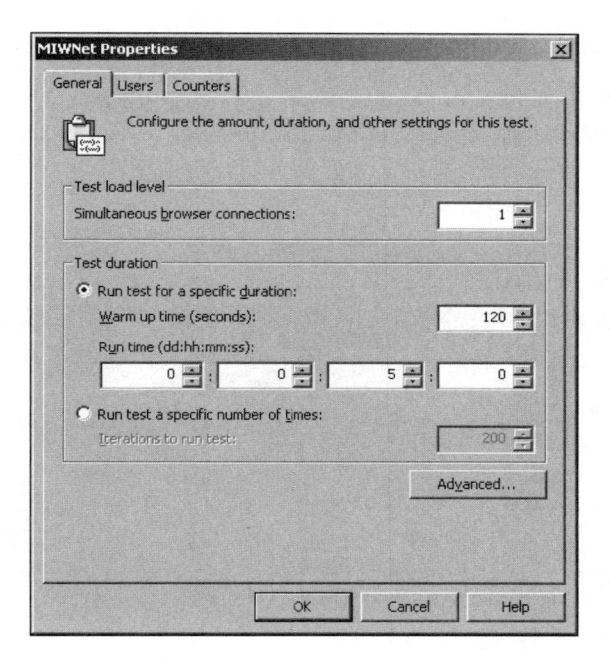

Before we run the test, we also want to set up the Performance Monitor to monitor application counters. ACT allows you to monitor Performance Monitor counters while running the script from within the tool (click on the Counters tab to set up Performance Monitor counters). In our example, we are going to monitor the performance counters from within the Performance Monitor interface already explained.

We have selected the following counters to monitor:

- Processor: % Processor Time – monitor CPU activity during stress.

- ASP.NET Application: Anonymous Requests/sec – gives us an indication of how many requests per second are being executed. This is the same counter as we will see in the test execution window's "RPS" counter. We want to monitor this counter to use as a measuring stick with the other counters. We want to see at what request per second the application becomes over stressed.

- Physical Disk: Disk Transfers/sec – I/O usage. Since this was our limitation before, we want to see how the counters perform in overall usage traffic.

- Physical Disk: % Disk Usage – monitor I/O usage. Correlated with Disk Transfers/sec.

323

Chapter 6: Measuring Scalability

With the test created and the performance counters ready for monitoring, we can now stress the application by executing the script. The following screenshot shows the script while the test is executing. We are issuing around 40 requests per second without any user delay between the requests. If you look closely at the generated script, there is a global script variable called `fEnableDelays` that can be set to `True` to mimic the user delay between requests. Mimicking delay would give us a better approximation of actual user activity. At this point, we are simply trying to find our system's limits and are more concerned with total requests per second. Note that the ACT tool should not be run on the server being tested. The ACT tool requires resources and if executed on the server being tested, would detract from the server's ability to handle the simulated user load.

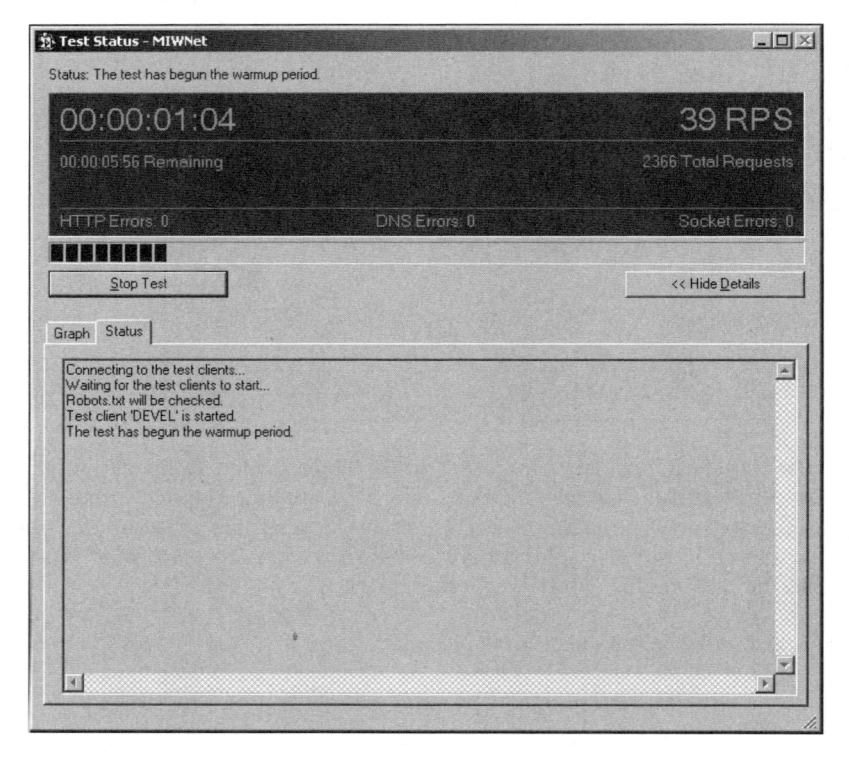

![Test Status - MIWNet screenshot showing status of test that has begun the warmup period, elapsed time 00:00:01:04, 39 RPS, 2366 Total Requests, 0 HTTP/DNS/Socket errors, with status messages: Connecting to the test clients..., Waiting for the test clients to start..., Robots.txt will be checked., Test client 'DEVEL' is started., The test has begun the warmup period.]

The **Test Status** screen shows us the current statistics for the test. Here, we are issuing 39 requests per second with no errors. In order to see how our application is performing, let's take a look at our server performance counters.

Application Monitoring Tools

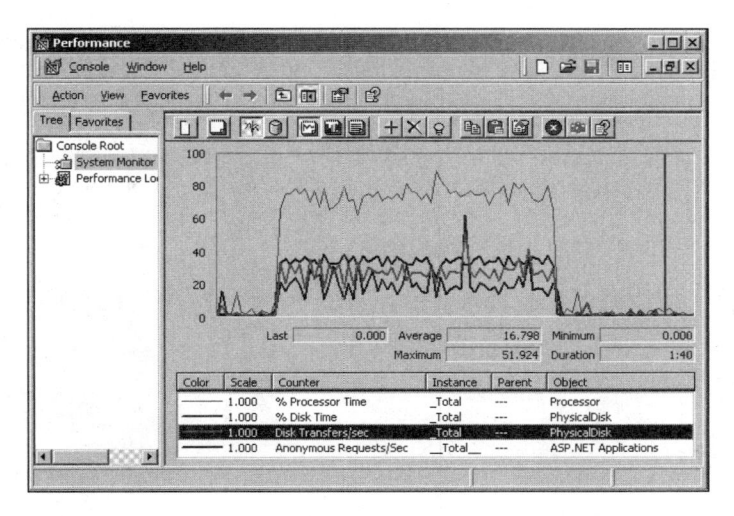

[Performance monitor screenshot showing System Monitor with graphs of % Processor Time, % Disk Time, Disk Transfers/sec, and Anonymous Requests/Sec counters]

During the test, we notice a healthy but not overwhelming stress on the system. As an interesting point, we notice that the I/O usage that was a bottleneck is not yet becoming a relevant source of concern in overall stress testing. Keep in mind that the same test can produce different output when different parts of the application are being monitored. In this scenario, we notice that the processor is running quite high, signifying CPU usage may be reaching capacity.

In order to really stress the system, we'll change the number of connections from 1 to 3. This will open the floodgates a bit more against our system.

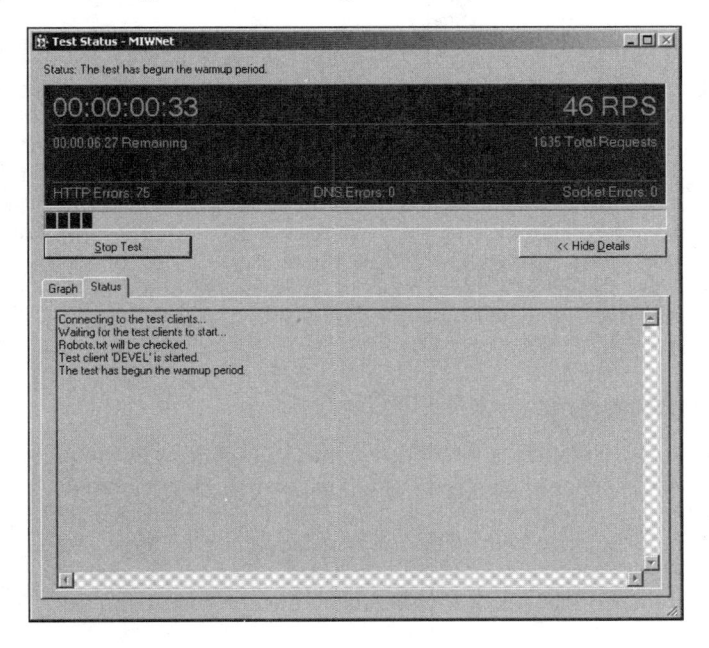

[Test Status - MIWNet screenshot showing 00:00:00:33 elapsed, 46 RPS, 1635 Total Requests, HTTP Errors: 75, DNS Errors: 0, Socket Errors: 0]

325

Chapter 6: Measuring Scalability

Notice that we have increased our requests per second from the upper 30's to the upper 40's, about a 25% increase in stress. Since our processor was reaching its limit before, adding an additional 25% overhead should stress the system completely out.

Looking at the testing output, we have issued 1,635 requests, but have received 75 errors. The errors are related to the system stress. The server is not able to keep up with the incoming requests and is throwing HTTP errors to us because of the high traffic. Let's take a look at our performance counters.

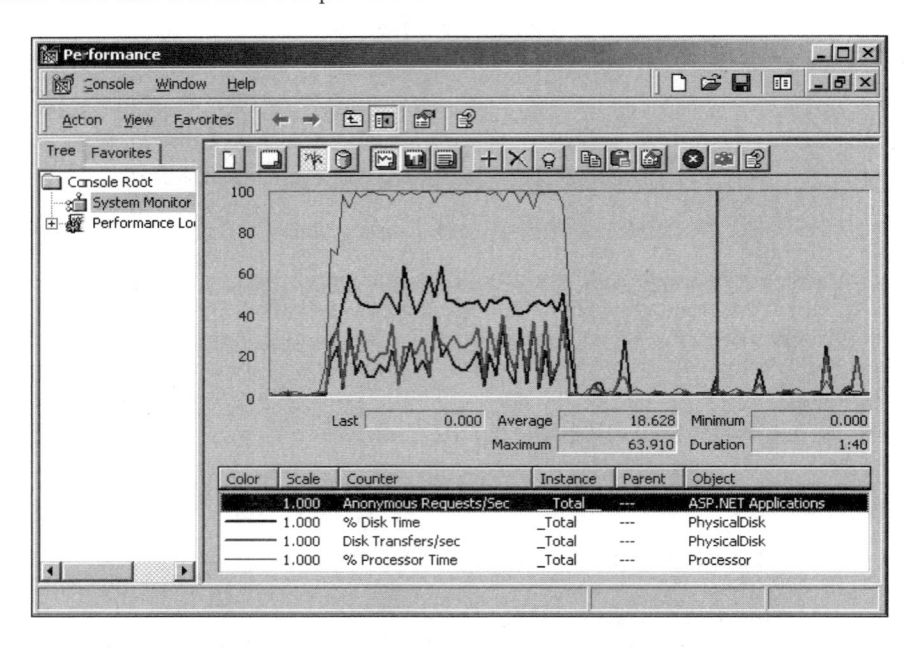

We can see that our CPU usage is at its peak for the lifetime of the application. We can be assured we have hit our system ceiling somewhere between 40 and 46 requests per second. Remember, this does not mean we can handle only 46 concurrent users. Since we are issuing requests without a user delay and within a LAN environment, we are able to issue requests many times faster than a true user base. In order to get the estimated user count, a test could be created to mimic user timing in page submission and flip the Boolean script switch to simulate the delay between pages.

Tools Summary

Measuring scalability is greatly improved with the use of tools. In the previous example, we have the ability to change the user load to simulate various numbers of users and determine how our application performs under the differing user loads. We have just begun to scratch the surface with our brief introduction to the code profiler, Performance Monitor, and ACT tools. The software industry has created many proprietary as well as open source tools available for download and purchase.

Understanding tools and their respective purpose in software development allows you to create more scalable and higher performing code. Just as a mechanic is assisted with automotive diagnostic tools to fix engines, the application developer is assisted with code diagnostics and performance monitoring tools to build and troubleshoot code.

Understanding the tools involves understanding their role in the software development lifecycle. Each tool has particular strengths:

- **Code Profiler** – These tools profile application code, including a detailed analysis that spans to the method or line level of analysis. The code profiler is useful when building algorithms and unit testing specific application blocks for performance.

- **Performance Monitor** – This is responsible for monitoring system-wide events including system hardware, operating system, and application performance counters. It is useful throughout the lifecycle; however, the counters monitored will differ depending on the resources affected by the test.

- **Application Center Test** – This is a stress tool useful for stress testing a piece or entire web application. It is useful for automating test cases while providing the ability for the developer to alter or write the test scripts.

Code Instrumentation

So far in this chapter, we have discussed the theory behind testing and have implemented a few tests to measure the performance of our application. We have also looked into some monitoring tools that allow us to enhance our abilities to test and monitor our software.

Measuring performance and scalability does not stop when development ends. In fact it increases. When the application is released into the production environment, we must have the ability to monitor the application performance, locate and troubleshoot defects, and watch for places within our system that could benefit from scaling.

Of all the tools mentioned, only the Performance Monitor is of any real value for monitoring the application once it is in a production environment. While monitoring the system counters gives us important data on how the system is performing, the counters are generic in nature and often do not correlate with how the application internals are performing. Later in this chapter we will discuss how to implement our own performance counters which will give us tailored, meaningful counters we can monitor.

Imagine we are creating an online retail system accepting orders online. Using the Performance Monitor allows us to monitor the SQL server, ASP.NET, and system resource counters. While these metrics are great for system administrators and overall capacity planning, the developer is much more interested in finding out which parts of the application are used and how frequently code events happen. A few possible metrics that we might be interested in monitoring for in our online retail system include:

Chapter 6: Measuring Scalability

- How many orders are being placed?
- How many custom errors are being fired?
- How many product searches are being done?
- How many orders are being calculated but not necessarily ordered?

In order to provide true application-specific metrics, we need to include **code instrumentation** within our source code. Code instrumentation is the process of making our application capable of publishing events of interest to a listening application such as Performance Monitor, the event log, a debug window, or a listening code tracer.

Code instrumentation consists of writing statements within code that can be listened to while the application is running. For example, we could implement a listener to write text messages to a text file when a code action occurs. When the action occurs, the code would send a message to anyone listening for messages. If we have a listener, the listener would accept the message and append it to a text file.

Code instrumentation is an important technique for measuring scalability. If certain components or functionality are being used extensively, we can consider scaling techniques to improve the performance of such code. Without code instrumentation, we must use other metrics including custom reports or excessive data logging, which is expensive to perform in a real-time environment.

Tracing

Tracing is the process of capturing actions that occur in code and writing them to a resource that we can monitor. Tracing is performed by writing `Trace` statements into the code that can be listened for and captured by outside trace listeners.

The .NET Framework exposes a set of classes in the `System.Diagnostics` namespace that allow us to add tracing statements into our application code. The `Trace` class within this namespace provides methods similar to those of the `System.Console` namespace that allow us to write statements to any trace listeners. The most frequently used methods are `Write()` and `WriteLine()`.

Tracing 101 – Establishing Tracing

Implementing tracing in an application is very easy and can be explained best with a small sample application. The following code is the same `Account` class as was used earlier in the chapter during the discussion of unit testing. Setting up the test code in a sample application allows us to focus on the issues around tracing. Implementing tracing in our production application would dilute the text with unnecessary code not related to tracing. Implementing trace code in our production application would follow the same procedures as explained in the following code.

Code Instrumentation

Notice that we must import the `System.Diagnostics` namespace in order to use the `Trace` class without the namespace qualifier. We then add `Trace` statements to the code when an important action occurs. In our case, we would like to write trace statements when someone withdraws from their account. Before we exit, we tell the `Trace` class to flush its output to its listeners:

```
Imports System
Imports System.Diagnostics

Module Module1

  Sub Main()

    'Add the system console and text file as trace listeners
    Trace.Listeners.Add(new TextWriterTraceListener(Console.Out))
    Trace.Listeners.Add(new TextWriterTraceListener( _
                  System.IO.File.Create("test.txt")))

    Dim acct As New Account(1000)
    Debug.Assert(acct.InitialBalance = 1000)
    Debug.Assert(acct.Balance = 1000)
    Debug.Assert(acct.Activity = 0)

    acct.Withdraw(200)
    Debug.Assert(acct.InitialBalance = 1000)
    Debug.Assert(acct.Balance = 800)
    Debug.Assert(acct.Activity = -200)

    acct.Deposit(2000)
    Debug.Assert(acct.InitialBalance = 1000)
    Debug.Assert(acct.Balance = 2800)
    Debug.Assert(acct.Activity = 1800, _
              "Deposit activity assertion failed, check deposit")
    Trace.Flush()
  End Sub
End Module

Public Class Account
  Private _initialBalance As Double
  Private _balance As Double

  Public Sub New(ByVal InitialBalance As Double)
    _balance = InitialBalance
    _initialBalance = InitialBalance
  End Sub

  Public Sub Withdraw(ByVal Amount As Double)
    If Amount > _balance Then
      Throw New ArgumentException( _
           "Withdraw amount cannot exceed current balance")
    End If
    _balance -= Amount
```

329

Chapter 6: Measuring Scalability

```
        Trace.WriteLine("Account withdrawal of " & _
                        Amount.ToString("c") & " at " & _
                        System.DateTime.Now())

    End Sub

    Public Sub Deposit(ByVal Amount As Double)
        _balance += Amount
    End Sub

    Public ReadOnly Property InitialBalance() As Double
        Get
            InitialBalance = _initialBalance
        End Get
    End Property

    Public ReadOnly Property Balance() As Double
        Get
            Balance = _balance
        End Get
    End Property

    Public ReadOnly Property Activity() As Double
        Get
            Activity = _balance - _initialBalance
        End Get
    End Property

End Class
```

By importing the `System.Diagnostics` namespace, we have abbreviated access to the set of tracing classes. The `Trace` class is the heart of tracing and is the central class used when implementing trace statements.

In order for trace statements to be processed, we first must add listeners to the `Trace.Listeners` collection. We can attach as many listeners as we need to report. Listeners are typically streams capable of processing text. There are currently three types of trace listeners:

- `DefaultTraceListener` – The default listener is automatically added to the `Trace.Listeners` collection. In Visual Studio .NET, the default trace listener is typically the Debug output window.

- `EventLogTraceListener` – Writes trace messages to the Windows event log.

- `TextWriterTraceListener` – Writes to any stream objects including text files, the console window, or another class deriving from `System.IO.Stream`.

Code Instrumentation

In our example, we implement two `TextWriterTraceListener` listeners. The first writes to the console output stream, the other writes to a text file.

One interesting thing about the `Trace` class is the ability to control if tracing is enabled via a compiler directive. Using the `/define` directive, we can set `trace=true`. Compile the `Account` class with the following to enable tracing. If we did not include tracing, the compiler would not compile the trace statements into our resulting IL code:

```
> vbc /r:System.dll /define:trace=true Account.vb
```

Executing the application proves the console writer was attached as a trace listener:

```
C:\Scalability\Chapter 6\Tracing 101>Account
Account withdrawal of £200.00 at 24/09/2002 13:48:24

C:\Scalability\Chapter 6\Tracing 101>
```

The second trace listener wrote to a text file as well:

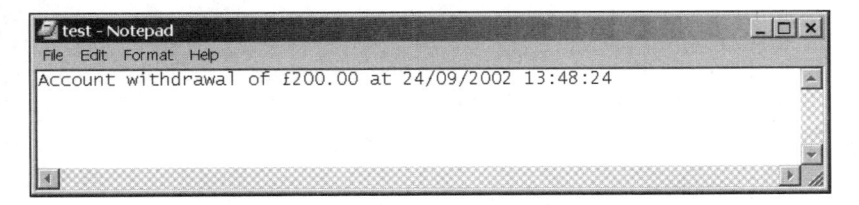

```
Account withdrawal of £200.00 at 24/09/2002 13:48:24
```

From this simple example, we can see how instrumenting code with tracing is an effective technique for measuring code-level activity. However, there are some shortcomings with our current scenario. Writing to an output stream is not an activity we want to do constantly. In our previous example, we wouldn't want to write to a text log during normal application operation since we would incur the associated performance hit. We could compile the executable without tracing enabled. If at some later point we decided to implement tracing, we would be forced to recompile. What is needed is a method to dynamically add trace listeners to our application when we want to begin tracing and remove them when finished, all without needing to change code or recompile.

Another shortcoming with the previous example is the fact that tracing is all or nothing. Perhaps we would only like to monitor a subset of trace statements, perhaps only those with a high priority.

Perhaps some trace statements are higher priority than others. For example, perhaps we would like to monitor only the critical error messages when debugging and log all trace statements when monitoring overall performance. We need to have the ability to set a level for which we would like to monitor.

331

Tracing 102

Fortunately, tracing has the ability to overcome the limitations imposed in the previous example. Tracing allows us to configure which trace statements we would like to listen for, or if we want to listen at all. For example, perhaps we would like to shut off tracing or only monitor error events. We also would like to be able to change what we trace for without needing to change any code or recompile.

The ability to give a trace statement a precedence level is accomplished with a `TraceSwitch`. A `TraceSwitch` is a configurable parameter that we include in a configuration file that controls which statements are to be monitored. By changing the switch value in the configuration file, we can change what the tracer listens for.

Let's edit our previous code to illustrate the use of a `TraceSwitch`. In particular, we would like to change the `Withdraw()` method to write a trace message to all trace listeners if an error occurs, regardless of what level they are listening at. We would like to write a trace statement on a successful withdrawal only if they are listening to every trace message being written. Because a successful withdrawal is rather common, we don't want to write the message in all scenarios. Only when the tracer is listening for all trace messages would we want to write that message. If the tracer was listening only to the error messages, including successful withdrawal messages would dilute the more important error responses.

In order to implement levels of tracing, we define a `TraceSwitch` called `defaultSwitch`. Notice that we check the level of `defaultSwitch` before we write error messages. The levels of trace switches include:

- `TraceError` – traces only error messages
- `TraceInfo` – traces error and info messages
- `TraceWarning` – traces error, info, and warning messages
- `TraceVerbose` – traces error, info, warning, and verbose messages

Before we call `Trace.Write()`, we check the switch to see what its current value is. The current value is set in a configuration file, which we will view shortly. The switch's value determines if the trace message is to be logged. Rewriting the `Withdraw()` method to take into account the trace switch looks like the following:

```
Public Sub Withdraw(ByVal Amount As Double)
  Dim defaultSwitch As New TraceSwitch("DefaultSwitch", _
                                       "Default tracing switch")
  If Amount > _balance Then
    If defaultSwitch.TraceError Then _
      Trace.Write("An account was attempted to be overdrawn")
      Throw New ArgumentException( _
           "Withdraw amount cannot exceed current balance")
  End If
```

Code Instrumentation

```
    _balance -= Amount
    If defaultSwitch.TraceVerbose Then _
        Trace.WriteLine("Account withdrawl of " & _
            Amount.ToString("c") & " at " & System.DateTime.Now())
End Sub
```

Since the error is of high priority, we make sure that `DefaultSwitch` is set to `TraceError` or higher. In contrast, the successful withdrawal trace message is only written if the `TraceSwitch` is set to `Verbose`. If the `TraceSwitch` is set to warning, info, or error, it will not be written to the trace output.

In order to trigger the error trace message, we must alter our `Main()` method to try to withdraw more than the current balance. For simplicity we just catch the error and continue processing:

```
Sub Main()
    'Add the system console and text file as trace listeners
    Trace.Listeners.Add(new TextWriterTraceListener(Console.Out))
    Trace.Listeners.Add(New TextWriterTraceListener( _
                System.IO.File.Create("C:\test.txt")))

    Dim acct As New Account(1000)

    Debug.Assert(acct.InitialBalance = 1000)
    Debug.Assert(acct.Balance = 1000)
    Debug.Assert(acct.Activity = 0)

    acct.Withdraw(200)
    Try
        acct.Withdraw(9999)
    Catch
    End try
    Debug.Assert(acct.InitialBalance = 1000)
    Debug.Assert(acct.Balance = 800)
    Debug.Assert(acct.Activity = -200)

    acct.Deposit(2000)
    Debug.Assert(acct.InitialBalance = 1000)
    Debug.Assert(acct.Balance = 2800)
    Debug.Assert(acct.Activity = 1800, _
            "Deposit activity assertion failed, check deposit")
End Sub
```

Configuration

In order for our application to stay as configurable as possible, we implement the `TraceSwitch` value in the application's configuration file. Using the configuration file for specifying the switch's value allows us to change the value without recompiling:

333

Chapter 6: Measuring Scalability

```xml
<?xml version="1.0" encoding="UTF-8" ?>
<configuration>
  <system.diagnostics>
    <switches>
       <!-- Set value property of the Arithmetic switch to one of the
following: 0(off) 1(error), 2(warning), 3(info), 4(verbose) -->
       <add name="DefaultSwitch" value="1" />
    </switches>
    <trace autoflush="true" />
  </system.diagnostics>
</configuration>
```

There are two points to note in this configuration file. First, we set the `DefaultSwitch` trace value to 1, which tells us to listen for only the error trace messages. We are also able to configure the trace class to `autoflush` itself so we do not need to call `Trace.Flush()` manually to write trace statements.

Compiling the application with the new changes requires the same command line as previously used. Keep in mind that the configuration file must be named `Account.exe.config` and be placed into the same directory as the resulting executable:

> **vbc /r:System.dll /define:trace=true Account.vb**

We can then run the application as we did before:

```
C:\Scalability\Chapter 6\Tracing 102>Account
An account was attempted to be overdrawn
C:\Scalability\Chapter 6\Tracing 102>
```

Notice that only the error message was traced. This is by design, since we only wanted to trace the error messages and disregard the other varieties. In order to see the successful withdrawal statement, we will change the `DefaultTrace` value to 4 to enable verbose tracing:

```xml
<?xml version="1.0" encoding="UTF-8" ?>
<configuration>
  <system.diagnostics>
    <switches>
       <!-- Set value property of the Arithmetic switch to one of the
following: 0(off) 1(error), 2(warning), 3(info), 4(verbose) -->
       <add name="DefaultSwitch" value="4" />
    </switches>
    <trace autoflush="true" />
  </system.diagnostics>
</configuration>
```

Code Instrumentation

Without recompiling, we can re-run the executable with the configuration changes made. Both the error message and the verbose message will be traced in verbose mode:

```
C:\Scalability\Chapter 6\Tracing 102>Account
Account withdrawal of £200.00 at 24/09/2002 13:51:36
An account was attempted to be overdrawn
C:\Scalability\Chapter 6\Tracing 102>
```

Tracing and Performance Monitor

Tracing to a text file or stream is nice for debugging and detailed system diagnostics. For example, if we would like to examine the data manually or perhaps import the data into a spreadsheet or database for further analysis after the data has been collected.

From an analysis perspective, the text file is rather limited since it does not provide any summation or visual representation. In order for good statistics to be calculated, the text file must be altered or perhaps run though a parser that has the ability to provide more rich performance feedback. Also, it does not lend itself well to immediate analysis since it must be translated from its text form into meaningful data. What we would like to do is analyze immediate performance statistics in a similar fashion to how we monitor our CPU or system resource usage via Performance Monitor.

Knowing what we do about trace listeners and understanding how to create a performance counter is all that is necessary to implement a custom trace listener to log its information to the newly created custom performance counter.

Creating a Custom Counter

Before we can implement a trace listener to write to a counter, we must first create a performance counter on our system to which the trace listener will write its data. Typically, creating the necessary system performance counters would be included during the application installation routine and prepared before the application is executing. The code to create a custom performance counter looks like the following:

```
Imports System
Imports System.Diagnostics

Module CreatePerformanceCounter
  Sub Main()
    If PerformanceCounterCategory.Exists("AccountPerf") Then _
      PerformanceCounterCategory.Delete("AccountPerf")

    Dim ccd As New CounterCreationData("AccountApplication", _
      "Performance counter for the account application", _
      PerformanceCounterType.RateOfCountsPerSecond32)
```

335

Chapter 6: Measuring Scalability

```
    Dim ccdc As New CounterCreationDataCollection()
    ccdc.Add(ccd)
    PerformanceCounterCategory.Create("AccountPerf", _
        "Account performance counters", ccdc)
End Sub
End Module
```

The `PerformanceCounterCategory` is an object that has a set of static methods for interacting with the `PerformanceCounter` objects located on the local system. Located in the `System.Diagnostics` namespace, the object has static methods for creating, deleting, and checking to see if the performance category exists. In the following Performance Monitor screenshot, the `PerformanceCounterCategory` corresponds to a Performance object.

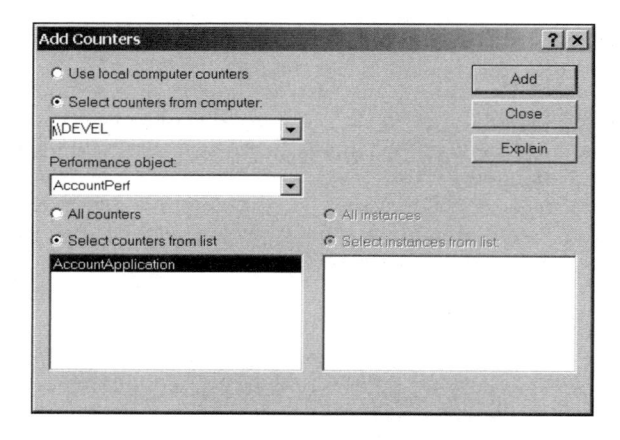

Before we create the counter, we make sure it does not already exist. If it does exist, we make sure to delete it and the counters it has already established to make sure we have a correct set of counters within the performance object. In our small app, we want to make sure we start with a clean slate within our performance category. If the `AccountPerf` category had been previously created, we would like to delete the counters and start fresh with a new category.

Each counter we wish to create needs to have its own `CounterCreationData` object that holds its counter information. In our case, we create a `CounterCreationData` for an `AccountApplication` counter. Besides the name, we also pass a textual description for the counter and what type of counter it is. In our case, the counter indicates the total instances created in the last second. This type of counter is similar to the CPU counter in that the current value is the activity within the last second. There are a multitude of counters found in the `PerformanceCounterType` enumeration that represent different counter types. Another common type of counter is one whose value keeps a running total and is not continually being reset to zero as the `RateOfCountsPerSecond32` counter would be if no activity was issued in the last second.

Code Instrumentation

Once the `CounterCreationData` object is created and has information related to our counter, we add it to the `CounterCreationDataCollection` object, which is necessary for creating a new performance counter category. The `CounterCreationDataCollection` is a strongly-typed collection object for holding instances of `CounterCreationData` objects.

Creating the performance counter is one line of code; we pass the `CounterCreationDataCollection` object to the `PerformanceCounterCategory.Create()` method.

In order to compile this application, save the code into a file called `pc.vb` and compile it with the following command line:

```
> vbc /r:System.dll pc.vb
```

After executing the application, check Performance Monitor and you will see that the `AccountPerf` category has been created with a single `AccountApplication` performance counter.

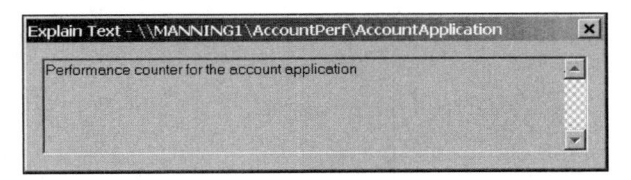

Explain Text - \\MANNING1\AccountPerf\AccountApplication

Performance counter for the account application

Implementing a Custom Listener

Perhaps the most useful feature of the tracing functionality is the ability to create our own `TraceListener` objects. The .NET Framework exposes an abstract class appropriately called `TraceListener` (`MustInherit` in VB.NET) which we can inherit from to implement our own `TraceListener`. All three standard trace listeners within .NET inherit from this base class.

Inheriting from `TraceListener` requires us to implement our own `Write()` and `WriteLine()` methods for our listener at the bare minimum. When someone writes a message to our `TraceListener`, we want to increment our performance counter.

Logging data to a performance monitor is slightly different from logging to a text file. Since the performance counter only understands increment and decrement values, it cannot interpret the difference between two text messages. When any message is written to the performance counter trace listener, we will simply record that as a single activity and increment our custom counter one unit of measure.

The following code implements a trace listener to write to our newly created `AccountApplication` performance object:

```
Imports System
Imports System.Diagnostics
```

337

Chapter 6: Measuring Scalability

```
Module Module1

  Sub Main()

    Dim rand As New System.Random()
    Trace.Listeners.Add(New AccountPerfMonTraceListener())

    Dim acct As New Account(1000)
    acct.Withdraw(200)

    Dim i As Integer
    For i = 0 To 100000
      Try
        acct.Withdraw(9999)
      Catch
        'stall the thread to slow the performance counter
        System.Threading.Thread.CurrentThread.Sleep(rand.Next(1, 50))
      End Try
    Next
  End Sub
End Module

'Account Class omitted for brevity

Public Class AccountPerfMonTraceListener
  Inherits TraceListener

  Private pc As PerformanceCounter

  Public Sub New()
    pc = New PerformanceCounter("AccountPerf", _
                                "AccountApplication", False)
  End Sub

  Public Overloads Overrides Sub Write(ByVal Message As String)
    pc.Increment()
  End Sub

  Public Overloads Overrides Sub WriteLine(ByVal Message As String)
    pc.Increment()
  End Sub
End Class
```

Inheriting from `TraceListener` is all that is necessary in order to implement our own trace listener. In our `AccountPerfMonTraceListener` class, we simply attach to our performance counter when the class is created and increment the counter.

In order to provide some meaningful data to view via Performance Monitor, we put the `Withdraw()` method within a loop to produce a larger number of trace messages via the error thrown. In the `Catch` statement, we stall the thread a bit in order to prevent our performance counter from becoming overwhelmed with messages.

338

Code Instrumentation

Note that the `Account` class has been removed from the application in order to shorten the code. Pasting in the `Account` class in our code module and saving the file as `Account.vb`, we are able to compile the application via the following command line:

```
> vbc /r:System.dll /define:trace=true Account.vb
```

Before we run our application, we start Performance Monitor and add our custom counter. Running the application gives us a similar output to the following:

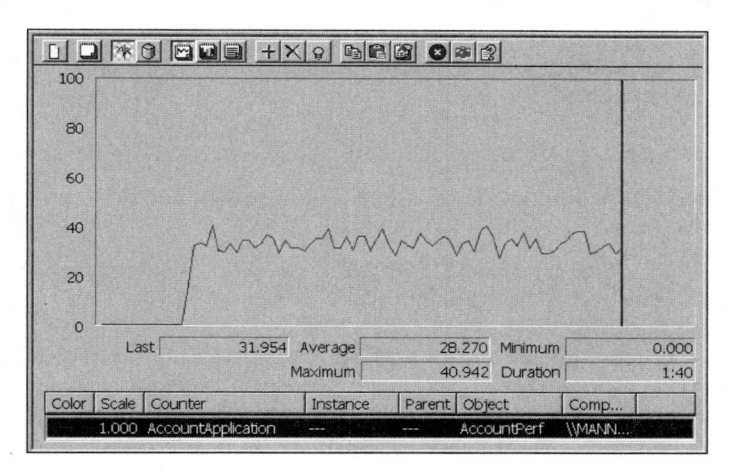

[Performance Monitor screenshot showing a graph with Last: 31.954, Average, Maximum: 40.942, Minimum: 28.270, Duration: 1:40, Counter: AccountApplication, Object: AccountPerf, Computer: \\MANN...]

Our random thread delay gives us some variance in the logging count as shown in the output graph.

Instrumentation and Scalability Measuring

By instrumenting our code with tracing and performance counting metrics, we increase our ability to measure our application's performance and scalability. Instrumentation provides a real-time data feedback from our application whose data can be monitored and analyzed for scalability metrics.

Code instrumentation is an effective technique, especially in distributed systems since we can measure how our application performs on different architectures and configurations. The default Windows operating system metrics can give a general indication as to how our application is performing, but cannot be used to establish why our application is performing the way it is. Instrumentation allows us to understand why our application is taking up resources and what actions within the code users are performing to stress the system. Assume we are working with the online retail scenario and our system is performing poorly. We use the Performance Monitor and notice that our SQL Server CPU usage is extremely high. We assume that we have quite a bit of queries going through. At this point, we could use SQL Profiler to examine the actual queries entering the system; however, SQL profiler cannot tell us what actions are users are taking within the application.

Attaching a trace monitor to the application allows us to retrace or monitor usage patterns and pinpoint where in code the action is taking place. Keep in mind that we can have multiple performance counters within the application and monitor the different counters in parallel. Understanding how the code is performing while the system is being stressed gives us the ability to plan and prepare for scalability improvements in our application.

Summary

Throughout the application's lifecycle we are presented with scalability questions we must be prepared to answer:

- How many concurrent users and requests per second can the system handle?
- Which parts of the code can benefit from scaling and how can we write scalable code?
- Will additional memory, CPU, servers, or a combination of resources be the most effective in the scaling process?

In order to answer these involved questions, we must understand how to test, monitor, and instrument our application with scalability in mind. Creating tests, using monitoring tools, and instrumenting our application will help us to effectively measure our application and determine which pieces of the application can benefit from scaling.

Creating test cases is the fundamental concept used to measure performance and scalability. Keeping a set of consistent test cases allows us to test our application in a wide variety of environments. Executing a uniform set of tests in different hardware environments allows us to attribute all performance changes to the hardware. From our test results, we can begin to determine how well our application scales under different architectures.

Writing tests involves creating a set of unit tests that target differing parts of the application. Unit tests can be as focused as testing a particular method or can be as high-level as simulating a user interaction. The goal of creating unit tests is to provide a wide variety of tests against the system to ensure it is performing correctly.

Along with being an excellent tool for measuring performance, unit testing greatly eases regression testing duties when changing code. Running the tests on changed code assures that the changes made did not break previous functionality.

Stress testing is the process of simulating a user load on the system to determine the system capacity. Stress testing allows us to test for common performance-limiting factors including bandwidth consumption, memory leaks, resource locking, and bottlenecks.

Tools play an important part in the testing process. Having a solid understanding of the tools increases our productivity by providing a rich set of performance feedback not easily obtainable from writing our own custom code.

Summary

Code profilers allow us to view code-level statistics including method execution time, the number of times a method has executed, the method stack, and the amount of execution time each line of code took to execute. Code profilers are excellent for detecting bottlenecks and can shed light on poorly performing algorithms.

Monitoring scalable applications, particularly in distributed systems, involves monitoring at the operating-system level. Windows Performance Monitor is a graphical tool used to monitor operating system and application-level metrics at the computer level. The Performance Monitor can monitor virtually all of the important operating system subsystems including processor, memory, I/O, and networking counters.

Using Performance Monitor while running tests allows us to view the system load and determine if our code has a bottleneck and what part of the system could be affected by the bottleneck.

Microsoft Application Center Test (ACT) is a script generator and stress testing tool for testing web applications. By using ACT, we are able to write or generate scripts and execute the script to simulate a large concurrent user base. ACT has an underlying object model and is based on scripts that the developer can customize for more detailed control of the test cases.

Code instrumentation is a technique used to provide performance monitors with the necessary information as to how the code is executing. By writing trace statements and implementing our custom `TraceListener` classes, we are able to tailor the output by severity level and send data to multiple sinks. By creating a `TraceListener` that writes to a custom performance counter, we are able to monitor our application's performance in real time via windows Performance Monitor.

VB.NET

Scalability

Handbook

Appendix A

A

MyInvestmentWatch.com Database Layout

MyInvestmentWatch.com is an application specifically constructed for the book so that we can illustrate how to create an n-tier application capable of scalability. The purpose of this appendix is to explain the design of the database that serves MyInvestmentWatch.com and provide enough information to assist you with understanding the design decisions and layout for running the application. In this appendix, we will show a high-level diagram of the data tables that compose the application as well as a more detailed analysis of each data table.

Database Design

The MyInvestmentWatch.com database is quite simple. One of the goals of the application was to keep it simple so as not to draw attention away from the scalability focus of the book with an overwhelmingly complex application. The database, in its entirety, looks like the screenshot over the page.

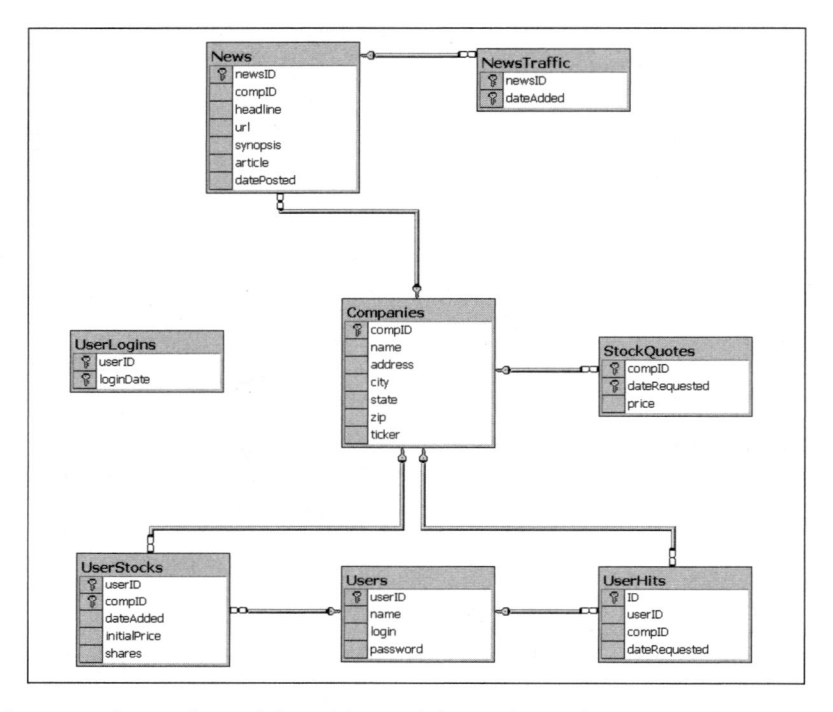

Appendix A: MyInvestmentWatch.com Database Layout

For a better understanding of the tables and their relationships, we will now take a look at each table individually.

Users

The first table we will examine is the `Users` table. The `Users` table is responsible for keeping very minimal login and password information as well as the user's name for display.

The `Users` table contains a `userID` column, which is an identity column (auto-incrementing) and a foreign key used in other tables to identify a user.

When a user logs into the site, the `Users` table is responsible for validating the user's credentials. When new users are added to the database, a new row is created for each user.

Field	Data type	Length	Description
userID	int	4	Primary key and identity field unique for each user
name	varchar	50	The user's name
login	varchar	20	The user's login ID
password	varchar	8	The user's password

344

Companies

The `Companies` table contains information for each individual company. For the context of the application, a company has an ID, an address, and the stock ticker symbol. Our example assumes that a company can have only one stock ticker symbol. If a single company has multiple stocks (which is entirely possible), multiple records would need to be entered for that company. If multiple stocks were a common occurrence, it would be better to put the stock ticker symbols into a separate table.

The user interface does not interact with the `Companies` table directly. In order to use this application, company information must be pre-entered into the database. From the user perspective, the `Companies` table is read-only.

Field	Data type	Length	Description
compID	int	4	Primary key and identity field unique for each company
name	varchar	50	The company's name
address	varchar	50	The company's address
city	varchar	50	The company's city
state	char	2	The company's state
zip	varchar	5	The company's zip code
ticker	varchar	10	The company's ticker symbol

StockQuotes

In order to provide quote information related to the ticker symbols, the `StockQuotes` table is used. The `StockQuotes` table contains a record for every stock quote that we obtain from an outside source. Like `Companies`, our user interface cannot update or insert into the `StockQuotes` table.

Our application does not provide the functionality to obtain stock quote prices. In a real-world scenario, the `StockQuotes` table could be populated (or replaced) by an additional source. Perhaps a direct feed from the stock market or a nightly download (if real-time quote info is not important) would populate the table.

If we had a direct link to an outside quote vendor, perhaps they would allow us to query into their database directly, avoiding the need for us to maintain continuous quote information in our database. Having historical data on a stock is nice; however, the space requirements are significant if the data is kept in this table.

345

Appendix A: MyInvestmentWatch.com Database Layout

Field	Data type	Length	Description
compID	int	4	Foreign key field referencing the compID primary key of the Companies table. Combines with the dateRequested field to for a composite primary key.
dateRequested	datetime	8	Combines with the compID field to form a composite primary key.
price	money	8	The current price of the stock.

UserStocks

UserStocks is responsible for maintaining user stock information. When the user adds records to or deletes records from their portfolio, the UserStocks table is updated to reflect the change. The userID and compID fields make up the composite primary key. The userID is a foreign key to the Users table and compID is a foreign key to the Companies table. At most, a single user can have only one record for each company.

The UserStocks table makes up the user's 'portfolio' and is fully editable from the user interface. When a user adds or removes a stock from their portfolio, the UserStocks table is edited.

Field	Data type	Length	Description
userID	int	4	Foreign key field referencing the userID primary key of the Users table. Composite primary key with the compID field.
compID	int	4	Foreign key field referencing the compID primary key of the Companies table. Composite primary key with the userID field.
dateAdded	datetime	8	The date and time the stock was added.
initialPrice	money	8	The initial price of the stock.
shares	int	4	The number of shares owned.

Database Design

UserHits

In order to keep track of site metrics, we keep a table called `UserHits` that holds information as to which stocks are being viewed by the users. Every time a user retrieves a stock, we add the `userID` that requested the stock, the `compID` that they requested, and the time the stock was requested. From this information, we are able to obtain the following metrics:

- What stocks are frequently viewed?
- What time of day are the most quotes requested?
- What stocks does user 'X' frequently examine?

Field	Data type	Length	Description
ID	int	4	Primary key and identity field unique for each user hit
userID	int	4	Foreign key field referencing the userID primary key of the Users table
compID	int	4	Foreign key field referencing the compID primary key of the Companies table
dateRequested	datetime	8	The date and time of the request

News

The `News` table is responsible for keeping a list of news articles related to a stock. When a user is retrieving information on a stock, we give them a current list of news articles as taken from this table. Similar to the `StockQuotes` table, data for this table would typically be provided by a news vendor. Perhaps the news vendor would expose a web service that could return the latest news articles. Having an alternative data source would allow us to get rid of this table.

Field	Data type	Length	Description
newsID	int	4	Primary key and identity field unique for each news item
compID	int	4	Foreign key field referencing the compID primary key of the Companies table
headline	varchar	100	The headline of the article
url	varchar	500	The URL of the article, which can be NULL

Table continued on following page

347

Appendix A: MyInvestmentWatch.com Database Layout

Field	Data type	Length	Description
synopsis	varchar	1000	The synopsis, or brief outline, of the article
article	text	16	The full text of the article
datePosted	datetime	8	The date the article was posted

NewsTraffic

The `NewsTraffic` table is kept to record news viewing traffic. Whenever a news article is viewed, we record the viewing. Keeping the record of hits allows us to keep track how many viewings each of the stories has. If the news articles are provided from a third-party source, we could record how many times their stories were viewed. Perhaps this would lead into a revenue stream.

Field	Data type	Length	Description
newsID	int	4	Foreign key field referencing the newsID primary key of the News table. Composite primary key with the dateAdded field.
dateAdded	datetime	8	The date the news article was added. Composite primary key with the newsID field.

UserLogins

In order to record user login activity, we maintain a `UserLogins` table. Whenever a user logs into the site, we add a record to the table. Having login metrics, we are able to calculate our usage patterns, busy times, and our frequent users.

You may have noticed that we do not maintain a relationship between the `Users` and `UserLogins` tables. The reason we have decided not to maintain the relationship deals with removal of users from the database. When we remove users from the database, the user record is deleted. We could have kept an 'active' property on the user record; however, we simply delete the record. If we had a relationship between the `Users` and `UserLogins` tables, we would need to delete the `UserLogins` information for that user. However, since we want to maintain all the login information regardless of whether the user is deleted, we keep no relationship between the two.

Field	Data type	Length	Description
userID	int	4	The userID from the Users table. No foreign key relationship is maintained to avoid cascading deletes.
loginDate	datetime	8	The date and time of the login.

VB.NET

Scalability

Handbook

Appendix B

Support, Errata, and Code Download

We always value hearing from our readers, and we want to know what you think about this book and series: what you liked, what you didn't like, and what you think we can do better next time. You can send us your comments, either by returning the reply card in the back of the book, or by e-mailing us at feedback@wrox.com. Please be sure to mention the book title in your message.

How to Download the Sample Code for the Book

When you log on to the Wrox site, http://www.wrox.com/, simply locate the title through our Search facility or by using one of the title lists. Click on Download Code on the book's detail page.

The files that are available for download from our site have been archived using WinZip. When you have saved the attachments to a folder on your hard-drive, you will need to extract the files using WinZip, or a compatible tool. Inside the Zip file will be a folder structure and an HTML file that explains the structure and gives you further information, including links to e-mail support, and suggested further reading.

Appendix B: Support, Errata, and Code Download

Errata

We've made every effort to ensure that there are no errors in the text or in the code. However, no one is perfect and mistakes can occur. If you find an error in this book, like a spelling mistake or a faulty piece of code, we would be very grateful for feedback. By sending in errata, you may save another reader hours of frustration, and of course, you will be helping us to provide even higher quality information. Simply e-mail the information to support@wrox.com; your information will be checked and if correct, posted to the Errata page for that title.

To find errata, locate this book on the Wrox web site (http://www.wrox.com/ACON11.asp?ISBN=1861007884), and click on the Book Errata link on the book's detail page.

E-Mail Support

If you wish to query a problem in the book with an expert who knows the book in detail then e-mail support@wrox.com, with the title of the book, and the last four numbers of the ISBN in the subject field of the e-mail. A typical e-mail should include the following:

- The name, last four digits of the ISBN (7884), and page number of the problem, in the Subject field
- Your name, contact information, and the problem, in the body of the message

We won't send you junk mail. We need the details to save your time and ours. When you send an e-mail message, it will go through the following chain of support:

- **Customer Support**

    Your message is delivered to our customer support staff. They have files on most frequently asked questions and will answer anything general about the book or the web site immediately.

- **Editorial**

    More in-depth queries are forwarded to the technical editor responsible for that book. They have experience with the programming language or particular product, and are able to answer detailed technical questions on the subject. Once an issue has been resolved, the editor can post any errata to the web site.

- **The Author**

    Finally, in the unlikely event that the editor cannot answer your problem, they will forward the request to the author. We do try to protect the author from any distractions to their writing (or programming); but we are quite happy to forward specific requests to them. All Wrox authors help with the support on their books. They will e-mail the customer and the editor with their response, and again all readers should benefit

The Wrox support process can only offer support for issues that are directly pertinent to the content of our published title. Support for questions that fall outside the scope of normal book support is provided via our P2P community lists – http://p2p.wrox.com/forum.

p2p.wrox.com

For author and peer discussion, join the P2P mailing lists. Our unique system provides Programmer to Programmer™ contact on mailing lists, forums, and newsgroups, all in addition to our one-to-one e-mail support system. Be confident that the many Wrox authors and other industry experts who are present on our mailing lists are examining any queries posted. At http://p2p.wrox.com/, you will find a number of different lists that will help you, not only while you read this book, but also as you develop your own applications.

To subscribe to a mailing list follow this these steps:

- Go to http://p2p.wrox.com/
- Choose the appropriate category from the left menu bar
- Click on the mailing list you wish to join
- Follow the instructions to subscribe and fill in your e-mail address and password
- Reply to the confirmation e-mail you receive
- Use the subscription manager to join more lists and set your mail preferences

VB.NET

Scalability

Handbook

Index

Index

A Guide to the Index

The index is arranged hierarchically, in alphabetical order, with symbols preceding the letter A. Most second-level entries and many third-level entries also occur as first-level entries. This is to ensure that users will find the information they require however they choose to search for it.

Symbol

.asmx pages, 202
.NET and scalability, 6, 59
  see also scalability planning.
  caching, 36
  CLR, 60
  COM+, 60
  enhanced scalability, 7, 29
  hardware scalability issues, 47
  interoperability, 59
    layer to existing COM components, 92
  middle tier, 34
  need to understand framework, 91
  n-tier applications, 94
  session management, 32, 60
  threading in .NET, 30
  versioning compared to DLL Hell, 173
.NET Framework
  pre-installed channels, 185
.NET landscape, 76
  assembly deployment, 79
  CLR, 77
  code migration, 78
    ASP applications, 78
  language selection, 77
  retraining, 76
    libraries, 76
    OOA&D, 76
    OOP, 76
.NET Remoting
  see Remoting.
@OutputCache directive
  see OutputCache directive.

A

AboveNormal value, CacheItemPriority enumeration, 269
absolute timespan, 266
abstract factory design pattern, 151
ACT (Application Center Test), 320
  configuring, 321
    dynamically generated script creation, 321
    running the test, 322
    New Test Wizard, 321
  not run on server being tested, 324
  scalability planning, 57
    Component Load Balancing, 57
  strengths, 327
  stress testing, 296
  Test Status screen, 324
  testing ASP.NET web applications, 321
  using with Performance Monitor, 323
actions and events
  logical middle tier functionality, 172
activated objects
  can be stateful, 190
ADO.NET
  communicating with database, 106
  DataSet, 116,129
    DataRelations, 130
      and scalability, 136
    ForeignKeyConstraint object, 134
    object hierarchy, 129
    UniqueConstraint object, 133
    working with constraints, 133
  DataView, 136
    and scalability, 140
    creating, 136
      with relationships, 138
    updating DataTable, 140

ADO.NET (continued)

ADO.NET (continued)
  design goals
    familiar programming model, 122
    native XML support, 123
    support for n-tier programming, 122
  introduction, 122
    data providers, 122
    design goals, 122
  object model, 123
    .NET data providers, 124
      objects that make up, 124
  scalability recap, 141
  stored procedures, 115
Advanced Server
  required by NLB, 70
ALTER TABLE statement
  changing database schema, 115
Application Center Test
  see ACT.
Application class (ASP.NET)
  see HttpApplicationState class.
application integration
  database integration, 97
  event-based integration, 98
  integration between applications, 98
  real-time integration, 97
  schedule-based integration, 97
application logic
  logical middle tier functionality, 172
application monitoring tools, 306
  code profiler, 296, 311
  importance of, 305
  Performance Monitor, 296, 317
  summary, 326
Application object, ASP
  using Visual Basic objects in ASP, 17
  problems with, 17
application scalability
  benefit of availibility in scaling out, 73
  function of hardware and software, 56
  scalability planning, 74
  using DMZ for security and restricting access to internal resources, 73
application testing, 296
  benefits, 297
  creating a relevant test, 306
  first test, 306
  identifying scalability limitations, 311
  monitoring in a production environment, 327
  stress testing, 302
  unit testing, 297
application tier
  see middle tier.
ArrayList class, System.Collections namespace, 212
  Capacity property, 212
  data storage structure, 227
ASP
  HTML and logic are severely intermixed, 241
  IIS, 16
  no inherent caching support, 22
  state management, 273
  using Visual Basic objects in ASP, 16
    ASP Application object, 17
    ASP Session object, 17
    misusing Visual Basic objects, 27
    storing state outside session, 19
ASP.NET
  separating code from presentation, 241
  state management, 274
ASP.NET Application: Anonymous Requests/sec
  monitoring with Performance Monitor, 323
ASP.NET applications
  benefits from middle architecture, 180
  caching, 36
    @OutputCache directive, 36
    programmatic cache access, 37
  session management, 32
  testing with ACT, 321
  using Visual Basic .NET, 38
ASP.NET scalability
  features, 233
    caching, 234
    compiled code, 234
    session management in a web farm, 234
assembly deployment, 79
  versioning in .NET, 79
average usage, trends within, 86

B

bandwidth consumption, 303
BelowNormal value, CacheItemPriority enumeration, 269
benchmarks
  benchmarking an existing system, 86
  benchmarking before rollout, 87
  goal of, 86
  prototype during design, 87
Beowulf and scaling out, 71
Big Iron solutions
  scaling up, 63
binary and SOAP formatters compared, 184
bottlenecks, 304
boundaries, reducing crossing of, 94

C

C# compared to Visual Basic .NET, 8
Cache class, System.Web.Caching namespace, 245
  functionality, 245
  Insert method, 269, 270
  programmatic caching access, 37, 265
    key features, 265
  Remove method, 271

cache events, 270
  CacheItemRemovedReason enumeration, 271
cache item dependencies
  absolute timespan, 266
  benefits of, 269
  file-based dependency, 267
  key-based dependency, 268
  multiple dependencies, 269
  sliding timespan, 266
  time-based dependency, 266
cache item priorities, 269
CacheItemPriority enumeration, System.Web.Caching namespace
  values, 269
CacheItemRemovedReason enumeration, System.Web.Caching namespace
  values, 271
caching, 242, 243
  .NET caching functionality, 36
    output caching, 36
    programmatic cache access, 37
  best practices, 272
  description, 22
  expensive data with ViewState, 286
  no inherent support in ASP, 22
  output caching, 246
  page-level caching, 23
  partial page caching, 262
  programmatic caching, 265
    cache events, 270
    cache item dependencies, 266
    cache item priorities, 269
  scalability and, 22
  SPM, 22
  where the cache fits, 244
    cache object, 245
    Session object, 245
Capacity property, ArrayList class, 212
Cascade value
  DeleteRule property, ForeignKeyConstraint class, 135
  UpdateRule property, ForeignKeyConstraint class, 135
channels
  .NET Frameworks pre-installed channels, 185
  channel/formatter guidelines, 185
  creating, 185
  remoting clients and servers must agree on, 184
Charles Shwab example
  hardware scalability issues, 15
  unplanned growth and scalability, 14
CLB (Component Load Balancing), 57
  impact on planning, 77
code instrumentation
  and scalability measuring, 339
  monitoring applications in a production environment, 327

performance monitoring, 296
tracing, 328
and performance monitoring, 335
code migration, 78
  tlbimp utility, 78
code profiler, 311
  DevPartner profiler, 312
  establishing the profiler, 313
  limitations, 317
  measuring application scalability, 312
    analyzing results, 313
  strengths, 316, 327
  using in conjunction with Performance Monitor, 317
code, downloading samples, 351
CollectionBase class, System.Collections namespace, 212
  provides collection enumerators, 226
COM
  extended by DCOM, 19
  SPM, 22
COM+
  enhanced scalability, 7
  enhancements to DCOM, 22
  features, 61
  System.EnterpriseServices namespace, 61
Command classes
  see also SqlCommand and OleDbCommand classes.
  making up .NET data provider, 124
Common Language Runtime
  see CLR.
Component Load Balancing
  see CLB.
Component Role-Based Security, COM+, 61
Connection classes
  see also SqlConnection class and OleDbConnection class.
  making up .NET data provider, 124
Connection Lifetime connection string parameter, 128
connection pooling
  lifetime of resources, 49
  SQL Server .NET Data Provider, 127
connection string parameters
  list of, 128
Constraints property, DataTable class
  determining constraint, 133
control-level caching in .NET, 60
Cookieless attribute, sessionState element, 275
cookieless browser support
  session management in .NET, 33
cookies
  determining if cookies accepted, 17
  required for using ASP Session object, 17
cost reduction, 297
CounterCreationData class, System.Diagnostics namespace, 336

357

CounterCreationDataCollection class,
    System.Diagnostics namespace, 337
Create method,
    PerformanceCounterCategory class, 337
CreateChildView method, DataRowView
    class
    creating DataViews with relationships, 138
critical path, determining, 95
cross process communication, 181
current baseline indicators
    planned growth and scalability, 12
customer support, 352

D

DAL (Data Access Layer)
    benefits in middle tier, 213
    CRUD operations, 143
    object model, 143
Data Access Layer
    see DAL.
data validation
    logical middle tier functionality, 172
DataAdapter class
    see also SqlDataAdapter and
        OleDbDataAdapter classes.
    making up .NET data provider, 124
database access
    granularity, 93
database design, 106
    choosing a platform, 107
        understanding design principles and your
            platform, 107
    First Normal Form, 146
    indexes, 116
        clustered indexes, 116
        nonclustered indexes, 117
        performance tuning tips, 117
    MyInvestmentWatch.com, 40
    normalization, 145
    Second Normal Form, 146
    SQL Server, 107
    stored procedures, 114, 147
        lifecycle, 114
    Third Normal Form, 147
database replication, 100
database tier, 40, 105
    database design, 106
    MyInvestmentWatch.com, 40
    scaling out, 71
    start small, 72
Datacenter Server
    hardware scalability issues, 47
DataColumn class, System.Data namespace
    Unique property, 133
DataReader classes
    see also SqlDataReader and
        OleDbDataReader classes.
    making up .NET data provider, 124

DataRelation class, System.Data
    namespace
    adding constraints, 130
    adding to DataSet object, 130
    creating, 130
DataRow class, System.Data namespace
    GetChildRows method, 132
DataRowCollection class, System.Data
    namespace
    returned by GetChildRows method,
        DataRow class, 132
DataRowView class, System.Data
    namespace
    CreateChildView method, 138
DataSet class, System.Data namespace
    adding DataRelation object, 130
    can act as a relational data model, 122
    EnforceConstraints property, 133
    object hierarchy, 106, 129
    populated by SqlDataAdapter class, 126
    populating XmlDataDocument class, 123
DataTable class, System.Data namespace
    Constraints property, 133
    DefaultView property, 136
    viewing data with DataView, 136
DataView class, System.Data namespace,
    136
    building index, 137
    compared to SQL Server view, 136
DCOM
    advantages, 20
    alternatives, 22
    and scalability, 19, 58
    compared to Remoting, 34
    dynamic port assignment, 21
        configuring port range, 21
        security problems, 21
    enhanced by COM+, 22
    extends COM, 19
    limitations, 20, 181
    RPC, 20
Debug class, System.Diagnostics
    namespace
    determining class level testing, 300
DefaultTraceListener class,
    System.Diagnostics namespace, 330
DefaultView property, DataTable class, 136
delegates
    .NET threading, 31
DeleteRule property, ForeignKeyConstraint
    class
    Cascade value, 135
    values, 134
Demilitarized Zone
    see DMZ.
DependencyChanged value,
    CacheItemRemovedReason enumeration,
    271

deploying new application
  to existing shared environment, 82
  to new environment, 82
design tips for database design, 108
designing for scalability
  application integration, 96
  design interchangeable objects, 96
  determining critical path, 95
  interchangeable objects, 96
  no shortcuts, 90
  reducing round-trips, 94
    code, 94
    output cache, 95
    stored procedures, 95
  reinventing the wheel, 91
  sequence around expected load, 96
  tiers, 92
DevPartner profiler
  establishing the profiler, 313
  measuring application scalability, 312
  analyzing results, 313
disconnected Recordsets
  advantages of using, 26
DLL Hell, 79
DMZ (Demilitarized Zone)
  isolating business objects, 70
  using for security and restricting access to internal resources, 73
Duration attribute, @OutputCache directive, 36, 248
  simplest method of caching data, 251
dynamic data
  problems with page-level caching, 23
dynamic SQL
  compared to stored procedures, 50
  MyInvestmentWatch.com, 50
  scalability issues, 50

E

encapsulation
  interface design, 176
EnforceConstraints property, DataSet class,, 133
environment growth plan, 89
errata, feedback on, 352
ETL tool
  providing a reporting database, 100
event-based notification
  Cache class, 245
EventLogTraceListener class, System.Diagnostics namespace, 330
ExecuteReader method, SqlDataReader class, 126
Expired value, CacheItemRemovedReason enumeration, 271

F

file-based dependency, 267
First Normal Form
  conditions to be met, 109
  database design, 146
ForeignKeyConstraint class, System.Data namespace
  adding to child table with DataRelation object, 130
  enforces rules when data in the related tables changes, 134
  UpdateRule property, 134
formatters
  channel/formatter guidelines, 185
  SOAP and binary formatters compared, 184

G

GET statement
  VaryByParam attribute, @OutputCache directive, 248, 253, 254
GetChildRows method, DataRow class
  returns a DataRowCollection object, 132
GetVaryByCustomString method, HttpApplicationState class, 250

H

hardware scalability issues
  .NET and scalability, 47
  Charles Shwab example, 15
  Datacenter Server, 47
  MyInvestmentWatch.com, 46
Hashtable class, System namespace, 227
High value, CacheItemPriority enumeration, 270
HTTP channel
  pre-installed on .NET Frameworks, 185
HTTP GET statement
  see GET statement.
HTTP POST statement
  see POST statement.
HttpApplicationState class, System.Web namespace
  accessing via WebService class, 198
  caching, 246
  GetVaryByCustomString method, 250
HttpRequest class, System.Web namespace
  Headers method, 259
HttpSessionState class, System.Web.SessionState namespace
  caching, 245
  session management, 274
  Timeout property, 275

359

IIS (Internet Information Services)

I

IIS (Internet Information Services)
 ASP, 16
 threading architecture, 16
 using Visual Basic objects in ASP, 16
IL (Intermediate Language)
 all .NET code compiled into, 77
in process session information storing, 276
 pros and cons, 277
Index Tuning Wizard
 automated approach to idea generation, 119
 example, 119
indexes, 108, 116
 clustered indexes, 116
 nonclustered indexes, 117
 performance tuning tips, 117
  design indexes to database function, 117
  index on search fields, 118
inline SQL
 see SQL statements.
in-process session model
 limitations, 33
 session management in .NET, 33
Insert method, Cache class, 269
 restoring removed cached item, 270
INSERT statement
 monitoring with Performance Monitor, 318
InstallSqlState.sql, 282
integration
 understanding integration points and methods, 85
IntelliSense
 and WSDL, 196
interface design, 173
 encapsulation
  benefits and drawbacks, 176
  increasing abstraction, 176
  reducing interface dependence between layers, 176
interface management
 logical middle tier, 173
Intermediate Language
 see IL.
intertwined design
 beware of, 93
item dependencies
 Cache class, 245

K

key-based dependency, 268

L

language selection, 77
lazy loading, 208
Level property, TraceSwitch class
 values, 332
lifetime of resources
 connection pooling, 49
 MyInvestmentWatch.com, 49
Listener property, Trace class
 returns TraceListenerCollection class, 330
load balancing
 scaling out, 68
Load method, User object, 44
 all or nothing design, 47
  memory consumpltion issues, 49
  problems with unnecessary loading, 48
load testing, 320
 compared to stress testing, 302
Location attribute, @OutputCache directive
 partial page caching, 263
 values, 248
logical middle tier
 interface management
  reducing interface dependence between layers, 176
 managing interfaces
  interface design example, 173
  interfaces and physical tiers, 177
 object model, 168
Loosely Couple Events, COM+, 61
Low value, CacheItemPriority enumeration, 270

M

machine.config
 session management, 274
mailing lists, subscribing to p2p.wrox.com, 353
maintenance
 support processes, 85
MarshalByRefObject class, System namespace, 168, 183
 creating, 187
 Remoting and middle tier, 193
Marshal-by-Value objects, 183
Max Pool Size connection string parameter, 128
measuring
 early and often, 89
 picks up from benchmarking, 89
 functionality, 297
 performance, 297
 scalability, 295
  application testing, 296
  importance of tools in testing, 305
  stress testing, 302
  unit testing, 297

memory leaks, testing for, 303
metadata, retrieving from remoting object, 191
Microsoft and scalability, 6, 15
  .NET and scalability, 6
    enhanced scalability, 7, 29
  caching, 22
  DCOM, 19
  improvements in NT and Windows 2000, 7
  issues with Visual Basic, 7, 15, 24
  issues with Windows DNA, 15, 24
  past problems with scalability, 6
Microsoft Message Queue
  see MSMQ.
middle tier, 167
  benefits realized at UI tier, 167
  logical middle tier, 168
  MyInvestmentWatch.com, 41
  physical middle tier, 168
  scaling out, 71
middle tier and .NET, 34, 180
  benefits of DAL, 213
  Remoting, 34, 181
    cross process communication, 181
  Web Services, 35, 193
    definition, 194
    reusing functionality, 202
middle tier definition, 169
  benefits, 169
    deployment, 171
    integration, 170
    reusability, 170
    scalability, 169
    summary, 171
  drawbacks, 171
    configuration, 172
    performance, 172
middle tier design, 172
  logical middle tier, 172
    functionality, 172
    managing interfaces, 173
  physical middle tier, 178
    and performance, 179
Min Pool Size connection string parameter, 128
Mode attribute, sessionState element, 275
monolithic applications
  beware of, 92
MSDataShape data provider
  Shape SQL syntax, 130
MSMQ (Microsoft Message Queue)
  application integration, 98
  how it works, 98
multiple dependencies
  creating, 269
MyInvestmentWatch.com
  application testing
    method performance, 314
    persistence model, 307

architecture, 39
database design, 40, 145, 343
  Companies table, 345
  First Normal Form, 146
  News table, 347
  NewsTraffic table, 348
  Second Normal Form, 146
  StockQuotes table, 345
  stored procedures, 147
  Third Normal Form, 147
  UserLogins table, 348
  Users table, 344
  UserStocks table, 346
data-tier, 40
  introduction, 40
data-tier application logic, 148
  creating interfaces, 149
  DAL object model, 148
  highlights, 162
  implementing interfaces, 152
    IHitsPersist, 157
    INewsPersist, 161
    IPersist, 154
    IPersistFactory, 152
    IStockPersist, 158
  possible improvements, 163
data-tier goals
  improved performance testing, 145
  providing abstraction, 144
  reusability, 144
  stateless design, 144
data-tier implementation, 106, 142
  benefits of improvements, 142
  goals, 143
introduction, 38
middle tier, 41, 168
  creating the object model, 205
    Hit object, 223
    Hits object, 221
    NewsArticle object, 220
    NewsArticles collection, 219
    Stock object, 213
    StockQuote object, 218
    StockQuotes object, 217
    Stocks object, 209
    User object, 206
  determining environment, 203
  possible improvements, 226
    error handling, 227
    searching/sorting techniques, 227
  using the logical middle tier, 224
possible method used to scale, 56
scalability issues, 46
  all or nothing design, 47
  dynamic SQL, 50
  hardware scaling, 46
  resource lifetimes, 49
  session state, 50
  web farms, 51

361

MyInvestmentWatch.com (continued)
- user interface, 41
  - caching, 243
  - code highlights, 237
  - design goals, 242
  - page flow, 235
    - *user login, 235*
    - *view individual stock, 236*
  - partial page caching, 262
  - revised version, 287
    - *code highlights, 287*
  - User object, 42
- Windows DNA, 39

N
- **network boundaries, reduce crossing of, 94**
- **Network Load Balancer**
  - *see* NLB.
- **New Test Wizard, 321**
- **NLB (Network Load Balancer)**
  - advantages and disadvantages, 70
  - scaling out middle tier, 71
  - software load balancing, 69
- **no state session information**
  - storing, 276
    - pros and cons, 276
- **Normal value, CacheItemPriority enumeration, 269**
- **normalization, 108**
  - and scalability, 112
    - OLAP, 113
    - OLTP, 113
  - benefits, 108
  - First Normal Form, 109
  - improves scalability, 105
  - Second Normal Form, 110
  - Third Normal Form, 111
- **Not Invented Here syndrome, 91**
- **NotRemovable value, CacheItemPriority enumeration, 270**
- **NT4**
  - DCOM and scalability, 58
  - enhanced scalability, 7
- **n-tier applications**
  - architecture
    - scaling out, 66
    - scaling out across a single tier, 67
    - scaling out across tiers, 66
  - designing for scalability
    - .NET and tiers, 94
    - beware of intertwined designs, 93
    - beware of monolithic applications, 92

O
- **Object Pooling, COM+, 61**
- **Object-Oriented Analysis and Design**
  - *see* OOA&D.

- **Object-Oriented Programming**
  - *see* OOP.
- **OLAP (Online Analytical Processing)**
  - characteristics of OLAP system, 113
    - SELECT queries, 113
  - normalization and scalability, 113
  - read-intensive, 105
  - summarization and reporting capabilities, 113
- **OLTP (Online Transaction Processing)**
  - normalization and scalability, 113
  - write-intensive, 105
- **Online Analytical Processing**
  - *see* OLAP.
- **Online Transaction Processing**
  - *see* OLTP.
- **OOA&D (Object-Oriented Analysis and Design)**
  - need to learn, 76
- **OOP (Object-Oriented Programming)**
  - bad practice in Visual Basic, 29
  - limitations in Visual Basic, 7
  - need to learn, 76
  - Visual Basic .NET, 37
- **Oracle provider**
  - creating, 162
- **out-of-process session model**
  - scalability advantages, 33
  - session management in .NET, 33
- **output caching, 36, 95**
  - @OutputCache directive, 36, 247
  - description, 36
  - sequence for page requests, 246, 250
  - using, 251
- **@OutputCache directive, 36, 247**
  - Duration attribute, 36, 248
    - simplest method of caching data, 251
  - Location attribute
    - values, 248
  - VaryByControl attribute, 249
    - using, 255
  - VaryByCustom attribute, 249, 260
  - VaryByHeader attribute, 249, 258
  - VaryByParam attribute, 36, 253
    - values, 248

P
- **p2p.wrox.com mailing list, 353**
- **page-level caching, 23**
  - advantages, 23
  - in .NET, 60
  - problems with dynamic data, 23
- **partial page caching**
  - @OutputCache directive, 263
- **performance**
  - compared to scalability, 10
  - peak and non-peak performance, 12
- **performance and load monitoring, 89**

RPC (Remote Procedure Call)

Performance Monitor
 and distributed applications, 318
 and tracing, 335
 monitoring applications in a production environment, 327
 monitoring SQL Server, 318
  analyzing results, 319
 strengths, 327
 using in conjunction with code profiler, 317
 using with ACT, 323
 variety of counters for different subsystems, 320
performance monitoring
 code instrumentation, 296
 code profiler, 296
PerformanceCounterCategory class, System.Diagnostics namespace, 336
 Create method, 337
PerformanceCounterType enumeration, System.Diagnostics namespace
 counters, 336
Physical Disk: % Disk Time
 monitoring with Performance Monitor, 318
Physical Disk: % Disk Usage
 monitoring with Performance Monitor, 323
Physical Disk: Disk Transfers/sec
 monitoring with Performance Monitor, 318
Physical Disk: Disk Transfers/sec – I/O usage
 monitoring with Performance Monitor, 323
physical middle tier, 178
 and performance, 179
 communicating with UI, 179
 determining the UI, 180
  understanding client architecture, 180
 hardware architecture, 168
 Remoting, 168
planning for scalability
 see scalability planning.
Pooling connection string parameter, 128
ports
 dynamically assigned by DCOM, 21
  configuring port range, 21
  security problems, 21
POST statement, 249
 VaryByParam attribute, @OutputCache directive, 248, 253, 254
presentation tier, 231
 see also UI (user interface).
 ASP.NET scalability, 233
 caching, 243
  best practices, 272
  output caching, 246
  partial page caching, 262
  programmatic caching, 265
 state management, 273
 Web-based UI, 231
  advantages, 231
  disadvantages, 232
process boundaries
 reduce crossing of, 94

Processor: % Processor Time
 monitoring with Performance Monitor, 318, 323
programmatic caching, 37, 265
 Cache class, 37
 Cache Events, 270
 Cache Item Dependencies, 266
 Cache Item Priorities, 269
 Cache object, key features, 265
 explicit access, 265
 implicit access, 265

R

read-only output
 and ViewState, 286
ReadOnlyCollectionBase class, System.Collections namespace, 218
 provides collection enumerators, 226
Recordset object
 bad Recordset practice and scalability, 26
 disconnected Recordsets, advantages of using, 26
reliability
 compared to scalability, 11
Remote Procedure Call
 see RPC.
Remoting
 and middle tier, 193
 channel/formatter guidelines, 185
 compared to DCOM, 34
 compared to Web Services, 35
 creating a remoting-accessible object, 186
  creating the client, 191
  creating the server, 188
 cross process communication, 181
 flexible infrastructure, 35
 framework, 182
 implementing remoting scenario, 182
 middle tier and .NET, 34
 terminology
  channel, 184
  formatters, 184
  MarshalByRefObject class, 183
  Serializable (ByValue), 183
Remove method, Cache class, 271
Removed value, CacheItemRemovedReason enumeration, 271
Request object
 see HttpRequest class.
resource locking, 303
 considerations, 304
resource management
 Cache class, 245
RowFilter property, DataView class, 137
RowStateFilter property, DataView class, 137
RPC (Remote Procedure Call)
 and DCOM, 20.

363

S

scalability, 5
  .NET and scalability, 7
    enhanced scalability, 29
  caching, 22
  compared to performance, 10
  compared to reliability, 11
  definition, 6
  description, 9
  design problems with Windows DNA, 25
    misuse of Visual Basic objects, 27
    misusing external resources, 26
    OOP bad practice, 29
    Recordset bad practice, 26
    resource intensive tier interfaces, 27
    SQL statements, using instead of stored procedures, 25
  hardware and scalability, 15
  importance of scalability, 5
  introduction, 5
  measuring, 295
  Microsoft and scalability, 6
  overview, 8

scalability planning
  .NET landscape, 76
  aligning with business vision, 82
  benchmarks, 86
    benchmarking an existing system, 86
    benchmarking before rollout, 87
    prototype during design, 87
  benefits of .NET, 57
    CLR, 60
  constraints of company, 56
  creating a reporting environment, 99
    database replication, 100
  creating environment growth plan, 89
  define requirements, 81
    actionable and measurable, 81
  design guidelines, 90
    application integration, 96
    design interchangeable objects, 96
    determining critical path, 95
    no shortcuts, 90
    reducing round-trips, 94
    reinventing the wheel, 91
    sequence around expected load, 96
    tiers, 92
  determine expected load on system, 83
    concurrent users, 83
    integration, 85
    maintenance, 85
    transactions, 84
    trends, 85
  determining growth of system, 88
    plan for unexpected, 88
  importance of holistic view, 83
  key traits, 55
  lack of planning leads to failure, 55
  limitations of pre .NET Microsoft technology, 57
    Application Center, 57
    DCOM, 20, 58
    Windows DNA, 15, 24, 59
  measuring early and often, 89
  MyInvestmentWatch.com, 46
  planned growth and scalability, 12
    current baseline indicators, 12
    trends, 12
  sequence ourt non-user processing, 99
  systems architecture
    need for, 55
  tying it together
    grow big, 74
    scaled system example, 74
    start right, 73
    start small, 72
  types of scaling, 62
    scaling out, 66
    scaling up, 63
  understanding environment
    deploying new application to existing shared environment, 82
    deploying new application to new environment, 82
    upgrading an existing system, 82
  unplanned growth and scalability, 13
    Charles Shwab example, 14

scaling down, 89

scaling out, 66
  across a single tier, 67
    hardware load balancers, 69
    round-robin DNS, 68
    software load balancers, 69
  across tiers, 66
  benefits and costs, 71
  best practices, 70
  n-tier architecture, 66

scaling up, 63
  best practice, 64
    databases, 65
  making servers bigger, 64
  making servers faster, 63

SCM (Service Control Manager)
  introduced with advent of COM, 58
  using other objects, 58

Second Normal Form
  database design, 146
  example, 110

security problems with DCOM, 21

SELECT * FROM statement, 126

serializable objects, 168

<Serializable> attribute, 183

servers
  making bigger, 64
  making faster, 63

Service Control Manager
  see SCM.

session management
  best practices, 283, 286
    only use session if required, 283
    only use session when required, 283
    plan for SQL Server, 284
  HttpSessionState object, 274
  in a web farm, 234
  machine.config, 274
  storing session information in ASP.NET, 274
    in-process, 276
    no state, 276
    SQL Server, 281
    state server, 278
  ViewState
    and scalability, 285
session management, features in .NET, 32, 60
  cookieless browser support, 33
  ease of use, 33
  hosting sessions, 33
    in-process session model, 33
    out-of-process session model, 33
    SQL Session mode, 34
session object (ASP.NET)
  see HttpSessionState class.
Session object, ASP
  alternatives, 18
  cookies required for using sessions, 17
  MyInvestmentWatch.com, 50
  problems with scalability, 18, 51
  using Visual Basic objects in ASP, 17
    problems with, 17
  web server process required for maintaining session, 18
Session_OnEnd, 283
Session_OnStart, 283
sessionState element
  attributes, 275
  modifying for storing
    SQL Server session information, 281
    in-process session information, 276
    no state session information, 276
    state server session information, 278
shadow deployment, 80
Shape SQL syntax, 130
Shared Property Manager
  see SPM.
Simple Object Access Protocol
  see SOAP.
single call objects, 168
  wellknown mode, 190
Single-Threaded Apartment Model
  see STA threading model.
singleton objects, 168
  wellknown mode, 190
sliding timespan, 266
snapshot replication, 100
SOAP (Simple Object Access Protocol)
  example, 196

SOAP and binary formatters compared, 184
soapsuds.exe
  retrieving metadata from remoting object, 191
Sort property, DataView class, 137
SPM
  caching, 22
  limitations, 22
SQL Compilations/sec
  monitoring with Performance Monitor, 318
SQL Profiler
  purpose and effectiveness, 118
SQL Re-Compilations/sec
  monitoring with Performance Monitor, 318
SQL Server
  Index Tuning Wizard, 119
  monitoring with Performance Monitor, 318
  scaling out, 71
  SQL Profiler
    purose and effectiveness, 118
  SQL Session mode for session management, 34
  support for replication, 100
SQL Server .NET Data Provider
  connection pooling, 127
  parameters, 128
  contained within System.Data.SqlClient namespace, 125
  enables application to speak in SQL Server TDS format, 127
  using, 125
SQL Server authentication
  used throughout book, 128
SQL Server database design
  normalization, 108
  tools and language features specific to, 107
SQL Server session information
  storing, 281
    pros and cons, 282
    setting up, 282
SQL Server view
  creating logical tables, 136
SQL Session mode
  session management in .NET, 34
  uses SQL Server database, 34
SQL statements
  compared to stored procedures, 25
  dynamic SQL, 50
SqlCommand class, System.Data.SqlClient namespace
  executing stored procedures, 126
SqlConnection class, System.Data.SqlClient namespace
  only one SqlDataReader can be attached at any one time, 126
sqlConnectionString attribute, sessionState element, 275

**SqlDataAdapter class,
 System.Data.SqlClient namespace**
   populating DataSet object, 126
**SqlDataReader class,
 System.Data.SqlClient namespace**
   ExecuteReader method, 126
SSL requests
   processing and servers, 65
STA threading model
   limitations, 16
   required by Visual Basic objects, 16
   thread affinity, 16
Start method, Thread class, 31
state management, 273
   ASP.NET compared to ASP, 274
   session management, 274
   ViewState, 284
state server
   setting up, 279
state server session information
   storing, 278
      pros and cons, 280
      setting up state server, 279
**stateConnectionstring attribute,
 sessionState element, 275**
**stateNetworkTimeout attribute, sessionState
 element, 275**
stored procedures, 108
   advantages, 25
   and ADO.NET, 115
   and scalability, 25, 115
   compared to dynamic SQL, 50
   compared to SQL statements, 25
   database design, 147
   lifecycle
      compile, 115
      execute, 115
      parse, 114
      recompile when necessary, 115
   reducing round-trips, 95
stress testing, 295, 302
   ACT (Application Center Test), 296
   common performance limitations, 302
      bandwidth consumption, 303
      bottlenecks, 304
      memory leaks, 303
      resource locking, 303
   compared to load testing, 302
support processes and maintenance, 85
System Analysis, 62
System Design, 62
system growth
   determining, 88
   unplanned growth, 88
System namespace
   Hashtable class, 227
   MarshalByRefObject class, 168, 183, 187, 193

System.Collections namespace
   ArrayList class, 212, 227
   CollectionBase class, 212
   ReadOnlyCollectionBase class, 218, 226
System.Data namespace
   DataColumn class, 133
   DataRelation class, 130
   DataRow class, 132
   DataRowCollection class, 132
   DataRowView class, 138
   DataSet class, 106, 122, 123, 126, 129, 130, 133
   DataTable class, 133, 136
   DataView class, 136, 137
   ForeignKeyConstraint class, 130, 134, 135
   UniqueConstraint class, 130, 133
System.Data.SqlClient namespace
   SqlCommand class, 126
   SqlConnection class, 126
   SqlDataAdapter class, 126
   SqlDataReader class, 126
System.Diagnostics namespace
   CounterCreationData class, 336
   CounterCreationDataCollection class, 337
   Debug class, 300
   DefaultTraceListener class, 330
   EventLogTraceListener class, 330
   PerformanceCounterCategory class, 336
   PerformanceCounterType enumeration, 336
   TextWriterTraceListener class, 330
   Trace class, 328, 330, 331, 332
   TraceListener class, 296, 337
   TraceListenerCollection class, 330
   TraceSwitch class, 332, 333
System.EnterpriseServices namespace
   accessing COM+, 60
<system.runtime.remoting> node
   remoting runtime configured with contents, 189
System.Threading namespace, 32
   Thread class, 31
System.Web namespace
   HttpApplicationState class, 198, 246, 250
   HttpRequest class, 259
System.Web.Caching namespace
   Cache class, 37, 245, 265
   CacheItemPriority enumeration, 269
   CacheItemRemovedReason enumeration, 271
System.Web.Services namespace
   WebService class, 198, 202
   WebServiceAttribute class, 198
System.Web.SessionState namespace
   HttpSessionState class, 198, 245, 275
systems architecture
   application scalability, 56
   need for, 55

T

Tabular Data Stream
see SQL Server TDS format.
TCP channel
  pre-installed on .NET Frameworks, 185
testing environment, 86
**TextWriterTraceListener class,
System.Diagnostics namespace, 330**
think-time, 84
Third Normal Form
  database design, 147
  example, 111
thread affinity
  problems with, 16
  STA threading model, 16
Thread class, System.Threading namespace
  Start method, 31
threading
  .NET threading, 30
  advantages, 30
  delegates, 31
  System.Threading namespace, 32
  IIS, 16
  using Visual Basic objects in ASP, 16
  limitations in Visual Basic, 15
  STA threading model required, 16
time-based dependency, 266
Timeout attribute, sessionState element, 275
Timeout property, HttpSessionState class, 275
tlbimp utility
  code migration, 78
tools for scalability testing
  see application monitoring tools.
Trace class, System.Diagnostics namespace
  controling via compiler directive, 331
  methods, 328
  Write method, 328, 332
  WriteLine method, 328
trace statements, 329
  performance monitoring, 296
  precedence levels, 332
TraceError value
  Level property, TraceSwitch class, 332
TraceInfo value
  Level property, TraceSwitch class, 332
TraceListener class, System.Diagnostics namespace
  creating custom listeners, 337
  performance monitoring, 296
  Write method, 337
  WriteLine method, 337
TraceListenerCollection class, System.Diagnostics namespace
  adding listeners to, 330

TraceSwitch class, System.Diagnostics namespace
  values put into application configuration file, 333
TraceVerbose value
  Level property, TraceSwitch class, 332
TraceWarning value
  Level property, TraceSwitch class, 332
tracing
  configuration, 333
  established tracing, 328
  monitoring higher priority trace statements, 331
  precedence levels, 332
  Trace class, 328
tracing and Performance Monitor, 335
  creating a custom counter, 335
  implementing a custom listener, 337
transactional replication, 100
transactions
  determining throughput, 84
trends
  peak and non-peak performance, 12
  planned growth and scalability, 12
Two-Phase Transactional Support, COM+, 61
types of scaling, 62
  scaling out, 66
    n-tier architecture, 66
  scaling up, 63
    best practice, 64
    making servers bigger, 64
    making servers faster, 63

U

UI (User Interface)
  see also presentation tier.
  communication with physical middle tier, 179
  deployment scenarios, 180
  MyInvestmentWatch.com, 41
  User object, 42
  Web-based UI
    advantages, 231
    disadvantages, 232
Underused value, CacheItemRemovedReason enumeration, 271
UninstallSqlState.sql, 282
Unique property, DataColumn class
  setting constraint, 133
UniqueConstraint class, System.Data namespace, 133
  adding to parent table with DataRelation object, 130

unit testing, 295
  and performance and scalability, 301
  class level, 298
    determining the test, 299
    example, 298
  methods level, 297
  strengths of, 300
    industry support, 301
    regression, 301
UpdateRule property, ForeignKeyConstraint class
  Cascade value, 135
  values, 134
upgrading existing system, 82
user interface
  see UI.
User object
  description, 42
  inefficient use of resources, 44
  Load method, 44, 47
  MyInvestmentWatch.com user interface, 42
user profiling, 84

V

VaryByControl attribute, @OutputCache directive, 249, 255
  partial page caching, 263
VaryByCustom attribute, @OutputCache directive, 249
  using, 260
VaryByHeader attribute, @OutputCache directive, 249
  using, 258
VaryByParam attribute, @OutputCache directive, 36, 253
  best caching practices, 273
  example, 253
  using with GET and POST statements, 248, 253, 254
  values, 248
  varying cache information by parameter, 253
ViewState and scalability, 285
  best practices, 286
    caching expensive data, 286
    read-only output, 286
    recreating controls, 286
    use sparingly, 286
Visual Basic .NET
  compared to C#, 8
  compared to VB6, 8, 76
  enhanced scalability, 8
  introduction, 37
  OOP, 37
  threading, 30
    example, 30
  using with ASP.NET, 38

Visual Basic 6
  bad OOP practice, 29
  compared to Visual Basic .NET, 8, 76
  design problems, 25
  limitations, 7, 24
  popularity, 24
  scalability problems, 7, 15, 24
    misusing Visual Basic objects, 27
    threading issues, 15
  using Visual Basic objects in ASP, 16
    ASP Application object, 17
    ASP Session object, 17
    misusing Visual Basic objects, 27
    storing state outside session, 19

W

Web Application Stress tool
  see ACT.
web farms
  MyInvestmentWatch.com, 51
  pinning users to web servers, 52
  scalability issues, 51
  session management, 234
web servers
  pinning users to web servers, 52
  processing SSL requests, 65
Web Services
  and middle tier, 202
  compared to Remoting, 35
  defined, 194
  definition
    requirements for client server interaction, 194
    SOAP, 196
    WSDL, 195
    XML, 197
  description, 35
  example, 197
    creating the client, 200
    creating the Web Service, 198
    testing, 199
    WSDL service description, 200
  middle tier and .NET, 35
  reusing functionality, 202
Web Services Description Language
  see WSDL.
web tier
  scaling out, 71
  start small, 72
Web-based UI
  advantages, 231
    consistent deployment platform, 232
    easier collaboration with external partners, 232
    easier support for multiple clients, 232
    fewer deployment targets, 232
  disadvantages, 232
    client processing power not leveraged, 233
    less functionality, 233
    slower response time, 233

WebService class, System.Web.Services namespace
gives access to Application and Session objects, 198
Web Services and the middle tier, 202
WebServiceAttribute class, System.Web.Services namespace, 198
wellknown objects
modes
singleton and singlecall objects, 190
Windows 2000
Datacenter Server, 47
enhanced scalability, 7
Windows authentication
benefits, 128
Windows DNA
and scalability, 15, 24, 59
design problems, 25
misuse of Visual Basic objects, 27
misusing external resources, 26
OOP bad practice, 29
Recordset bad practice, 26
resource intensive tier interfaces, 27

SQL statements, using instead of stored procedures, 25
MyInvestmentWatch.com, 39
Winforms applications
benefits from middle architecture, 180
Write method, Trace class, 328, 332
Write method, TraceListener class, 337
WriteLine method, Trace class, 328
WriteLine method, TraceListener class, 337
WSDL (Web Services Description Language), 195
and IntelliSense, 196
can be read by IDEs, 196
WSDL service description, 200
wsdl.exe tool
creating proxy classes forr web methods, 201

X

XML (Extensible Markup Language), 197
XmlDataDocument class, System.Xml namespace
populating with DataSet object, 123

369

Visual Basic .NET Threading Handbook:

Author(s): K. Ardestani, F. C. Ferracchiati, S. Gopikrishna, T. Redkar, S. Sivakumar, T. Titus
ISBN: 1-861007-13-2
US$ 29.99
Can$ 46.99

All .NET languages now have access to the Free Threading Model that many Visual Basic Developers have been waiting for. Compared to the earlier apartment threading model, this gives you much finer control over where to implement threading and what you are given access to. It does also provide several new ways for your application to spin out of control.

This handbook explains how to avoid some common pitfalls when designing multi-threaded applications by presenting some guidelines for good design practice. By investigating .NET's threading model's architecture, you will be able to make sure that your applications take full advantage of it.

What you will learn from this book
- Thread creation
- Using timers to schedule threads to execute at specified intervals
- Synchronizing thread execution - avoiding deadlocks and race conditions
- Spinning threads from within threads, and synchronizing them
- Modelling your applications to a specific thread design model
- Scaling threaded applications by using the ThreadPool class
- Tracing your threaded application's execution in order to debug it

Visual Basic .NET Text Manipulation Handbook:
String Handling and Regular Expressions

Author(s): François Liger, Craig McQueen, Paul Wilton
ISBN: 1-861007-30-2
US$ 29.99
Can$ 46.99

Text forms an integral part of many applications. Earlier version's of Visual Basic would hide from you the intricacies of how text was being handled, limiting your ability to control your program's execution or performance. The .NET Framework gives you much finer control.

This handbook takes an in depth look at the text manipulation classes that are included within the .NET Framework, in all cases providing you with invaluable information as to their relative performance merits. The String and Stringbuilder classes are investigated and the newly acquired support for regular expressions is illustrated in detail.

What you will learn from this book
- String representation and management within the .NET Framework
- Using the StringBuilder object to improve application performance
- Choosing between the different object's methods when manipulating text
- How to safely convert between String and other data types
- How to take advantage of .NET's Unicode representation of text for Internationalization
- The use of regular expressions including syntax and pattern matching to optimize your text manipulation operations

Visual Basic .NET Class Design Handbook:
Coding Effective Classes

Visual Basic .NET Class Design Handbook: Coding Effective Classes

Author(s): Andy Olsen, Damon Allison, James Speer
ISBN: 1-861007-08-6
US$ 29.99
Can$ 46.99

Designing effective classes that you do not need to revisit and revise over and over again is an art. Within the .NET Framework, whatever code you write in Visual Basic .NET is encapsulated within the class hierarchy of the .NET Framework.

By investigating in depth the various members a class can contain, this handbook aims to give you a deep understanding of the implications of all the decisions you can make at design time. This book will equip you with the necessary knowledge to build classes that are robust, flexible, and reusable.

- **What you will learn from this book**
- The role of types in .NET
- The different kinds of type we can create in VB.NET
- How VB.NET defines type members
- The fundamental role of methods as containers of program logic
- The role of constructors and their effective use
- Object cleanup and disposal
- When and how to use properties and indexers to encapsulate data
- How .NET's event system works
- How to control and exploit inheritance in our types
- The logical and physical code organisation through namespaces and assemblies

p2p.wrox.com
The programmer's resource centre

A unique free service from Wrox Press
With the aim of helping programmers to help each other

Wrox Press aims to provide timely and practical information to today's programmer. P2P is a list server offering a host of targeted mailing lists where you can share knowledge with four fellow programmers and find solutions to your problems. Whatever the level of your programming knowledge, and whatever technology you use P2P can provide you with the information you need.

ASP — Support for beginners and professionals, including a resource page with hundreds of links, and a popular ASP.NET mailing list.

DATABASES — For database programmers, offering support on SQL Server, mySQL, and Oracle.

MOBILE — Software development for the mobile market is growing rapidly. We provide lists for the several current standards, including WAP, Windows CE, and Symbian.

JAVA — A complete set of Java lists, covering beginners, professionals, and server-side programmers (including JSP, servlets and EJBs)

.NET — Microsoft's new OS platform, covering topics such as ASP.NET, C#, and general .NET discussion.

VISUAL BASIC — Covers all aspects of VB programming, from programming Office macros to creating components for the .NET platform.

WEB DESIGN — As web page requirements become more complex, programmer's are taking a more important role in creating web sites. For these programmers, we offer lists covering technologies such as Flash, Coldfusion, and JavaScript.

XML — Covering all aspects of XML, including XSLT and schemas.

OPEN SOURCE — Many Open Source topics covered including PHP, Apache, Perl, Linux, Python and more.

FOREIGN LANGUAGE — Several lists dedicated to Spanish and German speaking programmers, categories include. NET, Java, XML, PHP and XML

How to subscribe
Simply visit the P2P site, at http://p2p.wrox.com/

WROX PRESS INC.

Wrox writes books for you. Any suggestions, or ideas about how you want information given in your ideal book will be studied by our team. Your comments are always valued at Wrox.

Free phone in USA 800-USE-WROX
Fax (312) 893 8001

UK Tel. (0121) 687 4100   Fax   (0121) 687 4101

NB. If you post the bounce back card below in the UK, please send it to:
Wrox Press Ltd., Arden House, 1102 Warwick Road, Acocks Green, Birmingham. B27 9BH. UK.

Registration Code : 78844K4N2I6Y4HC01

How did you rate the overall contents of this book?
☐ Excellent ☐ Good
☐ Average   ☐ Poor

What influenced you in the purchase of this book?
☐ Cover Design
☐ Contents
☐ Other (please specify)

What did you find most useful about this book?

What did you find least useful about this book?

Please add any additional comments.

What other subjects will you buy a computer book on soon?

What is the best computer book you have used this year?

Note: This information will only be used to keep you updated about new Wrox Press titles and will not be used for any other purpose or passed to any other third party.

Name
Address

City
Country   Postcode/Zip
State/Region
E-mail
Occupation
How did you hear about this book?
☐ Book review (name)
☐ Advertisement (name)
☐ Recommendation
☐ Catalog
☐ Other
Where did you buy this book?
☐ Bookstore (name)   City
☐ Computer Store (name)
☐ Mail Order
☐ Other

wrox
PROGRAMMER TO PROGRAMMER™

BUSINESS REPLY MAIL
FIRST CLASS MAIL PERMIT #64 CHICAGO, IL

POSTAGE WILL BE PAID BY ADDRESSEE

WROX PRESS INC.
29 S. LA SALLE ST.,
SUITE 520
CHICAGO IL 60603-USA

NO POSTAGE
NECESSARY
IF MAILED
IN THE
UNITED STATES